Returned Exile

George James Christian

Returned EXILE

A Biography of George James Christian
of Dominica and the Gold Coast, 1869–1940

MARGARET D. ROUSE-JONES
and
ESTELLE M. APPIAH

 THE UNIVERSITY OF THE WEST INDIES PRESS
Jamaica • Barbados • Trinidad and Tobago

The University of the West Indies Press
7A Gibraltar Hall Road, Mona
Kingston 7, Jamaica
www.uwipress.com

Republic Bank Limited
9–17 Park Street
Port of Spain, Trinidad
Trinidad and Tobago
www.republictt.com

© Margaret D. Rouse-Jones and Estelle M. Appiah, 2016

All rights reserved. Published 2016

A catalogue record of this book is available from the National Library of Jamaica.

ISBN: 978-976-640-588-5 (print)
978-976-640-589-2 (Kindle)
978-976-640-590-8 (ePub)

Cover and book design by Robert Harris
Set in Adobe Garamond Pro 11/14.5 x 27
Printed in the United States of America

Contents

List of Illustrations **vii**

Foreword by Kwesi Kwaa Prah **ix**

Preface **xv**

Acknowledgements **xix**

1. Migration and Documentary Heritage **1**
2. Antecedents and Early Years in Dominica, England and the Gold Coast **9**
3. Christian as Father and Family Man **30**
4. Achimota College, Dr J.K. Aggrey, Christian and His Family Experiences **80**
5. "Lawyer Christian" **104**
6. Christian's Multifaceted Life **134**
7. Christian's Contribution to the Political and Social Development of the Gold Coast **169**
8. Christian and His Compatriots in the Gold Coast: Community, Identity and Heritage **195**

Appendix 1. List of Oral History Interviews Related to George James Christian **227**

Appendix 2. Published Articles and Conference and Lecture Presentations on George James Christian **229**

Notes **233**

Selected Bibliography **309**

Index **313**

Illustrations

Unless otherwise credited, all images courtesy the George James Christian Papers, Alma Jordan Library, the University of the West Indies, St Augustine, Trinidad and Tobago.

P.1. Official handover of the George James Christian Papers to the University of the West Indies, St Augustine, 22 June 2005 **xviii**

2.1. Dominica House, Sekondi **27**

2.2. Map of the Caribbean **28**

2.3. Map of Ghana showing Accra, Sekondi-Takoradi, Tarkwa and the Ashanti Region **29**

3.1. Family tree of George James Christian – Dominica-born children **74**

3.2. Family tree of George James Christian – Africa-born children **75**

3.3. Mary Aba Ackon, wife of George James Christian **76**

3.4. Abba Lucy French (Mami Abba), wife of George James Christian **76**

3.5. Peter Christian, George James Christian, Joseph and Josephine Christian in back row; Sarah and Howard Christian in front row **76**

3.6. Herminie Eccuah Christian **76**

3.7. Maude Mary Christian **77**

3.8. Howard Christian and Essi Christian **77**

3.9. Clara Marguerite Gordon **77**

3.10. Ebenezer Kwesi Christian **77**

3.11. Joseph (Joe) Christian **78**

3.12. Josephine Martha Christian and Dr Joseph E. Armah on their wedding day **78**

3.13. Howard Kojo Christian 78
3.14. Essi Matilda Forster 78
3.15. Ferdinand Francisco Christian 79
3.16. Edward Clifford Christian 79
3.17. Spectators at the Accra Race Course, Ghana, including John Mansour 79
4.1. Edward Christian, Mami Abba and Howard Christian 102
4.2. Sarah Helena Christian 103
4.3. Angela Ambah Christian 103
4.4. Descendants of George James Christian and Dr James Kwegyir Aggrey participate in a celebration of the founding of Achimota School 103
5.1. George James Christian, barrister-at-law, in wig and gown 133
5.2. Franz Dove, barrister-at-law, who communicated with the Colonial Office on George James Christian's behalf 133
6.1. Angela Christian, George James Christian, Essi Christian and Netelka Packwood 166
6.2. Joseph, Howard, Sarah, Josephine and George James Christian 166
6.3. Clara Gordon and her six children 167
6.4. George James Christian in Freemason regalia, W Bro. Hon. G.J. Christian 168
7.1. George James Christian, member of the Legislative Council, Accra, Gold Coast 194
8.1. George Francois, formerly of St Lucia, and his family 225
8.2. George Stanley Lewis, formerly of St Lucia, Accra, Ghana, 1994 226
8.3. George James Christian 226
8.4. Graves of Maude Mary Christian and George James Christian, European Cemetery, Sekondi 226

Foreword

THE EMERGENCE OF MODERN AFRICAN NATIONALISM AND THE growth of an articulate intelligentsia from the late nineteenth century onwards cannot be fully grasped or appreciated without an understanding of the place and role of the African diaspora in seeding and shaping its gestation. The existentially harrowing implications and consequences of their involuntary transport and bondage in various locations across the Atlantic prompted in negation the rise of a lore of resistance in mind and spirit, and the wish to return to the motherland became an indelible part of the psychology of the diaspora. In his famous poem "The Outcast", the Jamaican bard Claude McKay, one of the icons of the Harlem Renaissance, poignantly captured this mood in affective language:

> For the dim regions whence my fathers came
> My spirit, bondaged by the body, longs.
> Words felt, but never heard, my lips would frame;
> My soul would sing forgotten jungle songs.
> I would go back to darkness and to peace,
> But the great western world holds me in fee,
> And I may never hope for full release
> While to its alien gods I bend my knee.
> Something in me is lost, forever lost,
> Some vital thing has gone out of my heart,
> And I must walk the way of life a ghost
> Among the sons of earth, a thing apart;
> For I was born, far from my native clime,
> Under the white man's menace, out of time.

Most did not find their way back, but some did. Some of those who found their way back, mainly professionals, carved honourable roles for themselves and their progeny in the wider society in the motherland. Some others have divided their time between both sides of the Atlantic. This historic drama of the "Atlantic African" continues to the present and affirms the organic nature of the historical and cultural bonds between continent-based Africans and their diaspora.

This text is the story of one of those whose life and legacy in Africa bristles with honours, someone who created a living, recognizably consanguine network both in the Caribbean and West Africa, a man who was part of the group which ushered in the Pan-African Association and movement in 1900. In short, a person who, in a lifetime, united around himself the diaspora and the motherland, and resolved the historical quandary which McKay so evocatively expressed. *Returned Exile* is a testimony of courage and determination in the face of trying conditions.

Within the covers of this book, a superbly crafted narrative has been rendered by Margaret D. Rouse-Jones and Estelle M. Appiah on the life and times of George James Christian (1869–1940). The text is a well-researched and expertly fashioned portrait of a man who, in the best of the "back to Africa" tradition, came to West Africa in 1902 when he was in his thirties and stayed on until he passed in 1940. It is a lucid and insightful biography written in language free from unnecessary verbal adornments and presenting in one unbroken stream of historical snapshots the life of a successful African diaspora returnee who made a grand re-entry into African society after a long, so to speak, historical exile from home. Others have followed him "back to Africa". Christian took his life's decisions with calculated and single-minded rationality. Almost inadvertently, the text provides a rich compilation of glimpses into Gold Coast society seen through the life and times of George James Christian. This would be useful for a historian of the Gold Coast looking at the first half of the twentieth century.

George James Christian arrived in a pacified Gold Coast. Captain C.H. Armitage, acting for the colonial secretary, reported in the Annual Colonial Report at the end of 1902 that the Ashantis had, more or less, recovered from the last war; refugees had returned and many towns and villages had been rebuilt. The Anglo-German Boundary Commission, which started its demarcation exercise in December 1901, had finished the work. An Anglo-French Boundary Commission was also nearly finished. The authorities were improving the township of Sekondi; sanitation, water storage and new public buildings were being constructed. A new African neighbourhood to the southwest of the old town was also under construction.

Christian came from the sunny idyllic Caribbean island of Dominica. Many people in his position would have wanted to go back there after legal studies in the United Kingdom. But for Christian, the call of Africa was too strong. He and his friend Henry Sylvester Williams, who coined the term pan-Africanism, both came to Africa at about the same time. Williams went to Cape Town, and George James Christian ended up in Sekondi; both were legal practitioners. Williams did not last; after two years he left. Christian stayed on to establish a successful legal practice; he made some money and lost some, and he became a highly respected member of Gold Coast society.

Reading his history in this text, one forms the opinion that Christian, for all intents and purposes, was undaunted by any challenges to his standing in Gold Coast society and his access to whichever office or position he may have been suitable for. He had the pluck and confidence to stand against J.E. Casely Hayford for office in the Legislative Council. He lost the first time, but after Hayford's death, he was comfortably elected to office. His contributions to the work of the Legislative Council were enormous, and he always had the mettle to advance his views without fear or favour.

Christian was for about a quarter of a century Liberian consul in Sekondi, a task he performed with zeal and for which he was highly appreciated by the Liberian presidency. He was an enthusiastic Freemason, well-cultivated in the craft. This was an affiliation he shared with his father in the West Indies and continued in the Gold Coast. By degrees and diligence, he rose in the hierarchy of the organization and was given international recognition for his contributions to its growth in the Gold Coast and the West Indies. He had little doubt about the virtues of Freemasonry. His many social activities included school management, which he performed with keenness and attention, standing up always for what he thought was right. He was not convinced that the idea of Achimota School* as originally conceived was a sound one and had many questions in this regard. He interacted extensively with Kwegyir Aggrey about

---

*In 1948, Achimota College became three separate institutions: the University College of the Gold Coast (which was subsequently moved to a separate campus at Legon and is now known as the University of Ghana), the Achimota Teacher Training College, and Achimota School. Achimota College still operates today as Achimota School under the oversight of the Ghana Education Service, providing a senior high school education to young women and men.

the school. It is also worth noting that Christian's interest in agriculture dated back to his early years in the Caribbean. He continued to pursue agricultural projects in the Gold Coast.

Among other things, law reform for a long time preoccupied him, and Christian was involved in discussions around the possible extension of judicial facilities into Ashanti. His contributions in this regard were crucial in creating the introduction of better legal representation in the Ashanti region. Also notably, Christian tried his hand in a range of business activities. He appears to have been more successful in his early years than in later ones. It is clear that he combined a full range of activities and public engagements which would intimidate many people. He took to these challenges like a duck to water. No challenge was too big for Christian. His support of the West Indian Club in the United Kingdom, Harold Moody's League of Coloured Peoples, also in the United Kingdom, and other West Indian organizations deserves mention. It attests to the fact that he never weakened his links to the Caribbean and Caribbean affairs. It is also interesting to observe that he actively supported a recruitment drive during the First World War for the Gold Coast regiment.

By all accounts, Christian was a convivial, warm-hearted and friendly person who lived life to the full. He was never averse to expressing himself in clear and unadulterated terms. He obviously felt comfortable and at home in the Gold Coast, and continued until his final years the espousal and pursuit of pan-Africanist objectives. There is evidence that he, together with Henry Sylvester Williams, was particularly interested in the problems of Africans in Southern Africa. Christian's grandson Bankie Forster Bankie, who continues in his grandfather's inspirational vein, drew my attention to this.

George James Christian's illustrious life in the Gold Coast reminds Africans on this continent in our times of the need to push for the rapid implementation of diaspora rights to citizenship in any country in Africa, on demand. We must with speed address and resolve this issue of right of return. When we achieve this goal, our national sense will deepen and become entrenched. We shall have recognized and successfully retrieved the unity of the fabric of our historical character as Africans in a global order, which has been truncated by the centuries of slavery. It would be a consequential way to honour the life of George James Christian and his ilk. Above all, it will also be in our collective interest.

The writing of this biography, *Returned Exile*, has been helped by the numerous letters George James Christian left to posterity. His records have been well-maintained, and their safekeeping in the archives of the University of the West Indies is fortunate. This book is eminently readable and consistently engaging. It is advised reading for pan-Africanists and the wider audience of people concerned with the lot of Africans in the world.

Kwesi Kwaa Prah
Cape Town
9 October 2015

Preface

RETURNED EXILE HAD ITS GENESIS IN A FRIENDSHIP which began more than forty years ago in 1974, when Estelle and Margaret met as postgraduate students of history and law at William Goodenough House, London, a residence for Commonwealth students. At their first meeting, Estelle, a Ghanaian, mentioned her West Indian heritage and shared details about her grandfather, George James Christian, originally from Dominica in the Eastern Caribbean. Christian had trained as a lawyer in London, migrated to the Gold Coast (now Ghana) in 1902 and contributed to the development of society in that country. He had also documented his experience and left behind a collection of papers. Margaret, of Trinidad and Tobago, was immediately intrigued by the story of this West Indian who had gone back to Africa. It was this initial conversation, and a long-lasting friendship faithfully maintained by snail mail in the pre-technology era, that convinced Estelle and Margaret they were meant to co-author this biography about Christian's life and legacy, a unique testimony of reverse migration.

In 1991, seventeen years after that first meeting, the co-authors began to research Christian's life in the Library at Gray's Inn, London, where he had studied law. In the ensuing years, oral-history research was conducted in Dominica and Ghana with Christian's surviving children, other relatives and friends. This included an interview with one of the later migrants, George Stanley Lewis of St Lucia, brother of the Nobel laureate Sir Arthur Lewis and personal friend of Christian, who migrated to the Gold Coast in 1929. (A list of people interviewed is given in appendix 1.) In 1994, twenty years after that first meeting in London, Estelle and Margaret reunited in Ghana to continue the research in the National Archives in Accra, Cape Coast and Sekondi.

This first full-length biography of Christian chronicles his experience as a student in London and his migration to the Gold Coast, where he had a successful life as a lawyer, father and family man, businessman, philanthropist and politician. He also served as honorary consul for the Republic of Liberia, was very involved in Freemasonry and was engaged in a wide range of public service activities. Christian left a legacy through his service and involvement in the society, as well as through his descendants who were also professionals. He was the central figure among a small group of doctors, lawyers, businessmen and other West Indian professionals who migrated to the Gold Coast in the early decades of the twentieth century. This biography also highlights the migration process and aspects of the lives of these other West Indians. Included among this disparate group is Bishop Joseph Oliver Bowers, also of Dominica, who migrated to the Gold Coast shortly before Christian's death. Christian kept his connections with his homeland alive with visits every few years and maintained contact with friends and relatives there until the end of his life in 1940.

Apart from the detailed narrative of Christian's experience in the Gold Coast, some chapters provide contextual information that will have a wide appeal to readers with an interest in the legal profession and Gold Coast history. Chapter 4, for example, provides details about the establishment of Achimota College (formerly Prince of Wales College and Achimota School) and the friendship between Christian and Dr James Kwegyir Aggrey, known as "Aggrey of Africa", which is documented by correspondence. Chapter 5 deals with the celebrated case of Dr Benjamin Knowles, a British doctor who was charged with the murder of his wife.

Over the years, as the research evolved, the authors took advantage of opportunities to make presentations about Christian, either singly or jointly, at conferences on both sides of the Atlantic. The first paper on Christian was presented at a conference in Trinidad and Tobago on "Henry Sylvester-Williams and Pan-Africanism: A Retrospection and Projection", hosted by the University of the West Indies, St Augustine, and Oberlin College, Ohio, in the United States, January 4 to 13, 2001. Christian was one of the delegates who had attended the first pan-African conference organized by Williams in London in 1900, and it was considered appropriate to present the results of the research at this conference. Other presentations were made in the Dominican Republic (2006), Ghana (2007), Barbados (2007) and South Africa (2010). Extracts from the research on Christian have been used in professorial and other memorial lectures presented at the University of the West Indies campuses in 2007, 2008, 2011 and 2012. (A list of the publications and presentations that feature Christian is given in appendix 2.)

The major source of information for this biography, as substantiated by the copious notes and references provided, is the George James Christian Papers (GJC Papers), created and amassed by Christian and maintained by his family, especially his daughter Essi Forster, after his death. The GJC Papers and associated oral-history interviews served as unique reference sources that profile the contributions made by Christian and other West Indians who went to the Gold Coast in the first three decades of the twentieth century. The majority of photographs used in the book are included in the GJC Papers and have been reproduced with permission of the West Indiana and Special Collections Division, housed at the Alma Jordan Library, the University of the West Indies, St Augustine, Trinidad and Tobago. Those sourced from other collections are referenced in captions.

The GJC Papers were donated to the University of the West Indies, St Augustine, on 22 June 2005, when Estelle Appiah officially handed over her grandfather's papers and signed a deed of gift to the university, with Dr Maude Christian-Meier, another granddaughter of Christian, as the witness. This decision to donate the collection came as early as 1991, after a visit by Estelle to the university, and consent was given by her mother, Essi Forster. The collection will be available for use by scholars and researchers from 2016.

The authors hope that this biography, which profiles the life, legacy, professional and personal contributions of "'returned exile" George James Christian to Gold Coast society, will be a useful source of information for students, teachers and researchers, in support of studies on the African diaspora, pan-Africanism and Gold Coast history in the first half of the twentieth century.

Margaret D. Rouse-Jones and Estelle M. Appiah
30 March 2016

Figure P.1. Official handover of the George James Christian Papers to the University of the West Indies, St Augustine, 22 June 2005

Acknowledgements

THIS BIOGRAPHY HAS HAD A LONG GESTATION PERIOD, and we pay tribute to the many people and institutions that have played a part to bring this project to fruition. We wish to convey thanks and appreciation for the contributions made by relatives, friends and associates of George James Christian, listed in appendix 1, who responded positively to requests to be interviewed. Other family members shared useful information or assisted the authors in other ways during the research process. In this regard, we are indebted to the late Mrs Essi Forster, his daughter, and granddaughters Margaret Busby, Phyllis Christian, Dr Maude Christian-Meier, Veronica McNeil and Aileen Ewuradwoa Conteh. We are also extremely grateful to Dr Susan Craig-James, fellow researcher, who discovered considerable information on George James Christian Sr in the National Archives in London and drew it to our attention.

Our very special thanks are expressed to Leeanna Stewart, a University of the West Indies history honours graduate and law student, who was our research assistant. Her input on this project was invaluable. She assisted, as she said, "to bring to life the story of a distinguished West Indian man".

We owe a debt of gratitude to the staff in libraries and archives in the United Kingdom and Ghana where we did considerable research. The staff at Gray's Inn Library, London; National Archives, London; National Archives, Accra; Cape Coast Archives; and Sekondi Archives, Ghana, were extremely helpful in response to our requests for information and photocopies.

We are deeply grateful to Jennifer Joseph, university and campus librarian, St Augustine, and the staff at the Alma Jordan Library of the University of the West Indies, St Augustine, for the many courtesies extended. In particular, staff in the Secretariat and the West Indiana and Special Collections Division were supportive of the project and were tireless in their efforts to respond to our requests for documents. They offered a listening ear, collegial discussion, encouragement and practical help as necessary, over the many years of research and data gathering in the GJC Papers. Thanks are due to Aisha Baptiste, Dr Karen Eccles, Floris Fraser, Neisha Hyatali, Lorraine Nero, Indira Ramroop-Chadee, Lucille St John Soso, Larraine Seales, Maud Marie Sisnette and Dr Glenroy Taitt. We apologize to all those whom we may have omitted to mention by name.

We appreciate the input of our other colleagues and friends who either participated in social and intellectual exchanges and interactions or offered prayers and spiritual support that encouraged the research, writing and publication process: Doreen Baptiste, Jacqueline Cameron-Padmore, Dr Maude Christian-Meier, Phyllis Christian, Gabriel Christian, Dr Roslyn Cooper-Trim, Claire Craig, Dr Susan Craig-James, Stephney Ferguson, Kathleen Helenese-Paul, Dr Alma Jordan, Annette Knight, Karen Lequay, Evadne McLean, Professor Paula Morgan, Vera Nibbs, Dr Laura Roberts-Nkrumah, Deborah Souza-Okpofabri, Sherma Quamina-Wong Kang, Janice Thomas, Genevieve Vincent, Margot Warner and Professor Valerie Youssef.

Special thanks go to Dr Kweku Appiah, Dr John Campbell, Professor Franklin Knight and Cheryl Peltier-Davis, who read the manuscript at different stages and offered constructive criticism. Dr Emmanuel Evans-Anfom, who was a student at Achimota College in 1935, read the draft of chapter 4 and added relevant information and interesting perspectives based on his first-hand experience. While we acknowledge and appreciate their invaluable advice, we accept full responsibility for what we have written.

We are grateful to Professor Kwesi Kwaa Prah, director of the Centre for Advanced Studies of African Society (CASAS), who encouraged the research through his invitation to participate in one of the CASAS Back-to-Africa workshops in 2010. We especially thank him for his insightful foreword to the book.

Our editor, Maureen Henry, patiently journeyed with us through the lengthy process to bring the manuscript to the required standard for submission to the publisher. We are indebted to her for this task.

Dexnell Peters, graduate student at Johns Hopkins University, meticulously verified reference sources at the final stage of publication. His diligence has added value to the work.

We say a heartfelt thank you to our husbands, Rupert Jones and Dr Kweku

Appiah, our children, siblings and other close relatives, who in one way or another have lived with this project over the decades. They are undoubtedly as happy as we are that it has finally come to a successful conclusion.

A very special thank-you is due to Republic Bank Limited, through its Power to Make a Difference programme, for its willingness to collaborate with us to publish and disseminate the life story of this West Indian pioneer. Its generosity is greatly appreciated.

We are extremely grateful to Linda Speth, Shivaun Hearne and the staff at the University of the West Indies Press for their diligence and efficacy during the publication process.

Finally, we acknowledge the divine hand of the Sovereign God, through Jesus Christ, who brought us together over forty years ago and who has undoubtedly guided us throughout the research, writing and completion of this biography. To Him be the glory!

CHAPTER 1

Migration and Documentary Heritage

> Providence has ordained it that we the descendants of those unfortunate exiles should return to the father-land and give the benefit of our experience to the descendants of those who were responsible for the cruelty inflicted upon our ancestors.
> —*George James Christian*

WITH THESE WORDS IN ONE OF HIS LAST letters before he died, George James Christian of Dominica in the Eastern Caribbean welcomed his fellow countryman, a young priest, Reverend Joseph O. Bowers, to his first appointment in the Gold Coast.[1] Both had migrated from Dominica to the Gold Coast during the first half of the twentieth century and would make a significant contribution to the host society; they died there in 1940 and 2012 respectively. Christian's letter to Bowers, which also reflected on the horrors of the slaves' journey as "human cargo" during the transatlantic crossing, is instructive as it shares insights into his ideology of return and his experience as a migrant. He concluded that they were privileged to be there and that they had a duty to perform, even if they were sneered at as "returned exiles".[2]

The construct of the returnee as an exile is not uncommon. Kwesi Prah's recent studies of the ideology and practice of the African returnee phenomenon have indicated that "throughout history and in diverse locations, the members of many diasporas, large and small, old and new, who have been forcibly or involuntarily removed from their native lands, have seen themselves as exiles and have cultivated and expressed ideas of return – or successfully returned – to the motherland".[3] Fitzroy André Baptiste, in a brief commentary on the Caribbean antecedents of the "back to Africa" movements, mentioned four

West Indians: John Russwurm and Robert Campbell of Jamaica; Edward Blyden of the Danish West Indies, and Canon Philip H. Douglin of Trinidad, who made the return journey in the post-emancipation period. Other West Indians, namely, Robert Love, Marcus Garvey and Claude McKay of Jamaica, Richard B. Moore of Barbados, and Henry Sylvester Williams and George Padmore of Trinidad, were contributors to the "back to Africa" and pan-Africanist movements of the late nineteenth and early twentieth centuries.[4]

More recent research by Waibinte Wariboko examines the return of West Indians, predominantly Jamaicans, who voluntarily migrated as Christian missionaries to Nigeria in the late nineteenth and early twentieth centuries. Their aim was to improve "the spiritual and moral conditions of Africans". At the inception of the scheme, a programme of "homecoming" had been launched "on the assumption that racial affinity, including shared racial characteristics between black West Indians and West Africans, would persuade the former to embrace the program enthusiastically".[5] The scheme "fell through because . . . the black West Indians rejected the homecoming idea and declared their desire to be treated and perceived as foreigners". The research concludes that "conflicting perceptions of race and racial identity . . . ruined this missionary enterprise of employing West Indians to proselytize Africans".[6]

Prah has identified two main traditions in the history of the "back to Africa" experience, one of which is relevant to this study. It can be identified among Africans in the diaspora, individuals or groups, who reckoned that their future would be "strategically bleak, problematic and undesirable" and that return to the motherland was the better option. Significant among these were Paul Cuffee of the United States, who made early attempts to return groups to Sierra Leone. Others who had a similar purpose included Martin Delany and Robert Campbell, who investigated settlement options in Nigeria. Chief Alfred Sam from the Gold Coast and Marcus Garvey of Jamaica also spearheaded schemes to return groups of African Americans and other diaspora Africans respectively, during the early decades of the twentieth century.[7]

There were also West Indians, mainly from Jamaica and Barbados, who went to parts of Africa under the auspices of various missionary societies. Two such missions that involved Jamaicans – the Baptist Missionary Society mission to Fernando Po and Cameroon in 1841, and the Scottish United Presbyterian mission to Old Calabar in 1846 – were first initiated in Jamaica and then effected by the home boards in Britain. The third venture, which also used

Jamaicans, was the mission to the Gold Coast of the Swiss-based Basel Missionary Society in 1843. In this case, Jamaicans were sent to work as teachers, settlers or labourers. A fourth experiment, which has become known as the Rio Pongas Mission, originated with the Anglican Church in Barbados in 1855.[8]

Contemporary research by Maureen Warner-Lewis, on the work and contribution of West Indians to the development of West Africa in the early twentieth century, has highlighted that the activities of the Rio Pongas Mission of the Senegambia region were the result of the active interests of British officials who served in the colonies. These included Richard Rawle, principal of Codrington College, Barbados, and Dr William Walrond Jackson, bishop of Antigua, who was a member of the English Committee of the Anglican Church. Colonel S.J. Hill, who served as governor of Freetown in the 1850s and was later appointed governor of Antigua, also strongly supported the mission. In successive years, missionaries, both men and women, from other parts of the West Indies – St Kitts, Nassau, Barbados, Grenada, Antigua and Trinidad – joined this mission and gave valuable service. Warner-Lewis notes that "the corporate history of the evangelical work of the missionary endeavour includes its quota of fore-shortened lives – both of missionaries and their children – due to adverse health conditions. On the other hand, it offers evidence of marathon years in the field. And while the documentation shows that several missionaries eventually returned to the Caribbean, there are indications that some of the missionaries and their descendants settled in Africa."[9]

The group of West Indians who came from Jamaica to the Gold Coast in 1843 and settled in the town of Akropong are among the earliest recorded West Indian returnees to the Gold Coast. They had responded to a request made by Moravian missionaries for African Christians who, it was believed, would have a greater influence on their fellow kinsmen. Their experience has been documented in the general histories of the Moravian Church in the West Indies and also in an autobiography by a son of one of the migrants.[10]

Research done by Samuel Boadi-Siaw has identified Afro-Brazilian returnees, known at present as "Tabom", who returned to West Africa, including Ghana, in the post-emancipation era and throughout the nineteenth century. They left Brazil for a variety of reasons. These included their desire simply to return home, or to avail themselves of opportunities for education and self-improvement, or to escape a hostile environment under which free Africans existed in Bahia, or, for those who became Christians, to share their faith in the homeland. They came on their own, without sponsors or official support, and on their arrival on the West African coast, they "had to quickly adapt to the society to which they had come, and to accept whatever would enable them to survive – the food, language, religion and general way of life". These returnees have become "completely absorbed into Ga society – in political organization, social patterns, language and in religious beliefs and practices", although they have retained "a few traces of Brazilian and Nigerian (Yoruba) cultural remains".[11]

Ray Jenkins's work also identifies the presence of "Brazilians and West Indians" in the Gold Coast during the second quarter of the nineteenth century. In particular, the introduction of West Indians was linked to the soldiers, relatively few in number, who were recruited to the First West India Regiment stationed at Cape Coast and English Accra after 1844, and two ministers, the Reverends T.B. Freeman (1809–1890) and H. Wharton (1819–1873), who were the founders of Methodism in the Gold Coast. The development of the British Gold Coast and, in particular, the towns of Accra and Sekondi, created an increased demand for military personnel, which resulted in the employment of civilian colonial officers from the Caribbean to fill senior positions after 1880. Jenkins has cited "evidence accumulated by Jeffrey Green" that points to a substantial increase in the number of West Indians in the colonial administration after 1901. They included people from Jamaica, Barbados, St Lucia, St Vincent and British Guiana (now Guyana) who were employed in the Post and Telegraph Office, the Police, Prisons and Customs departments, the government schools at Cape Coast and Accra, where women teachers from the Caribbean were prominent, and the Accra Teacher Training Institution, which opened in 1909. Newly arrived West Indians also joined the "communities of businessmen in the coastal towns of Axim, Sekondi, Cape Coast and particularly Accra". Included in this "expanding elite" were lawyers, engineers, bankers and traders. G.J. Christian of Dominica, and J.S. Bonitto of Jamaica, the manager of the Accra branch of the Colonial Bank who was also the vice-president of the Accra Chamber of Commerce, are mentioned in this group.[12]

Obiagele Lake's work, which focused on contemporary repatriates, sees Ghana as "a kind of mecca" to which returnees have continued to be attracted. In the post-emancipation period, they came as a reaction to slavery. In more recent times, they have been attracted by the attainment of "African independence and a sense of pride in their ancestral land". Lake's research, which was conducted in 1989, was based partly on interviews with 84 of the approximately 120 "diaspora Africans", mainly African Americans, living in Ghana at the time. They went there owing to marriage, in pursuit of business opportunities, or to offer their skills.[13]

Another small group of recent returnees to Ghana in the twentieth century, who might be considered religious returnees, are the family of the late Rastafarian reggae superstar Bob Marley, who died in 1981. His widow, Rita Marley, also a Rastafarian, wanted to return to Africa. She had actually visited Ethiopia, but when she finally had to make a decision, the considerations were varied. Ghana was chosen because that was "the country that opened its heart and its arms. Its stable government was attractive, as well as its embrace of development."[14] As a further explanation for her choice of country, Rita Marley commented that Nigeria was reminiscent of New York, whereas Ghana met her expectation of how an African country should be. Rita Marley and her entire family, including thirty-seven grandchildren and the household staff, settled in Konkonuru, in the Aburi mountain district outside Accra, and in 2000, established the Rita Marley Foundation, a non-governmental organization, with the aim of giving to the community.[15]

This biography examines a relatively unknown case of reverse migration in the early decades of the twentieth century. It chronicles the life and times of a Caribbean student who went from Dominica to England and then "back to Africa". George James Christian (hereafter Christian or GJC) went to London to study law in the 1890s. On completion of his legal training in 1902, he migrated to the Gold Coast, established a large family, became a prominent lawyer and active member of society, and remained there until his death in 1940. The role of education, especially foreign education, as pursued by Christian, who obtained a law degree, is considered to be of particular value and significance for Caribbean migrants as a means to acquire a profession and improve one's social status. This view has been documented by Elizabeth Thomas-Hope, who further stated that such students have been characterized as one category of long-stay migrants who have, as their major goal, the acquisition of education.[16]

Christian was one of a small group of West Indian professional migrants to the Gold Coast during the first four decades of the twentieth century. He realized early that he had deviated from the norm and considered it extremely important to document his experience as it happened. The papers he left are a rich source of primary data, and they were the majority of research materials for this study of Christian's life. They paint the picture of an extraordinary human being who gave full measure to each aspect of his existence – plans, career, family, friends, public service – despite the fact that he faced challenges such as the death of children, financial difficulties, ill health and family problems. He also recognized the importance and value of this information for posterity and passed it on to his next generation of kin, who in turn ensured the protection and provenance of his papers.

The George James Christian Papers (GJC Papers) comprise more than fifty-three hundred items dating from 1890. They include a variety of documents – correspondence, legal briefs, financial documents, pamphlets, election manifestos, Legislative Council submissions and notes, information about his children, newspaper clippings, funeral programmes, photographs and other background information. Christian was meticulous in his record-keeping and had a filing system for his correspondence. He kept letters he received as well as copies of his replies. In some instances, he even had important letters retyped on better-quality paper to ensure their longevity. He wrote to his children and encouraged them to respond to him as well as to write to each other.[17] He kept in touch with his relatives and friends in Dominica right to the end of his life.[18]

The GJC Papers are also a source of information about the other individuals who came to the Gold Coast at the time. Like Christian, these were mainly professionals who would most likely have come to offer their skills or to make a better life for themselves, as was mentioned by Lake. Although few official statistics on the size of the West Indian community in the Gold Coast at the time are available, a 1931 census document indicates that there were 3,182 non-Africans in the Gold Coast, of whom twenty were West Indians – seventeen males and three females.[19] A 1937 source identified three "legal practitioners" and six of the thirteen "African" medical practitioners in the Gold Coast in 1937 as West Indians.[20] Fortunately the oral data collected in support of the research on Christian, combined with the scattered references throughout the GJC Papers, have allowed more light to be shed on this small community of West Indians who settled in the Gold Coast in the first four decades of the twentieth century.[21] Christian played a leading role among them, and this will be dealt with in chapter 8.

During the time that Christian lived in the Gold Coast, his contribution penetrated different walks of life, and he was recognized as an outstanding member of the society at several levels. In his homeland, John-Baptiste Charles (1875–1983), father of Dame Eugenia Charles, Prime Minister of Dominica from 1980 to 1995, who purchased Christian's bicycle, described him as "the famous Christian . . . who left to go to England to study law and who became one of the foremost lawyers of West Africa".[22] Henrietta Peters, an African-American missionary who was headmistress of the West African Industrial Academy in Sekondi,[23] was on the receiving end of Christian's generosity of spirit during a difficult period in her life. She pointed out to Christian that his name would "live on in Gold Coast history", and she hoped that through the school, she would be the catalyst to ensure that this would happen.[24] Christian also received recognition from the colonial secretary as one of those presented with a medal, "forwarded by command of His Majesty, the King . . . to be worn in Commemoration of Their Majesty's Silver Jubilee 1935".[25] Samuel Richard Wood, author of *Handbook of the Gold Coast*, invited Christian to send a sketch of his life and a photograph to be included in the "Biography" section as "one of those prominent persons who, in their respective spheres, have contributed to the progress of the country within the last few decades".[26]

During her tenure in office as prime minister of Dominica, Dame Eugenia Charles endorsed the contribution of men like Christian in the context of heroes and nation-building from a Caribbean perspective. In a 1990 address on the subject of national pride on the twelfth anniversary of independence, Dame Eugenia identified the types of people who should qualify as national heroes. She cited four categories, three of which related to those whose efforts resulted in the development of Dominica society in various ways over time:

1. The "Carib and Arawak" ancestors, who "fought valiantly against the mighty powers of Spain, France and Britain to preserve and protect our birthright".
2. The forebears "of African descent who fought relentlessly and gave their lives for freedom and the inalienable rights of man".
3. The "latter day heroes of the twentieth century who fought against the colonial powers to uphold the rights and privileges of the society".

Christian fits into the fourth group, which included those "who achieved fame, not necessarily in Dominica, but in other parts of the world, where their accomplishments caused others to take notice of Dominica". Dame Eugenia further stated that "these sons and daughters of Dominica, many of them living abroad, have helped to build our reputation as a proud and hard-working people, and we must recognize their worth and their contribution to our nationhood. We must be proud of them."[27] Christian therefore deserves to have his story told, and it is in this context that the details of his life are being brought to light.

CHAPTER 2

Antecedents and Early Years in Dominica, England and the Gold Coast

GEORGE JAMES CHRISTIAN WAS BORN IN THE PARISH of St Joseph on the island of Dominica[1] on 23 February 1869[2] to George James Christian Sr and Sylvanie Laudat. Christian Sr was born in Antigua in the parish of Green Bay,[3] allegedly "to a female slave and an unnamed member of the Christian family". He was a descendant of Robert Christian, a wealthy slave-owner who arrived in Antigua in 1699 and owned six plantations, with several hundred slaves, located close to a bay that carried his name, Christian Bay.[4] Sylvanie was a descendant of the French aristocrat Laudat,[5] and her mother's name was Herminie.[6] Christian Jr apparently grew up within an extended family system and had at least one full sister[7] and one half-brother on his father's side, William Nathaniel Alexander Christian.[8] Sylvanie sold baked goods to assist in providing for the family. An older female cousin, Jeanvillia Romain, lived with them and assisted Sylvanie with their care and other duties.[9]

On account of his mixed heritage, Christian Sr was permitted certain privileges that resulted in his ability to read and write. After slavery was abolished, with the help of the Moravian Church, he was able to qualify as a teacher[10] at the Mico Training College,[11] which had been established in Antigua by the Trustees of the Mico Charity for the education of "young persons of the negro and coloured races for service as schoolteachers among their own countrymen". The college was used particularly by the Moravians for this purpose, as well as to train staff to evangelize in Africa, "where there was a pressing need for Negro missionaries".[12] Christian Sr allegedly worked as a teacher in Antigua[13] and was also reported to have been actively involved in community work[14] before he moved to Dominica, possibly in the late 1850s.[15]

Christian Sr, like his son after him, had ensured that some aspects of his life experience were documented for posterity. He was a "serial petitioner" to the governor, secretary of state and other colonial officials during the decade of the 1860s and left records in the National Archives of the United Kingdom.[16] These documents confirm that he was originally from Antigua, had been educated at the Mico Training College there[17] and was subsequently resident in Dominica. He was described by the chief justice of the time as someone "with ability and intelligence above the average of his rank". He had been formerly employed in Dominica "down the coast" as master of a co-educational school, but he had been "dismissed in 1860 by the Board of Education for gross immorality". According to the chief justice, "he was someone without position, character or property, except for a few acres of land given or acquired for election purposes".[18] After his dismissal as a schoolteacher, he earned his living "chiefly, if not entirely by drawing deeds and other papers for persons in the lower ranks of life".[19] Christian Sr described himself as a "writing clerk".[20]

The Dominica to which Christian Sr migrated was the only island in the British West Indies where rule by white planters in the wake of emancipation had been successfully challenged. A group of coloured[21] families controlled the legislature for two generations before the introduction of Crown colony government. There is evidence to support the view that the second half of the nineteenth century has been described as "a period of social and political reorganisation".[22] In a particular complaint in 1863, the governor of Dominica, in a letter to his superior in Antigua, drew attention to newspaper articles that suggested that the chief justice meddled in local politics. The governor realized that this officer should not be involved in such matters and wrote to him via the colonial secretary. He was also of the view that the chief justice should withdraw from cases of a political nature.[23] The colonial secretary in turn brought the controversy to the attention of the chief justice.[24] In light of the political situation, the governor reported that given its size, few British colonies "have given so much trouble to the Secretary of State and to the local Governors as this little island of Dominica".[25] Similarly, an 1866 newspaper reported that Dominica, "for many years had the unenviable reputation of being one of the most turbulent and unsettled of these colonies and of its politics being directed by a singular absence of honesty and right principle . . . without even a semblance of justice or wisdom".[26]

The multiple petitions that Christian Sr submitted to the Colonial Office authorities seem to have had a common theme, namely, a disagreement with the chief justice of Dominica, His Honour Thomas Sholto Pemberton. In 1864, Christian Sr was required to attend court to answer "for unlawfully and contemptuously composing, writing and publishing as well as causing and procuring to be written, published and delivered to the Chief Justice, whilst he was presiding in the Court, the said paper . . . in contempt of court and to the obstruction of public justice". It was felt that he had allowed himself to become "a victim of political partisanship".[27] Christian Sr admitted that he was involved in the writing of the articles and that he had been encouraged by others.[28] As a result, he was sentenced to three months' imprisonment and fined £25 for contempt of court, with further imprisonment until the fine was paid.

With regard to this matter, he wrote to Her Majesty Queen Victoria to plead his case further. He described vividly a prison breakout and the prevailing circumstances that took place during his incarceration. One of the prison guards was injured, and the other went in pursuit of escaped prisoners. As a result, he was virtually in command of the jail for ten minutes and did not exercise his option to escape. He was subsequently praised for his actions by the inspector of prisons.[29] He further explained that he did not possess the means to go to the mother country to prosecute the appeal in person or to retain counsel or agent to act on his behalf. He accused the chief justice of being a political partisan and contributor to a newspaper of inflammatory articles against a certain measure of the government called "The Constitution Act 1863".[30] The chief justice denied all these charges and claimed that Christian's objective was not merely to obtain a review of his sentence but to assail the chief justice with charges and imputations, with the intention to bring about his dismissal, and that he was encouraged "by some half dozen persons of the same stamp as himself".[31] Christian Sr was subsequently released on the grounds of his inability to pay the fine and his good conduct at the jail during the breakout.[32]

In other correspondence between Christian Sr and the secretary of state, he accused the chief justice of miscarriage of justice in two cases against Alexander Robinson for assault, battery and perjury. At the root of the matter was an issue related to the 1862 struggles by one class to exclude participation by the other in the legislation of the country. His lengthy letter with enclosures was

230 pages and included complaints of nepotism and control of the legislature by people of colour who were related to one another. He called for the removal of the chief justice and questioned whether

> the partisan and fervid politicians of today may be trusted to assume tomorrow the calmness and freedom from bias and passion which are essential to the office of Judge, whether consideration is not due to the parties whose rights are being dealt with and whether it is desirable to continue in an office a gentleman who by virtue of that office has to decide on the political rights of persons who have not a shade of a shadow of confidence in him in any capacity whatsoever.[33]

Christian Sr apparently had not been authorized to make a claim on Robinson's behalf and was expressing his private views and opinions. His letter had been transmitted to the chief justice, who was in the process of preparing his statement on the matter.[34]

Another petition submitted by Christian Sr and Thomas Doyle in 1868 related to the issue of printing contracts. Thomas Doyle came originally from England but had lived in Dominica since his youth. He was the proprietor of the *Dominica Colonist* from 1840 and was its editor from 1855. He had also held unsalaried positions on the island as admeasurer of vessels and master-in-chancery. Christian Sr was also an editor of the newspaper. In 1862, the new assembly established a committee to address the issue of escalating costs of government printing in the preceding fifteen years since 1847. Consequently, a decision was taken that the award for government printing contracts should be advertised for tender. In response to the advertisements in 1865, Doyle put in the lowest bid and was awarded the contract for three years from 1 April 1865, with liberty to terminate after two years by either party. In December 1866, Doyle was told that by a resolution of the Legislative Assembly his contract would terminate on 31 March 1867, on account of alleged conflict of interest due to the positions he held, although these were non-salaried posts.[35] Doyle and Christian Sr submitted another tender that was unsuccessful. The gist of the memo submitted by Doyle and Christian was that the tender process for the government printing contract was unfair and not transparent and that there was favouritism that worked to their disadvantage.[36]

Christian Sr's penchant for writing to the colonial authorities certainly earned him a reputation at that level of the administrative system. Chief Justice Pemberton, against whom the petitions were directed, was of the view that

Christian Sr's motive was to leave his name in the records. He commented to this effect to the governor, after Christian's request for a review of his prison sentence in 1864: "Should he however fail in obtaining a review of his sentence he will nevertheless have attained that which I believe is of equal, if not greater importance to him and his abettors . . . the Petition and Doleance will remain a memorial against the judge in the Archives of the Colonial Office in Downing Street and of the Privy Council office at Whitehall."[37]

Towards the end of the decade, Governor Freeling, who was responsible for the administration of Dominica from 1869 to 1871,[38] made a similar observation to his superior, Governor Pine.[39] He wrote as follows: "I regret that I have so frequently to forward petitions every one of which emanate from the same individual George James Christian . . . I imagine that your excellency as well as the Colonial Office are fully aware of the character of the man and how he has assailed every Governor and nearly every public officer here for some years past."[40]

In this instance, Christian Sr alleged an illegal act on the part of the provost marshal in an issue related to the levy he made on a house. He considered the matter to be of such importance that "the style and tone" of the officer's communication was inappropriate even "to the meanest of Her Majesty's subjects".[41] The governor, on the other hand, described the provost marshal as "one of the most conscientious and best among the public officers".[42] In the final analysis, however, the governor reported that he could not interfere in the matter.[43]

Christian Sr explained why he had submitted these multiple petitions to one of the colonial officials. His actions were "in pursuance of a plan to appeal successively to every constitutional protective authority with a view to obtain redress for the Wrongs and Grievances" which he had "sustained at the hands of the Chief Justice of this island".[44] Generally the text and tone of his petitions demonstrate that he was a highly literate and well-informed man who had the courage of his convictions and was willing to confront the might of the empire.

CHRISTIAN'S EARLY YEARS IN DOMINICA

These activities of Christian Sr give an oblique insight into the kind of paternal influence to which the young Christian was exposed during his formative years in Dominica. Christian Sr most likely encouraged his son to follow in his footsteps and train as a teacher at the Mico Training College in Antigua in the late 1880s. While there, GJC's roommate was Sheriff M. Bowers, also from Dominica. He would also have been exposed to other students, many of whom came from other parts of the Caribbean, including British Guiana.[45] GJC did use his Mico training and served as a schoolteacher in the government of Dominica at St Joseph School. From 1891, he also worked as registrar of births and deaths for the parish of St Joseph.[46] Christian indicated that his father had introduced him to the Oddfellows organization,[47] and he continued to be active as a Freemason throughout his life. His father, who was concerned about the failure of the judicial system in the administration of justice, would undoubtedly have supported his son in his choice of the legal profession.

It would seem that Christian's exposure and his education had contributed to his consciousness of the experience of the enslaved Africans and of his African heritage.[48] At the Mico Training College in Antigua, he was apparently influenced by one of his teachers, Charles Farquhar, who had spent fifteen years as a teacher there before serving as a priest in Guinea.[49] In an 1890 letter of congratulation to Farquhar on his ordination to the priesthood and assignment to a posting in Africa, Christian and Bowers expressed their pleasure at his success.[50] They described themselves as "recently trained Instructors", the only ones in Dominica, and expressed the hope that his experience in that "distant land" would encourage others to follow in his footsteps.[51] The Reverend Farquhar, in his reply, stressed that his main goal was to be a teacher and that he was "happy in the knowledge that by far the larger portion of [his] time will be spent in humble efforts to lift Africa's sable sons to a higher intellectual level". At the same time, however, he also recognized his other mission as a black man in the service of God:[52] "I am pleased to know that, while my mission will be so to act upon the hearts of those among whom I go, that it will be realised that the image of the dear Master is stamped as indelibly upon ebony as upon ivory, still I shall be most literally a teacher, and only your reverend brother."[53]

After his ordination as a deacon, he sailed with his wife and family to the Îles de Los, an island group off Conakry, Guinea, and arrived there in October 1890 to become the headmaster of a boarding school that was still to be built and established on the island of Cassa. The school was formally opened in July 1892.[54] Christian and Farquhar remained in contact in the ensuing decades.

The year 1899 was a turning point in Christian's life. Apart from the fact that it was the year that he attained the age of thirty and left Dominica to study in England, it was also the only year for which he kept a specific record of the events of his life. The diary has permitted a close-up look at his life and character. It clearly shows that he was someone with a plan for his life and that he put measures in place to ensure that it would be realized.[55] He evidently had intentions to further his studies, and he wrote to England "for papers" early in the year.[56] He continued to seek out the relevant information for study abroad and also discussed his plans with people who could advise him.[57]

On 14 March 1899, a day on which he was in town engaged in the purchase of limes, he recorded that Mr Harris advised him to go to England and study law. Five days later, he had made up his mind to do so and "told Thomas of his intention to go abroad". In preparation for his studies overseas, he made a timetable for his work and began taking extra lessons from Thomas, including lessons to acquire or improve his proficiency in Latin.[58]

He also engaged in a variety of economic ventures, undoubtedly to fund his study abroad. He therefore travelled throughout the island by various means of transportation – bicycle, horseback[59] or boat – depending on where he was going. He generally recorded where he spent the night. Throughout the year, he was busily engaged in trade: the purchase and sale of various products, for example, salt and cattle.[60] He planted crops – nutmeg, pumpkins, melons and other plants.[61] He was also involved in the sale and shipment of the produce from his land – limes, coconuts, mangoes and other fruits. For example, in June, he spent one day in the preparation of mangoes and other fruits for shipment to Bermuda, and the next day, he shipped twelve barrels of limes to New York.[62] Similarly, on 11 August, he took two boatloads of mangoes and limes for shipment. He continued to ship his produce abroad until his departure for England. In preparation for his studies abroad, he discussed with his father his plan to secure a loan and received his father's approval to do so. He was promised a loan of £15 by "Howard" [Shillingford].[63]

He also provided quasi-legal services to people in the community. These included measuring land, writing deeds and preparing wills.[64] He reported having consulted with lawyers and searched records in the registrar's office, as regards a case of trespass on the Syers Estate.[65] He was also summoned as a juror and empanelled on a case.[66]

Christian seemed to be a well-rounded person, and apart from his work and study, he attended to the spiritual and social aspects of his life. He recorded his attendance at church services on important days that year. Having partied on New Year's Eve of 1899 and arrived home late, he nevertheless got up early and went to the Roman Catholic Church at St Joseph for devotion, as 1 January 1899 was a Sunday. He also attended Divine Service on Easter Sunday.[67] He kept in touch with friends and family and had an active social life. He received visitors, periodically entertained his friends, attended picnics and hosted quadrille parties. The latter took place for the New Year, Easter and Whit Monday bank holidays.[68] Before he travelled to England, he made sure to say goodbye to all his friends, relatives and associates throughout the island, starting with his friends at Portsmouth a month before his departure date. A week before he left, he spent a morning with "dear Laura", the mother of his deceased infant son, Ulric, and Felina [Serrant], the mother of his son Peter.[69]

Christian never lost his focus as the days and weeks passed, and it is evident that he had carefully worked out his plans. He exported his final shipment of fruits on the SS *Zaymouth* on 10 September 1899, and later that day, he embarked on that ship for the first leg of his journey to England to study law. He was thirty years old. They set sail at 8:30 p.m. for Bermuda. The first stop was Antigua, where he spent a night, and then he sailed on to St Kitts, where the ship landed. En route, they stopped at St Croix, and Christian was inspired to study history as he journeyed, as he found it "more congenial" and the fellow passengers agreeable.[70] From Bermuda, he travelled on the SS *Trinmarer* to New York, where he secured a passage to England on the SS *Lucania* of the Cunard Line.[71] He was unable to study on this leg of the journey, as there were too many people on board and excessive movement. He was also not feeling well.[72] As they continued on their journey, it was cold and foggy. They first stopped in Ireland, and the next day they arrived in Liverpool. From there, he travelled by train to Euston, London, where he was met by Fred Reeves.[73]

The young man who was about to embark on his legal training in London had a characteristic which would be an asset throughout his life, the ability to make an impact on and to keep in touch with colleagues and friends. During the stopover in St Kitts, Christian met with two brother Oddfellows, and he also visited the Reverend Everard, rector of St George's, who gave him a recommendation.[74] The Reverend Everard indicated that he had known Christian of Dominica "for many years". He held "a high opinion of his qualities both morally and mentally" and confirmed that Christian had "shown indomitable perseverance in struggling for the end he had in view".⁷⁵ Shortly after his arrival in England, one of his neighbours from Dominica wrote with a request to purchase a plot of land from him, because Christian was the only one who had the "right to sell". This neighbour extended greetings and "best compliments" from "all friends".⁷⁶

There is no doubt that in the thirty years he had lived in Dominica, Christian was well known and highly esteemed in his home community. His travel to London to pursue legal training was indeed a significant milestone in his life. On the one hand, he had left his native land of Dominica, to which he would return only as a visitor. At the same time, he was poised to lay the foundation for his future career as a lawyer and a life-changing experience in the Gold Coast.

STUDENT LIFE IN LONDON

Christian arrived in London to begin his studies at Gray's Inn at a most interesting time. The first section of the Central London Railway's line was opened in mid-1900, and its Chancery Lane tube station served Gray's Inn.⁷⁷ It was reported that in 1901, the revival of Gray's Inn "stood on the threshold of a century rich with the illimitable promise of inconceivable progress" and that "never before had living been so cheap, so affluent and so lavish". All classes of people were able to enjoy the opulence in varying degrees. There were 250 inhabitants at Gray's Inn, which was still considered to be "an island of quiet", although "it was not immune from the intrusions of the outside world".⁷⁸ Christian spent the first few days in London becoming acquainted with his new surroundings and with the contacts he had there, as well as writing to his mother, other relatives and friends in Dominica.⁷⁹ Fred Reeves, who had met him on his arrival in London, was instrumental in his settling-in process, showed him around and introduced him to people and places of interest. During these early days, Christian also acquired appropriate clothing and kept a close eye on his finances. He went to Gray's Inn for the first time on 4 October 1899, when, he recorded, he met Dennis Douthwaite, steward of Gray's Inn, and students Henry Sylvester Williams and Francis Stanislaus Leung.⁸⁰

Christian's initial application to Gray's Inn, which included his qualifications from the Mico Training College, was not successful, but he persisted until he achieved his aim. He had submitted a petition to request admission "without passing the preliminary examination in Latin". This was apparently contrary to the regulation, but the steward of Gray's Inn did indicate that he would be pleased to meet with Christian if he so desired.[81] Initially his petition for the exemption from the Latin examination requirement was not granted. The steward promised to ask the treasurer whether he could be tested in French instead.[82] In the meantime, Christian duly resumed his Latin studies under Reeves's tutelage and devoted considerable time to it, although he acknowledged feeling miserable and low in his spirit over the disappointment.

Christian was eventually granted the exemption from Latin[83] and was allowed to do the examination in French, which he passed satisfactorily. Williams assisted him to secure an outstanding signature on relevant documents, and in due course, within the first few weeks, he secured his certificate of recommendation for entrance to Gray's Inn and admission to the Inns of Court. Christian also successfully completed the Inns of Court examinations in English Language and English History. He began his reading, borrowed materials from other students and started to work on his assignments.[84] He was officially admitted to Gray's Inn after he paid the relevant fees on 20 November 1899. He attended his first dinner there the same night. On his admission to Gray's Inn, he was described as a retired schoolmaster, "the first son of George James Christian, writing clerk".[85] His two referees were Arthur Langridge, barrister of Middle Temple, and Tho. J. Greenfield, barrister of Gray's Inn. Henry Sylvester Williams had introduced him to Greenfield.[86]

Christian was mindful of who was supportive to him during this period of his life. Many years later, when Mr D.W. Douthwaite, the steward who dealt with Christian in these early days, was retiring after thirty-eight years of service at Gray's Inn, Christian was pleased to be part of the celebration. He duly signed the testimonial slip, sent the required donation of five shillings and indicated that he could not sufficiently express his appreciation of Douthwaite's role in his life during his student days. He felt that were it not for Douthwaite's "kindness and sympathetic encouragement", he "might never have qualified".[87]

In the midst of his anxiety as well as intense study during this period, Christian sensibly continued to take time out for recreation. He took the opportunity to enjoy other aspects of life in London – the theatre and music halls, in particular the Palace and Metropolitan theatres. He wrote letters, took walks (for example, in Regent's Park), bought tobacco and began the habit of smoking a pipe before going to bed. He also recorded certain health challenges during these early days in London – a fresh cold, painful boil over his left eye, constipation, influenza and fever.[88]

As recorded in the latter weeks of his 1899 diary, Christian settled well into student life in London, giving it his full participation. He continued to correspond with his relatives at home, although he reported disappointment at not receiving sufficient correspondence frequently and expressed the concern that his letters home might have been tampered with.[89] He also had his pipe engraved, went to Fenchurch Street to the sale room for turtle shells (which were used to make jewellery and decorative items), and had success in selling shells which he had brought with him. He completed the six dinners at Gray's Inn for the term, began his reading in the area of Roman law and participated in a debate in the common room at the Inn. He bought dumbbells and boots and began to exercise. He kept up his social life and his friendship with Reeves. He took out "Miss S" to the theatre in Drury Lane, attended two other plays and bought and wrote Christmas cards.[90] When he passed his first exams, he informed T.H. [Howard] Shillingford in Roseau, and the latter, who had "published [the news] to all friends", also passed on their congratulations and encouraged him to study hard to pass his final examinations.[91]

As was to be expected, he also experienced some challenges in his new environment. In terms of the weather, he recorded on 10 December 1899 that it was very cold, and he could not read. He had a fire in his room, but he still felt cold. He also had a disagreement with Leung over an outstanding loan and sent him a "sharp letter" asking Leung to indicate the day on which he intended to repay him. He reported that Leung was annoyed at being "dunned". Christian summed up the experience in the following note in his diary: "<u>Lent money – lost friend</u>",[92] although Leung did repay the loan by the set date as promised.

There is no doubt that Christian missed home. As Christmas approached, he anticipated that it would be "a dull one" being away from his friends. He spent the entire Christmas Eve day in his room, and bought himself a bottle of whisky for his Christmas treat. On Christmas Day, he wrote several letters to relatives in Dominica, including Felina and his mother. His Christmas Day entry in his diary stated as follows: "Christmas in England, a dull time – plenty of food and kissing under the mistletoe." He attended a party at Mrs Marvin's, where there was a large gathering of ladies and gentlemen. He enjoyed himself with them, returning home at 3:30 a.m. He was ill with the cold for the next few days, however, and had several sleepless nights that the rainy and foggy weather did not help. Campbell, a friend from Demerara (Guyana) who was studying medicine at King's Hospital, prescribed a mixture, which he took. He spent the rest of the week mostly indoors, reading the newspapers and the *History of Gray's Inn*. On 30 December, he went out for a walk and visited the National Portrait Gallery. He began to feel better the next day.[93] He reported that London was quiet but anxious.

CHRISTIAN AND THE PAN-AFRICAN ASSOCIATION

Given his interest in African affairs, it is not surprising that as a student in London, Christian immediately embraced an opportunity to become involved in the African Association. It was founded in 1897 by Henry Sylvester Williams from Trinidad, whom Christian had met shortly after his arrival. Williams had enrolled as a student at Gray's Inn two years prior to Christian's admission to the Inn.[94] The African Association was intended to be "a body of Africans in England representing native opinion in national matters affecting the destiny of the African race".[95] Williams had been planning for the famous first Pan-African Conference at least a year before Christian arrived in London.[96] Among the other West Indian students at Gray's Inn at the time was Richard Emmanuel Phipps of Trinidad, who also participated in the activities of the African Association and served as secretary for the West Indies on the Pan-African Conference Committee.[97] Christian's former teacher from the Mico Training College, the Reverend Charles W. Farquhar, who had been posted to West Africa in 1890, also attended and addressed a function of the African Association in 1898.

The Pan-African Conference which took place in July 1900 was originally intended to address the "widespread ignorance . . . in England about the treatment of Native Races under British rule".[98] However, it was expanded to deal with the subject as it related to "European and American rule" in South Africa, West Africa, the West Indies and the United States.[99] Christian attended the conference and, together with Henry Sylvester Williams, he addressed a session devoted to South Africa on the theme "Organised Plunder and Human Progress Have Made of Our Race Their Battlefield". Christian's contribution was a "wide-ranging survey of conditions in Africa", which clearly demonstrated that he had knowledge and understanding not only of the atrocities of slavery, but also of the continued domination and exploitation of African states by the colonization process.¹⁰⁰ Christian, who was described by one newspaper as "of pure negro type", stated that

> the Dutch farmer looked upon the negro as a beast of burden inferior to humanity. . . . The Negro in Rhodesia, as in the British West Indies, was compelled to work without adequate wages and in Rhodesia the chiefs were forced to find gangs of black men for the mines, where they have to work for months at the absolute mercy of a company. . . . (The men were) compelled to work without wages. . . . Payment was in things for which they had no use and they returned to their homes with nothing in return for their work. What was this if not the revival of slavery? It was part of the white man's civilisation in South Africa.
> The natives were stolen from their native shores in the 16th century and were now jostled out of their lands. . . . They are not allowed to own land, or even to be at large without a pass, no matter what position they might attain to in wealth, character, and intelligence. They could only travel in a part of the train more fit for beast than man, and the franchise is out of the question. . . . The treatment of native races in South Africa, particularly in Rhodesia, was a more degrading form of slavery than that which the English nation had done so much to abolish. . . . And now it was proposed that they should adopt more stringent measures in regard to native labour, so as to lessen the expense of the mines and give larger dividends to the shareholders. . . .
> If justice was to be done in the coming settlement in South Africa, the Imperial Government must guarantee protection by laws that no local legislation could alter, and no prejudiced Judges and juries could pervert. In addition, territories should be reserved for the natives and native chiefs be given some measure of home rule over their tribes. With justice and fairness the natives would become a loyal people of the empire, ready to fight for its cause and die for its flag.¹⁰¹

Christian's active participation in the conference confirmed that he identified with Williams and the pan-African interests. In his suggestions for a solution in South Africa, he recognized that a legal system supported by the means of implementation was an avenue by which the situation of the African could be changed. The *Lagos Observer* reported that Christian "had struck the key note". It was "a perplexing question" as to "whether the source of trouble was the system of Administration or with the men sent out as Governors". According to the newspaper report, "the larger share Native Chiefs have in the administration of their internal affairs, the better it would be for peace and prosperity".¹⁰² An observation was made that the overseas delegates to the conference left behind "those like Williams and Christian who had to complete their studies".[103] In the wake of the conference, a permanent Pan-African Association was formed, into which the African Association was subsumed.[104] Christian served as treasurer of the new association.[105]

During his student days in London, Christian worked assiduously towards his goal to become a lawyer. In the process, his entrepreneurial tendencies were also revived and served him in good stead. He recounted to his son Howard that even before he had successfully completed his examinations in Roman law or constitutional law, he had "the cheek" to tutor two Indians in those subjects. He was practical about it, as he noted that the fees he charged came in useful, and as he coached them, it helped him to learn the subjects.[106] On 22 and 23 May 1901, less than two years after his admission to Gray's Inn, Christian had successfully completed his "final examination, preliminary for call to the Bar". He had "previously passed in the second class the examinations in Constitutional Law and Evidence and Procedure".[107] Having duly paid the princely sum of £89 2s. 4d. "for Bar and Bond Stamp, Fees and Americaments on Call to the Bar",[108] he was called to the Bar on 11 June 1902.[109] Fellow West Indian Henry Sylvester Williams of Arouca, Trinidad, eldest son of Henry Bishop Williams, architect, was also called to the Bar on that occasion.[110]

Christian secured recommendations and began to look for a job as soon as he had completed his examinations. In one testimonial, a fellow law student who had been a practising solicitor for many years wrote of Christian that "his appointment to any position connected with the Law or administrative affairs would be highly satisfactory" and that "he would acquit himself with great credit".[111] Unfortunately Christian was advised that his application for "a legal appointment in the Colonies" could not even be considered until he could submit testimonial evidence of his working experience as a practising barrister.[112] Christian, however, was not deterred. He maintained the same focus on his vision combined with determination that brought him successfully through the fulfilment of his educational goals. He was ready to continue to the next leg of his migration journey.

FROM GRAY'S INN TO THE GOLD COAST

If Christian's participation in the 1900 Pan-African Conference was a means to express his consciousness of the experience of the enslaved African and the ramifications of his African heritage, his identification with Africa went much deeper. His migration to the Gold Coast on completion of his legal training was in fulfilment of a goal he had set for himself when he left his homeland. This is confirmed in a speech that he made when asked to propose a toast at a farewell function in 1929 for the then chief justice of the Gold Coast, Sir Philip Crampton Smyly.[113] He reported that on the night when he was called to the Bar in 1902, he "had some idea of coming to Africa as [his] home". He therefore summoned the courage to ask Smyly, who was serving in Sierra Leone at the time, where in Africa he would recommend.[114] Smyly had replied as follows: "Well, I would not advise you to go to the Gambia, Sierra Leone is overcrowded, Nigeria I know nothing about, but if you are worth your salt, try your luck on the Gold Coast." According to Christian, he considered the suggestion and "within a short time, [he] was on the briny and landed at Cape Coast on Coronation Day 1902",[115] which was 9 August.[116]

It is possible, however, that apart from the advice he received, other prevailing circumstances would have made the Gold Coast a favourable option for the young lawyer from Dominica. Towards the end of the nineteenth century, there was a "small but interesting group of people from the Gold Coast" who were living in London. They were mainly "students, businessmen and a mixed group of sportsmen, theatrical impresarios and ministers of religion".[117] It is significant to note that the only African-born person identified at an 1898 meeting of the African Association at which the Pan-African Conference was discussed was Dr E. James Hayford of the Gold Coast.[118] Similarly, among the delegates listed as attending the Pan-African Conference was J. Buckle of the Gold Coast.[119] It is therefore reasonable to conclude that Christian may also have had friends and associates from the Gold Coast.

Having decided to go to the Gold Coast, Christian sought to establish contacts there. Henry Sylvester Williams gave him letters of introduction to other West Indians – Maurice Reece of Trinidad and Dr Simmonds. Williams described Christian as "a general favourite of his Inn" and anticipated that he would be a success.[120] He also indicated that if Christian maintained the reputation with which he had left the Inn, he would certainly gain the esteem of all with whom he came into contact.[121] Williams, who was fluent in the French Creole spoken in Arouca, Trinidad,[122] made reference in both letters to the ease and the fluency with which Christian spoke patois (Creole). This was undoubtedly a bond between them. Williams mentioned to

Reece that it recalled "happy associations of our dear old home Trinidad".[123] Shortly after his arrival in the Gold Coast, Christian contacted Smyly and requested from him a letter of introduction to an official of the court. Smyly, who had never been to the Gold Coast, received the request while in Switzerland and explained that not only was his only contact there on extended leave at that time, but also he had no access to the list of officials. He was sorry that he could not accede to Christian's request and "very sincerely" wished him "every success in [his] new venture".[124] Years later, Christian acknowledged that he owed a debt of gratitude to Smyly for having given him the advice initially.[125]

Christian's arrival in the Gold Coast in 1902 presented some challenges, but this phase of his experience was short-lived. When he first landed at Accra, he stood on the beach that Sunday morning, a "stranger amongst strangers". Although he had sufficient money to pay for accommodation, there were no hotels, and he did not know where to go to spend the night. One of the Customs officers, who discovered Christian's origins, reported his plight to his superior officer, a fellow West Indian, Leonard Muss. Muss then invited Christian to join him for lunch, together with the agent of Swanzy Limited who was present at the time, and allowed him to stay at his house until the following day. Muss also helped him to establish his legal career in the Gold Coast by introducing him to the then chief justice, who served as a referee and provided verification of Christian's legal certificate.[126] Christian subsequently helped Muss's son to get into school and to buy the necessary books, and he considered it a privilege, honour and blessing to return in some small way the kindness which he had received on his arrival.[127]

Christian also reported that he had to spend his first night in Tarkwa "on a naked counter", but, as he himself indicated, this did not prevent him from making good progress.[128] He eventually settled in the town of Sekondi,[129] a busy port on the coast, which served as one of the main import and export terminals of the country. It was known as "the Liverpool of Western Africa" on account of the number of ships that used the harbour.[130] Originally established by Europeans in 1900, the old Sekondi European Town and railway terminus was at one time "a commercial, residential, trading and political centre". It was a hub of economic activity and a thriving commercial area. Some historians have noted that the building of Takoradi Harbour in 1927 marked the beginning of the decline of Sekondi.[131]

Generally it will be seen that Christian's involvement in Gold Coast society demonstrated a conscious attempt to use his legal training and other skills and abilities for the advancement of society.

DOMINICA HOUSE

Despite the fact that he had chosen to settle in the Gold Coast, Christian remained overtly conscious of his West Indian heritage. He demonstrated this in a tangible way when he became a property owner and landlord in 1908 and gave the name Dominica House to the property he acquired, a constant reminder of the land of his birth. Located at number 4 Poassi Road in Sekondi, Dominica House was rented out for five years from 1 July 1908 at the annual rent of £200 to Gottlob Siegfried Rottmann, a merchant of Hamburg trading in the Gold Coast Colony. One of the witnesses to the lease was Christian's law partner, barrister-at-law F.S. Leung.[132]

In April 1915, just over thirteen years after coming to the Gold Coast, Christian undertook construction to extend the existing property to include a large family residence, retaining the name Dominica House. The African Union Company was contracted to erect a two-and-a-half-storey residence, an addition to the building located at Poassi and High Court Road, Sekondi, at a cost of £169, for which Christian supplied all the material. Described as a "mini castle" by one of his sons, Dominica House was a unique edifice architecturally. It was designed by an African-American architect, Charles W. Chappelle, and was built of imported timber from Canada. The building materials were shipped from Montgomery Ward and Company in Chicago at a price of approximately US$700.[133] It was such an outstanding structure that even before it was complete, Christian and the African Union Company received congratulatory remarks for the aesthetics and uniqueness of the building. In one of the newspapers, the *Gold Coast Leader,* in the section General News for Sekondi, it was reported that

> the African Union Company are putting [*sic*] a three storied house for Lawyer Christian. It may seem as if we were rather too quick with our recommendations, but the fact remains that although the building is not yet completed, the architecture and beauty thereof are unequalled and unquestionable. Owing to the situation of the land, the corner part of the building leading to the Gold Coast Machinery side has been so rounded from the bottom all way up that the view

from afar projects to the eyes as peculiarly astern, the only one such building in Seccondee. We congratulate Lawyer Christian and the Company.[134]

Throughout Christian's life in the Gold Coast, Dominica House was an outstanding feature of the Sekondi landscape and facilitated his career and lifestyle. Apart from providing accommodation for his family, he often entertained his friends at Dominica House. The degree to which Christian became well-known and respected in the society can be seen from the fact that he offered hospitality to many at his home. For example, Dr James Kwegyir Aggrey,[135] Bishop J.W. Brown and his wife of the African Methodist Episcopal Zion Mission,[136] and Mr and Mrs George Padmore of Liberia[137] were some of Christian's friends who visited or stayed at Dominica House. Similarly K.W. Todd, who worked at Achimota College (formerly Prince of Wales College and Achimota School), planned on doing some sightseeing before leaving the colony. He intended to visit Kumasi, Cape Coast, and then travel to Sekondi by train, and was depending on Christian to accommodate him.[138]

An extant printed programme indicated that a full-fledged concert, including twenty-two items – solo and choral performances, piano solos and duets and recitations – by male and female friends of GJC was held at Dominica House on 21 December 1929. Christian also received requests to use Dominica House as the location for meetings[139] and other events from time to time. For example, in 1938 the Bar Association requested the use of his residence as the venue for a luncheon party in honour of two judges, Barton and Savary.[140] During the Christmas and Easter holidays, Dominica House was the venue for many annual gatherings of the West Indian community in Sekondi and the surrounding areas.[141] It was reported that "Jamaican cocktails" were famous at Dominica House.[142]

Although the building no longer exists, Christian ensured that there would be a photographic record. In 1925, he had arranged for postcard photos of Dominica House to be printed in England, through Mrs Leung, who sent the samples in the post from London.[143] Described as "a very imposing structure",[144] the house consisted of a ground floor which was rented out to commercial enterprises and two upper floors where the family lived.[145] The interior of Dominica House included a veranda, bedrooms, dining room, sitting room, a huge living room with a billiard table and a drawing room with a corridor leading to it from the back steps.[146] There was also a four-car garage.[147] The furnishings included a dining table with an additional leaf, piano, carpets, elephant tusks and a showcase of silverware.¹⁴⁸

After Christian's death in 1940, his wife Abba Lucy French, popularly known as Mami Abba,¹⁴⁹ his children and extended family continued to live at Dominica House.¹⁵⁰ In 1949, a fire broke out on the ground floor of the house, which was rented out to Kingsway Chemist. The floors, walls and some furnishings in upper rooms occupied by the family were burnt, or damaged by heat, smoke or chemicals from the fire extinguishers.¹⁵¹ The property was acquired by the government of Ghana in the 1960s for public purpose and was subsequently demolished.¹⁵²

Figure 2.1. Dominica House, Sekondi

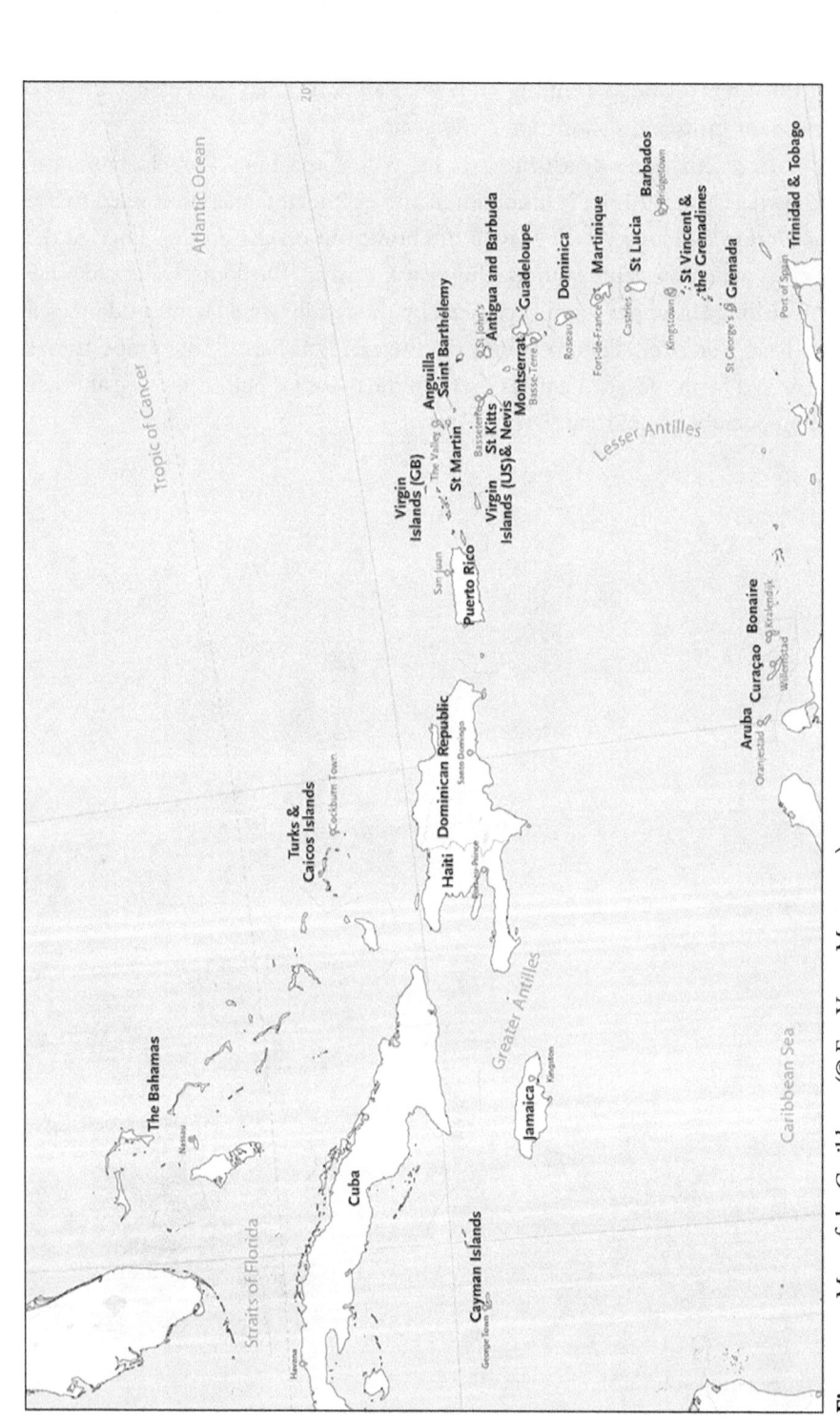

Figure 2.2. Map of the Caribbean (© FreeVectorMaps.com)

Figure 2.3. Map of Ghana showing Accra, Sekondi-Takoradi, Tarkwa and the Ashanti region (http://www.nationsonline.org/oneworld/map/ghana_map.htm)

CHAPTER 3

Christian as Father and Family Man

AN IMPORTANT FOCUS OF THIS STUDY IS THE personality of Christian the patriarch and central figure in his community and among the West Indians, which is best elucidated in the context of his role as father and family man. Christian established his home and a large family in the Gold Coast, but he did not forget or neglect his three children and two nieces from Dominica. It is evident from his dealings with his children that his upbringing and experience had taught him the value of education. He was committed to the process of raising progeny who would be self-sufficient and useful to society. Consequently he ensured that each of his children received the best possible education. Most of them were educated in England, and he kept in touch by letters and periodic visits.

He had many challenges along the way – children who did not meet his expectations, as well as the illness and death of four of his offspring. His son Howard, who had qualified as a lawyer shortly before his father's death, became the family patriarch. Generally Christian's children, among whom were two doctors, two lawyers, a nurse and a teacher/diplomat, went on to lead successful lives in the Gold Coast.

CHRISTIAN'S CHILDREN

Dominica-Born

Considerable correspondence left by Christian combined with the oral records[1] give an insight into his progeny and family life in Dominica and the Gold Coast. When he left Dominica in September 1899 at the age of thirty to go to England to study law, he was already the father of two children, had buried a third, and a fourth was on her way. Clara Marguerite, his eldest child, was born in May 1895.[2] His second child, a son, Peter Charles, was most likely born in 1895.[3] Early in 1899, a son named Ulric, presumably born in 1898, fell ill and was seen by a doctor on 3 January, in Roseau, the capital of Dominica. However, over the next two weeks, his condition deteriorated, and he died of "infantile indigestion"[4] on 22 January 1899. He was buried the next day at St Joseph.[5] Christian, in a 1934 letter to a friend in Dominica, Mr Hypolite, reminisced on this incident in his life: "I sometimes take my mind back to the days when Laura and I were planning great things for the future but it pleased God to take away 'My Son' and the whole scheme of our respective lives was changed. Let me hope that she is well and prosperous and when you do write her give my loving regards."[6] His fourth Dominica-born child was Maude Mary, whose date of birth is given as 24 December 1899.[7]

There is scant information about the mothers of these four children. The mother of his deceased infant son, Ulric, was most likely Laura Lecointe. She was mentioned twice in Christian's 1899 diary simply as "Laura". On 19 March, he wrote her "a reproachful letter". In the week before his departure from Dominica to commence his studies in London, he rode down to Coulibistrie and spent the morning "with dear Laura and friends".[8] He apparently kept in touch with her throughout his life and sent her remittances, which she acknowledged. In a March 1925 response to correspondence from Miss Laura Lecointe of Coulibistrie, he addressed her as "my dear coumere"[9] and discussed whether it was possible for his niece Christiane (Chrissie) Burke, who was her godchild, to stay with her. He wished her the best of good health and luck.[10]

Christian's niece May Christian gave the names Felina Serrant and Virginia Boland[11] as the mothers of the other children and confirmed that Christian was not married before he left for England.[12] Felina Serrant was evidently the mother of his son Peter, as it was later reported that he had a half-brother named George Serrant.[13] Christian visited Felina shortly before his departure for England in 1899, and she, together with another female friend, came and assisted with the work to be done at his home.[14] Peter also reported on her health in correspondence between father and son in the 1930s.[15]

Africa-Born

In the Gold Coast, Christian fathered another twelve children with six different mothers. According to a granddaughter, "he became an African in the true sense of the word. He had children by more than one woman and he was married to the mothers of those children by what was called at the time, native law and custom".[16] Christian himself also noted that he had "so many African children" that he was an African and would "fall or rise" with them. He also expressed the view that he did not want his children "to be wage earners and landless" and that he wished "them to be treated as human beings".[17]

Four children born to two mothers between 1905 and 1908 were Christian's first set of children in the Gold Coast. Sarah Helena and fraternal twins Joseph (Joe) and Josephine Martha were the offspring of Mary Aba Ackon.[18] Ebenezer Kwesi Christian, born on 20 March 1906, was the son of Frances Maame Franswa Boham of Elmina.[19]

Five other children, Howard Kojo, Herminie Eccuah,[20] Essi Matilda, Ferdinand Francisco and Edward Clifford, were born to Abba Lucy French (Mami Abba),[21] between 1915 and 1930. Another child, Angela Ambah, born in 1916, was the daughter of Cecilia Ajuah Fenyi from Ajumako Owane.[22] She grew up with her siblings at Dominica House.

There were two other Africa-born sons about whom there is brief information in the written and oral records. In particular, there is no direct specific data about their mothers. A son, George Kwesi Christian, was born in 1906 and was educated in Sierra Leone before his return to the Gold Coast, where he died at a relatively young age.[23] Another son, John Mansour, whose mother was Lebanese, did not carry his father's surname. He was taken to Lebanon, where he was educated, and he subsequently trained as a lawyer in France. He returned to the Gold Coast in the 1950s, by which time Christian had already died.[24]

CHRISTIAN'S AFRICAN WIVES

Mary Aba Ackon

The records left by Christian give little information about the mothers of his children. Mary Aba Ackon was born at Cape Coast in 1868 to Opanyin Kow Kra and Madam Amba Yarba of the Adwenadze family. Her mother was a trader who moved from Cape Coast and settled in Sekondi in 1880. Mary Aba followed in the tradition of her mother and became established as one of the leading traders. Described as "industrious and persevering", she travelled long distances on foot to transact business, sometimes as far as Kumasi.[25] In addition to her trade in general goods as a passbook holder of Messrs Millers, Russell and Swanzy,[26] she was also a baker and an active Grand Lodge member of Mount Zion. She was most likely married to Christian under customary law.[27] After their relationship ended, she remarried and had several other children, including two sets of twins.[28]

In a discussion about the welfare of his daughter Sarah, who was at school in Sierra Leone in 1923, Christian compared her delicate appearance with that of her mother, who he noted had been able to withstand a "rough and demanding life".[29] Sarah supported her mother with a monthly allowance, and together with her siblings, Joe and Josephine, purchased a home for her at a cost of £200. Christian advised them that the house bought for their mother would be safer if placed in Joe's or either of their names instead of their mother's name, since he personally knew "that these ladies are bad traders" and feared that their mother "might get into debt and the property levied upon".[30]

Frances Maame Franswa Boham

Maame Franswa, a baker and trader at Chapel Square in Elmina, had been introduced to Christian by friends, and after a few visits to Sekondi, he was betrothed to her. During her pregnancy, she returned to her family in Elmina for their assistance, as it was her first child. It is alleged that initially, Christian denied paternity based on rumours of promiscuity. He only accepted responsibility when he was told of the child's resemblance to him. Consequently the family was upset, and as a result, this son, Ebenezer Kwesi, grew up with his mother. He was christened at the Methodist Church, and he attended Elmina Methodist Primary and Middle School, where he obtained the standard seven school-leaving certificate. His mother worked in the family bakery business to provide for him. On completion of his middle-school education, he went to Sekondi in search of his father.[31]

Abba Lucy French

The only wife for whom there is information about her relationship with Christian was Abba Lucy French (Mami Abba). Her father, J.W. French, a Portuguese man of mixed race, from Shama, close to Sekondi, was Christian's friend. She was considerably younger than Christian and was the wife with whom he had a long and close relationship. According to her Nigerian daughter-in-law, Grace Christian, she must have been about twenty years old when Christian married her. Mami Abba, who never knew her date of birth, observed her birthday on the same day as Christian's.[32] Mami Abba spoke Fante and encouraged her daughter-in-law to speak it. Christian understood the language but did not speak it. Mami Abba had clothes, shoes and jewellery in abundance, some of which Christian had bought her on his overseas trips. She was an excellent cook, and apart from traditional West African dishes such as palm soup and groundnut soup, her repertoire included West Indian dishes such as callaloo and souse pork, which Christian taught her to prepare. Christian entertained frequently, and there were many occasions at Dominica House for which Mami Abba prepared the food that was served. Christian was very proud of her.[33]

Christian was open in his expression of care and attention to Mami Abba, and this was noted by no less a person than Dr James Emmanuel Kwegyir Aggrey, who had stayed at Dominica House in 1926. He was impressed by Christian's show of devotion to his wife and wished that more African men would be as "tender and kind" to their "sisters, mothers and wives".[34] In 1935, Mami Abba was in a vehicular accident, and although no limbs were broken, she suffered bruises on her neck, face, arm and leg.[35] When she continued to experience pain on her right side and in the ear, Christian sent her to the Korle Bu Hospital in Accra for an X-ray.[36] The following year, she suffered two bereavements. Her father, Mr J.W. French, died on 13 March 1936, and two weeks later, her "oldest and dearest sister", Essi, also passed away.[37] The double sorrow brought on a return of the pains in the side and ears that she had experienced after the motor accident. Christian did his best to cheer her up because he recognized that good health was required "all round" to meet their heavy responsibilities.[38]

Mami Abba in turn was also attentive and caring to Christian, who was plagued with bouts of illness. He commended her as the good lady who had looked after him all these years and nursed him back to health.³⁹ Some years later, when he was unable to move from his bed, his doctors also congratulated her and said that they did not have any nurse that "could so well attend" to Christian.⁴⁰

Mami Abba was a most supportive partner, who was also generous with her finances when it was necessary to be of assistance for the upkeep of Christian's other children. For example, when Christian was faced with the responsibility for the education of his grandchildren,⁴¹ Mami Abba offered to help pay the children's dues in England.⁴² She indicated her willingness to dispose of an investment to help Clara and her children, despite the fact that she also had her own daughter, Essi, for whom she had to provide. Christian deeply appreciated her generosity.⁴³ Mami Abba had her own income from the purchase and resale of rice and smoked and salted pig flanks, which were sourced from Cheapside Syndicate Limited.⁴⁴ Christian ordered as many as a hundred bags of rice from George Francois for Mami Abba to sell.⁴⁵ Her mother, who was also involved in the retail business, assisted her with the sale of the cases of pig flanks.⁴⁶ Mami Abba contributed one pound sterling towards the duty on the Christmas box being sent to Clara's sons.⁴⁷ She was also "willing and anxious" to help finance Windsor House, a property in Bermuda that Christian intended to renovate for rental in order to assist Clara.⁴⁸

Christian, not unexpectedly, did experience some challenges with his complex extended family. For example, in 1923, Sarah, Joe and Josephine were being educated in Sierra Leone,⁴⁹ because he was not satisfied with the available educational opportunities in the Gold Coast then, and he could not at the time fulfil his intention to send them to Europe. He was concerned about their health, and at the same time, their relatives in the Gold Coast wanted to see them. The solution was to bring them to the Gold Coast for a holiday and a change and then send them back to continue their education, because he was "determined not to have them among the surroundings on the Coast".⁵⁰ Years later, he admitted to Clara that the other children were not pleased with Mami Abba being there, as they would have preferred to have their own mother around. He was of the view that Mami Abba's inability to read or write was "her misfortune".⁵¹ On the other hand, Christian also noted that it was to her credit that "unlike [his] other crowd", her interest was genuine and not merely for what she could get out of him.⁵² She had been close to his daughter Maude.⁵³ Peter also found her to be "genuine" and became fond of her during the time that he visited his father in the Gold Coast.[54] Christian noted that Peter had "certainly endeared" himself to her and wished that "others had done likewise", because it would have been "far more pleasant for all concerned".[55]

IMPORTANCE OF EDUCATION

Christian held strong views on education, which he always rehearsed to his children whenever an appropriate occasion arose. His upbringing and experience in the West Indies had taught him the value of education as an agent of social mobility. Generally he felt that it was the only means whereby the person of African descent could attain a decent lifestyle. This topic takes centre stage in his correspondence. Not only did he ensure that all his children received good-quality education, but he continuously instilled in them the importance of having a worthwhile career as the means of self-advancement and a better standard of living.[56] For example, he reinforced his advice and encouraged his daughter Angela as follows:

> I note that you are not keen from moving from teaching to law . . . I do not want to suggest to any of you children [a] particular line of work . . . so long as you have some qualification by which you will be able to earn a living on your return to Africa and be able to make yourselves useful to your country and your race. Bear in mind this always. Ours must be a life of service and by so acting the example set will perhaps make others do likewise.[57]

Similarly, when his son Ebenezer connected with his father on completion of his school-leaving certificate, Christian encouraged the young man to learn a trade. This son acquired skills in metalwork and later secured a job at the Gold Coast Railway in the Western Province.

Christian shouldered his responsibility and aimed to ensure that his children were given an opportunity to qualify for their chosen careers, although he experienced some disappointment in this regard. He had kept in contact with his family in Dominica and provided for the education of his children there. His eldest child, Clara, was sent to a convent school in Edinburgh at the age of eleven, after the death of her mother, and from there she went to Hampton Institute[58] and Oberlin College in the United States, where she trained as a singer.[59] In 1915, she returned to Edinburgh, where her father initially intended for her to take a course in optometry, but according to him, "she obstinately insisted on taking a full medical course at Edinburgh University".[60] At Edinburgh she had the distinction of being the first black woman to enrol as a student.[61] It was also at Edinburgh that she met Edgar Gordon, a fellow medical student, from Trinidad, who, in her father's words, "persuaded her to give up [her studies] and go in for matrimony".[62] A year later, they were married. In 1939, Christian, as he was inclined to do in moments of reminiscence, outlined the circumstances which led to Clara's marriage. He was of the view that if she had had access to less money during her student days, she would not have been "in the position to help Edgar" as she did,[63] and "he would not have been drawn" to marry her in the hope that her father would support him and his children all of his life as his actions had proven.[64] She would have been "a qualified doctor and not Mrs. Gordon without a qualification".[65]

In the early days of the marriage, Clara and her family returned to Dominica. In 1920, her husband, Edgar Gordon, hoped to secure a government job and joined her there. The "sole reason" for their return at this time was that they hoped their presence in Dominica would be an incentive for Christian himself ultimately to settle there. They were also willing to offer Maude a home, under their "protection and chaperonage". Edgar obviously felt the need to reassure his father-in-law that he should "always endeavour to prove his worth", so that Christian would be able to "absolutely and unconditionally dispense with any prejudice or ill feeling that Clara's irregular matrimonial escapade" might have engendered. He confided to Christian that Clara's health was cause for "grave concern", but that he intended to restore her to perfect health. Without any intention to excuse himself or to condone her behaviour, he also wanted to state "a fact", that Clara's "health would never have permitted her to stand the climatic and other conditions that a medical course at Edinburgh involved". He wanted to ensure that Christian saw things in their true perspective. He also offered his assistance if Christian wanted anything done with his property in Dominica. He was prepared "to do whatever" to further Christian's interests, as he was grateful "for the manly and timely help" he had received from him.[66]

The Gordons had six children, who were born between 1917 and 1927.[67] The family subsequently moved to Bermuda. Unfortunately they separated later due to "irreconcilable matrimonial problems".[68]

Christian's experience with his second child, Peter, who was educated in the United States, showed his determination to do everything possible to assist his children to become established in their careers. Peter's education included two years at Hampton Institute and four years each at Howard University itself and at the Medical and Dental School[69] before he graduated with a bachelor of science and doctor of dental surgery in 1925.[70] Despite Peter's qualifications, attempts to have him certified to practise both in the United Kingdom and in the Gold Coast were unsuccessful, owing to the non-recognition of American tertiary degrees in British colonies at the time. The vice-dean of the medical school at Howard University had not been able to secure a decision in Peter's favour with the British embassy, probably on account of Howard University's "B" classification with the Dental Educational Council of America (DECA). The situation could not be altered until a re-survey of the dental college was done by the council.[71] The director of medical services in the Gold Coast had consulted with the attorney general, and the interpretation of the existing law meant that only those who held degrees registered with the General Council of Medical Education in the United Kingdom were eligible to practise in the Gold Coast.[72] Dr Scott of Howard University, with whom GJC had kept in touch throughout Peter's student days, was "pained beyond measure" that Peter, having qualified, was not able to begin his practice.[73]

Christian was not deterred. He also wrote to the governor on the matter, in view of the shortage of dentists and "their utter disproportion to the population of the Colony and dependencies". He asked that the rule related to registration be relaxed in order to recognize and admit qualified dentists from known dental institutions outside Great Britain.[74] The response from the governor expressed regret that the Gold Coast laws could not be relaxed in favour of any person. It did suggest that although Nigeria's laws were equally strict, there was a possibility that he could be accepted for registration there.[75] Peter also explored the possibility of practising in Liberia and was greatly encouraged to do so by the Liberian consul general in Liverpool, who explained that there was a dire need for trained dentists.[76]

In the wake of these hindrances to Peter's ability to practise in the Gold Coast, Christian sent him to England with the intention for him to qualify there and submit his case to the Board of Examiners in Dental Surgery. The requirements to qualify entailed further study and examinations in medicine and surgery, as well as practising at a dental hospital and school – in reality, two one-year programmes that he was expected to undertake concurrently.[77] Unfortunately Peter had health challenges while in England and had to give up his studies and return to Dominica.[78] He was subsequently certified as a dentist within the Leeward Islands[79] and eventually set up his practice in Dominica, where he also looked after matters related to the tenancy and maintenance of his father's properties.[80]

Christian had also persisted to have Peter registered to practise in Africa, and in 1937, he secured a temporary licence for him to register as a dentist surgeon and to practise dentistry in Nigeria. Peter was required to produce his dental diploma for scrutiny at the Medical Headquarters in Lagos on his arrival in Nigeria.[81] Having visited the Gold Coast but never practised there, Peter confessed to his father that he was "loathe" to join him. He found the atmosphere uncomfortable, did not feel "at home" with the grown-ups and feared that he would suffer the same fate as his sister Maude.[82] He was emphatic that he preferred to remain and die in poverty in Dominica rather than live in Africa and have cause to regret it. Christian read Peter's letter "with great interest" and replied that he never realized that Peter was so "faint-hearted" and that his son almost made him feel ashamed.[83]

Christian's daughter Maude also received a well-rounded education from an early age. In 1913, she attended the Convent of the Faithful Virgin in Roseau, Dominica, together with her cousins Marjorie and Christiane (Chrissie) Burke, the daughters of Christian's sister. Apart from his expenses for their board, lodging, tuition fees and allowances, Christian also paid for tickets for them to attend the circus and theatricals, library subscription fees, dresses for special occasions such as Easter, and trimmings for hats and handkerchiefs.[84] Maude had her secondary education in Edinburgh, Scotland, at St Margaret's Convent between 1916 and 1919, after which she successfully completed the examinations of the Education Institute of Scotland in English, geography, history and French.[85] She subsequently studied chemistry in London and went on to qualify as a midwife in 1921, with certification from Clapham Maternity Hospital and Clapham School of Midwifery in the principles and practice of midwifery as well as the certificate of the Central Midwives Board, London.[86]

As a father, Christian was not spared from the position of having to make tough decisions to bring a child to his or her senses. For example, in 1924, Maude was in England being supported by her father with £75 a year, plus a dress allowance of £25. She also requested a monthly allowance of £10, which caused her father to express the view that he felt that "everyone should earn their own living and learn to be independent after the parents have done their share and not to rely always on the parents or the matrimonial market".[87] She eventually returned to Dominica, against her wishes, as her father could not "afford to have her doing nothing in England".[88] He threatened to discontinue her allowance because of her attitude. She was "too proud to work for the peasants", while she kept company with people who did not meet his approval.[89] He further commented that Maude seemed oblivious to the fact that he had "other responsibilities besides her" and that "although he was not inclined to force her to consider marriage to someone she did not care for as an option", he wondered whether "it would have been wiser for her to have accepted lawyer Burke's offer" instead of "playing the fool in Dominica" with the expectation of her father's continuous support.[90]

Christian, however, never lost sight of his goals for his children. When Maude was unable to find suitable employment in the West Indies, he then proposed that she take a short course which would equip her to work alongside her brother Peter in his dentistry practice.[91] In March 1925, she enrolled at the Bodee School of Mechanical Dentistry in New York to do a three-month course. Christian went so far as to enlist the assistance of Emmett Scott of Howard University, where his son Peter was a student, to impress it upon Maude that her father was no longer able to provide the level of support to which she was accustomed when she was in England.[92]

Maude eventually joined her father in the Gold Coast in 1926 and took up a government appointment at Sekondi as a maternity nurse. She was subsequently transferred to Accra, Christiansborg District, in 1928, where she was required to visit expectant mothers. Her father was concerned that the authorities had not provided her with proper or suitable accommodation, so she was forced to find her own, which was costly. Her father was practical, in that he encouraged her to stick it out so as "not to prejudice the chance of the others". He hoped that later on, the authorities would reconsider the situation and reassign her closer to Sekondi in more suitable conditions.[93] After a few months, however, she tendered her resignation and returned to Sekondi to take charge at home and possibly set up a private practice.[94]

The education of his children was an expensive exercise, and there were times when Christian was hard-pressed to meet all his commitments owing to fluctuations in the economy that affected his finances. For example, in 1923, he complained about the increase in fees at the convent in Sierra Leone where two of his children were students. He summarized his situation at the time as it related to the education of his family:

> It is all very fine when a man has only one child, but it becomes a matter for consideration when he has two at the Sierra Leone convent, one in Dominica, one in St Joseph's convent in Grenada, one in the convent in Elmina, one in London with Mrs Leung, one in America at Howard University, and two grown up ones in the West Indies to be provided for. I think they ought to show me some consideration. You might find an opportunity of mentioning this to the good lady when you see her, and besides those I have enumerated, I have three with me here to provide for.
>
> It is not every man that would do as much for his children as I am doing for mine – both African and West Indian, and I assure you, recent losses and disappointments have pressed hard on me, and as I do not believe in false pride, I want it known.[95]

Eventually most of his children were educated in England, and Mrs Hedwig Leung, widow of his law partner Francis Leung, was their guardian while they were there. Christian was naturally delighted when he received positive reports on the children's progress, and he reiterated to their guardian his goals for their education. He felt that the disadvantages of race increased daily, and "the poor black man did not have a chance in any walk of life which the white man wanted for himself". He cited the situation of some lawyers who did not earn much money because law was overcrowded, and one had to be above average to do well. He repeatedly asked Mrs Leung to emphasize to the children that it was important that they should "each qualify in some calling" and take up a profession by which they would earn a good living and be self-supporting.[96]

Christian recognized his indebtedness to Mrs Leung for looking after his children and was appreciative of all her kindness. He believed without her assistance, he would not have been in a position to have so many of them in England together. In 1929, when she indicated her intention to be away from London for a year, he described it as a "bomb-shell". He hoped that she would continue to take an interest in their welfare and, in particular, make suitable arrangements for "some good folks" to oversee his son Howard and assist with his character development.[97]

The twins, Joe and Josephine, were a source of concern to him as they seemed less academically inclined than the other children. However, they were sent to England to train in agriculture and millinery respectively.[98] Christian was concerned that he could not afford to keep them indefinitely in England if they did not progress in their studies. It would be a disgrace if they were to return to the Gold Coast without a trade or any means of earning a living.[99] Christian even considered dentistry as a possible profession for his son Joe. He recognized that Joe was "by no means brilliant" and subject to illness, and although he did not wish to "look down on the brain power of the dentist", he felt that dentistry, unlike law or medicine, required "less of the grey matter" to be successful after one was qualified.[100] Christian eventually conceded that Joe wanted to study agriculture and agreed to his pursuit of this course of study, although Christian felt that he should study at Kew, because it would put him in an advantageous position on the job market.[101]

Christian, however, was always inclined to push his children to the outer limit of their capability.

In 1928, seven of his Africa-born children were being educated in England and France. Sarah was at Queen Mary's Hospital, Carshalton; Joe had left King's School, Rochester, and was being tutored privately;[102] Josephine, who was at one time not very happy, eventually attended a convent in France, Institution De Melles L'Anzag Poitiers; Howard was at Dulwich College; and Angela and Essi were at the La Sagesse Convent School at Romsey near Southampton.[103] Josephine, who acquired proficiency in French, was subsequently sent to another academy,[104] where she earned a diploma in millinery and dressmaking.[105] Joe eventually attended the Seale-Hayne Agricultural College in Newton Abbot, Devon, where he completed a diploma in agriculture.[106]

Christian could also be an indulgent father, and he did as much as he possibly could to enable his children to develop their full potential and give them positive life experiences. In 1924, his daughter Herminie Eccuah, at the age of seven, accompanied her godparents, Mr and Mrs R.E. Dick, who were originally from Barbados, on a four-month visit to the West Indies and England.[107] Essi, whose education in England began when she was five years old, recalled that her father generally came to England every two years. He would visit the school, but they also came to London and stayed at Mrs Leung's, and he took them out to restaurants and showed them a good time.[108] On an occasion when he did not visit or write to his children in England during the holidays, he instructed Mrs Leung to "indulge them" with extra pocket money.[109] The following summer, he requested Mrs Leung's assistance to organize his summer travel schedule to England, which would include some holiday time, "in part with the children and in part by [him]self". The issue to be decided was whether he should go to Vichy with or without them and for how long.[110]

As a father he had a vision for his children and stopped at nothing to give them the tools to accomplish the goals he had set for them. For example, in 1937, he was willing to pay for Angela, Essi and Howard to holiday in France, because he desired for them to learn the language.[111] He had hoped that Essi would become equally proficient in French as Josephine.[112] He sent an ivory necklace, to be used a gift, as a source of encouragement to Peter in his pursuit of the young lady he was "anxious to please" at that time.[113] He would use the offer of an increase in their pocket money as an incentive to his children for them to improve their performance in particular areas of study.[114] On the other hand, he could be hard when necessary to bring a child in line with his wishes. Christian was concerned about his son Howard's behaviour in school. A remark in Howard's school report placed much emphasis upon the college's requirement that boys be well-behaved. Christian warned Howard that the report on his behaviour had caused him great distress, and he would not hesitate to make a change in his life that he would not like.[115]

IMPORTANCE OF FAMILY RELATIONSHIPS AND PATERNAL WISDOM

Christian invested considerable time and effort to have a relationship with all his children, and his attentiveness and caring for them was consistent and exceptional. He had been raised in the Catholic faith, and although he confessed that he had got "an overdose of the Scriptures and church-going" as a student at the Mico Training College,[116] there is evidence that he aimed to instil in his children values which were in harmony with his religious upbringing. He emphasized sound family and moral values at every opportunity, even though the children were educated abroad.

He was careful to treat all his children the same, and he corresponded with each of them individually. He was also practical, because when time did not permit him to do so, as happened when Maude and Joe were both ill and caused him much concern, he wrote to the eldest child, Clara, and sent copies of the same letter to all the others.[117] He also encouraged his children to develop and maintain relationships with each other by correspondence. On one occasion, he asked Peter to write "nicely and encouragingly" to Howard to urge him to aim for success in his school certificate examination so that he might start his professional course. He confessed to Peter that with his advancing years, he wanted someone to help him, but instead he still had to help everyone. In this regard, he made reference to the fact that Peter was not able to practise as a dentist in the Gold Coast, where he would have been much better off financially than in Dominica.[118]

Despite the fact that they had different mothers and were educated in different places, GJC's children did develop strong bonds among themselves. For example, Howard pointed out that because of the way he exchanged letters with Angela, he became more familiar with her than with any other member of the family. He further stated that they, more than any of the others, had lived and grown up together, for which he was thankful. They had always shared each other's "secrets, joys and woes".[119] Howard was pleased to hear how his mother had taken to Angela, for he had always considered his sister as a part of him.[120] In the tribute from her family on Angela's demise, it was noted that as siblings, they had separated at an early age for educational purposes. When they returned to Ghana in the pre-independence era, however, "a renewed closeness" quickly developed among them, and despite their diverse experiences growing up apart, they "cherished the bond of family".[121]

Christian kept his finger on the pulse of all his children's activities through his letters. He always aimed to be positive in his advice and to encourage them to excel. GJC held strong views and maintained high standards, which he tried to impart to his children. When his son Peter successfully completed his studies at Howard University and qualified as a dentist, his father indicated that the news had brought him joy, but he was quick to point out to Peter that "it [was] one thing to graduate and quite another thing to be a successful practitioner. There are some lawyers whom I could not engage as junior clerks in my office although they have been qualified and called to the Bar. Everything depends upon your own efforts and integrity."[122]

He did not reprimand them when they failed, but instead offered encouragement and practical suggestions. Among his many words of advice to his children was the adage, "If at first you do not succeed, try, try, try again." He gave this advice to both Howard and Essi, when they had difficulty in passing their examinations. He pointed out to Howard that not everyone is apt in passing exams and advised him to understand the subject and not just trust to memory.[123] He encouraged Essi not to squander a golden opportunity, but to gird up her loins and persevere until she was successful.[124] He was concerned about the details of the education of his children and was willing to provide extra coaching to ensure that they met the necessary standards. For example, when Essi expressed concern about her readiness to take a Latin exam, he responded to her that, "Mother and I are very perturbed about your Latin. Will you please consult the Revd. Mother on the subject and let her take all necessary steps to ensure your success."[125]

When his daughter Angela, who was on staff at Achimota College, had to take a Fante exam, his suggestion to Essi, who spoke only Fante when she left for England, was that she should try to avail herself of opportunities to practise the language so that she would still be fluent. His concern was for the future, in anticipation of her return to the Gold Coast.[126]

Christian believed that there was a tendency for Africans who had been in England for any length of time to lose touch with their own kind and on their return to be apt to look down on their fellow countrymen, even to the extent that they professed not to understand the language of their motherland. Christian described such people as "artificial individuals" and noted that he "despised" them, and he warned Howard that he should not return to the Gold Coast with any verbal affectation.[127] Christian felt that heaven knew what sacrifices he had to make for his children, and he would like to feel that when he was gone, they could take their place in the community and be more useful than he was.[128]

Christian was tireless in his efforts to respond to his children whenever they sought his guidance. For example, he advised and encouraged Howard, Sarah and their siblings in England to become affiliated with the League of Coloured Peoples. He explained that there was no harm in their meeting and knowing other coloured people in England.[129] There were decent Africans and West Indians with whom it was desirable to associate, and those otherwise should be given "the wide berth".[130] Christian indicated that he was even willing and prepared to pay for the subscription.[131] He pointed out that the members were noteworthy people, such as the brother of George Stanley Lewis,[132] who worked with Mr Francois in the Gold Coast. Christian acknowledged that Drs Moody and Brown, who were involved with the League of Coloured Peoples, could be of assistance to them with the placement of his granddaughters in hospitals.[133] Christian saw the value of their meeting other people of African descent. He believed that it was to the advantage of black students in England, who were mainly in contact with white people, to meet and get to know other people like themselves.[134] Sarah in fact recollected that as a trainee midwife in Scotland, children often called out to her as "Blackie nurse". She stood out, as there were virtually no other black people around, but she generally ignored them as she was usually on the way to deliver a baby.[135]

He used every opportunity to advise his children and would suggest positive mechanisms to deal with difficult situations. When the Second World War was imminent, for example, he suggested to Essi that she should use the three months of disquiet to read and keep her mind occupied rather than get excited over the rumours being circulated in the daily newspapers.[136] As the situation became more serious, he urged her "to keep within bounds". He anticipated that if the war broke out, their correspondence would most likely be curtailed. In such a case, he advised, they should exercise patience, take all precautionary measures and do what they could to obey orders and restrictions.[137]

At the outbreak of the Second World War, Essi asked her father to bring them home. Her concern was for the number of people who would be killed. Her examinations had been postponed indefinitely, and although she was prepared, she anticipated that she would have forgotten by the time the examination was due.[138] After the outbreak of the war, Christian continued to impress upon her that it was important to continue her studies.[139] He discussed with Howard the issue of volunteering to fight and related that his mother did not want him to take undue risks without her consent. Furthermore, he warned Howard to keep company only with those who were loyal to the king of England and advised him that the safest place for him, Essi and his grandchildren to be was the countryside. He wisely pointed out that sea travel would be more dangerous, since English boats would be at the mercy of submarines and aircraft.[140] When he heard that Howard was part of a delegation to the secretary of state on the subject of the colour bar, he cautioned him not to speak out on a subject about which he did not know enough, apart from which, he did not want him to be a politician. He emphasized that although criticism could be either constructive or destructive, since the empire was at war, there was a need to be careful not to do or say anything which might cause embarrassment to the government.[141] Howard thanked his father for this advice and conceded that he knew nothing of the conditions in the Gold Coast. It was because of this lack of knowledge that he decided not to participate in any discussions again.[142]

Christian also took the opportunity to advise and encourage his children with good values and principles by which to live, and at times he was eloquent, graphic and humorous in the process. When Howard reported that he had enjoyed holidays with the parents of a schoolmate from his prep-school days at Dulwich, his father quoted from "the old philosopher" to remind him that school friends are for life and should always be valued: "The friends thou hast and their affection tried grapple them to thy soul with hooks of steel."[143] Similarly, when Howard expressed misgivings about his ability to cope when Angela and his other siblings/relatives left England,[144] his father advised him that when Angela left, like the young eagle who when dropped in mid-air by its mother recognized it had wings and began to fly to save himself, he must reconcile himself to the situation. Christian also encouraged him with, "Do not be a coward, be a Howard."[145]

Christian continued to take responsibility for his niece in Dominica, Chrissie Burke, as he was concerned about the long-term prospects for her independence. He asked Peter to explain to her that his aim was to educate her so that she would become self-supporting, because he would not be around forever.[146] He eventually sent her to America to learn a trade, and after she qualified "in Beauty Parlour business", he arranged for her to go to Bermuda and helped her get established. He also asked Clara to assist in this regard,[147] although Chrissie's preference was to join him in the Gold Coast.[148] Christian's aim was that Chrissie and Clara would live and work together and be "mutually helpful to one another", especially as it related to the Gordon children. He envisaged that they could assist Chrissie in their after-school hours and thus increase the family earnings. Two years later, Chrissie, however, wrote that she preferred to live in New York, but Christian informed her that she would not be allowed to stay in the United States without citizenship and that she should consider herself lucky to be permitted to practise in Bermuda.[149] He continued to encourage her to make the best use of opportunities that came her way. He hoped that things would improve and that she would remain in Bermuda rather than hold on to her desire to return to New York, where the hairdressing business was overcrowded.[150]

As he did with all his children, Christian took the opportunity to counsel Chrissie on the basis of his experience and reasoned with her in the course of his advice and guidance: "Do not distress yourself about my finding fault with you. . . . I have tried to outline to you the difficulties and dangers which beset a young girl in a strange land and I wish you therefore to bear in mind what I say."[151] With regard to money matters, he was straightforward: "My dear child, it is wrong for me to encourage you into believing that I can conveniently send you £4 for rent every month when such is not the case. Sometimes it will be possible at others not. However, I am hoping that your takings will be sufficient to meet your expenses."[152]

Chrissie Burke was certainly a challenge to her uncle, who later wrote: "As regards Chrissie, well, it is unfortunate that the child is of such a temperament. I cannot remedy the evil and since she will not be advised then she must paddle her own canoe and not blame me hereafter. . . . Well, if she will not listen to Clara what can I at this distance do but to let her please herself and perhaps regret her indiscretion hereafter."[153]

She continued to try his patience, and after he received a report of unsatisfactory behaviour on her part, he said to Peter that he had "discharged" his obligation to Chrissie and that she could "go to the devil if she wanted to misconduct herself". He believed that he could not spend all his life "looking after others with never any appreciation even from the likes of her".[154] Chrissie did eventually admit that if anything was to happen to her uncle, she would "feel it also", and she expressed her gratitude to him for everything he had done for her.[155] He in turn explained to her that Mami Abba's concern for her was based on the African tradition that traced inheritance from the mother's side, since one's maternity could not be questioned and she was his sister's only living child.[156]

Christian also encouraged another niece, May Christian, who had trained as a teacher, and he demonstrated paternal concern over personal details of her life. He commiserated with her over the fact that a teacher had to function at a second-class level for five years before being permitted to sit for the first class. He sent her money for the purchase of books and a lamp.[157] He was concerned about her weak eyesight and warned her not to put too great a strain on her eyes.[158] May did purchase the lamp and was particularly happy to have it to prepare for her exams, as she generally read by night.[159] He also inquired from her about his half-brother William and explained that the relationship between them was strained on account of their different views of the roles and responsibilities of fatherhood.

> When next you hear from your father I will be glad to learn if he is holding his own. He seemed very bitter against me when I suggested using a part of the £100

which your grand-mother left to him, towards your going to Antigua, etc. I do not mind what he chooses [to] think of me, my whole object was to see you qualified and able to earn a living, having discharged that duty he is at liberty to think of me what he likes; it does not make me the worse for it.[160]

IMPORTANCE OF SOCIAL AND PROFESSIONAL CONTACTS

Although Christian was always concerned about his children's welfare and never passed up an opportunity to assist them to become established in their careers, he did have some reservations and concerns as to what was professionally correct, given his position in the society. For example, in 1927, in a letter to Dr James Kwegyir Aggrey, who had travelled to the United States, Christian asked him to bring it to the attention of the authorities at Howard University, if the opportunity presented itself, that his son Peter, despite his qualifications from Howard University, was not allowed to register as a dentist in the Gold Coast. Christian further reflected that he "made a mistake in not approaching Sir Gordon Guggisberg personally on the matter, but jealous of my professional reputation and knowing what my colleagues might say, I avoided him to my regret".[161]

On the other hand, Christian used his professional contacts to advantage whenever possible to seek guidance for his children. For example, while Chrissie was in Bermuda, Christian sought the advice of Mrs Henrietta Peters, an educator, on whether Chrissie's training and equipment were sufficient to enable her to make a living there.[162] He asked if she would periodically "write a friendly letter" to Chrissie, to advise her of the best course of action.[163] He further suggested that she discuss the possibility of Chrissie's return to New York with the Cockburns.[164] Christian also exchanged correspondence with Mrs Peters about the possibility of the four Gordon granddaughters attending school in America, as it was costly to keep them in England.[165]

His concern for his granddaughters' education certainly occupied his attention, and he also discussed it with Mrs Leung. He intended to write to his daughter Clara to impress upon her that the eldest girl should train for nursing or "forfeit whatever chances the others might have". He was concerned and caring but at the same time practical. He explained that he could not "afford to pay for them always and I certainly do not intend to use what I have put by for old age or illness in educating my grand children, for if I got ill for a long time I might find myself requiring money for my upkeep as I certainly would not want my children to support me".[166]

Similarly, when his son Howard was training to be a lawyer, he asked his friend Horace Douglas, a London-based barrister, to "keep an eye on the boy affording him the benefit of advice and experience" after his entry to Gray's Inn.[167] He further asked Douglas

> to persuade Howard to join the Gray's Inn Debating Society and to mix more with his fellow students and so be drawn out of himself. I see he has passed his constitutional and my programme would be as soon as he has passed his final, without waiting for him to be called, to let him begin reading with you or anyone you recommend, so as to fulfil the requirements of the regulation to the effect that newly qualified people should read one year in Britain or two years out here before they can practise. I naturally want him to come and relieve me if God spares our lives, as soon as possible.[168]

In 1940, three years after this initial request, he reminded Douglas to pass on his "fatherly advice" to Howard whenever they met, as well as to Essi, who also wanted to become a lawyer.[169]

CHALLENGES FACED BY CHRISTIAN AS A FATHER

Christian experienced many trials as a parent, as he continued to be intimately involved in his children's lives. As a father, his children were always his responsibility, and although he aimed to educate them so that they would be self-sufficient, he consistently showed paternal concern and offered assistance to each child as necessary as they dealt with their various challenges.

Clara's Divorce

Christian was concerned about the fate of his oldest daughter, Clara, who had given up her studies at Edinburgh University to get married. He considered as part of his troubles the possibility of Clara's separation from her husband, Dr Gordon, who had gone to Bermuda to practise, but who, according to Christian, had refused "to do his duty by her". He advised that if the situation escalated, a deed of separation could be signed between them and provision made for the custody of their children. He also felt that the children could be placed in a convent while Clara should proceed to America to take her course in optometry, which was his original plan for her.[170] If she accomplished this, she would be able to support herself instead of being dependent on a husband who neglected her. She could not depend on her father to support her and her children, for he already had his other children to look after. He pointed to Clara's "bad luck" and lamented that the "young and giddy . . . decline the advice of . . . elders and suffer the consequences in later life at leisure".[171] He confessed that he was sad that Clara was so far from him and not happy in her domestic life.[172]

After the dissolution of her marriage, Christian demonstrated his willingness to assist Clara in every possible way, even when he himself was in financial difficulty. In 1935, when Sarah invited Clara to visit her in New York for a few weeks, Christian asked his son Peter to go round and look after the house and the children during Clara's absence.[173] Christian also used his legal expertise to ensure that Clara and her family would not lose any of their entitlements in the wake of her failed marriage. During a period of ill health, he encouraged her to make a will, to secure what she had for her children and to nominate trustees to administer the estate. In 1938, he engaged Hollis Hallet, a lawyer in Bermuda, to meet with Clara for that purpose. He advised Hallet that Windsor House, which he had acquired for Clara, should be put in her name, and in any event at her disposal, so that she would get the benefit of it for herself and her children. Christian undertook to pay all charges for Hallet's services.[174]

Clara's situation continued to be a source of concern to Christian, and he was grieved at the turn of events in her life in Bermuda and deplored the difficulties that had beset her. She suffered a nervous breakdown in the wake of a court order which decreased the sum of money paid to her by her husband and required her sons to spend an hour per week with their father.[175] Christian asked a colleague in Bermuda to impress upon Clara the need to rise to the occasion and remain strong to defeat her ex-husband's plans.[176] Clara, with the encouragement of her sister Sarah, sent her four daughters to La Sagesse Convent in England. Her father was annoyed that they had done this without his consent and was concerned when they got into financial difficulty and turned to him for help. He was forthright in his explanation that he had done his part to educate his children, and they should not depend on him to support his grandchildren as well.[177] He was concerned that Edgar was not doing his duty, and Clara was making a sacrifice and must have had to "starve herself" to keep her children at Romsey.[178]

Christian was willing to give whatever help he could, but he considered it a burden, due to the fact that he had been ill, his law practice was not what it used to be, and he still had children in England being educated and two younger ones who were still in the Gold Coast.[179] The issue of the children's holidays was also cause for concern. He asked Mrs Savage to confer with Mrs Leung and work out the most economical way to provide them with a suitable place for their holidays. He would have liked them to go to France because of the opportunity to learn French, but it would have been difficult for Howard, who would have had to look after the girls. He was nevertheless willing, if possible, to arrange to meet some of the expenses.[180]

In 1938, Clara expressed regret that she had ever met Edgar Gordon and did her best to suppress feelings of bitterness at the thought.[181] Gordon accused Christian of unwillingness to hear the other side of the case between him and Clara, who he said was "nothing of the paragon of virtue that her father imagined her to be". He had wanted to discuss the education of the two boys, Edgar and Kenneth, with him, because he did not wish them to be "handicapped" in the same way as their sisters had been because of their mother's "delusion that she was self-sufficient and knew everything". He also complained that Clara had allowed his daughters to leave Bermuda without saying goodbye to him, and despite the fact that he had written to Barbara twice, their mother had forbidden them to respond. He wondered what Christian as a father would think of such treatment.[182] Christian often thought that it was "a pity" that Clara married as she did, because as a result, he had to discharge Gordon's obligations to Clara and their children, as well to his other children. This was "painful" for him, as he was unwell at the time and money was "so scarce".[183]

Dr Edgar Gordon became involved in politics in Bermuda and served as a member of parliament. His motivation was to confront the racism he had witnessed in England and Bermuda, and he became a leading activist for the rights of Bermuda's workers. He was a founding father of the Bermuda Workers Association and played a role in protests when black citizens were excluded from the civic commemoration of Queen Elizabeth II's coronation tour of 1953.[184] Dr Gordon changed his name to "Mazumbo" with the intention to frustrate white racists, who would not honour him, when they referred to him, either with his title of "Doctor" or even the prefix of "Mr". He died in 1955.[185]

Peter's Personality

Christian continued to encourage Peter, who he felt was too timid[186] and not willing to use his initiative to exploit all the professional opportunities available to him as a dentist in the West Indies. As a result, Peter never made enough money to support himself. His father had offered to help him to travel periodically to the other islands – St Lucia and St Vincent initially, and later Antigua and St Kitts, to offer his services.[187] Peter was not keen to travel as he felt that those islands had their own dentists. His father pointed out to him again, on Dr O.C. Arthur's advice, that "a new person visiting occasionally was preferred to the local man as the people generally wanted something new". His father urged him to give it a thought rather than to stagnate in one place.[188]

When Dr Beausoleil made the same suggestion three months later, Christian pleaded with Peter: "Why will you not try your luck as others do. It is time for you to get out of your shell."[189] His father strongly suggested that it was fear, false modesty and lack of confidence and courage that prevented him from going to the other islands to work as a dentist.[190] His father took the opportunity to draw reference to his own experience and reminded Peter that when he was called to the Bar, he did not allow the fact that he was a stranger to Africa, or that other professionals were already established there, to prevent him from competing against them. He conceded that although he had not yet reached the pinnacle of his success, at the same time, he had not gone under nor been defeated by his rivals.[191]

Peter's pecuniary state was a constant source of concern to his father.[192] He continued to struggle as a professional in Dominica to the extent that he described himself as "catching hell" and wondered how long he could cope with the increased debt. His impoverished state forced him to postpone one of the Freemasonry rites of passage, as he could not afford to host "the proper kind of dinner".[193] His father ordered the apron on his behalf but advised him not to spend money for the purpose of a "big show".[194] Christian continued to encourage Peter to follow the example of the dentists from Antigua and Guadeloupe who had come to work in Dominica, and "invade their territory as they do yours".[195] He was blunt enough to point out to Peter that he was almost at the age when he should be earning enough to meet his requirements, even if it meant that he had to "try another field" to achieve this. He often encouraged Peter to get married[196] and continued to hope that this son would not "go on all [his] life being a bachelor". He suggested that a wife would put some "vim" into him.[197]

Christian, however, was shrewd and had thought through all the ramifications of his having chosen to live in the Gold Coast. He confessed to Peter that although he very much wanted him to come to the Gold Coast, at the same time, he realized that if Peter did relocate, there would be no one in Dominica to look after their interests. Therefore he was not inclined to persuade Peter one way or the other and was willing to give whatever support was needed for him to make it in Dominica.[198] For example, he undertook to assist Peter with the purchase of a car, with which he could transport tourists when they visited Dominica.[199]

Illness and Death of Children

Some of Christian's children had ongoing health concerns that put a strain on their father's pocket as well as his peace of mind. Peter's bouts of illness, for example, were reported as early as 1925, when he had health challenges while in England after his graduation from Howard University and had to give up his studies and return to Dominica.[200] In 1928, Christian remitted funds for his niece Chrissie to have her eyes attended to in Barbados.[201] Peter, who had been experiencing bouts of dysentery,[202] made the trip to Barbados with Chrissie. Christian hoped that both had derived full benefit from treatment in Barbados, but suggested to Peter that he should consider going to Washington for medical attention if his problem persisted. Christian was aware that health was "the first consideration", and he was willing "to find the funds ... for that purpose".[203] In the wake of the visit to Barbados, Peter reported that his health was restored and his father cautioned that he should pay attention to his diet in order to avoid a recurrence.[204]

Within three months, however, Peter's health challenges recurred. His father, who clearly understood that health was "more precious than money",[205] offered to finance his trip and made repeated suggestions that Peter should take a break and visit Washington for medical attention.[206] In 1932, Peter was ill to the point where he had gone to Trinidad for a change. The following year, Christian sent him some money to take a health trip, either to "St Kitts, St. Thomas, Antigua, St. Lucia or Trinidad", but the money was to be returned if it was not used for the stated purpose.[207] His father subsequently suggested

Bermuda as an alternative, reaffirming his belief that despite the costs, one's health had to be given priority.[208] Peter spent a month in Bermuda in 1934 and thanked his father for the "much needed" change of environment.[209]

Five years later, on Christian's return visit to his homeland in 1938, he travelled back to London with Peter and one of his granddaughters (Joyce), both of whom were hospitalized.[210] Peter was hospitalized for about ten weeks at the French Hospital in London.[211] He was suffering from stricture of his intestines.[212] He was treated by the consultant and physicians at the hospital and was visited each week by Dr Clarke.[213] He was finally released on 16 December 1938 after "the stricture had been successfully dilated" but he remained in England for a while longer.[214] He was discharged with medication and other supplies to continue with his treatment on his return to Dominica, as directed by the doctors.[215] He was also cautioned "not to drink for a while and [to] take things easy".[216] Peter returned to Dominica early in the spring of 1939.[217]

Initially Joe had a problematic right leg that occasioned several long periods of hospitalization. This continued throughout the decade of the 1930s.[218] For example, in 1932 he was hospitalized in Korle Bu Hospital, Accra, for a couple of months, and although his leg was healing slowly, it was necessary for him to remain an additional two or three weeks before his discharge.[219] A year later, he went to England for experts to decide whether it was necessary to amputate his leg.[220] He was accompanied by Sarah, when she travelled for her holidays. He underwent an operation for skin grafting, which indicated that the doctors in England hoped to save the leg and not have it amputated as had been suggested by medical personnel in the Gold Coast.[221] By the start of 1934, his leg was reported as "cured", and he was due to return to the Gold Coast.[222] However, Joe was readmitted into hospital and had a successful operation on 31 January for osteomyelitis of the upper end of the tibia of the right leg. This was a new development, since it was his left leg that had been the problem before this, but the infection had apparently spread from one leg to the other.[223] Joe's problems with his legs continued to the end of his father's life. In September 1939, when the scar on one leg became infected again, he lamented to his father that he felt "like having the blasted thing taken off and a wooden leg put in place" to save him from "the worry for a lifetime".[224] He was being drained of his substance, while the doctors were being enriched. He wanted to have a family of his own and felt that it could not be attained if he was unable to work and earn a living because of his leg.[225]

As a father Christian dealt with the whole gamut of experiences, not the least of which was the death of four of his children, an experience which has been described as "unnatural".[226] Apart from his having buried his infant son Ulric in Dominica in 1899, three of his other children, Africa-born George Kwesi, Herminie Eccuah and Dominica-born Maude Mary all predeceased him in 1922, 1926 and 1933 respectively.

George Kwesi Christian (1906–1922)

There is virtually no information about how Christian was affected by the death of his first Africa-born son, George Kwesi. This son had received his early education in Sierra Leone, where he was described as a "very brilliant boy".[227] He was moved to Richmond College, Cape Coast Castle, merely four months before his death. He fell ill and was being treated for inflammation of the liver, vomiting and seizures, but he died within a few days. His father was ill and confined to bed at the time of his death, but his mother attended the funeral.[228] At the memorial service, it was reported that at the college, he had "many and varied" interests and "made excursions into the realms of chemistry, of photography, and of butterflies" – subjects which did not generally interest boys of his age. He was a full member of the Wesleyan Methodist Church, and his life, which was "full of promise and not blighted", would find "its fulfilment in eternity". This was "assured because he had the love of God in his heart". It was noted that he had "sought to be a peacemaker between those he most loved" and that "perhaps what he failed to accomplish in this life, he may be able to bring about by his death".[229] In 1938, Christian sent a photograph of the late George Kwesi to his brother Howard in England to have it enlarged, so that he could have it mounted.[230]

Herminie Eccuah Christian (1917–1926)

Christian was "overwhelmed with sorrow" when his daughter Herminie Eccuah died a couple months short of her tenth birthday.[231] She had suffered a fall in 1924 and broken her thigh bone. Her leg was put in splints, but she was not in any danger.[232] Her illness set in six weeks after she began her education at the convent in Elmina at the age of eight in 1925.[233] She suffered with "fever night and day", and had an enlarged spleen, which the doctor said might have been "due to worms and malaria".[234] In the latter part of 1926, she suffered from bronchopneumonia, which occasioned multiple visits to the doctor and medication via injections.[235] She died of pneumonia on 21 December 1926.[236] At the time of her death, she was being considered for entry to the newly established Achimota College as a companion for her younger sister Essi, who had already been accepted as a pupil there. However, Herminie's death resulted in a change of plan for Essi's education, as her father was not inclined to send Essi to Achimota without her older sister.[237]

Maude Mary Christian (1899–1933)

Despite already having had to bury a child on at least three previous occasions, Christian was deeply affected by the death of his daughter Maude Mary at the age of thirty-three. This was understandable, because she was older and had had a longer relationship with her father than her deceased siblings.

Maude had joined her father in the Gold Coast in 1926, and as early as 1927, Christian reported that she was "getting a cold in her head" too often for his liking.[238] Her first bout of fever occurred in 1928, two months after she was assigned as a visiting maternity nurse to expectant mothers in Accra, Christiansborg District.[239] Her father felt that her living conditions were not appropriate, but he encouraged her to be patient. She eventually resigned and returned to Sekondi.[240] In 1932, Maude was ill with an attack of blackwater fever, and her life was in danger.[241] The doctors believed that when the crisis was over, she would have to recuperate in bed for at least three weeks, followed by a change of environment in Europe.[242] Once she recovered, Christian arranged for her to travel to England and possibly the West Indies for a change.[243] Maude did travel to England for recuperation,[244] but on arrival there, she was admitted to Endsleigh Hospital "under observation".[245] She made a good recovery, put on weight and had a holiday in Scotland during the time.[246] She returned to the Gold Coast at the end of October 1932 and appeared to be fit.[247]

Maude fell ill again in June 1933 with a temperature for a few days, which they thought was an ordinary fever. On 23 June, she suddenly developed blackwater fever. Dr Ribeiro was called in, and when he observed the severity of the attack, he immediately summoned Dr F.S. Paterson, medical officer in charge of the local branch of the Red Cross. Christian's friends Drs R.A.

Hoyte, A.E.C. Beausoleil, J.H. Murrell and E.L. Auguste were also contacted. Drs Hoyte and Beausoleil immediately left Nsawam and Tafo respectively to assist and remained in attendance and in collaboration with Drs Ribeiro and Paterson. It is reported that this medical team did all they could possibly have done. Dr Selwyn-Clarke, who was the assistant director of medical services in Ashanti, happened to be in Sekondi on the Sunday, and on hearing of Maude's illness, he too engaged in consultation with the attending physicians. Dr Duff, director of medical and sanitary services, and Dr Byrne, senior medical officer of Takoradi, who were also in Sekondi, offered advice as well.[248] The doctors were initially hopeful of her recovery and planned to send her to England again as soon as she was able to travel.[249] Despite the skill of the seven doctors in attendance, however, Maude Mary did not recover.[250]

She had previously received the last sacrament of the Catholic Church from the Reverend Father Bouchier. Twenty minutes before she passed away, she repeated the opening lines of the Girl Guides taps: "The day is done, The sun is gone", followed by her final words, "My time has come."[251] Her father, who was kneeling at her bedside when she passed away, could not reconcile himself to the loss. He lamented, "It seems all so strange to me and desolate. My plans are all upset. She was my confidential secretary and right hand."[252]

He described her death as "the greatest shock" of his life, as she was his "dearest and best".[253] Christian confessed that she "looked after" him and that "by her charm she won and controlled" his every action.[254] He was distressed that she was "cut down even before she reached the prime of life".[255] A year later, he bemoaned the fact that there was no warning that she would die within three weeks. He could not understand why she was taken away when she was proving her usefulness, but he conceded that in the final analysis, he had to "bow to the inevitable".[256]

The *Times of West Africa*, in a full-page report on her passing, noted that her funeral, which took place the following afternoon, was "one of the largest ever seen in Sekondi". This was a clear indication that the community held her in high esteem. The acting commissioner and other senior police officers led the cortège, which consisted of "friends and sympathisers" from "all classes and sections of Sekondi". There were several wreaths from relatives, friends and the many organizations in which she was involved. Condolence messages were also received from His Excellency the Governor and Lady Thomas, the colonial secretary, the secretary for native affairs, several justices and other notable people.²⁵⁷

Christian's response to Maude Mary's death indicated the important role children and family life held for him. With her passing, new traditions were established in the household. The anniversary of Maude's birthday was 24 December, and therefore the Christmas season automatically brought back memories of her death. Christian confessed that it was no longer the same for him, and from that time forward, the season was no longer celebrated in their household.²⁵⁸ Five years after her demise, Christian continued to be deeply affected by the experience of his loss.²⁵⁹ On the other hand, on alternate Sundays, Mami Abba continued to show her undiminished love for Maude and took the choicest flowers available to her grave. She was usually accompanied by Maude's good friend, Mrs Nora Awoonor-Williams.²⁶⁰

Celebration at Age Seventy

When Christian attained the biblical age of "three score and ten" in 1939, he held a special celebration. His children who were overseas went to great lengths to show their appreciation, and they prepared a unique birthday gift for him. It demonstrated their thoughtfulness, love and gratitude and also the standard of living to which they had become accustomed. Peter, who had been hospitalized in England at the time, Howard, Essi and granddaughter Evelyn came together and prepared a gramophone recording of their greetings as a present.²⁶¹ Christian reported that he and Mami Abba were equally pleased to hear their voices.²⁶²

Christian invited several friends and colleagues to join him for "wine and small chop" at noon. The party included Mr Justice Barton; all the members of the Bar, namely, Messrs Nichol, Abbensetts, Williams, Gwira, Carter; Major Kingsford, Captain Peele, the provincial commissioner, Commander Saxton, district commissioners Beeton and Morley, and the police magistrate. In the evening, he had a party "at home" for the younger people with the police band to entertain everyone with "sweet music".²⁶³ At the end of the gathering, he played the record sent by Howard and the others, which was "to the surprise of all the guests". Christian expressed the hope that his life would be "spared", so that Howard would be able to join him for his next birthday in the Gold Coast.²⁶⁴

Shortly after his seventy-first birthday, Christian anticipated that he would be able "to regain health sufficiently to return to harness". His finances were low owing to his inability to work since the previous summer, although he still had to "discharge his obligations" to his children and three grandchildren in England.[265] He looked back on his life with the hindsight of experience and warned against the "burden" of a large family, until one was in a position to discharge one's obligations. He opined that it was no use to give such advice to young people, who were not willing to listen to their "elders" but wanted "to try the experience for themselves".[266]

Christian must have eagerly anticipated the day when he would achieve his goals for his children. He believed that they should follow his example and use opportunities and fortunes earned to assist other family members. For example in 1927, he admonished Peter to disregard his niece Chrissie's "so called foolishness and help to care [for] her", because he expected members of the family "to do by each other in return for what [he had] done for all".[267] In 1939, when Howard completed his Bar exams, Christian was overjoyed and looked forward to his return the following year, ready to start practice.[268] He was explicit in his advice to Howard and what he expected of him during the post-qualification year in London. He had no objection to his extra-curricular activities such as lessons in boxing, dancing, or singing, as long as they did not interfere with his reading in chambers and his attendance at court. The latter were necessary to acquire practical knowledge that would give him an advantage in the Gold Coast. He recommended that Howard should develop skills in typing, as this was useful in practice. Generally Howard should aim to "merit the probation" of the two Benchers who had nominated him for his call, in the same way that he (Christian) had done.[269] He also cautioned him not to entertain any friendships that might encumber his position. He further advised that in their family, the one who qualified first had to help the others to get through. Owing to the change of circumstances as well as the many obligations he had as a result of his age and illness, he was unable to offer the same assistance to Essi as he had to Howard. He expected Howard to earn enough money to support himself and discharge his obligations to his mother and to Essi.[270]

Generally, Christian's focus was to raise his children to be useful citizens who would be self-sufficient and make the world a better place. However, not every child had met the mark and satisfied his expectations. His *cri de coeur*, in a letter to Peter, mere days before his demise, poignantly expressed the pain and the frustration he must have experienced at the turn of events in the lives of Clara, Peter and Joe.

> You are getting to be that age when you should be earning all that you require and if you cannot get it at home then try another field. It is like that boy Joe who is hanging on my neck as a weight. Must all my life go on supporting my children when I have spent so much on their education and their profession? It is like your sister [Clara] having a large family without finishing her Medical Course to earn money.[271]

Despite his efforts to educate them to be self-sufficient, they were still dependent on him for support. But such are the vicissitudes of life as a father.

Christian's Legacy

Christian had done all in his power to achieve the goals he had set for his family. He took full responsibility as a father and family man, and what he accomplished was exemplary. It would have been unreasonable to find fault with him in this regard, and the majority of his children fulfilled his general goals and attained success. When Christian died, his friend Dr Beausoleil reflected on the sudden nature of his death and brought to Howard's attention the fact that his father had gone "without the climax of his life, the great day to introduce [Howard] to the Gold Coast Bar". This "painful pleasure" would now be "reserved to his friends Abbensetts, Dove and Korsah". This was indeed a great disappointment for all concerned.[272] Christian did think seriously about his children who would follow him in the legal profession. For example, he had conferred with Howard as to what career Essi should pursue[273] and had indeed mused at the thought of what it would be like to see both Howard and Essi in court on completion of their legal training: "I would like to see Barrister Christian (Howard) holding a brief in court against Barrister Christian (Essi). I wonder if they would go for [one] another as sometimes fellows go for one another when I attack them. Ah well, it is a fair cry, so let us be diligent, self-confident and trustful."[274]

Although Christian did not live to see the fulfilment of this particular dream, both Howard and Essi became established in their legal careers. Similarly his other children were successful in the Gold Coast and continued in the tradition of family life and responsible service to their fellow man. Sarah and Angela both worked initially at Achimota College, then went on to further study and made a valuable contribution in other spheres. The twins, Joseph and Josephine, each got married, raised families and for the most part became productive citizens. Christian's two youngest sons, Ferdinand and Edward, who unlike their siblings received their primary and secondary education in the Gold Coast, both qualified for the medical profession. They had successful careers locally and internationally and died within a few months of each other. The achievements of Christian's children who survived him are summarized below.

Clara Marguerite Gordon (1894–1964)

Clara settled in Bermuda and, despite her challenges as a single parent, was highly respected by both white and coloured Bermudians. Peter felt, however, that even with the support she received from her former husband, she would not be able to maintain herself and the six children without sustained assistance from her father.[275] Christian continued to contribute financially and helped her to improve her property, Windsor House, with the hope that the rent from the house would help with some of her daughter Barbara's expenses. But he could not meet her request for £900 to convert Windsor House into a clinic, where her daughters could be employed when they qualified as nurses and midwives.[276]

In the final analysis, Clara's four daughters were successfully educated in England, with financial support from Christian, although he was not consulted on this decision. Barbara studied music at the Royal Academy of Music, married an American and moved to the United States. Joyce trained as a nurse in England and also went to America, where she practised privately. Evelyn trained in beauty culture and returned to New York.[277] Marjorie became a nurse and in 1943 was engaged to Harold Stuart, a solicitor from Barbados who lived in London, whom she subsequently married. In 1991, their daughter, Moira Stuart, was the first black female newsreader employed with the BBC. She was awarded the Order of the British Empire in 2001.[278]

Clara's two sons, Edgar (Teddy or Hakim) and Kenneth, were initially educated in Bermuda, and in 1944 they entered Edinburgh University, Scotland, to pursue studies in medicine. Despite the fact that Christian had purchased annuities for their education, they had to discontinue their university programme owing to financial difficulties. They both began to use their musical talents, inherited from their mother, to earn a living, and Kenneth eventually became well-known on the London jazz scene.[279] Hakim became a world traveller. He decided to investigate his maternal ancestry, and from his base in the United Kingdom, he travelled to Africa and then to Dominica to trace his grandfather's roots and to find out about his estate. Clara Gordon died in Bermuda in September 1964.[280]

Peter Charles Christian (1895–1945)

Christian's son Peter never attained the self-sufficiency that his father desired for him and remained dependent on remittances from him until his death. After Christian died, Peter cabled a request to Howard to have the estate "wound up quickly so that he could get some of his share of the money", since he was in dire circumstances.[281] When Howard returned to the Gold Coast to begin his career as a lawyer, Peter encouraged him to be loyal to the values and principles which he had chosen for self-motivation and "to remember father". He confessed that he wished for another chance to start again and regretted that he had not done his best.[282] Peter, whose mother died seven months after his father, acknowledged that he saw himself as the senior male of the family.[283]

Reports from other relatives in Dominica indicated that Peter began to act irresponsibly with regard to money matters, especially after the death of family friend Constance Lockhart. Francois, with whom Howard had discussed the situation, noted that Peter seemed "to have wrecked his life" and considered that it was "just as well GJ" was not around to be "distressed over his family".[284] Peter died in 1945, at the age of fifty, after a long and painful illness. His body was taken from Sekondi House, Roseau, to the town of St Joseph, where he was born, and he was buried alongside his mother, as he had requested.[285] The grant of probate of his will was recorded on 29 November 1945. He willed his lot of land and premises in Hanover Street, Roseau, called Sekondi House, to his brother Howard Christian, and his share in the Dominica House property in Sekondi, Gold Coast, was left to "Mrs Aba Christian". He bequeathed all other "real and personal estate", which was not "otherwise specifically disposed of", to his brothers Howard, Ferdie and Teddy "as tenants in common in equal shares absolutely".[286]

Sarah Helena Busby (1905–1991)

After her stint at Achimota College, Sarah returned to England and attended the Royal Infirmary, Stirling, Scotland, where she qualified as a midwife within six months.[287] She returned to the Gold Coast and worked for a year with Drs Hoyte and Busby at Nsawam.[288] She subsequently married Dr George Busby[289] and worked with him in his private hospital at Suhum. They had three children – one son and two daughters. Their younger daughter, Margaret Busby, writer, editor and publisher, who co-founded Allison and Busby in 1967, was the first black female publisher in the United Kingdom. She was awarded the Order of the British Empire in 2006. Sarah died in London in 1991 at the age of eighty-five.

Ebenezer Kwesi Christian (1906–1969)

Kwesi Christian, who worked initially with the Gold Coast Railway, returned to his hometown of Elmina after a few years and established his own business, Ochesco Industries. The company specialized in the repair of mechanical and electrical items. He also engaged in the sale of imported goods, a venture which proved to be so lucrative that he opened an outlet in Andado, a village close to Elmina. In his free time, he took up vegetable farming and used his produce to cater for his friends on special occasions or for social events. He was well-known for his salads.

Kwesi Christian lived a full life at Chapel Square in Elmina. He was a devout member of the Methodist Church, where he held a leadership position. He was also a member of the Freemason Lodge. He married Elizabeth Akosua Baffoe, and they had seven children in addition to one stepchild. His children were Ebenezer Kojo Adams, Ebenezer Nana Banyin Christian, Ebo Christian, Francis Augustine Boham Christian, William Plange Christian, Frances Victoria Maame Franswa Christian, Christiana Nana Ahema Boham Christian and Veronica Nana Aduaba Janet Christian. He died on 26 December 1969.[290]

Joseph (Joe) Christian (1908–1956/58?)

Joe Christian, who wanted to be a farmer, had been trained in agriculture at the Seale-Hayne Agricultural College in Newton Abbot, Devon, England.[291] Christian had done as much as he could to help Joe to become established in his chosen career. In January 1931, he had arranged for him to start at a training centre in the junior service at a nominal salary with the possibility of getting a promotion within two to three years, once Joe applied himself.[292]

Joe secured employment from time to time, but unfortunately, as was mentioned earlier, he was plagued with an injured leg throughout most of his life, and this negatively affected his ability to establish a career. For example, in 1932, he was worried that his job with the Accra Ice Company might be terminated, since he was away for a long time because of the leg injuries.[293] In 1934, he worked as a salesman under the supervision of Mr Brett.[294] In January 1935, Joe Christian was employed as manager for the Accra Ice Company at Obuasi.[295] The following year, however, he received notice that he had to leave the ice company on the grounds of economy.[296]

In 1939, when Joe planned to resign from his job because of dissatisfaction, Christian thought this was a "rash" decision. Furthermore, Joe's desire to open a drugstore merely underscored his immaturity and lack of experience.[297] Later that year, he was drafted to Kumasi, which was a disappointment, as both he and Josephine wanted to be stationed at Sekondi.[298] Less than half a year after Christian's death, Howard noted that Joe, who was partly dependent on his father "right up to his last days", had minimal resources of his own.

To his credit, however, Joe, who wanted to have a family,[299] made a step in this direction on 27 December 1941, when he married Lena Apatu, a qualified midwife, whom he had met in England.[300] In Nsawam, Ghana, they opened a maternity home/clinic. It was well known as the Christian Maternity Home, where mothers and pregnant women received care and assessment. Joe and Lena had three children – two sons and a daughter. Joe died while his children were young – between the ages of four and six – as a result of an injury to his leg, sustained during a cricket match.[301] His wife died in 2011 at the age of ninety-two.

Josephine Martha Armah (1908–1948)

Josephine had her education in Sierra Leone, France and England and was trained in millinery and dressmaking. She attended school in France and consequently spoke French fluently.[302] Josephine's sisters somewhat made fun of her, but her father noted she would be the first of his children to get married.[303] On 30 December 1936 Josephine married Dr Joseph Ersuah

Armah[304] of Axim, and according to Christian "everything was a success". She and her husband left the next day for Kumasi, where he was stationed in government employment.[305] She gave birth to her first child, a son who weighed nine pounds, in October 1939.[306] In April 1940, Christian went to Cape Coast to be "godfather to Josephine's hero".[307] Dr Armah became the personal physician to Kwame Nkrumah, the first president of Ghana. Josephine and Dr Armah had five children – four sons and one daughter. She died in 1948 at the age of forty.

Howard Kojo Christian (1915 –1963)

Howard had completed his training and was called to the Bar on 17 November 1939.[308] He was nominated for his call by two of his father's contemporaries, Lord Greenwood and N.L. McCaskie, KC. The former promised that he and the other Benchers would take the same interest in Howard's "career and success" as they had taken in his father's. Howard interpreted this as an expectation that he would assume the "dignity and responsibilities" of his father.[309]

At the time of Christian's death, Howard had embarked on the additional year in London to read in the chambers of W.A.L. Raeburn of 5 King's Bench Walk, Temple, on the advice and guidance of the Council of Legal Education and Mr Douglas.[310] During this period, he studied bookkeeping to increase his understanding of financial documents. He also pursued courses in typing and shorthand, because they would be useful in general and specifically to facilitate note-taking in court.[311] He was due to return to the Gold Coast during the winter of 1941.[312]

Howard was extremely happy when he returned to Africa. The sight of Freetown was "most impressive" after his seventeen-year absence from the Gold Coast, and when they landed at Takoradi, he wanted "to fall down" and "kiss" his "native soil". On his return to Sekondi, two of his father's barrister friends, Clarence Abbensetts and Franz Dove, facilitated his call to the Gold Coast Bar and introduced him to the chief justice and other legal luminaries. He naturally missed his sister Essi, his nieces and friends. He described life in Sekondi as "very lonely", since apart from his mother, there was only Abbensetts with whom he kept company.[313]

In his first case in the Gold Coast, Howard represented a man charged with murder. The accused received a two-year prison sentence from Judge McArthy instead of the death penalty. Howard was "very happy and kept wishing all the time" that his father could have been there in court to see him "safely launched" on his professional career. He felt that his profession was one in which it was possible to be independent of racial and political prejudice. He also knew that he could make "a better living" in the Gold Coast than in England, where his "colour" would be a disadvantage.[314]

Howard's professional training and other experience in London also facilitated his emulation of his father's leadership role in society. For example, he had joined the Air Raid Precautions service in London at the start of the Second World War and received the appropriate training, and there were many instances in London when his service and training were put to use. Consequently, on his return to the Gold Coast, he also functioned as an adviser to people who were or intended to be enlisted in one or another of the services.[315] He also reported that at a service of praise at the Methodist Church in Sekondi, he followed in his "father's footsteps" and undertook the function of chairperson at the harvest festival. It was the first time that he had addressed such a large gathering and he was "somewhat nervous at first", but he was informed later that he had performed "successfully".[316]

Howard was aware that he was expected to step into his father's role in the family. He described as "hellish" the reality that when folks looked at him, they always saw him in the light of his father, despite the fact that he was only twenty-six and had no money. Howard lamented that "this family custom" was "the scourge of the country" and was "what was keeping the people down". He had accepted that as the head of the family, it was his duty to look after his mother, his siblings and the household, but he refused to be swayed by those who claimed to be relatives ("hangers-on") and looked to him for monetary assistance. He also advised Essi that she should be careful whom she married, because a man might marry her for her money or her name and might not be a good husband. He believed that she should marry someone who was "strong enough to poo hoo all this damn nonsense of native custom, family palava, etc.".[317]

Howard became the family patriarch, and in the management of his father's estate, in response to concerns expressed by one of his older siblings, he gave the assurance that "all the pecuniary bequests" were paid off without the need to sell any of the properties. These properties were to be retained and leased so as to bring in a regular income, as they had when their father was alive. He expressed his thoughts not only as a lawyer but also in his capacity as "adviser" to his three younger siblings, Essi, Ferdinand and Teddy.[318]

In 1943, as a new lawyer in the Gold Coast, Howard claimed that he had fifteen years to make up, since there were six lawyers in Sekondi, and the last one had returned seventeen years earlier. He was still at that stage where he couldn't afford to have a clerk, and thus his time was filled with his work. Furthermore, he had the added responsibility of running the "mansion" that was Dominica House. He felt that his father was able to do so because he was "a rich man with seventy odd years of experience", while he was "a poor man" and "damn small", at least in the eyes of his staff, on whose knees he was "bounced when a babe".[319]

Howard, like his father before him, provided legal services to the West Indian community. For example, solicitors in London wrote to Howard in connection with the estate of the late Dr Beausoleil, who died in 1953, to secure his services as their agent in the Gold Coast, and they requested advice about the course to be followed to obtain the grant of probate of the will. Dr Beausoleil had bequeathed the property in the Gold Coast Colony to his son, Edwin George, as sole executor, while his daughter Cecile was executrix for his real and personal estate in St Lucia, Barbados and elsewhere in the British West Indies.[320] He ended his career as a judicial officer. Howard married Sarah Grant, and they had four children – two sons and two daughters. He died in 1963 at the age of forty-eight and predeceased his mother, Mami Abba, who died in 1964.

Angela Ambah Christian (1916–2000)

Angela had a clear understanding of her father's aims and expectations for his children, and she certainly did not disappoint him. While she was a student of education in London, she wanted to take a course in domestic science, "not so much for the purpose of teaching" but for her "own private use".[321] Angela felt that her father was afraid that she had plans to get married, and that was an influence to not take her studies seriously. She assured him, however, that this was not the case, and that she wanted to be qualified and to establish her "own independence at all cost".[322] Her father had also lauded her ability to speak Fante, unlike some of her siblings, who he felt were slow learners of the language and were not willing to learn "their mother tongue".[323]

Angela's contribution to nursery-school education in the Gold Coast Colony, based on her work at Achimota College from 1938 to 1945, where she taught at the kindergarten level, is widely acknowledged. She returned to England in 1946, where she continued to teach before she became involved in the establishment of the Gold Coast High Commission in London. In 1952, she served as the personal assistant and information officer to the high commissioner. In this capacity, she was responsible for appointments, protocol matters, and supervision of the administrative and clerical staff. During this period in her life, she began to pursue qualifications in law. Having completed courses in Roman and criminal law at Gray's Inn, London, however, she opted for a career as a diplomat and was then posted to the Ghana embassy in Paris.[324]

Her career with the foreign affairs ministry spanned many years. She served in Accra, where she established the cultural section of the Ministry of Foreign Affairs. She also represented Ghana at conferences overseas and fulfilled the role of cultural ambassador for visiting dignitaries at home. From 1962 to 1966, she was posted to the Ghana embassy in Washington, DC, and in the capacity of first secretary, she travelled extensively throughout the United States for speaking engagements, exhibitions and seminars. She returned to Accra in 1966 and continued her productive career with the reorganization of the cultural section of the Ministry of Foreign Affairs. Her dedication to the spread of her native culture resulted in her working to develop and assist in the preparation of exhibitions of Ghanaian arts and crafts in Brazil and Australia in 1970. In the closing years of her career, September 1970 to 1972, she served as a director of social and cultural affairs in the presidential household, after which she retired from the diplomatic service.[325]

Angela Christian certainly left her mark on Ghana society. After her retirement, she devoted the greater part of her time to voluntary work, either with social welfare and cultural organizations or in a private capacity. In 1973, she was consultant to the United Nations Economic Commission for Africa's Programme for the Advancement of Women, and their integration in the development process, a programme in which she maintained a great interest throughout her life. In 1973, she was awarded "the CERES Medal of the United Nations Food and Agricultural Organization (FAO) Food for All Programme".[326] She was also active in public service on the Ghana National

Freedom from Hunger Campaign Committee, the Women's Society for Public Affairs, Alliance Française D'Accra and the Church Council of Christ the King Catholic Church. She also wrote about Ghanaian culture – *Facets of Ghanaian Culture, Women in the Gold Coast, Modern Medicine in West Africa* – as well as stories and poems.

In a tribute, her family described her as "beautiful, graceful, poised and soft-spoken", and someone from whom they learned a lot. In addition to the "good graces and manners, appreciation of art, writing and other forms of creativity, and the rich insight into Ghanaian culture and heritage", she also taught them, by her deeds and example, how to be "good Christians".[327] Angela, who never married or had children, died in 2000 at the age of eighty-four.

Essi Matilda Forster (1922–1998)

Essi, who was sensitive to her father's priorities, hopes and plans for her education, aimed always to please him through her approach to her schoolwork.[328] By January 1940, she confirmed to her parents that she wanted to pursue law as a career, as she had been advised by her coach that it was possible for her to finish the law course and take the law degree all in three years.[329] After Christian's death, Essi discussed her career options with Howard. She was still in doubt as to which subjects she ought to study and contemplated a course in domestic science at Achimota College.[330] The professions of teacher, lawyer[331] and librarian were also under consideration.[332] Howard sought the advice of his father's friends on the subject, and Messrs Francois, Abbensetts and Judge Mr L.E.V. McCarthy all agreed that Essi should become a lawyer.[333]

In 1942, Essi followed in the steps of her father and brother, when she entered Gray's Inn, London, to read law. She was called to the Bar in London in November 1945 and became the first woman from the Gold Coast and the third in British West Africa to qualify as a lawyer.[334] Mami Abba had not seen Essi since 1927, when she left for England to attend school at the age of five.[335] She was "extremely proud" of her only daughter and eagerly looked forward to the day when Essi would return to the Gold Coast.[336] In December 1944, Essi married Gambian Dr Edward Francis Bani Forster, who was the first African psychiatrist south of the Sahara. She paid her first visit back to the Gold Coast in 1947.[337] During that year, she was called to the Bar in the Gold Coast and the Gambia.

Essi Forster practised law in the Gambia from 1947 to July 1951, and in Ghana from August 1951 as solicitor and barrister. She was also the acting registrar of companies, "Birth and Deaths", for six months in 1957. In 1957, she was invited by Mobil Oil Ghana Limited to become their corporate legal adviser, and she accepted. Her appointment "set a precedent in Ghana", and from then, "all large Corporations in the country" retained lawyers on their staff. She served in that capacity for more than twenty-five years, until March 1982.[338]

She continued in the tradition of her father with her participation in a wide range of professional and public service activities. From May 1954 to July 1959, Essi Forster was a member of the Accra Magisterial District Probation Committee. She served in different capacities in the following organizations: the Young Women's Christian Association, as the vice-president and secretary of the YWCA Hostel Committee; a foundation member of the International School Cantonments Committee from 1958 to 1963; secretary of the Ridge Church Sunday School from 1963 to 1980; member of the board of directors of the Ghana Broadcasting Corporation from 1968 to 1970; chairman of the Nurses and Midwives (Accra) Schools board of governors from 1969 to 1972; president of the Ghana Girl Guides and substitute member of the Constitution Committee of the World Association of Girl Guides and Girl Scouts from 1972 to 1975. Moreover, she was a founding member and president of the Ghana branch of the Federación Internacional de Abogadas (FIDA) and the Inner Wheel Club of Accra.[339] As a member of FIDA, she made recommendations to the Ghana Law Reform Commission on intestate succession, widowhood rites, maintenance of children and abortion.

Essi Forster concluded in a discussion that her professional and voluntary activities were essential to a full and interesting life.[340] She and her husband had three children – two sons and a daughter. Essi was described as "fiercely independent", and this may have contributed to her untimely death, when she was fatally knocked down by a motorcyclist on the Airport Road in Accra, as she crossed the road to the bank. She died in August 1998 at the age of seventy-five.[341]

Ferdinand Francisco Christian (1926–2002)

Ferdinand Francisco Christian was the older of Christian's two youngest sons in the Gold Coast. His father had decided to have him complete his primary and secondary education in the Gold Coast, so that he could "be moulded into local ways before going abroad so that he might be more in harmony and accord with his surroundings on his return".[342] Ferdinand entered Achimota College at the age of nine and completed his secondary education there.[343]

After Achimota, Ferdinand proceeded to the University of Dublin, Ireland, where he studied medicine and graduated in 1952. While at university, he met Grace Fehintola Phillips, daughter of Anglican bishop S.C. Phillips of Lagos, Nigeria. They were married on 19 June 1954 in Southport, England, and shortly afterwards returned to Ghana. On his return, he worked first at the Korle Bu Hospital and later at the Sekondi Hospital. He subsequently specialized in radiography at the University of Bristol and became a specialist radiologist at Korle Bu Hospital. He worked there until his retirement from the public service.[344] He was the recipient of a Commonwealth Fellowship in Canada from 1966 to 1968, and he travelled to the Caribbean for the first time in 1967, when he spent a fortnight, visiting Dominica, Trinidad and Jamaica.[345] After his retirement, he worked with Project Hope of America and served for two years as chief radiologist on the Caribbean island of Grenada.[346]

His family described him as "a quiet fulfilled man", who was "loving, handsome, astute and good" and who "will be remembered for his hard work and dedication to his family".[347] He and his wife Grace had three children – two sons and a daughter. He died in 2002 at the age of seventy-six.[348]

Edward Clifford Christian (1930–2002)

Edward Clifford Christian, known affectionately as Teddy, was the youngest of Christian's children. Like his brother Ferdinand, he attended Achimota College and left the Gold Coast in 1951 to pursue higher education in the United Kingdom. He qualified in medicine from the University College in Cork, Ireland, in 1957 and completed the diploma in clinical pathology in 1960. From 1960 to 1964, he worked as a doctor in Ireland, England, Ghana and the United States, before finally resettling in his homeland, where he made a substantial contribution. He is recorded as having "worked selflessly" at Korle Bu Hospital, Accra, from January 1965 to 1984. "Additionally, in 1966, he was appointed senior lecturer in Pathology at the Ghana Medical School, where he subsequently became professor and head of the Pathology Department in 1976." From the mid-1980s, he also held appointments in pathology at the King

Fahd Hospital in Jeddah, Saudi Arabia. During the time he lived in Saudi Arabia, he intermittently visited Ghana, London and Dominica.

He was described as a "gentle, modest and good-hearted man" who was "well respected by everyone". He was also an open, friendly and jovial person who readily welcomed everyone to his home. His hobbies included cooking, rose-gardening and fishing. He married Dorothy Hutton-Mills, with whom he had three daughters. He also had another daughter and a son.[349] He died in Saudi Arabia in 2002 at the age of seventy-two.[350]

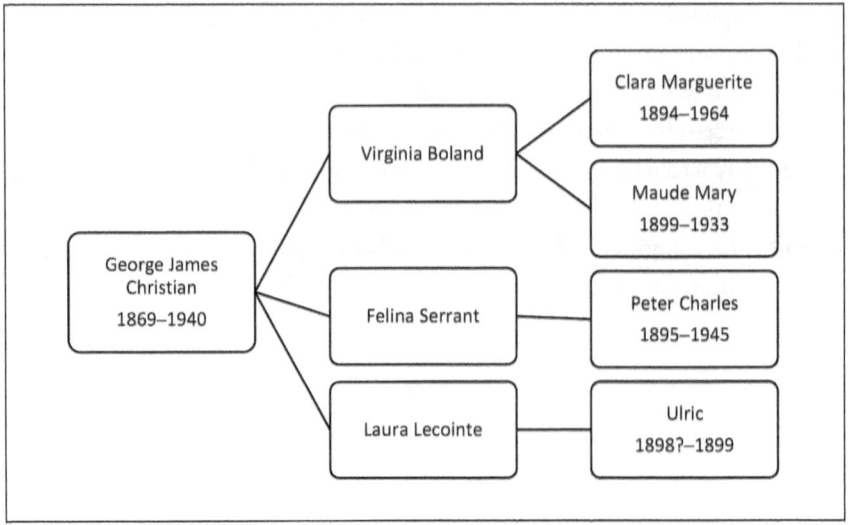

Figure 3.1. Family tree of George James Christian – Dominica-born children

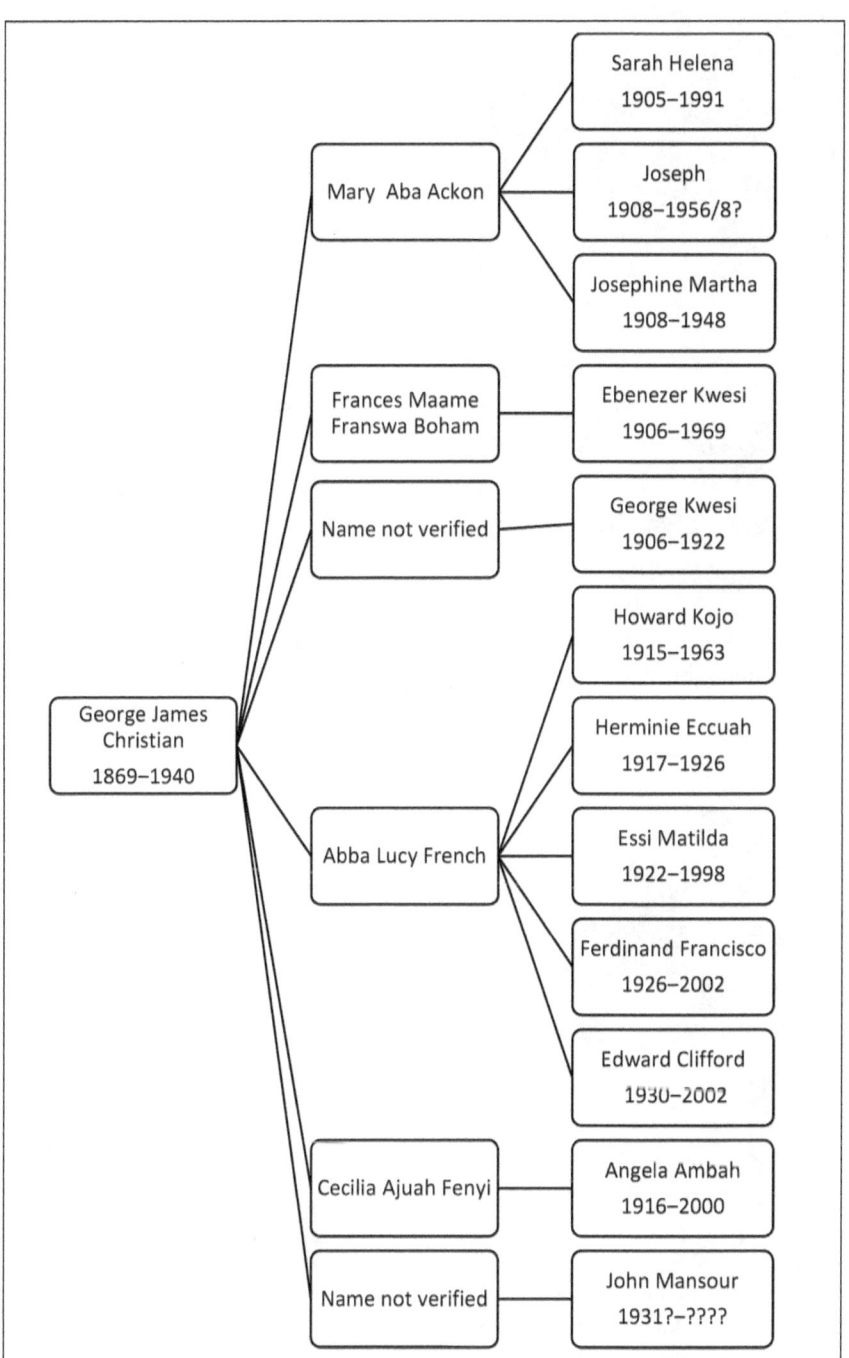

Figure 3.2. Family tree of George James Christian – Africa-born children

Figure 3.3. Mary Aba Ackon, wife of George James Christian

Figure 3.4. Abba Lucy French (Mami Abba), wife of George James Christian

Figure 3.5. Peter Christian, George James Christian, Joseph and Josephine Christian in back row; Sarah and Howard Christian in front row

Figure 3.6. Herminie Eccuah Christian

Figure 3.7. Maude Mary Christian

Figure 3.8. Howard Christian and Essi Christian

Figure 3.9. Clara Marguerite Gordon

Figure 3.10. Ebenezer Kwesi Christian

Figure 3.11. Joseph (Joe) Christian

Figure 3.12. Josephine Martha Christian and Dr Joseph E. Armah on their wedding day

Figure 3.13. Howard Kojo Christian

Figure 3.14. Essi Matilda Forster

Figure 3.15. Ferdinand Francisco Christian

Figure 3.16. Edward Clifford Christian

Figure 3.17. Spectators at the Accra Race Course, Ghana, including John Mansour, second from right in black jacket with black and white tie

CHAPTER 4

Achimota College, Dr J.K. Aggrey, Christian and His Family Experiences

ONE OF THE SIGNIFICANT OCCURRENCES IN THE GOLD Coast during Christian's time there was the establishment of Achimota College and School, which "came into being through the happy conjunction of three remarkable men, Guggisberg, Fraser and Aggrey".[1] Christian, with his keen interest in teaching and learning, was aware of Achimota and its possibilities for the education and future employment of his children. He became good friends with Dr James Kwegyir Aggrey, who had returned from the United States to assist with the establishment of the school. The exchange of correspondence between the two men highlights their disagreement on certain of the practices being instituted at Achimota, and Aggrey's inner conflict over his challenging personal circumstances at the time. Aggrey was disappointed that Christian had opted not to send his daughters to Achimota. However, Christian's two youngest sons had their primary and secondary education there, before they proceeded to university in the United Kingdom, and two of his daughters, who had been educated in England, worked at Achimota. The experiences of Christian's children provide insight into issues related to the establishment of the institution, student life during the early days of the college, and colonial policy on employment practices.

ESTABLISHMENT OF ACHIMOTA COLLEGE AND SCHOOL

Achimota College was the brainchild of Governor Frederick Gordon Guggisberg, who saw education as the keystone to progress.[2] The successful development of the cocoa industry and the related advances in trade meant that the government had resources to invest in education. There was also a need, because statistics indicated that in 1919, the 463 schools provided for only one-tenth of the children to be educated.[3] Guggisberg was committed to the education of Africans with the intention that they would eventually replace Europeans in the workforce. He therefore appointed a committee in 1920 to address all the relevant issues.[4] He believed that the increased material wealth of the people and their readiness for education provided an economic and social climate that would make the Gold Coast a favourite among the African territories for "a new and progressive educational policy".[5]

Guggisberg had great ideas and plans to build "the best school in Africa", and he invited Fraser and Aggrey to be part of the process.[6] The Reverend Alexander G. Fraser, who had previously served as a missionary in Uganda and as principal of Trinity College, Ceylon, brought to Achimota a profound suspicion of "Government-controlled education". It has been reported that he inspired Guggisberg to encourage the development of Achimota along the principles of independence and self-government, with a college council that would have an African majority.[7] Aggrey, the talented Gold Coast citizen known as "Aggrey of Africa" and considered "the greatest African of his day", was educated in the United States and became a member of a commission set up by the Phelps Stokes Fund that was charged with the responsibility to examine the school system of West and South Africa.[8] In preparation for this assignment, Aggrey wrote to his friends in the Gold Coast to enlist their support in the data-collection exercise.

Aggrey returned to the Gold Coast for the first time in 1920 as part of the Education Commission, whose mandate was to visit and examine schools and report on education.[9] During this visit, Governor Guggisberg and Aggrey met, and there was a mutual accord between them.[10] Guggisberg was aware of Aggrey and his abilities, and they became genuine friends. It is believed that Aggrey helped to reinforce Sir Gordon's determination to build a university college in the Gold Coast.[11] When Fraser and Aggrey did meet in London, they also expressed a mutual respect for each other's potential and a shared vision for the proposed school. Fraser and Aggrey were appointed principal and assistant vice-principal of Achimota respectively. Fraser was considered to be very experienced in the area of education and was in a position to influence government policy. He had accepted the appointment as principal of the new institution on the understanding that it would be co-educational. Aggrey reinforced this with his insistence on the importance of educating girls. Governor Guggisberg, a great visionary, threw his weight behind many novel and progressive policies advanced by his colleagues.[12] Thus the stage was set for the development of Achimota College and School, under the guidance of three formidable men.[13]

The school consisted of a kindergarten for boys and girls, a lower primary school for boys and girls up to the age of eight, and an upper primary school for girls only. The facilities included dining halls and dormitories. The Prince of Wales College consisted of a boys' upper primary school, a secondary school and a university college for advanced education. Secondary and university education would be available to girls who were resident in the Prince of Wales School.[14] The Legislative Council minutes recorded that the construction of the Prince of Wales School and the Prince of Wales College[15] at Achimota were "by far the largest work ever undertaken by the Public Works Department" in the country. The building commenced in October 1924, and the kindergarten was opened first on 28 January 1927, followed by the college and school, which commenced a year later, on 28 January 1928.[16] Initially accommodation and staff at the kindergarten were limited. There was space for sixty children under the age of eight who spoke Twi, Fante or Ga. The plan was that as additional accommodation became available, more children would be admitted.[17]

RELATIONSHIP BETWEEN CHRISTIAN AND AGGREY

The news of Aggrey's initial return visit to the Gold Coast in October 1920 to assist in data collection had been well publicized, and Christian and Aggrey most likely met each other fairly soon after Aggrey arrived.[18] The ship had landed at the port of Sekondi, and Christian sent Aggrey written communication on that occasion.[19] Less than a week later, the commission was given a public welcome in Sekondi "by a group of Africans engaged in various professional and clerical occupations, all dressed as Europeans and speaking English". A meeting to welcome him was also held in one of the churches.[20] It is quite possible that Christian was part of these events.

Aggrey's subsequent visits in 1924 and 1925, when he toured the Gold Coast to encourage support for the new school, included activities in Sekondi that provided opportunity for further interaction between them.[21] For example, during a January 1925 tour of the Western Province, Aggrey had considerable interaction with the Central Literary Club at Sekondi, an association of young people interested in the study of literature. He was appreciative of their efforts and "offered to become Patron of the Club", and whenever he came to Sekondi, he visited club members in their homes.²² Christian's daughter Maude was involved in this club.²³ An exchange of correspondence between Aggrey and Christian during 1926 and 1927 clearly indicates that by that time they had become close friends.

Aggrey, who had been a guest in Christian's home in 1926, sent him a thank-you letter in which he shared his heart and demonstrated the nature of the relationship between them. Aggrey compared the sense of welcome and comfort he felt in Christian's company with his understanding of the experience of the Christian faith, in which the believer yearns for his heavenly home, where the desires of the human heart for peace, perfection and the perpetual presence of loved ones will become a reality. Aggrey respected Christian for the qualities he perceived in him. He had taken notice of the atmosphere in the home, the attention Christian paid to his wife, the importance he gave to the education of his children, and his obvious potential as someone who had a valuable contribution to make to the development of society. Aggrey also offered to be of assistance to Christian's daughter Maude, if necessary.

Achimota University College
Accra
May 28, 1926

My dear Lawyer Christian

Just a brief note to emphasize my thanks to you and yours for the kind, cordial and generous hospitality that was mine to enjoy during the times that I recently was sheltered under your cultured roof. Never mind, I shall yet get even with you and yours for all these.

I somehow or other always feel at home in your home. There is an atmosphere there that sets one at ease and one's spirit seems to bask in the sunshine of an innate culture delightful to enjoy. Too bad that we must live so distanced by miles of ocean and of land. But I suppose it is such that deepens the yearning of one's heart for a heaven where loved ones are made perfect, where partings are at an end, and where true love blooms on to fruition in the eternal honeymoon.

I have written briefly also to "Miss Maude" and thanked her also.

Remember me kindly to Madam Aba French. I hope she is herself again by this time. You touched chords that vibrated deeply within my breast in your beautiful care for and attentions to her. I saw it all. I wish we had more of our people as tender and kind to our sisters, our mothers and wives. Someday when we two can in quiet think aloud to each other I want to ask you to help me solve or put plans that may help to solve many problems confronting the African who has never left home, or who if he has left home has yet to enter fully into all the choice spheres of the soul that develops [*sic*] the individual.

This is a tremendous time in the life of Africa. Before our eyes gigantic changes are taking place hurriedly, and unless our youth pause and consider much may be lost.

You are a lawyer, a barrister of the first water. I mean no flattery. But you are more than an ordinary barrister. There are other rich mines that perhaps only you know, and some of us are guessing and wishing that you had time to explore them and use their riches for the help of us all. You have read much, and thought more. And if you had the chance and felt that you were understood you would launch out more into the deep. No small heart that that [*sic*] has seen to the education of all of his children. No small brain that that [*sic*] shines piercingly through those eyes when half closed and the chin tipped up-ward. No small soul that continues to educate and educate and educate all and every child of his. I am thinking, Lawyer, if I could get a few more like you and all of us banded as one – each with his own divine gift, with souls aflame and hearts God-touched, who knows but that a nation may not be born in a day.

If you go on your furlough, you go with my heartiest bon voyage, and a great wish that you may be completely restored and as soon as possible return to Africa your Africa and mine – the land that reared the altars to our ancestral sires. In the meantime Maude seems to me a veritable sister and if there is anything I can do of help, of inspiration, of encouragement, or of protection should she need any such, it will be yours and hers to command and my pleasure to obey to the end – to the length of my cable bow (??) for I too am a widow's son.

Remember me to all friends including Lawyers Abinsett (I know not the proper spelling) and Mr Bratt.

Pray that the confidence imposed in me may not be betrayed and that I may be worthy of the company of all the best of all the lands. So make it be.

Yours very sincerely
J.E. Kwegyir Aggrey[24]

The correspondence between them focused on some of the issues related to the establishment of Achimota School. Christian was willing to support the fledgling school and attempted to enrol his younger daughters as students there. His youngest daughter, Essi Matilda, had been accepted and registered, but on account of her young age, Christian preferred her to have the company of her older sister, Herminie Eccuah.[25] There was no indication, however, that the latter would be accepted.[26] The headmistress explained that accommodation and staff at Achimota were limited, and that only sixty children of kindergarten age (eight years or younger) who spoke Twi, Fante or Ga would be admitted for January 1927. When additional accommodation became available, the intake would be increased, and he would be informed accordingly.[27] Unfortunately, Herminie died late in December 1926 after a brief illness. Christian therefore postponed Essi's attendance at Achimota School in the hope that another, older sister (Angela) would be accepted.[28]

Christian had doubts about how well the goals for the school would truly be attained. He had misgivings about the wearing of cloths[29] and the sleeping facilities, since his children were used to beds and mosquito nets. He therefore requested an invitation to the opening ceremony of the school, so that he and his daughter Maude would have an opportunity to examine the accommodation and sleeping facilities. At the opening ceremony, Christian, "inspired by His Excellency's manly speech", took the opportunity to "inspect various parts of the establishment" and made several "humble criticisms". In a letter to Aggrey, he expressed his views and concerns related to the accommodation and uniforms. He also voiced his apprehension about staffing issues, in particular the ratio of European to African staff, which he believed would have an effect on governance of the school and its ability to fulfil the aims of its founders:

> You paid me the honour of inviting me to be present at the opening of Achimota School, and after I had seen and heard you asked me to give you my views . . .
>
> In the first place sleeping accommodation is not all that is desirable and I would suggest that locally made cross frame camp beds with canvas tops would be better.
>
> Then as to clothing, the uniforms of blue material will be unacceptable to the wearers and despised by the general public whilst it will be a hardship to many of the scholars to be deprived of their cotton underwear and it cannot be seriously contended that a single sleeping cloth[30] is essential to keep the wearer "African".
>
> More important than these minor points is the necessity of permanency in His Excellency's ideal of preventing the college from being ruled by Local Government, or its policy shaped by Government. This can only be attained by the establishment of a board of independent ladies and gentlemen who together with the seniors of the staff would locally work to shape the principles of the institution on lofty lines.

> In the course of time the present staff will be replaced by others who may not be so sympathetic, and who may be affected by unsympathetic outside influence, and then Achimota will be anything but the place His Excellency aims to make it.
>
> No doubt Europeans can teach native languages as well as Africans, yet it is most desirable that there should be more Africans on the staff to assist with the teaching, tone the policy and help the single handed Aggrey in forming the esprit-de-corps which is desirable to win for Achimota the confidence of the community thus warding off all suspicion of ulterior motives and eliminating the danger of mutual misunderstanding leading up to discontent.[31]

The headmistress of the kindergarten extended sympathy to Christian on the death of Herminie and invited him to provide details about the other sister for consideration.[32] Both girls were eventually accepted into the school,[33] but on a doctor's advice, Christian decided not to send them to Achimota at that time, because of their "delicate health". The conditions under which the children would be accommodated did not meet his approval, and he was aware that it would be difficult to treat some children differently. In support of his decision, he further elaborated his views on the school's philosophy to Aggrey:

> There is so much for Africans to unlearn that I am at a loss to understand why it should be made a point to adopt some of the measures you propose for keeping them Africans.
>
> Competition is so great that I think the idea of making children stick to African customs is out of date. As well might the nations of Europe go back to the customs of centuries ago, yet because they keep ab[reast] with progress and civilisation they are able to hold their own in the battlefield of life. Fancy a Greek or an Italian being brought up to their ancient customs in clothes etc.
>
> I am afraid I understand too little of the subject to appreciate the raison d'etre of Achimota.
>
> Hoping you will forgive me for not seeing eye to eye with your authorities and with the best of wishes for the success of the experiment.[34]

Christian obviously felt strongly about these views, to the extent that a couple months later, on Aggrey's departure to the United States, he wrote again "to repeat his wishes and hope" and also to encourage Aggrey in his responsibility for the future direction of Achimota:

> This is to wish you bon voyage and to repeat my wishes and hope when I wrote you whilst in port here on the occasion of your first visit.

Now the seed is planted, the farmer must needs give all the care to the young and tender plant to make it thrive. The responsibilities of the farmer are great, and to be true to himself and his work he must make great sacrifice. The future of Achimota is not at all assured unless the old spirit is adhered to. Such influence as you have, please use it at all cost else the labour spent will be in vain.[35]

In Aggrey's response to Christian, he voiced his inner turmoil over his decision to return to the Gold Coast and become involved with the establishment of Achimota School. The letter, which was written aboard ship on his return to the United States via London to complete his book, was replete with biblical references and revealed his spiritual beliefs, aspects of his personality and some of the challenges he faced in this period of his life. He described Christian's letter to him as "fraught with thoughts that move and challenge one's seriousness" and indicated how much he needed and deeply appreciated Christian's counsel and advice.

Aggrey recounted the material comforts he had given up, the financial loss he experienced and the personal time and interaction with family that he had sacrificed in order to make himself available for the establishment of Achimota College. With regard to this assignment, he recalled the admonition of Jesus Christ to those who look back after they have "put their hand to the plough". He did not intend to renege on his commitment. He was extremely disappointed that Christian had decided not to send his daughters to Achimota, as he had hoped for the support of Christian and others of his ilk to give credibility to the school. Aggrey likened himself to Mary, who had poured out her precious jar of alabaster ointment for Christ. He was prepared to give his life "so that if there be any ointment of service the Master may have it". He also quoted from William Blake's poem "And did those feet in ancient time", adapting lines to reinforce his commitment to Africa. It was his last letter to Christian. Two months later, Aggrey's mortal life came to an end after a brief illness.

R.M.S. *Apapa*
May 10, 1927

My dear Lawyer Christian:

This is but a hurried note to acknowledge receipt of your letter fraught with thoughts that move and challenge one's seriousness.

I thank you. I will always need and deeply appreciate your counsel and advice.

I have been thinking thoughts, Lawyer. I am asking God to nerve me for the fray. I will answer you at better length later. I simply write to thank you and our Maude for your feelings toward me and toward Achimota.

For her and my country I have left an income of over Two Thousand <u>Pounds</u> [*sic*] a year. And now it looks as if I cannot see my dear family but only once in three years and then only for a short time. Over in America my place was made and income increasing and accumulating. Responsibilities were not so heavy. Your excellent daughter knows how I love my home and wife. It has been a question [*sic*].

I am but getting half what I used to get and spending more than twice what I used to spend.

But please God, I have set my face against the wind and cast my handful of seeds on high.

Future competency in finance is now uncertain. I sold my farm and five renting houses in America, leaving only my home and some vacant lots the price of which – the lots may or may not go up. My heart wants to bleed whenever I think of my home, my wife, my two children in Universities, one in a college, and one just 8 or nine months old that I have never seen. I must pause here. The very thought of it pains me.

Yet I have put my hand to the plough and I cannot turn back. I do not expect even my own people to understand me fully or realize what all of it is about.

It pained me that you could not send your two daughters. I had hoped that with the children of educated and cultured persons like you in Achimota forces might be united and massed to help bring about what in our heart of hearts we want. Fraser is genuine and sincere. He is a God send. There are some who have not yet caught the vision.

I am ready to lay even my life on the altar of sacrifice to my country and in the regard of my race. I am hopeful. God is not dead.

Like Mary's alabaster, I am dashing it, nay smashing my life so that if there be any ointment of service the Master may have it. I need you Lawyer Christian. I need such as you. Don't fail me. Who knows whether you are come to the Kingdom for such a time as this.

O Africa, my Africa
I will not cease from mental fight
Nor shall my sword sleep in my hand
Till <u>we</u> have built Jerusalem
In Africa's green and pleasant land
O Africa, my Africa.

Do come to London if you possibly can. My London address will be . . .
My regards to our Maude, Mamie Abba, Lawyer Abinsett & all friends

Yours sincerely
J.E. Kwegyir Aggrey[36]

Christian, however, was determined not to enrol his daughters at Achimota. In his response to Aggrey's letter, he indicated that "until certain changes are made at Achimota I will not be able to take advantage of it for the benefit of my children. Indeed I propose as soon as I can manage it to send them abroad in search of that type of training and enlightenment that would give them an advantage when they would have to compete for positions in the job market."[37]

This was Christian's last letter to Aggrey, who had taken up the position of assistant vice-principal of the Prince of Wales College in the fall of 1924 at the invitation of the British Colonial Office. However, his tenure in this position was short-lived. His wife, Rose Douglass Aggrey, a native of Virginia, United States, had accompanied him to the Gold Coast in October 1925, but owing to ill health, she returned to America six months later.[38] Aggrey was given leave of absence from May to November 1927 to write his book about British rule in West Africa in fulfilment of the outstanding requirement for the doctor of philosophy degree from Columbia University. He left the Gold Coast in May, travelled via London and arrived in New York on 16 June 1927. After a two-week visit with his wife and children in Salisbury, Maryland, he returned to New York to work on his book. He was engaged in this exercise when he fell ill and was hospitalized on 30 July 1927. He died of pneumococcal meningitis in the afternoon of the same day.[39]

The close relationship between Aggrey and the Christian family is evidenced by the fact that they were invited to participate in the celebration of his life. Maude Christian received a personal invitation to the memorial service for Dr J.E.K. Aggrey. It was held at the Chapel of the Wesleyan Methodist Church in Sekondi on 7 August 1927, and the Reverend Harry Webster, chairman and general superintendent of the Gold Coast District, officiated.[40] As one of Aggrey's "intimate friends", Christian received a copy of the statement issued by the Phelps Stokes Fund. His death was "universally lamented", as he was considered to be someone who had "ability as an interpreter of divergent groups to each other" and was an "inspiring influence towards a genuine faith in Africa and Africans as well as co-operation for his Native continent and peoples".⁴¹ As a tribute to his deceased friend, Christian penned these few lines:

> What one could feebly add to the many and varied testimony of the late Dr J. E. Kwegyir Aggrey was that he had the fear of love of God from his youth and died in the fear and love of God. He was a great interpreter and a bridge between the Black and White races and while constructing the bridge across the chasm between the black and white races as did the Apostle St Paul between the Jews and the Gentiles, he succumbed.
> Africa's Greatest Son in his day.⁴²

Christian associated himself with efforts to celebrate Aggrey's life and accomplishments. He was chairman of the board of founders of the Dr Aggrey Memorial High School, Sekondi, which was established on 26 November 1934 to perpetuate the late Aggrey's memory. Another West Indian lawyer, C.E.M. Abbensetts, was also a board member. The object of the school was to provide "an opportunity to boys for a sound training in Secondary School subjects by means of which the golden lessons of character-building and national consciousness might be inculcated. An opening for girls was created on October 15, 1935".⁴³ One of Christian's sons, Edward Clifford (Teddy), attended the school from the age of four.⁴⁴ He was still a student there in 1938.⁴⁵

CHRISTIAN'S INVOLVEMENT IN ACHIMOTA ACTIVITIES

Christian was also invited to take a leadership role in the organization of the tribute to the Reverend Fraser, the principal of Achimota College, on his retirement from the college and departure from the Gold Coast Colony in 1935. The plan was for a public reception to be held at the Rodger Club in Accra, during which the Reverend and Mrs Fraser would be presented with appropriate mementoes. A committee that was formed on behalf of the chief and people of the Eastern Province invited Christian to participate. They felt that as a member of the Legislative Council, he would wish to join in the effort to mark the debt that the country owed to the Frasers as "friends of Education". Not only was Christian's cooperation sought, but he was expected to secure the interest of the chiefs and citizens of the Western Province in this scheme and to ensure a successful outcome. The committee was confident that Christian would be willing to contribute the minimum of one guinea (£1 1s.), although there was no intention to limit him to this amount. Another West Indian, Dr J.H. Murrell, was also a member of the committee.[46]

Christian was in full agreement with the intentions of the committee, and he submitted a cheque for two guineas (£2 2s.) to assist them. He also arranged a meeting of the "Chiefs and the leading citizens" at his home to share the intentions of the committee for their "consideration and action". His hope was that they would not merely show their appreciation of Fraser's good work by means of monetary contribution but that they would be willing to put it in writing.[47] He promptly wrote to Chief Kwesi Andoh II, Tufuhene, in British Sekondi, to invite him to view the letter of request so that he could convey the message to his people.[48]

Christian also indicated his intention to bring together a subcommittee to pursue the matter as vigorously as it deserved.[49] He enlisted the support of fellow lawyer F. Awoonor-Williams and demonstrated his understanding of the significance of the occasion to the individuals concerned as well as to the wider society. He felt strongly that it was an excellent opportunity to express gratitude for the Reverend Fraser's significant contribution in such a way that he would have something tangible "to show to his friends and to say to them, [that] at least the African appreciates the good that is done for him". Christian also saw it as an opportunity to endorse the positive influence of Achimota School, which had produced many good citizens. He considered the school to be "the best investment" for monies that might otherwise have been spent on "salaries for more officials".[50]

There was at least one meeting at Christian's residence to discuss plans for the reception, which was to be held in Accra.[51] Christian was disappointed, however, by the support given and contributions raised, £2 12s. He blamed the outcome on political unrest at English Sekondi and the usual tardiness of the people. In order not to cause further delay, he submitted what was collected to the organizing committee.[52]

In the final analysis, Christian's efforts were successful. A tribute was sent to the Reverend Fraser, signed by the omanhene of the English and Dutch Sekondi,[53] as well as several barristers-at-law who were in agreement with the tribute of recognition for the excellent work he had done as principal of Achimota College. The letter made reference to "the conscious stand" which Fraser had taken to frame a constitution for Achimota College as an independent entity, free of governmental control, which maintained the spirit and scope of its founder, the late Sir Gordon Guggisberg, in conjunction with whom Achimota's foundation had been laid for its future development into a university, not only for the Gold Coast but for West Africa as a whole. The letter also drew attention to the fact that the work started under Fraser's supervision at Achimota was highly commended by the first inspectorate after a mere six years. They extended best wishes to Fraser and his family in their retirement and expressed the hope that they would maintain their interest in the school and make their experience available to the new principal and staff.[54]

CHRISTIAN'S CHILDREN AS STUDENTS AT ACHIMOTA COLLEGE

Despite the misgivings expressed by Christian when Achimota College was initially established, he recognized its potential as an institution of teaching and learning, as well as a place of employment. Several of Christian's children were exposed to the college either as students or employees. Their stories highlight aspects of life there that might otherwise have gone unrecorded.

Joseph (Joe) Christian, 1930 to 1931

Christian's son Joseph (Joe) was the first of his children to receive training at Achimota. He had completed the diploma in agriculture at Seale-Hayne Agricultural College in Newton Abbot, Devon, England and was interested in a job in agriculture. Principal Fraser had agreed to take him on as an intern at the farm at Achimota College. He would be taught aspects of general Gold Coast farming and poultry farming in particular. He was due to spend no more than nine months at Achimota, after which, as soon as he understood the Gold Coast context, he was to begin to farm on his own.[56]

Joe began his internship on 10 September 1930. Christian had made arrangements to pay for him to have his meals in the staff mess with his sister Sarah, and he was given a bed.[57] However, the brother and sister intended to arrange their own meals in Sarah's bungalow.[58] After three months, Fraser reported an improvement in Joe, as evidenced by the courteous and considerate treatment and understanding extended to the labourers. His knowledge of local marketing and money transactions had also improved.[59] Joe wanted to return to England, however, to become a partner in a dairy and pig-breeding venture. His father confessed that he had "neither the money nor the inclination to indulge him".⁶⁰ The authorities on the farm were unsure whether the work there was beneficial to his long-term plans, but they were willing to take him back for a further trial.⁶¹

Christian, who was not financially able to acquire land to establish Joe on his own farm, acknowledged that his son was a problem and sought advice from the Reverend Fraser as to what would be the best course of action for him.⁶² Fraser suggested that rather than leave Joe idle at home, it would be better to send him back to Achimota, with the expectation that if he continued to improve, he would undoubtedly become useful, either to Achimota or to the government. He cautioned, however, that it would mean harder work than Joe had been in the habit of doing.⁶³ By February 1931, Christian had sent Joe back to Achimota as a student intern with the hope that later in the year he would secure employment in the Agricultural Department, where his name was on a waiting list, and eventually, after years of employment, get a promotion.⁶⁴ Those hopes never materialized. In April 1931, Joe unceremoniously left the college to go to Assuantsi. He borrowed three pounds from the acting principal to pay his lorry fares. The money was eventually repaid to the college by his father.⁶⁵

Ferdinand and Edward Christian, 1934 to 1947

Contrary to the education choice he made for his daughters, Christian decided to allow his younger sons to have their initial education in the Gold Coast. As early as 1932, when Ferdinand Francisco and Edward Clifford, born 20 August 1926 and 29 November 1930, were six years and fourteen months old respectively, their father began to explore the possibility of purchasing insurance to pay for their education. He expressed his intention to send them to a school like Achimota until the age of ten or twelve, after which he would then send them to England.⁶⁶ Two years later, his plans for their education, now more concrete, were again expressed in a letter to the Reverend Fraser, who was then principal of Achimota College, to inquire about what insurance policies were available to provide for their training until they attained the qualifications for law, medicine or dentistry. He wanted them to be trained "among their own people" until they were about fifteen years of age. He would then send them "to Europe to equip them with the necessary qualifications to meet present day competition in the field . . . in whatever line they chose to take". He wanted them "to be so equipped as to have a fighting chance".⁶⁷

When Ferdinand (Kwamina) attained the age of nine, Christian transferred him to Achimota from the West African Industrial Academy, which had been established by the Reverend and Mrs Henrietta Peters.[68] Christian left nothing to chance when he arranged for the transfer to Achimota College and requested that the document should state what level his son had attained, his "form or standard", in order to ensure that he would be placed appropriately at Achimota.[69] Dr Emmanuel Evans-Anfom, who was then a joint house prefect with the late Modesto Apaloo, remembered Ferdinand Christian among a group of boys that he referred to as "My House 6 boys", namely, "Victor Owusu, Silas Dodu, Peter Renner and R.S. Amegashie". House 6 was a junior house "where the under aged boys were housed".[70]

Ferdinand corresponded with his parents during his student days at Achimota. His letters kept them abreast of his experiences there and also reported on his younger brother Teddy.[71] For example, he gave a detailed account of the earthquake of 1939, which he thought at first was "the end of the world", and as it continued, he wondered whether it was the Nazis trying to destroy the country.[72] As a son, his sensitivity to the individual function and needs of both his parents was expressed in his letters. For example, he reported to his mother that they were glad to have their sweaters when the temperatures dropped, and also that they were being served "gari"[73] for lunch and dinner because of the shortage of rice and flour.[74] He expressed concern to his father about the latter's health issues and also directed his request for allowances to him.[75]

He also corresponded with his brother Howard in England during the period. His letters show that he was quite happy at Achimota, was fully engaged in school life, enjoyed the outings, collected stamps and maintained an interest in his older brother's activities. He reported on one occasion that when their father came to Accra for a meeting of the Legislative Council on 11 March 1940, he sent the car to meet them. Ferdinand, together with his younger brother Teddy and their sister Angela, visited him on 16 March 1940. According to Ferdinand, his father was in good health at that time, though Christian died a month later.[76]

Ferdinand also reported on arrangements for the use of Achimota School premises during the Second World War. The college was asked to give up part of its space for the use of "black and white soldiers". The students were given six weeks' vacation. Some could not be accommodated, and Teddy attended "home school" with John Francois (son of George Francois of St Lucia). It was also uncertain whether Angela would go back to the college.[77] Two years later, he shared the news that the army was in need of even more space from the college, which resulted in the permanent relocation of the kindergarten and lower primary students and their teachers to Aburi. This move included both Angela and Teddy.[78]

The letters, which cover the period 1939 to 1942, give a good picture of the extracurricular activities at Achimota, outings to the different parts of the country and the boys' visits back home. They reveal a close relationship between Ferdinand and his older brother Howard, and a genuine concern for other members of his family and the household staff. In one letter, he reported a discussion with his mother over how he spent his pocket money, which was fifteen shillings per term. She asked what he did with the five shillings which was left after he put aside some money in his savings account and paid for his laundry. He reported his reaction to Howard: "Well am I not to have any pocket money at all? I was very bitterly shocked that Friday morning, and for the first time since the death of Father, I saw my tears."[79]

In his response, his brother reminded him that his mother might not always see the "man's point of view", that she had more experience of life, and her advice was usually correct. It was most important, however, that regardless of his age, he owed his mother respect.[80] His letters also indicated that the bonds formed between and among the West Indians in the community were lasting. Mention was made of contact and visits with Mrs Murrell, Mr Phipps and Drs Hoyte and Busby.[81]

Christian's youngest son, Edward (Teddy), also attended Achimota while Ferdinand was there. He began his formal education at Aggrey Memorial School and completed both his primary and secondary education at Achimota between 1939 and 1950.[82] In 1947 he was a resident at Guggisberg House and corresponded with his brother Howard, who by this time had completed his law studies and returned to the Gold Coast. He too was interested in the activities at home and was excited about the return home of his sister Essi, whom he had never met.[83] His letters reveal that he was a serious student of Latin. He also played cricket at Achimota, "bowling for our house first cricket team".[84] After he left Achimota, Teddy went to Great Britain to pursue studies in medicine.[85]

EMPLOYMENT EXPERIENCES AT ACHIMOTA COLLEGE

Christian, who was concerned that his children should be educated and trained for a profession, considered Achimota College and School as an appropriate employer for them. Two of his daughters, Sarah and Angela Christian, worked there as a nurse and teacher respectively, and a third, Clara Gordon, applied for a position there. Their experiences shed light on issues and practices at the time with regard to the employment of Europeans versus Africans for positions in the colony.

Sarah Christian, 1930 to 1938

While his daughter Sarah was a student nurse at the City of London Maternity Hospital, Christian enlisted the assistance of a colleague, who travelled to England to advise her that she should contact the Reverend Fraser, the principal of Achimota, in order to secure an appointment there on completion of her training for the nursing profession.[86] Principal Fraser persuaded Sarah that Achimota needed her "at once", and she was hired as senior staff even though she had not completed her training in England.[87] In the long run, this worked to her disadvantage.

Sarah took up an appointment as nursing sister at the Prince of Wales College and School in 1930. Her terms of service included first-class passage on the commencement of her appointment and on return from approved leave of absence. Her initial salary was £400 per annum with annual increments of £25 to £450 during a three-year probation period, and thereafter at the rate of £475 per year.[88] According to the Reverend Fraser, Sarah won everyone's heart with her charming ways and the manner in which she settled in to her position. There was no one to show her what was expected, as the doctor himself was new, and the assistant nurses had worked without supervision for some months. Sarah made a good start, however, and was clearly up to the task.[89] She received good reviews from the Reverend Fraser, who informed her father that he was satisfied, because Sarah was the first African to whom he had given a European position, and he felt his choice was justified.[90] It is reported that "from the students' point of view, she was a highly competent worker and brought great discipline to the hospital". On the other hand, she was not very popular, as "students thought she was too prim and proper and too serious".[91]

Two situations demonstrate that Sarah's work at Achimota was highly valued at different levels. During the illness of her sister Maude, a request from Christian for Sarah to be allowed to return home to assist with the care of her sister was refused by the acting principal of Achimota College. Instead, Dr Selwyn-Clarke arranged with the Ministry of Health that the Sekondi midwife should be put at Christian's disposal. It was hoped that this would be a satisfactory arrangement.[92] The sons of another West Indian, George Francois, also benefited from Sarah's motherly care during their early years at Achimota. The boys, George and Edward, had entered the upper and lower primary classes respectively. Their father was conscious that it would take them much longer to settle because of the size of the school, but Sarah assured him that they were doing well.[93]

Several years into Sarah Christian's assignment at Achimota, there was a discussion on reorganizing the hospital, and there was a possibility that her position would be abolished. Since she was on contract, she was entitled to remain for its duration, although if the position was discontinued, she would not qualify for any gratuity. Sarah was advised that the decision was in the hands of the school council. The finance committee put forward a counter-suggestion that the position should not be eliminated, but that the salary and overseas-leave entitlement be reduced.

Sarah's communication to her father on the subject revealed the disparate views held by the European and African members of staff. The former felt that Sarah, "being an African" and not fully qualified, should be "kept in [her] place". The Africans felt that she had access to privileges that they did not enjoy. Sarah, on the other hand, found it a lonely experience despite the comfortable wages. The hours of work were long, with no regular off-duty time and no one to relieve her, as happened with her European counterparts.[94] With the proposed retrenchment, there was also a suggestion from her employers that she should complete her studies.[95]

In correspondence with her father on the matter, Sarah not only sought his legal advice but also expressed the humiliation and shame she would feel if she was required to settle for a lower salary without proper termination of the former position, including some kind of gratuity for her seven years' service. She felt that no one cared whether happiness was included in her existence. She concluded her letter as follows: "I leave it to you to handle as you think fit, bearing in mind I am almost 30 years old, a woman with desires of enjoying all that life offers."[96]

Christian in turn sought an opinion from his friend and colleague Francois, who felt that there was "a question of principle involved in the abolition of the appointment of an African with European privileges". He felt, however, that Christian's relationship to Sarah stood in the way of his fighting it "tooth and nail". Francois was of the view that there was sufficient justification for a gratuity or retirement allowance, in view of the fact that she had given up her studies and lost her deposit in the process, and was being advised, by the same employers, to continue her interrupted studies.[97]

Christian's strategy was to use all his professional contacts to resolve the issue. He wrote four letters on 11 December 1936, one each to Franz Dove and E.C. Quist, barristers-at-law, L.E.V. McCarthy, solicitor general, and a diplomatic letter to Canon Grace, principal of Achimota.[98] In his letter to Grace, he suggested that if Sarah had given satisfaction, and the only motive was economy, they should consider a reduction of salary only and not of status. He also alluded to the fact that her lack of qualifications should not be held against her, given the circumstances surrounding her appointment. He also expressed his confidence that the matter "could not be placed in fairer hands". A copy of the letter to Grace was sent to his other three contacts, with a request that it be brought to Canon Grace's attention before the relevant meeting of the Achimota Council. He also requested their support to ensure that justice prevailed and that advice was available to all relevant parties.

Each of the letters to his three friends/colleagues was different according to their role in the matter. He asked Dove to advise Sarah as well as McCarthy, Quist and any others who might have a voice in the council. In his letter to Quist, he expressed his views freely concerning the race issue in the matter: "If it were not of my personal interest . . . I should fight it out to the bitterest end, as this is vital to ourselves as a race. It is simply that an African is being denied a position which she is entitled to. If she were a European there would be no questioning about it."[99] His letters to both McCarthy and Quist indicated that he wanted to have the matter on record so that thereafter if justice were not done he would have at least that much to refer to[100] "so that in years to come if needs be, one can use the precedent as [he was] sure it is not economy at the bottom of this thing".[101]

The Achimota Council insisted that Sarah Christian's position was no longer necessary but offered to retain her services if she would take on additional duties, but with a reduced salary and leave entitlement. Alternatively they would give her a year's salary and return first-class passage to England, so that she could complete her studies, acknowledging that she had given "valuable services" during her time at Achimota.[102] Christian felt that she should accept the reduced salary and stay on, but he had heard that she was not in agreement.[103]

Sarah was not inclined to make a "rushed decision" on the matter, because she realized that her entire future depended on it. In her view, her father had assured her that whatever decision she made, he would accept it with no ill feeling, although there were rumours that her father wanted her to stay on at Achimota, and that he intended to cut her off if she did otherwise.[104] She eventually resigned, as she was unwilling to remain at the reduced salary.[105] She returned to the United Kingdom and completed her studies at the Royal Infirmary in Scotland in 1938. According to her father, she qualified "in record time".[106]

Clara Gordon's Quest for Employment, 1937

A brief exchange of correspondence between another of Christian's daughters who sought employment at Achimota College also indicated that there could be claims of discrimination against non-European staff. Christian's Dominica-born daughter, Clara Gordon, had applied for a position as assistant matron at Achimota in 1937. There was no pensionable post for this position, and the salary was not high – £200 a year would be the maximum. The intention of the college authorities was to train up a young woman to do the job, but the principal acknowledged that a married woman of Clara's age "would possibly be more satisfactory" for the position. In the response she received, she was asked to consider coming in a junior capacity, without any provision for leave abroad. There was the possibility that if her performance was exemplary and the senior position became available, she could be considered for it, but nothing was guaranteed. Her leave entitlement would be some of the school holidays, but she was expected to be prepared to live in the Gold Coast until her assignment at Achimota was completed.[107] Clara subsequently withdrew her application, as personal circumstances prevented her from accepting the position.[108]

Angela Christian, teacher at Achimota, 1938 to 1945

Christian's daughter Angela was appointed a member of the senior staff at Achimota College from 1938 to 1945, taught kindergarten and contributed immensely to nursery education in the Gold Coast. She had been trained as a teacher and obtained the National Froebel Foundation Teachers Certificate "A" at Maria Grey Teacher Training College, a constituent of the Institute of Education, University of London, England.[109] Two of her brothers, Ferdinand and Teddy, were students at Achimota College at the time she was teaching.[110] Angela is remembered as being "well respected at Achimota".[111]

The agreement between Angela and the school stipulated that she was appointed in the capacity of mistress at the Prince of Wales College and School and was provided with furnished quarters and all necessary medical attendance. She was to be paid a salary of £250 per annum for a period of two years' probation from 12 October 1938 and could be reappointed for a further period of service, whereby the first period of years should count towards the first seven years of service if she were to be placed on the regular staff of the college.[112]

Howard Christian's Views on Achimota's Employment Practices

Howard Christian, in the course of advising his sister Essi whether she should seek employment as a teacher at Achimota, provided details about the perceived injustices in the terms and conditions of employment for European versus African staff there. He drew reference to the fact that "on paper", no distinction was made between the whites and the blacks on the staff. In reality, however, Europeans were given numerous preferences, while Africans got "the dirty end of the stick". A European and African with the same qualifications might be hired at the same time as senior staff and be treated differently. Howard pointed out that in such a scenario, the white person would be assigned a house to himself. His or her appointment would be calculated from the date of travel from England and confirmed on arrival. The qualifying period would begin immediately and would be pensionable after seven years.

He then reflected on the experience of his sister Angela, who was hired from England. Unlike what would obtain for a white counterpart, she was assigned to second-class travel, and at Achimota she had to share accommodation with a junior member of staff. She was required to serve a probationary period of two years before her appointment was confirmed, so that in order to earn a pension, she would have to serve eight or nine years, while the European would work for seven. Howard's letter pointed out that for his family members, opportunities for employment were generally limited: "Achimota is the only place for people like the Christians – and the 'powers-that-be' there know it. Having this upper hand they can call their game."[113]

Howard warned Essi that she would be the envy of others. He also pointed to the anomalous position to which his family was sometimes relegated. They were the envy of people in the Gold Coast who considered them to be foreigners, while the English saw them as natives. He opined: "What the dickens are we? We are a family most envied by both blacks and whites."[114] In this regard, Howard was voicing sentiments his father would have understood. In a subsequent letter to Essi on 18 June 1942, Howard, on reflection, wondered whether he had a "bad liver" when he wrote that 23 April letter and confessed that if he had to do it again, he would write "in a much milder tone".[115]

Christian's response to the "Achimota experience", both as a friend of Aggrey and as parent to children involved in the school, was consistent with his lifestyle, professional training and philosophy. The correspondence between Christian and Aggrey, although relatively brief, was nonetheless meaningful and revealing. Aggrey was disappointed in Christian's apparent lack of support in the early days of the establishment of Achimota. Still, the mutual respect and admiration that they had for each other were without question.

Aggrey's early death did not diminish Christian's active interest in the school and its possibilities as an educational institution for his children. He weighed the pros and cons at every stage of the process and acted in accordance with the goals he had set for himself and his family in the Gold Coast. He was willing to take advantage of whatever the school had to offer only if it was in the best interest of his family. He supported the development of the school and encouraged his children to join the Achimota staff, despite the challenges they faced as non-European expatriates.[116] He was also keenly aware of where they stood in society and was an advocate for good sense to prevail in the circumstances. His decision to have his two youngest sons educated in the Gold Coast at Achimota had a successful outcome. The experience of the Christian family at Achimota College, as recounted here, however, brings to light a frequently overlooked but significant dimension of the early days of this much-celebrated Ghanaian institution as it was established and developed in colonial times.

Figure 4.1. Edward Christian, Mami Abba and Howard Christian

Figure 4.2. Sarah Helena Christian

Figure 4.3. Angela Ambah Christian

Figure 4.4. Descendants of George James Christian and Dr James Kwegyir Aggrey participate in a celebration of the founding of Achimota School at a reception at the Golden Tulip Hotel, Accra, Ghana, on 4 February 2014. *Courtesy Saki Publicity, Accra, Ghana.*

CHAPTER 5

"Lawyer Christian"

THE GOLD COAST IN THE EARLY TWENTIETH CENTURY was a good prospect for people trained in the legal profession. In the 1860s and 1870s, in the absence of formally trained barristers and solicitors, a few educated Africans presented cases in court. They were required to acquire licences and became the first semi-professionals in this capacity, although they soon came into conflict with the chiefs.[1] The court system, which was based on the British system, stipulated that murders, robberies and other offences should be tried before the royal judicial officers and the chiefs of a district. Trial by jury was also established in the Gold Coast Colony. By the mid-1880s, however, qualified lawyers from Sierra Leone and England dominated the courts. In 1887, John Mensah Sarbah of Cape Coast qualified as a barrister-at-law at Lincoln's Inn and earned the distinction of being the first African from the Gold Coast to be called to the Bar.[2] The legal profession became increasingly attractive, and by the 1920s, there were active Bar associations in Accra, Cape Coast and Sekondi.[3]

Christian had made a conscious decision to study law, and therefore the practice of his profession would have been extremely important to him. He had earned a good reputation at Gray's Inn, and during his participation as a student, in discussions about South Africa at the 1900 Pan-African Conference in London. It is instructive that he was outspoken about the importance of legal systems, supported by mechanisms for implementation, as a means to effect change in African society. Within a year of his arrival in the Gold Coast in 1902, it was reported from Tarkwa that Christian had established a legal firm, "Messrs Christian and Leung".[4] His partner, Francis Stanislaus Leung, of Chinese descent, came originally from British Guiana.[5] He had practised in Calabar, Nigeria, until 1905, when he left there and went to the Gold Coast.[6]

The firm had in its employ Mr J.E. Dadson, a former registrar in the Concessions Court.[7] Within three years, the workload had increased, and Christian placed an advertisement in the local newspaper for "a lady typist and shorthand writer".[8] The fact that the applicant could state the salary she wanted was a clear indication that business was booming. Christian also became a "concessions" lawyer dealing with franchises for gold mining, and he had a successful private practice in Sekondi as well as Tarkwa.[9] A chronological survey will demonstrate the range of legal matters with which Christian was involved.

CHRISTIAN'S LEGAL CAREER

Christian's legal career was established on a successful footing from the start. As early as 1903, cases in which he was involved on either side came to public attention through newspaper reports. The *Gold Coast Leader* carried favourable reports of two cases in which Christian provided legal counsel. One case in which he appeared for the prosecution involved three European men. They took advantage of a young local woman, who had been offered accommodation at the quarters of a "kind-hearted European" with his permission. The three "rascals" went to the house and made certain "proposals" to the young woman, who did not assent. They responded by "beating her and destroying her personal effects before vacating the premises". According to the news report, this was one of many similar incidents that happened along the railway line, where the white officials were converting the country into "a mining camp and its lawlessness".[10] At the end of an impassionate address in which Christian referred to "violation of sacredness of hospitality and the evils that might follow as natural consequences of such maltreatment practised on poor natives", judgment was given in favour of the plaintiff for £50 and costs. It was further reported that this was "a remarkable case which will long be remembered by those who were interested".[11]

The other 1903 case was the "Essiamuah murder case", which ended with the acquittal of the accused. The Crown had not produced substantial evidence to send the accused to trial at the assizes, and the evidence rested on suspicion. Christian was congratulated in the media for his able defence.[12] Some years later, in "the Broomassie robbery case in Tarkwa", it was reported that on account of the "able defence of Mr. Barrister Christian", the majority of prisoners were discharged.[13]

Christian was relentless in his pursuit of justice for his clients and availed himself of every opportunity to assist the downtrodden. He took cases that dealt with property law as regards legal ownership through the possession of land title deeds.[14] He also secured the agricultural rights of land on behalf of clients. For example, on one occasion he successfully fought a land case on behalf of a local by the name of Joseph Daddy. The land, called Gayin Kromeis, was 4,992 acres, located at a sawmill and suitable for the cultivation of oil palm.[15] In another instance, his knowledge of property law was of assistance to a friend who had become a widow and was subsequently in a dispute with her late husband's brother over her entitlement to a share of the proceeds from the sale of a plot of family land.[16]

In another significant land issue during the 1920s, Christian represented the Amanful chief in a matter about the acquisition of the whole of Takoradi and the Amanful lands for the construction of the Takoradi Harbour Scheme. Initially, in April 1920, the government was granted an option to the land on condition that it paid the Amanful people for the right of use. The compensation was to be decided by the colonial secretary. The balance of the land was to be laid out in a township, plots were to be leased by the government to merchants and others and the rents were to be paid to the chief. Subsequently a sum was paid to the chief of Amanful, not to renew or extend the option but as consideration to release the government from its obligation.[17] The government then acquired the land under the Takoradi Harbour and Town (Acquisition of Lands) Ordinance 1921, specifically drafted to enable seizure of the Takoradi and Amanful lands.[18] As compensation, the government offered the owners the sum of £2,000 plus 10 per cent of the rent derivable from the plots, which were to be let out to merchants and others.[19] Christian described this acquisition of land and the subsequent compensation as an "injustice".[20] He believed that the sum offered was an unreasonable figure. He wanted a higher figure based on the proposed income to be generated from the area in its improved state. He also believed that the loss of fishing and agricultural rights and the like should be taken into consideration, and therefore a ten-year purchase plus 10 per cent for compulsory acquisition should have been offered.[21] Christian therefore made a claim for a much greater sum on behalf of his client, based on the proposed ten-year profits from the fishing and ferry rights and the transportation of logs in the Whin River, which passed through the land. The agricultural rights with respect to the production of yams, groundnuts, cassava, pepper, tomatoes, onions, tiger nuts and cocoa were also considered in his claim.[22] The Takoradi people originally filed a separate claim for £50,000, as did other parties who owned different portions of the land outside the Takoradi–Amanful area but within the area required for the Takoradi Harbour Scheme.[23]

Christian, at the request of the Crown solicitor, was also in negotiation with the Takoradi people, who at the same time had an action pending in court against the Amanful. The Takoradi people claimed all Amanful land on the ground that they had given the Amanful ancestors permission to settle on the land in ancient times.[24] Christian negotiated with the Takoradi people to pool their interests, whereby the Amanful would be satisfied with one-third of the compensation and the Takoradi two-thirds.[25]

Eventually, Christian came to a settlement with the government on behalf of his clients.[26] The chiefs were granted 50 per cent of the rents and £10,000. He wanted to hold out for twice that amount (£20,000), but because of the anxiety of the lawyers of the other claimants, he accepted the offer.[27] He subsequently indicated, however, that the settlement was unjust and noted that the government was "the richer for it".[28]

In this case one sees the extent of Christian's professionalism, and that his concern for justice took precedence over the importance of remuneration. He had sought advice from a consulting engineer, L.A. Smart, who was critical of the Takoradi Harbour Scheme,[29] and also from an English lawyer, J.R. Cardew Smith, whom he paid for his services,[30] often from his own pocket, since his clients were unwilling to pay.[31] In fact, Christian experienced great difficulty in obtaining his legal fees from the Takoradi people. Despite the fact that they owed him, he continued to provide legal counsel in the matter, because according to him, he had given them his word that he would see them through, and because he realized that "a mean advantage will be taken of them", he had "to stick to [his] guns".[32] Though Christian was dedicated to helping the Takoradi people, he developed ill feelings towards them because of their greed and unappreciative nature.[33]

In another land-use case, which lasted over six years, Christian demonstrated commitment to ensure that his client received what was due to him, although another lawyer had been engaged in the appeal process. Christian was originally retained as counsel for the defendant, Chief Awotwi, in an action brought by Chief Odikro Kwaw Koom for damages in the sum of £250 for trespass committed by the defendant and his people on the plaintiff's stool lands.³⁴ After a trial which extended over a four-year period, January 1923 to April 1927, judgment was entered in favour of the plaintiff Kwaw Koom for a sum of £75 damages and costs, which were afterwards taxed at approximately £140.³⁵

The defendant, Chief Awotwi, lodged an appeal, with Robert J. Hayfron as his counsel, and won with costs on 25 March 1929.³⁶ The judgment allowed the case to be sent back to be heard by the Divisional Court, and the defendant's costs in the appeal were assessed. Under the initial ruling, damages and costs as allowed were deposited in the Divisional Court at Sekondi to await the result of the defendant's appeal to the full court. On the success of the appeal, Christian, as the defendant's original counsel, applied for a refund of the money deposited in the court and discovered that it had been withdrawn by the plaintiff. Christian then made a formal application to the Divisional Court for an order authorizing payment to the defendant.³⁷ The application was successful.³⁸

From early in his career, Christian demonstrated that he was thorough in his approach to his work, going to any lengths necessary to understand and interpret the law. In one particular matter, however, he seemed to represent dual interests and eventually faced a conflict-of-interest situation with his client. The issue involved Henry Dietrich, a German, who traded at Tarkwa and gave Christian full power of attorney to represent his interests, when he left the colony in 1914.³⁹ He had been living in the Gold Coast from 1886 to 1914 and had worked at first with the firm I.K. Vietor of Bremen and later set up his own export and import firm at Tarkwa, Henry Dietrich and Company. At the outbreak of the First World War, he was in Sekondi and was removed from his private property and imprisoned, first at Sekondi and then in England, because as a citizen of Germany, he was considered as an enemy alien.

In dealing with this case, Christian had requested assistance from a colleague in England to purchase a handbook which dealt with "the position of alien enemies trading and owning businesses and property in this colony during the war". He explained that he was not in agreement with opinions expressed in the *Law Times* on the subject and therefore wanted to research it further. He questioned whether the closure of all German trading houses was lawful, given that martial law had not been proclaimed. The bank was also refusing withdrawals and payments, and objected to the endorsement of bills of exchange. Goods were being damaged in the process, and everyone seemed to be at a loss as to what to do. Christian was firmly of the view that all these actions were "contrary to law" and was anxious to do the research in order to establish the correct legal position on the matter.[40]

The dispute lasted several years and was complicated by Dietrich's absence from the Gold Coast and Christian's multiple roles as lawyer, public official and businessman. After two years' imprisonment, Dietrich's property was liquidated by the English. Christian, meanwhile, had been appointed by the government as the controlling officer of German property.[41] In this capacity, he was responsible for the sale of Dietrich's effects, which included an iron safe that Christian himself eventually bought at auction, and Dietrich's factory at Tarkwa.[42] According to Dietrich, at the end of his imprisonment in England, when the liquidation list of his property on the Gold Coast was given to him, he felt that his property had been squandered and most of his private possessions stolen. The liquidation list omitted mention of the most valuable furniture in his house, and subsequent requests for information directed to Christian were answered very shortly or evasively.[43] Dietrich felt that Christian "deeply abused" his confidence as a friend, solicitor and attorney, since he did not clear everything up despite knowledge of Dietrich's address for the last two years.[44] Christian, however, claimed that from 1920 to 1931, he had repeatedly written to Dietrich, who did not respond. He had confided this to Mrs Leung, who in turn attempted to contact Dietrich herself in 1922 without success and also informed Christian of this.[45] According to Christian, on the instructions of the government, all Dietrich's property was sold, and the money was paid to the treasury. This property consisted of his goods and household furniture not sold prior to his departure, his land at Sekondi and his factory at Tarkwa.

Christian continued to offer advice with the assistance of Mrs Hedwig Leung, German widow of his law partner, Mr F.S. Leung. The authorities had refused to reimburse the money paid into the treasury, and Germany declined to acknowledge Dietrich as a German, because he had forfeited his civil rights or was otherwise stateless by not joining the military at the proper age.[46] Christian then advised Dietrich to seek the advice of counsel on the matter of stateless people as to whether they should submit claims to obtain the money from their property sold during the war.[47] He advised him to speak specifically to Horace Douglas, and Christian also wrote to Douglas. However, Dietrich ceased correspondence with Christian until November 1932, when he wrote to Christian in German,[48] although he knew that the latter would not be able to read the letter.⁴⁹ Fortunately for Christian, Mrs Leung acted as a translator of Dietrich's letters and also as an informal mediator between the two during their dispute. She agreed with Christian that Dietrich's attitude was regrettable. She also hoped that Dietrich would realize his errors as regards Christian when he received his property.⁵⁰ In the course of her translated letters to Dietrich and Miss Grimm, Dietrich's fiancée, Mrs Leung emphatically repudiated the accusations and insults made against Christian and considered them to be "unfounded".⁵¹ She also informed Dietrich that his fiancée's letters were "awful, insulting and libellous". She noted that Dietrich knew that Christian was "incapable of disloyalty". She also added that Christian "never forgot a kindness, was a most trustworthy friend . . ., generous and very conscientious".⁵² The matter was eventually resolved, although the friendship between the two men obviously suffered as a result of the dispute.

In his dealings with another non-local client, the interplay among Christian's personal, professional and business relationships was again evident. This case involved John Mansour, a Syrian merchant who first went to the Gold Coast in September 1913 and engaged in trade at Sekondi, Kumasi, Accra and other parts of the Gold Coast Colony. He worked with accredited agents who were in charge of his business during his absence from the country. He was also a landed proprietor in Sekondi. His Syrian name was Hanna Abi Namih, and he was born in Beit El Chaar, Lebanon, on 19 October 1887. He married Mary Fares Francis on 26 August 1920.⁵³ Christian represented Mansour in his attempt to become a naturalized British subject. He submitted Mansour's documentation, his identity card and papers issued by his home authorities, to the provincial commissioner of the Western Province of Sekondi and also inquired what further particulars were necessary to complete the process.⁵⁴ The commissioner, however, returned Mansour's documents and pointed out that the name of the holder of the identity card appeared to be Hanna Bou-Nekme and not Mansour. The information given was also insufficient, he wrote, and he directed Christian to the notice on British naturalization which had been published in *Gazette* No. 70 on 1 September 1923, particularly paragraph 7.⁵⁵ Christian responded to the provincial commissioner and sent additional information supplied by Mansour, which he hoped would be sufficient to justify favourable consideration of the application. Christian also noted that the Arabic name appeared on the identification card, and Mansour would provide his passport to verify that he was the same person referred to on the card.⁵⁶

Despite the fact that this matter was apparently not successfully concluded, through it Christian demonstrated his ability to manage and maintain his personal, professional and business associations. Christian made an intervention on Mansour's behalf in the matter of a lease agreement with Mansour's landlady, who was proposing to lease a property to another client at a higher rent, contrary to the "terms and conditions of the agreement" into which they "mutually entered".[57] Christian informed her that what she was planning was a contravention of the lease agreement, and that Mansour would succeed if he took her to court. Subsequently the matter was settled "satisfactorily" between the two parties without the need for any litigation.[58] On another occasion, Christian arranged for Mansour, his wife and assistant to be allowed to travel from Beirut to Sekondi without a deposit of £60 each as required by the immigration regulations.[59] Mansour reported that Christian related to him as he would to "his own son or brother".[60] Christian had a power of attorney for Mansour's affairs during his absence from the Gold Coast and was also his landlord, being the owner of several premises occupied by Mansour for his business.[61] In this latter capacity, issues related to the rent charged for property and Mansour's ability to pay in times of economic hardship arose between them. Christian exercised compassion when necessary, and on one occasion, he offered to decrease the rent.[62] On another occasion, however, when Mansour was negotiating for a lower rent on a property of which Christian was the manager, he did not accede to the request for a reduction in rent.[63]

Christian availed himself of every opportunity to assist his friends as necessary in a professional and personal capacity. For example, he used his network of associates to assist Mrs Hedwig Leung in the sale of her rubber estate, a property of one square mile acquired by the late Mr Leung.[64] He advised Mr Daw, an associate with a syndicate that was acquiring several properties, to make an offer to Mrs Leung for her property.[65] He consulted with Innes Browne and Company on the sale of the property, and an offer was made.[66] He also helped Mrs Leung by arranging for the work and repairs[67] and with the leasing of her other property in the Gold Coast.[68]

Christian also acted on Mrs Leung's behalf with regard to rented properties which she owned in the Gold Coast. For example, Giles Hunt and Company, a firm of solicitors in Sekondi who represented Barclays Bank (Dominion, Colonial and Overseas), corresponded with Christian as necessary on the subject of the renewal of the lease on the premises occupied by the Colonial Bank on

Poassi Road, Sekondi. The original indenture of lease was made on 7 May 1917, and a further agreement had been made between Mrs Leung and the bank on 11 May 1925.[69] The premises were rented at a cost of £300 per annum. The draft lease was sent by Giles Hunt and Company for Christian's approval, after which the bank would have it engrossed for execution by both parties.[70] The lease was renewed for periods of two and three years in 1926 and 1928 respectively.[71] In the case of the renewal for three years, Christian also had the lease proved before the commissioner before signature and execution.[72] Generally he was prompt to take action and to keep his client informed throughout the process. The Colonial Bank eventually moved to its own quarters.

In another successful case that withstood two appeals, Christian represented the chief of Mpohor in a land dispute which began in the Provincial Council in Sekondi. After a prolonged trial, judgment was decided in favour of Christian's client. After that, the plaintiffs appealed to the West African Court of Appeal, which then dismissed the appeal with costs.[73] The plaintiffs appealed further to the Privy Council for special leave to appeal but were also refused.[74]

Christian was tireless in his effort to ensure that justice was served at all times. He took action in the case of Ernest Archer, a prisoner at the Central Prison in Sekondi, who wrote to seek his assistance as regards his sentence of fifteen months' imprisonment for defrauding the company where he previously worked. He was accused of instructing the clerks to put a carpenter named John Pebre and two timber contractors on the company's pay sheet, a charge he denied. He was tried in Kumasi without the aid of counsel. The principal witness for the prosecution had previously defrauded another company, and the witness for the defence, on arriving in Kumasi, was taken to the police commissioner's office and questioned. Christian, together with Franz Dove, a legal colleague, successfully had the sentence reduced by the acting chief commissioner of Ashanti from fifteen months to nine months.[75]

Christian often provided legal counsel in cases that dealt with the legal recovery of debt owed to companies. For example, he acted on behalf of Kumasi Garage Company and took out summonses against those who owed money to the garage and its associates – Mr Davidoff, Kwesi Bennah and Kweku Nti.[76] Christian obtained judgment against Davidoff, with the cost of the summons added to the amount.[77] Christian also successfully sued Bennah for £97 17s. that he owed to the Kumasi Garage Company.[78]

In a matter related to the Takoradi Town Acquisition of Land Scheme, Christian demonstrated his commitment to justice and fair play. He acted on behalf of Bekyire Yankeh II, Omanhin of Dutch Sekondi, the overlord of the stool, who claimed an interest in the land that the government intended to acquire for a cemetery and protective zone. It involved a plot of 514 acres, part of which was leased to Palm Oil Estates, for which Christian's client received a portion of the rent paid.[79] In a related matter, the Odikro, Kojo Edwin of Poassi, sought Christian's services for a complaint that there was an attempt to deprive him of his rightful share of the rents derived from Takoradi Town acquisition of land payable to him through his Omanhin, Bekyire Yankeh II of Dutch Sekondi. According to custom, the Omanhin should receive one-third of the amount paid to Kojo Edwin, and this arrangement had always been in effect. On this occasion, however, it was the intention to pay Kojo Edwin only half of his customary two-thirds. The matter of what proportion the Omanhin should retain then became the subject of an arbitration. Although it was decided in Kojo Edwin's favour, he alerted Christian to further attempts to withhold his payments.

Christian used his experience and expertise for the benefit of all concerned. In an effort to deflect further conflict between the parties and to "save their respective stools from unnecessary litigation and expense", Christian arranged an interview between Kojo Edwin and the district commissioner in Sekondi.[80] Christian also communicated with the manager of the branch of Barclays Bank in Sekondi to arrange for the collection from the authorities of the two-thirds due to Chief Kojo Edwin and to open an account for him. Christian took this initiative, with the intention to protect the interest of the chief and the stool and to ensure that the amount collected was not misused but left to accumulate as much interest as possible.[81]

In the course of his career, all kinds of people and organizations sought Christian's services, demonstrating that he was widely respected, and also that he did not discriminate. For example, the Western Province Teachers' Union expressed their "sincere thanks" for the "noble and successful" work he did on their behalf in "the reduction of the drastic cuts of twenty-six percent on teachers' salaries to only four percent on the increment for the year". The union noted that Christian was the "first person to obtain and shall ever obtain a superior place in the union's esteem and affection" because of the "indomitable efforts" he made "to convince the authorities to sympathise" with its situation and "the great interest" he took in the union by giving it "healthy suggestions each time a deputation from the Union was sent" to him.[82]

Christian also worked successfully as a concessions lawyer concerned with a wide range of professional activity associated with the mining industry. He was retained by the mining companies and the locals and always sought the best interest of his clients. In 1928, for example, Christian was the lawyer for the stool of Chief Kwamina Faibill II of Apintoe, which granted mining concessions to the company Abbontiakoon Mines Limited.[83] The company had requested a reduction in the rent paid by the company to the chief for the land on which the mining activity occurred. At the request of his client, Christian took over the matter and noted that "on no consideration whatever" was his client to "agree to reduce the rent" until his stool debts were paid. Christian further noted that if the company did not choose to "work the mines, they must pay rubber rent and then another Company can take up the mining".[84]

Early in 1929, Christian was made the attorney for the company Central Wassau Gold Mines Limited for their mining leases from Chief Kobina Angu and elders and councillors of the Mansu stool in the sections of Tarkwa known as Subilsu and Denkirawa.[85] In 1931, he was heavily involved in the acquisition of concessions, taking sixteen concessions for the Gold Coast Selection Trust Limited and several others after that for English clients such as Innes Browne, Kwahu Mining Company and the Tarkwa Banket West.[86] The records show that the chairman of Ariston Gold Mines (1929) Limited was so appreciative of Christian's work with the company that he recommended him to the West African Diamond Syndicate.[87]

According to Christian, with £300, he could "secure a gold mining lease of 99 years with occupation rent of £25 and working rent, when winning gold begins, of £300 per annum".[88] He even made the proposition to acquire mining concessions for his friends, including Mr Chappelle. He proposed to acquire "one of the old Concessions situated on the Tarkwa Banket Reef, which had previously been taken but abandoned, it being a 12 [hundredweight] proposition and the working cost per ton being then 38/-", and then "worked at 20/- per ton".[89]

Christian also won an appeal for Mr Thorton in the matter of Kumanwu–Agogo Concession-Enquiry No. 246 (Ashanti). He won the case because the appeal in the West African Court of Appeal in Kumasi, Ashanti, was dismissed after a three-day hearing. After the case, however, Christian required remittance from Thorton for the court fees[90] in order to pay for the appeal record or the retainer of the Honourable K.A. Korsah.[91] He stated that without the money, he could not obtain either the certificate of validity which was deposited in court or the certified copy of the judgment of the Court of Appeal in the matter.[92] According to Thorton, Christian, whom he had known for twenty years, was the only man in the Gold Coast that he would allow to handle his affairs.[93] Christian felt that "to have a man like Mr. Thorton" speak of him as he did was "compensation enough for doing the right thing and doing it always".[94]

Christian understood the nuances of the society and was able to use his legal expertise and his political position to take action for the greater good. In his capacity as a member of the Legislative Council, Christian wrote to the colonial secretary to bring to his notice some of the difficulties that he and his clients in the mining industry were experiencing as a result of the chaotic state of affairs in Upper and Lower Wasaw, particularly the latter. Almost all the "Chiefs in Lower Wasaw" were being "herded together at Tarkwa" and did not dare to go to their respective towns or villages, because some of their subjects had "purported to destool" them. This "destoolment" was not recognized by the government.[95] The subjects "did not stop at this" but contended that the omanhene, whose "enstoolment" was recognized by government, was not the "Omanhene" and refused "to recognise him or the State Council" over which he presided.[96] In a case in point, one of Christian's clients wanted to acquire a concession at Huni Valley but was "told by those on the spot, who are headed by one man called Enimil Kuma II, so called Chief of Huni Valley", that he did not "recognise the Omanhene Enimil V", whose "enstoolment" had been confirmed by government, but that he looked to "the Queen Mother's candidate as Omanhene". Furthermore, the chiefs were "threatened with violence if they dared go to their villages", and as a consequence, the chiefs asked Christian to "apply to Government for Police or Soldiers to protect them".

Christian advised the colonial secretary that this situation which obtained in Lower Wasaw was like a "volcano which may erupt at any time", if the government did not decide promptly on its course of policy. Christian described the situation as "similar" in Upper Wasaw but not as grave; however, it still hampered business. He requested that the colonial secretary bring the situation to the notice of the governor as a matter of urgency, bearing in mind the important role that the Western Province played in the mining industry and the provision of revenue for the colony.[97]

Christian also handled another high-profile concessions case in 1938 in Kumasi. Concession Obenemase "A" granted to his clients, the Nanwa Gold Mines, by one chief was at first opposed by another chief and then secondly by the king of Ashanti, the asantehene. Sir Mervyn Tew of the firm of J.J. Peele and Company, Franz Dove, and Christian represented different interests, but Christian led Sir Mervyn Tew for the Nanwa Gold Mines.[98] On the strong recommendation by the court and in order for the opposer to withdraw opposition, Christian and Sir Mervyn Tew paid them an increased premium or consideration money for each of the three concessions, Obenemase "A", Obenemase "B" and Ahire.[99]

As was to be expected, Christian also took cases that did not result in the desired outcome. For example, he was the defence lawyer in a case that involved a Syrian who was accused of murder. In that particular case, the deceased had attempted to recover money by force from the accused, who put up some resistance. A struggle ensued, during which the deceased fell and ruptured his enlarged spleen. Christian hoped to get an acquittal on the ground of accidental death.[100] The jury, however, by a verdict of five to two, found Christian's Syrian client guilty of manslaughter, and he was sentenced to six months' imprisonment. Christian attributed the verdict to the local practice of juries judging a case by rumours instead of testimony in court. There was ample evidence that there was a fight and that the man fell and ruptured his spleen, which the examining doctor found to be greatly enlarged and diseased. However, the rumour was that the white man had killed an African, and despite the fact that the evidence of the medical officer disproved the story that the deceased had been strangled, the jury found him guilty.[101] According to Christian, he lost "the Syrian case". His client was sentenced to six months' hard labour and abandoned the appeal that Christian proposed to lodge on his behalf.[102]

As with every other career, Christian experienced both high and low points. In 1932, for example, there was a period when Christian described business as "so dull" that the courts were practically closed and the judges and lawyers idle. The lack of legal work available to Christian at that time can be assessed in a statement he made in a letter to Mr Zaitzeff that "if litigation is an index of prosperity and its absence the contrary, then as our courts are practically closed, for want of work for the Judges, you will appreciate the position".[103] Similarly, as a concessions lawyer, Christian experienced professional disappointment despite his considerable expertise in this area of law, which included negotiations with chiefs and tribal institutions and the representation of shipping and other commercial interests.[104] By September 1936, most of the concessions work he did had "been given to a new firm of solicitors specifically sent out by the mining confraternity".[105]

Christian took his work seriously, and there were instances when work commitments had to take priority over personal matters. On one occasion, the status of one of his cases prevented him from travelling with one of his daughters. He pointed out that although there might be no court work for months, if he were to leave a particular case in its unfinished state, his reputation would be tarnished if in his absence, developments took place which were injurious to his and his clients' interest.[106] He described his motto as "Away with doubts and make way for success". According to him, "no case however small or ill supported with money" had "failed to command" his "energy and close examination and interest".[107]

Christian's humility allowed him to take advice and counsel from other professionals, and he did this throughout his career. As late as 1940, he reminded his friend Horace Douglas that owing to his illness since autumn, things had become unsettled in his office, and he could not trace remittances received for opinions given. Christian therefore asked Douglas to ensure and verify that he had paid all his outstanding bills. He also sought comments from Douglas on a Workman's Compensation Ordinance that was being introduced for discussion in the March session of the Legislative Council. He was doing this so that he would be in a better position to offer constructive criticism when the bill was being debated. He was not sure whether the bill was intended to cover each class of employers, domestic and otherwise, but he was aware that Douglas was experienced in these types of cases.[108]

George James Christian and the Benjamin Knowles Case

One of Christian's outstanding achievements as a legal luminary in the Gold Coast was the role he played in the right of appearance of lawyers in court in Ashanti, which was not part of the Gold Coast Colony. This came about as a result of his involvement in the case against Dr Benjamin Knowles, described as "arguably the most important murder case in colonial Ghana during the interwar years".[109] It was alleged that on 20 October 1928 at Bekwai, twenty-five miles from Kumasi and within the jurisdiction of the court, Dr Knowles unlawfully and with malice aforethought killed his wife, Harriet Knowles, by shooting her with a revolver.[110] Although the case was well publicized,[111] what is not widely known or acclaimed is the part which Christian played in having the matter brought before the Privy Council.

An important feature of this murder case related to where it was tried. The case was prosecuted in Ashanti, a colony of the Crown, obtained by conquest in 1901 and governed as a separate colony by the governor of the Gold Coast colony, which had been formed twenty-five years earlier. The Offin River served as a boundary between the Gold Coast and Ashanti. When Ashanti was conquered, it was not a requirement that it fall under the Crown Jurisdiction Act, the British Settlement Act or Order in Council. The governor of the Gold Coast was therefore not entrusted to legislate for the peace, order and good government of the Colony of Ashanti.[112]

Although the right to trial by jury existed in the Gold Coast Colony, Ashanti and other regions were outside the ordinary jurisdiction of the Gold Coast.[113] The Commissioners' Courts of the Ashanti were established in 1901 by the ordinance of the governor of the Gold Coast[114] and not by the Legislative Council of the Gold Coast. Trial by jury was practised in the Gold Coast but not in Ashanti.[115] It was acknowledged that this "extraordinary system" had escaped notice by the British public.[116]

The case was also considered to be significant because of the nationality of those people involved. Dr Knowles was originally from Aberdeen, Scotland, and he had served for many years as medical officer of the West African Medical Service, stationed in Bekwai,[117] where he was in charge of the hospital. He had had a distinguished military career during the First World War.[118] Knowles's wife, formerly Miss Madge Clifton, was a music-hall artiste. It is alleged that she probably had another husband at the time she went through the marriage ceremony with Dr Knowles. She died on 23 October 1928 in Kumasi Hospital from septic peritonitis, as a result of the wound she received from a bullet. In her dying deposition, she asserted that she had accidentally fired the revolver while getting up from a chair on which she had placed it.[119]

The case generated much interest and received extensive publicity in the British press. During the trial, which was heard by the police magistrate acting as the circuit judge, His Honour Frank John James Foster McDowell, the prosecution claimed that Mrs Knowles's deathbed testimony was a false attempt to protect her husband. Dr Knowles's defence was that he was falling asleep when he heard a shot and Mrs Knowles's cry: "Oh my God, I'm shot!" The case was tried without a jury, and the acting circuit judge considered the issue of whether Mrs Knowles accidentally shot herself or whether her declaration was the untruthful effort of a wife trying to save her husband from punishment for a serious crime.[120]

The trial lasted nine days, after which the judge, on 21 November 1928, found Dr Knowles guilty, on the basis of his belief that the evidence was overwhelming, and that there was no reasonable doubt of his guilt. It was reported that the circuit-court judge had decided not to accept the alleged declaration. He believed that there was no question of real premeditation, that the act was done suddenly in a dazed condition of semi-drunken frenzy and that there was evidence of great provocation.[121] Knowles was sentenced to death by hanging.[122] He did not have a right of appeal to a superior court under the law of Ashanti[123] but was at liberty to apply for special leave to appeal to the Privy Council. Dr Knowles objected to the fact that he was tried without the benefit of a jury and the services of counsel, which made him incapable of devising his questions properly.[124]

In the wake of the conviction and sentence, there was an outpouring of support on behalf of Dr Knowles. Inquiries were made by F.C. Thompson, MP, on behalf of a constituent, acting for Knowles's mother, as to whether an appeal was being proceeded with and whether all facilities had been afforded for the defence of the doctor. Other interventions were made by the British Legion by correspondence dated 29 November 1928 to Brigadier General Sir Samuel H. Wilson, KCMG, KCB, of the Colonial Office, which referred to the fact that the sister of Dr Knowles, Mrs Ashby, had made an approach to the legion for assistance due to the "somewhat irregular proceedings".[125] Doctors in London who were friends of Knowles also decided to present a petition requesting a reprieve.[126]

Considerable reporting of the Knowles case in the British *Daily Mail* kept the issues in the public eye. The circumstances related to the case were publicized, counsel for the defence had not been allowed, evidence of the prosecution was based on hearsay and the proceedings of the case were heard in camera with a cordon of police surrounding the building. It was also known that the challenge for the Gold Coast administration was to have a judicial system for white people in a country where white people were scattered.[127] Under the Ashanti Ordinance, lawyers did not have the right of appearance, and there was no appeal in any criminal matter. In capital cases, the notes of evidence were to be sent to the governor and the sentence confirmed by him.[128] Bekwai, where the crime was committed, was a hundred miles by train from Sekondi, and Knowles could have been brought there for trial, because Sekondi was part of the Gold Coast Colony, where lawyers had the right of appearance in court. Sir William Nevill M. Geary, barrister, attorney general of the Gold Coast, who had previously practised as a solicitor and barrister in Nigeria from 1897 to 1913, also thought it only fair that anyone, white or black, tried for his life should be properly defended by counsel.[129]

In a memorandum on the subject dated 28 June 1929, Captain R.S. Rattray, CBE, stated that he had always considered the advent of the native Bar into Ashanti as inevitable before the Knowles case, and that all the Knowles case did was to precipitate this step. He dismissed concerns that lawyers would encourage secession of Ashanti by the Ashanti chiefs. He was of the view that although the change in policy would be tantamount to "African Barristers" invading the domain of political officers of the Gold Coast Colony, it would only mean that these officers of the Crown would have to watch their Ps and Qs.[130]

On the subject of right of appearance of lawyers in Ashanti, the acting colonial secretary, Mr G.C. Boulay, noted on 1 August 1929 that at the time Ashanti came under British rule, there were good reasons to set up special machinery for the administration of justice there and for the exclusion of lawyers from the courts. The people had been ruined by prolonged wars, the country was undeveloped, conditions were primitive, there were no European traders and communication with the colony was difficult. The position had changed over time, however, and this necessitated a policy shift.[131]

The result of the dichotomy was that Europeans were amenable to the jurisdiction of the provincial courts in the Gold Coast, while hundreds of British subjects of African race had been sentenced to death under this procedure outside the Gold Coast Colony and been hanged. Those who handled these cases were "honourable gentlemen" who honestly endeavoured to administer justice. The fault was with the system that imposed duties on them for which they were not qualified. It was advocated that a commission be established to revise the judicial system, so that every British subject, whether European or African, charged with an offence, would be tried by a tribunal in accordance with British standards.

Reference was made to the fact that the matter had been the cause of frequent protests by ex-judges and members of the West African Bar, who would assist the commission to frame recommendations for reform to the criminal-procedure system. A former puisne judge in Nigeria, W.H. Stoker, KC, had pointed out that people in Britain were shocked by the procedure of the Commissioners' Court in Ashanti, and that even in wartime or under martial law, an accused person would not be tried as was Dr Knowles.[132]

Prior to the Knowles case, in fact as early as 1906, Christian brought the issue of the practice of law in the Ashanti region to the attention of the treasurer and master of the Bench of Gray's Inn. During a visit to the United Kingdom, he expressed his concern that members of the legal profession were deprived of any right of audience in Ashanti courts. He considered it a grievance to the lawyers, a grave danger to litigants and prisoners and questioned whether the practice was constitutional.[133] The Benchers forwarded the letter and its accompanying statement on the legal situation in the Gold Coast to the secretary of state for the Colonies and suggested that Christian's letter raised "an important constitutional question". After they complained of a lack of response, the Colonial Office informed the Benchers that Lord Elgin was in touch with the acting governor on the matter.[134] The next year, 1907, there were requests for lawyers to be allowed to practise in Ashanti.[135] In the system that obtained there at the time, the officer hearing a case could examine, cross-examine and re-examine a witness for the prosecution and the defence. The accused would then be asked to make a statement. The effect of this was that the judicial officer acted as the police, judge, jury, counsel for the prosecution and counsel for the defence. In the event of a guilty verdict in a murder trial, the president of the court was to forward to the governor a copy of the notes of evidence with a written signed report stating the recommendations of the court.[136]

Christian had persisted in keeping alive the issue of trial without jury and counsel in Ashanti. He had also brought it to the attention of the then president of the Bar Association, Lampard, who subsequently brought it to the attention of the Bar Association and the Council of Legal Education. When asked about it, however, the Colonial Office replied that Ashanti "was not ripe for it", and that the Benchers had better not press the matter then.[137] Christian also researched the subject and noted that there was one other place within the empire where this procedure had been followed for some years, but public opinion had been brought to bear on the matter and the law altered. This was in Balochistan,[138] a buffer state between Afghanistan and India on the Persian Gulf leased to Great Britain. Christian contested that this state – "even at its worst", when for years "its inhabitants were considered hostile and a form of military law obtained" – allowed a licensed "Indian (Pleader)". In Ashanti, however, "all egress" was barred from lawyers, even though some of the residents, who were "Britishers, others, British subjects and the Ashantis themselves", were a "law abiding people, and wholly devoted to the growing of cocoa and to trading".[139]

Christian kept his finger on the pulse of the entire situation and kept his colleague in London, Horace Douglas, informed about the course of action being pursued by the local professional body. He addressed a letter to the "Comrades of the Great War" about the case and its ramifications, which was to be read at an Armistice dinner in Sekondi. His appeal challenged the "Comrades" to take action in the cause of justice, so that this unfortunate man might be granted his entitlement as a British citizen under the Constitution of Great Britain. The letter was subsequently reproduced in the *Daily Mail*.[140] The local Bar association convened a meeting on 24 November 1928, with a view to taking steps to move the court to show cause why the members of the Bar were denied the right to practise in Ashanti (vide Laws of Ashanti 1920 – Ashanti Administration Ordinance No. 1 of 1902, Section 10 page 3) and to take the matter through to the Privy Council.

Christian was doubtful as to whether this proposed action on behalf of members of the Bar could be fought to a successful conclusion. His intent was to voice these matters and let public opinion force the authorities to do the right thing. His emphasis was not on the denial of audience to counsel but on ensuring that constitutional rights not be violated and the cause of justice not be obstructed, bearing in mind the motto "Justitia non est neganda non differenda".[141]

Christian also drew on his personal knowledge of the personnel involved in the system to provide further support for his views. Criminal appeals were made triable by the chief commissioner of Ashanti, who, at the time, was John Maxwell. He was a "Writer of the Signet",[142] and, according to Christian, "one of the ablest" among the administrators and political servants in the whole service. However, Christian felt that justice had a "better chance of being properly dispensed by the Chief Justice" of the colony, who had a "long experience in the Court of Criminal Appeals" as compared to John Maxwell, who had "not engaged in criminal practice" for the last twenty-six years and was chiefly "a Political Officer".[143]

Christian hoped that the Knowles case would draw attention to "the antiquated and unfair method of administering justice in Ashanti", and that it would receive the attention it deserved from the British public. This was important to him, because he felt that even though they were British subjects, blacks were "being tried for murder almost weekly in one part or another in Ashanti by inexperienced and often unqualified men without the help of counsel or the privilege of trial by jury". He believed it was "a scandal on the administration of justice", but since he was a member of the Bar, whenever he raised the issue, he was told that he had "an axe to grind", and that he wished the Bar was allowed to practise in Ashanti.[144]

The procedure in Ashanti, Christian thought, should be the same as in the Gold Coast Colony as far as it was practicable. He felt that the court should have obtained jurors, because there were hundreds of Europeans residing in Kumasi and thousands of Africans who were literate and fit to be jurors. It was not for lack of suitable men that Dr Knowles was not tried by a jury; it was "the perversity of the Authority", who felt that it would "derogate from their God-like powers to have a Jury or counsel".[145] He also believed that it was a disgraceful state of affairs that people in Ashanti were not afforded the same entitlement of protection as enjoyed in Britain and instead were tried for murder without the aid of counsel and without a jury.[146]

Christian became directly involved in the case after Knowles's conviction and sentence. Knowles, who had been incarcerated in Kumasi during the trial, received from the senior superintendent of prisons copies of depositions of the High Court and the summary of the judge and verdict, so that he could fully instruct Christian.[147] Condemned prisoners from Ashanti were usually sent to Sekondi, from where they were always allowed to see counsel if they wanted. This enabled Knowles to brief Christian, so after the trial and sentence, Knowles authorized Christian to take such steps as he might consider necessary on his behalf.[148] A petition was sent to the governor, as a result of which the sentence was commuted to life imprisonment.

The colonial secretary was concerned as to whether there was still a proposal to apply for special leave to appeal to the Privy Council in light of the fact that Dr Knowles's death sentence was not to be carried out.[149] Christian, however, intended to publicize the case and take the matter further.[150] As he had received instructions from Knowles to proceed, he forwarded the petition signed by Knowles for leave to appeal to the Privy Council to barrister Horace Douglas.[151] He also mailed a certified copy of the proceedings of the case to London on 2 and 11 December 1928, and the Privy Council granted the special leave to appeal.

Christian requested the services of solicitors Wynne-Baxter and Keeble, so that the matter would be "properly launched in the manner usually done of solicitor instructing counsel".[152] The petition for special leave to appeal was lodged on 13 March 1929, by Mr D.N. Pritt, KC, and Mr Horace Douglas, both of whom represented Dr Knowles[153] as appellant, while the attorney general, Sir William Jowitt, KC, and Mr C.H. Pearson appeared as counsel for the respondent, the Crown.[154]

According to the solicitors, Wynne-Baxter and Keeble, Dr Knowles did not appreciate the gravity of the situation. He thought that the trial on the coast was "a very mediocre affair, scantily conducted"; "he seemed to be "amazed at the sanction behind the conviction" and thought that he was brought to England "for the purpose of some trial", and in consequence he was "irritated at the delay" in what he considered to be "his real trial". The solicitors had to explain to him that though the conviction was "quite a fallacy", until it was shown to the contrary, it was still a "valid conviction and even any alteration in the law does not have a retrospective affect and that the one and only authority to review the decision [was] the Privy Council".[155]

There was support for Knowles both in England and in the Gold Coast. Some of his friends in London signed a petition asking for commutation of the death sentence. Dr J.J. O'Donnell, a colleague "with whom he once practised in London", noted that the petition was at the office of Mr Howard, "a solicitor of Gray's Inn-square", and that he hoped that "all Dr. Knowles friends, will sign it or communicate there as soon as possible". Additionally, "Mme. Madge Russell, a teacher of dancing and friend of both Knowles and his late wife, who was convinced of both his innocence and the veracity of his wife's dying statement that it was an accident, sent a letter to the King's secretary, asking that the King should intervene". The response was that this was not within the king's power, since the "prerogative of pardon" was delegated to the governor of the Gold Coast. The British Legion headquarters in London, on hearing that Knowles was a former serviceman, also helped his cause and put his sister "in touch with the legion's solicitors and counsel".[156] In the Gold Coast, "high legal authorities" assisted the governor, Sir A. Ransford Slater, "in reviewing the case". These included Chief Justice Sir P.C. Smyly. A full report would then be "transmitted to London by the Governor, together with any observations that he might think necessary to make to the Colonial Office".[157]

There were financial considerations related to the Privy Council appeal that had to be taken care of, before the matter could proceed. It was estimated that the appeal would cost at least £500. A proportion of the money had been subscribed by readers of the *Daily Mail*.[158] Former fellow students at Aberdeen University, who graduated in 1907 with Dr Knowles, collected about £100, which was spent to obtain leave to appeal to the Privy Council.[159] Forty copies of the printed record of the trial at Kumasi had to be provided for the Judicial Committee of the Privy Council at a cost of £100, and nothing could be done until the money was made available.[160] One of Dr Knowles's former student colleagues, who had participated in the earlier collection, expressed the hope that other students would subscribe towards the additional £100 needed for the copies of the proceedings.[161] It appears that a sum of seventy guineas was also sent to the *Daily Mail* by former fellow students of Dr Knowles to assist in his appeal.[162]

Christian was magnanimous and helped Dr Knowles "free of charge". In so doing, he felt that he was "carrying out the tradition of the profession" and hoped "that in future the law will be so amended" whereby the "employment of counsel" would be "allowed and such crimes are tried by Judge and jury".[163] Franz Dove, barrister-at-law in Accra, assisted by communicating with the colonial secretary on Christian's behalf.[164] At the end of the trial, the Crown agents for the colonies authorized payment of £863 1s. 1d. "from Gold Coast Funds" to Messrs Burchells of Westminster, London, who appeared as counsel for the respondent, the king.[165]

Christian also saw to it that the British public was informed and arranged for news about the case to be cabled to the *Daily Mail* in London. He reported on his role in a letter to Mrs Leung:

> I am engaged in a very important case at present, that of Rex V: Dr Knowles charged with killing his wife, found guilty and sentenced to death. Upon my

applying, the Governor has commuted his sentence to one of imprisonment, but I intend to appeal to the Privy Council all the same, because he was tried in Ashanti without the aid of counsel or Jury. No doubt you must have read this in the Daily Mail to which I caused the news to be cabled.[166]

Once the Judicial Committee of the Privy Council had granted leave to appeal the death penalty, Knowles was returned to London. He left Sekondi under escort on the Elder Dempster liner *Apapa* and arrived in Plymouth on 2 April 1929. During the journey, he was escorted by Major F.L. Hamilton, the commissioner of police, Accra, who used relays of second-class passengers to guard him during the day. He shared a berth with another prisoner and was not allowed to shave until towards the end of his journey. He was taken to the local prison in Plymouth pending the hearing of his appeal and was subsequently incarcerated at Maidstone Prison. It was reported that he was unable to attend the hearing of his appeal as he had been suffering from a mental disorder since his imprisonment.[167]

In the appeal before the Privy Council, it was considered that there was no reliable evidence upon which a capital conviction could safely and justly be based, and that the judge did not give effect to the paramount rule of law in a capital case. In addition, the Privy Council considered that the onus of proof was on the prosecution, and that it was not for the petitioner to prove his innocence. The fact that there was no power and jurisdiction under the Ashanti Administration Ordinance to refer the case to the Supreme Court of the Gold Coast Colony, where the petitioner would have been entitled to a jury and to be represented by counsel and solicitor, was also considered pertinent. The Privy Council determined that the case should have been referred.[168] The terms of the Ashanti Administration Ordinance 1 of 1902 and Section 118 of the Criminal Procedure Ordinance were also brought under scrutiny, with regard to the legal arguments to justify the trial's being held without a jury considered as a matter of criminal procedure.[169]

Christian maintained his interest and continued to seek information while the case was before the Privy Council. Christian hoped the case would receive as much publicity as possible to ensure a revision of the law whereby trial by jury would be allowed, at least in murder cases, where the accused would have access to counsel, or that Ashanti would be opened to the Bar. He also believed that the Privy Council would be persuaded to make a pronouncement on the matter, since it would force the authorities to amend the law.[170]

Christian sent a cable to the editor of the *Daily Mail*, London, in which he noted and compared the Knowles case with another murder case which was tried by jury. In that case, an African policeman named Fulani was shot dead in August 1927 without provocation, by a man named Anamen at Accra. The Koforidua jury disagreed among themselves, and the trial was sent to Sekondi. The defence was assigned to Christian, and he advised the accused to plead guilty to manslaughter, which he did, and the court sentenced him to only one year of imprisonment. Christian wanted to show the contrast of a murder trial in Sekondi with the aid of jury and counsel, with one in Ashanti without those aids. This was to emphasize the necessity to allow trial by jury in Ashanti with the aid of counsel.[171] According to Christian, the letter sent to the *Daily Mail* had made history.[172]

According to the Privy Council, the fatal flaw in the Knowles judgment was that after Mrs Knowles's account of it being an accident was set aside, the only alternative considered by the judge was murder. Manslaughter was not considered, and this would have been erroneous in the summing-up by a judge in the trial even if there were a jury present. The judge failed to consider the question of whether the evidence reached the standard of proof necessary for a conviction for murder. In the opinion of the Privy Council, it did not. On this account, the conviction was quashed.[173] On the issue of right to trial by jury, the Privy Council held that it was impossible for it to form a conclusion on the matter, which should be considered by a local tribunal in reference to its practicality and the state of local circumstances. The appeal was therefore not sanctioned on that ground.

In the aftermath of the case, Christian adopted a multi-pronged approach to set the record straight on the role that he had played, alluding to a related issue, namely, the non-recognition of the contribution of West Indians to Gold Coast society. Christian, detailing his role in the case, wrote to his fellow West Indian friend Francois as follows:

> Although I did not have any share in the hearing of the appeal before the Privy Council, yet it was I who made the first move in this Colony and succeeded in the first instance in getting the death sentence reduced to one of imprisonment, and afterwards I instructed my colleague in England to apply for an appeal there which was ended on Tuesday in favour of Dr. Knowles, the conviction being quashed by the Privy Council.
>
> This ought to secure a change in the law which will regulate the jurisdiction

and procedure and possibly lead to trial by jury and eventually counsel might be allowed to participate.

I have attained my end which was to expose the existing condition of the law and get public opinion in England to press for an amendment of the existing criminal law to the benefit of all concerned irrespective of race or colour.

I wonder what my local colleagues will say in the press commenting on the case and whether they will even mention my name as having set the ball a rolling, so very popular are the West Indians here.[174]

E.H. Ambaah of Kumasi, to whom Christian had sent a telegram with the news, responded that the information was received "with great joy". He had circulated the telegram to all concerned, including Europeans, with the hope that it would "help the opening of Kumasi for the Lawyers as early as possible".[175]

Christian also wrote to colleagues in England, demonstrating in the process that he had taken all the necessary steps to put the wheels in motion to take the outcome of the case to its logical conclusion by including all the relevant professional bodies involved. His letter is self-explanatory:

> I am sending you a copy of a letter I am sending to Broadhurst. Somehow or the other some of us West Indians are so unpopular that our names are never referred or published when you do anything worthy of praise hence I want both you and Broadhurst to know the truth of the movement to be used if occasion should require it.
>
> I may state that about July of this year I persuaded the local Bar to appeal to Sir John Simons and the Bar Association in England to help us to get Ashanti opened up and last week a letter has been addressed to the Governor by the local Bar Association to the same effect so we are awaiting developments. Doubtless our wishes will be granted upon our giving safeguards for the proper behaviour of all Members of the Bar. You know that to err is human, and just as we read of solicitors in England being disciplined for wrongful acts, so provision must be made here too in the event of any one misconducting himself which has been a great argument in the past against us.[176]

He continued to correspond with barrister Horace Douglas, who kept him abreast of how the matter was progressing. On the basis of what Douglas had reported, Christian expressed his pleasure and appreciation that the matter was still being considered by the Bar Council and that the Colonial Office seemed to be in agreement.[177]

Interestingly, although Christian wanted credit to be given where it was due, at the same time he was careful about how information was publicized and the effects it might have on his reputation. His West Indian colleague Abbensetts had written to the press emphasizing Christian's role in the case. Christian was not in favour of this course of action and had requested that the letter be recalled. He did not wish to be seen as someone who was "hankering after praise". He preferred to wait until, from the weight of circumstances, he, as well as Dove, who had helped to prepare the petition for the application and assisted throughout the process, would be given due credit. He felt that it would be better to let events take their course. He would be amply rewarded if his efforts eventually resulted in the desired end for the benefit of all concerned, irrespective of race and colour.[178] In a letter to Horace Douglas after the Privy Council's decision, Christian, who, as has been mentioned, agreed to take the case free of charge, said that he hoped "to get a letter of appreciation from Dr. Knowles or his people".[179]

Christian hoped that in the reasoning of the Privy Council's judgment, there would have been some recommendation of trial by jury with the help of counsel in the future; otherwise, inexperienced commissioners and judges might repeat the same error with people who would not be in a position to go to the Privy Council for redress. This, according to him, was indicative of a case of one law for the rich and another for the poor African.[180] As mentioned, however, the Privy Council did not rule definitely on trial by jury in Kumasi and thought of it as a question of practicality. Christian thought that the claim that it was not practicable to have trial by jury in Ashanti could be disproved by an affidavit that showed that there were as many as five hundred Europeans and a thousand or more literate natives available as jurymen in Kumasi and its suburbs and as many more within a radius of seven miles. Kumasi was the second largest town, if not the largest, in Ashanti and in the Gold Coast Colony.[181] Christian felt that the court shirked the point and kept excluding trial by jury in favour of occupants of the Bench who were hardly qualified or experienced.[182]

Further support for a change in the Ashanti justice system was embodied in a letter from the Gold Coast Bar Association to the General Council of the Bar which highlighted the issue of trial with jury and the service of counsel as seen in the Knowles case. It pointed out that for years the public had complained about it. The case of *Rex* v. *Dr Knowles* among others was used as an example of the consequences of this method of trial. According to the letter, the time had come to appeal for change in the relevant law.[183]

The matter eventually came to the attention of the British Parliament, and in 1931, the Colonial Office sent a legal adviser to West Africa "to inquire into the administration of justice in all the British colonies and to effect judicial reforms".[184] The recommendation for the Gold Coast called for unification of the legislation of the colony and associated territories and for the jurisdiction of the Supreme Court of the Gold Coast Colony to be extended to include Ashanti and the Northern Territories. Consequently, in 1933 the Colonial Government opened up Ashanti to legal practitioners, and C.E. Woolhouse Bannerman, an African who had served as police magistrate and puisne judge, was appointed acting circuit judge at Kumasi.[185] On account of the general dissatisfaction with the jury system as it operated, the colonial government implemented a system in which three assessors sat with a trial judge who was not bound by their opinions. Jurors only participated in the inquests which followed judicial hangings.[186]

H.G. Bushe, CMG, legal adviser to the Colonial Office, reported: "Kumasi no longer consists of a fort encircled by forest, but is a large and beautiful town capable of infinite development. Nor is there any reason to suppose that Ashantis are any less intelligent than the natives of the Gold Coast. The position today therefore, has no relation to that which existed thirty years ago when this ban was imposed." Bushe was not in favour of jury trials, but Sir R. Slater was in agreement "with the Judges and the Attorney-General and recommend[ed] that concurrently, with the admission of lawyers, the jury system should be introduced, but that it be restricted to capital cases".[187]

In this case related to Dr Knowles, Christian, with his dogged insistence and actions behind the scenes to effect change that would redound to the benefit of all, demonstrated that he was indeed a "chip off the old block". He used the power of the pen to advantage throughout the case and its aftermath.[188] Some ten years after the case, Christian wrote to the British press detailing his role, yet cleverly giving credit to the newspaper. In this letter, he was ostensibly reporting on the changes in the Ashanti legal system and practice.

> You will perhaps remember my name as it was I who took up Doctor Knowles' case a few years ago and sent you a long letter showing that he had been tried by an unqualified Judge in Ashanti, no jury and without the assistance of counsel.
>
> You will remember that the Privy Council when the case went before it quashed the sentence.

I am happy to say that since, the Court in Ashanti is presided over by a qualified judge and is made part of the Supreme Court of the Colony and legal practitioners are allowed to practise there. Thanks to the advocacy of the *Daily Mail* on the matter.[189]

Although Gold Coast lawyers were of the view that jury trial was a necessary condition of any meaningful change in the operation of the criminal-justice system in Ashanti, this took much longer to be effected. Gocking has indicated that "it was not until 1953, in the waning years of colonial rule, that the Convention People's Party government of Kwame Nkrumah finally introduced jury trial into Ashanti".[190]

After the Privy Council quashed Dr Knowles's life sentence, he was released from Maidstone Prison within twenty-four hours. His unusually rapid release was at the request of the agent-general for the Crown colonies, Mr J.R. Clynes.[191] Knowles was driven to a village in Buckinghamshire, accompanied by his solicitor, a friend, and Mrs Ashby, his sister, with whom he stayed.[192] He subsequently wrote to Christian informing him that he was sick with malaria and jaundice.[193] A few years later, Dr Knowles died at the age of forty-eight.[194]

The case of Benjamin Knowles was the first one emanating from the colonies that was recorded in the series "Notable British Trials".[195] According to Agyemang, who has documented several interesting court cases from the Gold Coast in the colonial period, there were rumours concerning the circumstances surrounding the incident which were not mentioned in the court. Forty years after the incident, however, it was still doubtful whether it was "a cold blooded crime, a hot blooded stupid blunder or an unfortunate accident occurring in an atmosphere of West Coast loneliness and constant bickering".[196]

REFLECTIONS ON CHRISTIAN'S LEGAL CAREER

In his reminiscences towards the end of his life, Christian described his first experience as a lawyer in the Gold Coast. He demonstrated fairness as a business partner and a sensible approach towards earnings and life in general. His first fee as a lawyer was for defending an Ashanti man in Cape Coast. Christian charged "six guineas", but the man paid "five sovereigns". Christian gave "two sovereigns to his partner, F.S. Leung" and kept two for himself, suggesting to Mr Leung that they should keep them "to show their children". With the fifth sovereign, they bought themselves champagne and drank that night.¹⁹⁷ Christian, in sharing the story with a young lawyer, acknowledged that he did not know what had become of his two sovereigns and advised against making resolutions that one could not keep, but said that he should follow his example "in saving half of your earnings but not to spend it unnecessarily afterwards".¹⁹⁸

Christian's career demonstrated that he had lived up to the expectations of his senior colleagues. In 1910, John Mensah Sarbah responded to a congratulatory letter from him and encouraged him "to continue to take that personal interest" which he had at times shown "in the welfare of the chiefs and people" with whom he came into contact.¹⁹⁹ In 1929, on the retirement of Sir Philip Crampton Smyly, who had recommended the Gold Coast to him, Christian confessed that Smyly's guidance remained a source of inspiration throughout his career. As a result, he considered it his "duty" to make himself "worthy" of Smyly's "approbation and good opinion".²⁰⁰

There is no doubt that Christian was an extremely competent and successful lawyer. As was reported on his demise, he was a "vigorous but generous and sportsman-like opponent" in his conduct of law cases. His concern for mankind at every level of society led him to defend many poor people free of charge.²⁰¹ It was also significant that he had maintained good relations with all strata of society, "both Europeans and Africans", and he was in no way discriminatory in the help he gave to all.²⁰² The colonial secretary, in an address to the Legislative Council, opined that no one who had the privilege of listening to Christian "could fail to observe the keen enthusiasm, the conviction and the deep sincerity that marked all his public work". He also noted that he acted with promptitude and consideration for all his clients, presenting cases "fairly, honestly and conscientiously".²⁰³

This survey of Christian's legal career has underscored the wide range of issues in which he was involved. He operated as prosecution or defence, and he served the whole spectrum of society. His clients included individuals and companies, the wealthy and the indigent, chiefs and the ordinary man, locals and foreigners. Indeed, Christian had truly earned the accolades showered on him at his death. His insistence that justice be served was reminiscent of his father's persistent dialogue with the Colonial Office authorities.²⁰⁴ His undocumented role in the Benjamin Knowles case led to eventual reform of the judicial system in the colony of Ashanti.²⁰⁵

Figure 5.1. George James Christian, barrister-at-law, in wig and gown

Figure 5.2. Franz Dove, barrister-at-law, who communicated with the Colonial Office on George James Christian's behalf. *Reproduced with permission of the Dove family of Accra, Ghana.*

CHAPTER 6

Christian's Multifaceted Life

CHRISTIAN, WHO HAD DEMONSTRATED FROM EARLY IN HIS life in Dominica and London that he had an astute business sense, engaged in a variety of money-making ventures during his time in the Gold Coast. This was necessary in order to support his lifestyle as well as the needs of his growing family, particularly the education of his children. His lifestyle included biennial trips to England and the Caribbean for vacations with his children and visits to his relatives and friends in Dominica with whom he kept in contact. In his public life, Christian was generous by nature and willing to contribute of his substance when there was a need, especially to assist younger people with their education. He demonstrated the same benevolence with a wide circle of friends, relatives and associates with whom he kept in contact. Three other significant roles he fulfilled in the Gold Coast Colony were as school manager, honorary consul for the Republic of Liberia and founding member of the Freemason Lodge in Sekondi. He managed these multiple roles with outstanding success, and although his financial status ebbed and flowed according to the economic state of the country, he amassed a substantial estate during his lifetime and thus provided for his family and loved ones after his death.

LANDLORD AND BUSINESSMAN IN DOMINICA AND THE GOLD COAST

Christian had been a property owner in Dominica before he embarked on his studies in London, and he continued to view property ownership as a productive form of investment. In 1894, he had invested in Mero Estate and Cassada Garden Estate in the parish of St Joseph, Dominica, for the support and maintenance of his Dominica-born children – Peter, Clara and Maude – and nieces Marjorie and Christianie Burke.¹ During his years in the Gold Coast, he maintained the property he owned in Dominica and acquired others. They were managed by his son Peter, to whom he periodically remitted funds for their upkeep and improvement.

In 1924, Christian, whose relatives in Dominica were dependent on him for monetary support, was anxious about the uncertain state of his financial affairs there. He owned several properties in Dominica which were rented through the assistance of Mr Howell Shillingford. These properties included his town house as well as plots in Cassada Gardens, Mero, Syers and St Joseph. He operated a share system with respect to crops on the plots that he rented to people on his estates.² In 1926, his estate in Mero was a great source of limes, which were sold by those who leased the plots.³ Christian was particular about the payment of rents, and he requested Shillingford to inform the tenants that they must absolutely pay their rentals or quit, because he was unable to support those who were dependent on him as well as outsiders.⁴ In 1927, he owned a town house, a cottage at St Joseph and a house at King's Hill.⁵ The rent from the town house was to be used as an allowance for his niece Chrissie.⁶ He also owned land at the "Pound" and premises at the Morne.⁷ Christian envisaged that he would send small remittances to Peter to be used to cultivate the various properties in Dominica. The income generated by them would then be used to relieve Christian of the obligation to support those at home, because he could not do that indefinitely. Christian was clear in his intent that the estates should generate sufficient income "to meet all local demands that might otherwise be made on [his] purse".⁸

These property investments in Dominica continued to be a source of income for Christian for the next decade. For example, in 1935, an indenture of lease was granted to the Roseau Town Council for a thirty-five-year tenancy in respect of a portion of Christian's land known as the Guinea Grass Piece or the "Pound". The lease was granted with an option to purchase the premises at $6 per square foot. This arrangement was made on behalf of Christian by his son Dr Peter Christian.⁹

Christian acquired property in Roseau that he named Sekondi House, which he bought for Peter.¹⁰ He and Peter purchased another house from a Mrs Shand in March 1939.¹¹ This property was placed in Peter's name as a convenience, but Christian, who contributed £300 towards the purchase, meant it to be an investment for himself, Peter and Clara.¹² Christian had to sacrifice his shares in the Gold Coast Main Reef, the Marlu and the Gold Coast areas in order to obtain funds to send to Peter for the purchase of the Shand property.[13] The house was renovated, insured and was to be rented out to prospective tenants.[14] Peter changed the name of that house from "Moss Lodge" to "Secondom House", since it was the "second house bought by good African money in Dominica".[15]

Christian began to acquire property in the Gold Coast within eighteen months of his arrival. In November 1903, he bought land situated on Poassi Road in the commercial sector of Sekondi for the price of £85 from Essau Entamah and other Krome farmers, and with the concurrence of Chief Kwamina Annasi, head chief of Dutch Sekondi, Chief Kobina Koomah and several other people from Sekondi. He originally held a lease of the land and then sought the "absolute sale" of the lot, which was granted to him. In February 1904, he bought a parcel of "stool land" situated in the village of Dunkwa from several people of the stool of Dunkwa for the sum of £5.[16]

As time went on, Christian took advantage of other opportunities to increase his financial base. In 1919, he was granted interest in several business propositions by the African Union Company (Inc.) because of his services in financing these concerns. They included one-eighth of the Prah River Falls Concession, three thousand or more logs of mahogany from the district of Darompom and one-sixth of net proceeds, two hundred or more logs of mahogany near Insu Siding and one-sixth of net proceeds, and one-quarter of one-third of the Shama land and Sawmill project.[17]

By July 1920, Christian owned a number of properties, some of which were rented out. These properties included no. 4 Poassi Road, Sekondi, and "Rust", which were rented by the French Company at £250 and £375 per annum respectively; Pickering and Berthoud, with a rent of £425; Bohams, which was rented by the African Association for £100; Swanzy, F. and A., which had a rent of £100; two pieces of vacant land valued at £5,000 and £500; and his own residence valued at £5,000.[18] In November 1923, the "Rust" property, which was situated in the marketplace, fetched a yearly income of £250 and was insured by the Bank of British West Africa Limited for £2,000.[19] At the same time, Christian was creative and practised a type of barter system with some of the tenants of his commercial properties. For example, with Messrs Robinson and Watt, he offered a deduction of rent based on the amount of goods they supplied him.[20]

Christian continued to acquire land, and by 1922, he was the holder of one square mile of land facing the railway line at 13.25 miles from Sekondi, adjoining Brett's sawmill. He had a ninety-nine-year lease of the agricultural rights and timber rights of the area, and he rented out the land for the purpose of agricultural schemes.[21] He also held a lease of agricultural rights over an area of about 10 square miles along the railway line to the Essauasu Bridge, 27-mile point, going to Akyem Station.[22]

The Takoradi Harbour Scheme in which Christian was involved as a legal representative was of concern to him because of the threat it posed to his properties. By 1924, his properties in Sekondi had decreased in value after his twenty years' experience as an owner.[23] He lamented that he had invested all his earnings in house property in Sekondi, and now that he was advanced in age, he was on the verge of losing everything. He was convinced, even apart from his own interest, that the Takoradi Harbour Scheme was immature.[24] Christian was in agreement with the other property owners and residents of the town of Sekondi, who believed that the construction of a harbour and new town at Takoradi would result in the abandonment of Sekondi, which would be a heavy burden on the community.[25] In his efforts to protect his finances, Christian sent a petition signed by himself and other property owners in Sekondi to the secretary of state to the effect that despite the development of Takoradi, they could not afford and were not willing to give up Sekondi and its infrastructure, since they had spent over £2 million to make it what it was.[26] Christian was also the spokesman for the Sekondi deputation during a meeting in which the property owners' views on the harbour were discussed.[27]

Christian's concern about the depreciation in value of his property because of the Takoradi Scheme was compounded by the paltry earnings he sometimes received from his legal practice. He lamented that all he owned was invested in house property in Sekondi, and that his legal practice was daily getting worse. Indeed, the commission of 10 per cent that he was due in the Takoradi case proved the point, because he considered it to be "truly inadequate for the services rendered".[28]

In his attempt to buy and sell properties, Christian sometimes faced challenges as to the right of ownership and incurred further expense in the litigation process. For example, in a particular situation in 1928, he obtained the property of a local chief named Adaja for the price of £70 at public auction.[29]

He was, however, unable to obtain possession, because the chief was unwilling to move, and the people around seemed to be afraid of the chief, who retained possession from 1926 to 1928. Christian sought the assistance of L.S. Gruchy to lay a complaint with respect to the matter before the district commissioner of Bekwai,[30] who ruled that Christian, as the owner of the house, was required to pay rent for the plot on which the house was situated to the owner of the property, the stool of Bekwai. This was regardless of the fact that the property was sold to Christian as freehold and not as leasehold.[31] Christian was concerned that Mr Brett bought the land for £70, transferred it to him, and now it had cost him around £100. He could not afford to lose the money he had invested in the property.[32]

The issue of paying rent was further compounded by the fact that the Public Works Department, on the suggestion of the building inspector at Bekwai, threatened to demolish the house. Christian believed this was due to advantage being taken by Adaja and others of his absence and inability to go to Kumasi and attend to the matter himself.[33] In fact, all buildings on the plot were being demolished, and compensation was to be paid to the person in charge of the property.[34] As a result, Christian attempted to negotiate to secure a lease of the plot of land, which he would then sell or sub-lease in order to benefit financially from the situation.[35]

The 1929 development of the harbour at Takoradi negatively affected his business as a landlord, since the town of Sekondi and its property greatly depreciated as a result. His "prospects were not very bright", because his tenants had "intimated their intention to terminate their leases", since they all had to build at the "rising town" of Takoradi.[36] Moreover, due to the amalgamation of Lever Brothers of Nigeria with African and Eastern Trade Corporation, Millers Limited, Swanzy Limited, Tarquah Trading Company, and others, some stores had been closed down and hundreds of storekeepers, cashiers and bookkeepers were fired because of the lack of work. This in Christian's view created an unsatisfactory outlook for the town of Sekondi.[37]

In the early 1920s, another business affair in which Christian engaged was the sale of timber. He partnered with Arthur Puls in the shipment of logs from the Gold Coast.[38] His connections to timber merchants were sought out by others interested in the timber trade.[39] Furthermore, as a result of these connections, he was also consulted by his friends about special deals on the consignment shipping of logs.[40]

During the period 1923 to 1926, Christian had a business relationship with the firm Curtis, Campbell and Company, which allowed him to purchase cocoa and other produce in the Gold Coast.[41] He had two credits with the firm, bearing interest at the rate of 8 per cent, opened in his favour at the Sekondi branch of the Colonial Bank. One was an unsecured credit for £10,000, which was to be used by Christian to make advances to his cocoa agent. The cocoa or any other produce when purchased was stored in Christian's private warehouse or the warehouse of the Colonial Bank at Sekondi. As soon as the cocoa or other produce was stored, it was legally hypothecated to the firm.[42] The second credit was a revolving one for £15,000, which was represented by cocoa or any other produce awaiting shipment either in the lighterage store or against bills of lading, which Christian handed to the Colonial Bank on behalf of Curtis, Campbell and Company. The amount advanced was only 75 per cent of the current local value of the cocoa or any other produce purchased. As collateral security, the title deeds of Christian's various immovable properties in Sekondi were deposited with the Colonial Bank to the firm's order. This gave Curtis, Campbell and Company the right to call upon Christian to mortgage the properties to the firm in the event that he was unable to repay the advances and accrued interests within six months after the date of arrival of the cocoa or other produce, if the firm was unable to effect a sale meanwhile. Furthermore, any shipment of cocoa or any other produce was to be consigned to Curtis, Campbell and Company, or their nominee, for sale on Christian's account, subject to a merchant's commission and other related fees.[43]

In his dealings with cocoa, Christian did not always benefit financially even after considerable investments. In one deal in 1923, he advanced £7,600 for cocoa which was to have been supplied to him at Sekondi Station.[44] However, he suffered a loss in this cocoa transaction. Some friends who intended to help him retrieve his losses bought three hundred tons for him in London.[45] Owing to the precarious state of the market for cocoa and the falling prices, he had to sell at a deficit rate.[46] Curtis, Campbell and Company then advised him that with the continued decline in the African cocoa markets, his suggested price was not sufficiently attractive to encourage them to proceed further in the business on his behalf. Christian later noted that this news upset him to the extent that it "unmanned" him, and that in addition to his other heavy losses, this news was "a stunner".[47] The shortfalls that Christian experienced during this particular period were a severe drain on his finances. He summarized the situation as follows: "I really cannot realise that I am in for so great a loss. It simply means that the savings of the last twenty years have gone in the last few months and I have to begin afresh."[48] As a result of the heavy loss incurred by Christian, the firm Curtis, Campbell and Company called for his collateral security, which was essentially his properties.[49]

Christian experienced another financial setback related to a one-hundred-ton shipment of cocoa he ordered and shipped through the SS *Badagry*, which was tied up in an arbitration process in London after being considered unfit for human consumption.[50] He admitted that this matter was particularly stressful and caused him to have sleepless nights and to indulge in self-pity.[51] His official financial position was precarious as a result, and he had to seek the assistance of G.H. Garford, of the firm Curtis, Campbell and Company, to provide funds to Mrs Leung for his child's needs, because he was overdrawn on his accounts.[52]

The following year, Curtis, Campbell and Company decided to discontinue operations on Christian's behalf to buy and sell cocoa on other markets except that of the Gold Coast and only up to a limit of "£5,000 open credit against Title Deeds deposited in the Bank of British West Africa, Ltd". Mr Garford was allowed to continue to help Christian, but the firm did not accept responsibility for whatever information was supplied.[53] Owing to the huge losses that he faced, by 31 December 1925, Christian's cocoa account with Curtis, Campbell and Company stood at a debit balance of £3,243 14s. 8d. He further withdrew £4,000 and with a previous £1,000 bought 150 tons of cocoa. He expected the cocoa to fetch a price of £7,000, so that he could balance his cocoa account with the additional transfer of the credit of his investment account of £522 12s. 6d. This would have prevented the necessity to sell or dispose of securities in order to pay the firm in full settlement.[54] By 1926, however, the firm Curtis, Campbell and Company ended the business relationship in cocoa with Christian after twenty-odd years because of what the company described as the firm's obligation in other directions.[55]

Christian subsequently had to resort to litigation on occasion in 1928 in order to secure his payments from the sale of cocoa. In one case, the middleman, Mr Otoo, who traded cocoa on Christian's behalf, was tried for outstanding money owed to Christian. Judgment was given in Christian's favour for £1,100 plus £20 13s., which was the cost of the summons.[56]

In the 1930s, Christian again considered involvement in the cocoa trade. He was cautious and sought the guidance of his fellow West Indian George Francois, whose business was the Anglo African Corporation. Francois advised him on which were the more competitive offers in terms of pricing.[57] Christian later became a share owner in Cheapside Syndicate Limited, which was registered on 19 September 1928. The company was run as a subsidiary of the Anglo African Corporation Limited, managed and directed by Franz Dove and George Francois up to the end of December 1935. Cheapside Syndicate Limited dealt in goods such as iron sheets, cement, ladles, sugar, tobacco, sardines, beef, biscuits, rice, earthenware, coal tar, men's suits, pigs' feet, machetes, and so on.[58] In March 1934, Christian and George Stanley Lewis were elected directors of the company. Christian was also the secretary of the company, and Francois was the chairman.[59] Unfortunately, the economic crisis of the later 1930s had a serious effect on the finances of Cheapside Syndicate Limited. Orders for goods continued to arrive even though commodities remained unsold, bills had to be met and duty paid.[60]

In January 1938, Christian described himself as "enjoying an enforced holiday", because the cocoa was not being marketed by the farmers as a result of the merchants having made a "pool" or buying agreement not to pay more than a given price. Farmers declined to sell and also boycotted all imported goods, which led to a cessation of business. Christian feared that there would be no revenue to run the administration. In his opinion, the outlook was "very bad".[61] He described the Gold Coast as being "dead quiet owing to the cocoa hold up" and said that they were suffering through a crisis that might be "worse than in 1931".[62]

When the world economy faced depression in the 1930s, so too did the Gold Coast, and Christian's financial situation also deteriorated at this time. By the latter part of the 1920s, it was evident to him that proceeds from his law practice were not sufficient to meet all his obligations, and he considered whether it should be discontinued. He noted that some of the practitioners were "charging a fiver for what one used to get fifty guineas easily".[63] His finances were also affected by delays he faced in payment of fees for murder cases.[64] In 1926, notice of termination of his concessions work on the grounds of the economy was particularly burdensome, because this was the most lucrative work available at the time.[65] In 1928, John Walkden and Company and Pickering and Berthoud ceased to rent his premises at the same time that the government chose to reassess properties on a higher basis, which gave him cause for financial concern.⁶⁶ Similarly, at the end of August 1932, Christian's premises, which consisted of two stores or shops downstairs with living quarters upstairs, were vacated by the United African Company on expiration of the lease, because Christian had not accepted the reduction in rent offered, from £500 to £200. As a result he continued to pay rates and other dues on an unrented property.⁶⁷ The income he had from that source was not sufficient to meet his obligations at the time. Mrs Leung also experienced the same fate, as both her properties were vacant. The Colonial Bank, her tenant, had moved to its own recently completed quarters.⁶⁸

Christian also experienced misfortune with his investments in Dominica. A hurricane on 1 September 1930 destroyed the great house on Christian's estate at Mero and the family house in Roseau. His personal house at King's Hill was also extensively damaged. Christian couldn't afford to re-erect the great house, and he requested that the family house and his house be attended to immediately.⁶⁹ Christian lamented how bad the timing of this hurricane misfortune was, given the state of his financial affairs. He requested a precise estimate of the damage to each of his properties. It was the "worst time" he had ever experienced in his professional career. The cocoa prices were so low that farmers did not think it worthwhile to pick cocoa.⁷⁰ The price had fallen from £40–£50 per ton to £23 per ton. Farmers preferred to burn their cocoa rather than sell at the low price, and as a result, there was a "general depression and suffering".⁷¹ The depression also meant a decrease in his court work, and he was finding it difficult to meet all his expenses.⁷²

Christian was therefore willing to try his hand at any new venture which would generate income, but for the most part these were unsuccessful. He explored the opportunity to invest in property in New York and sought the assistance of Captain Joshua Cockburn, who had a real-estate business there. He was, however, unable to afford the initial investment of US$20,000.⁷³ In 1930, he attempted to establish a rubber plantation near Mr Brett's sawmill. Since he was not able himself "to handle the axe and to personally supervise all the time, both the overseer and the labourers wasted time but claimed full pay". As a result, after spending over £100, he had to cut his losses and "give up the venture in great disgust".⁷⁴

In successive years, 1931 to 1933, Christian continued to explore various business possibilities. For example, he procured monkey, leopard and snakeskins for business owners for the purpose of trade. He sent samples to Europe and

America, but this business was a disaster, because the snake- and monkey skins sent to America were not sold, and he lost his capital in this venture.[75]

In 1932, Christian confessed to M.D. Reece that he had not written within recent times "due to indifferent health". He had experienced "such a crisis of depression and bad luck" that he thought it unfair to his friends "to worry them" with his troubles. His properties were still not rented, and there was no legal work coming in. Christian encouraged Reece not to complain about his circumstances:

> Why not be patient and bide your time as I am trying to do? There is always a silver lining . . . . It is no use getting despondent. If anyone had told me even a year ago that things would be as bad with me today all my investments gone I would not have believed. . . . Well, today is the day when the Irish Sweep draw takes place. I have got hope of drawing a prize, even a consolation will do me, and if I do I will send you a drink, whilst if you are lucky and I not, I shall expect you to do the same by me.[76]

Generally, Christian was the eternal optimist. Throughout the financial depression, he tried to look on the bright side. However, he continued to experience losses in his investments as the decade progressed. In 1935 and 1936, he had invested in shares with gold-mining companies,[77] but these investments did not bring the expected returns. In January 1938, Christian bought shares at 6s and to save a total loss, he had to sell at 1s. He had a similar experience with shares in a "diamond concern which he had to sell at a loss of 50%".[78] Because of his losses, Christian decided that whatever he saved "out of the wreckage", he would invest in the bank on fixed deposit at 2 per cent interest.[79]

BENEFACTOR AND SURROGATE FATHER

Despite his financial setbacks, Christian had sufficient reserves to stay afloat and was generally willing to assist his fellow man. His generosity had no geographic limitations, and he gave support to worthy causes in Dominica, the Gold Coast, the United Kingdom and the United States. In particular, he was also prepared to offer financial support to younger people who needed such help in order to equip themselves with a profession.

One such person was Vivian Harris, a student in England who sought Christian's help when he faced financial problems that jeopardized the completion of his studies in medicine. Christian responded positively to the request to enable Harris to qualify.[80] Earlier, Christian had informed Harris of an opportunity to work with Dr Simmonds, a private practitioner who was in search of young doctors as assistants. He also offered to make contact on his behalf.[81] Christian continued to inquire about his progress towards completion and subsequently advised of a similar opportunity with Dr Hoyte.[82] Christian also shared with Harris the experience of a Scottish friend and gave advice about working conditions for Europeans versus "coloureds". He explained that if the latter had "ability and tact", they could be successful.[83] Christian continued to provide support and to encourage Harris appropriately when his father died.[84] A year later, Harris explained to Christian that his lack of correspondence was due to intense preparation for his final exams, which included private tuition.[85] In 1932, however, Harris still had not completed his studies. Christian continued to assist with finances, conferred with Drs Beausoleil and Busby to offer advice and suggested that Harris do the examinations in Glasgow, where they were offered more frequently.[86]

Christian also extended moral support to the son of his friend and physician Dr Beausoleil, whose plan was to train as a lawyer. Christian wrote a letter of recommendation in support of Chery Beausoleil for acceptance as a law student at the Middle Temple.[87] Christian first knew him at his parents' home, and at the end of 1931, at his father's request, Christian took him to Trinidad and entered him at a college there. They met up again in New York on two occasions, and subsequently in London, where the young Beausoleil had gone to continue his studies in 1938. Christian endorsed the young man as "a gentleman of respectability and a proper person to be admitted as a student of the Honourable Society of the Middle Temple with a view to being called to the Bar".[88] He also inquired from his son Howard about the cost of admission.[89]

Christian was a contributor to needy causes irrespective of location. In 1924, he indicated that he had always wanted to make a small donation to Howard University to show his appreciation for the good work it did. The depression had caused him to postpone making the payment, but he was sending £12 as a first instalment towards the sum of $500 which he proposed to give to the university.[90] He anticipated that the instalments would be made quarterly, half-yearly, or yearly according to his circumstances.[91] It was subsequently agreed that the money would be used for the dental school, as this was the department from which his son Peter expected to graduate.[92]

Christian was liberal with his finances and his goodwill when he considered it necessary. For example, in 1927, he received letters of thanks from the secretary of the All Help League and the house governor of the Middlesex Hospital in London for his donation of three guineas towards maintenance. It was sincerely appreciated, since it was received at a time when the rebuilding of the hospital was a necessity.[93] Similarly, the government and people of Dominica were appreciative of his £5 contribution towards the relief of victims of a hurricane that affected Dominica in 1930.[94] In 1934, Mami Abba's father, J.W. French, experienced his son-in-law's magnanimity when he had surgery at Korle Bu Hospital in Accra. Christian contributed £15 towards the total bill of £28 3s.[95] In 1937, he also gave ten guineas to the Mico Chapel Fund, Jamaica, as part of the Mico College Centenary Fund.[96]

Christian noted that he wanted to collect money for the relatives of those who died in HMS submarine *Thetis*[97] and was part of an effort which raised £114 14s., for which he received a letter of thanks from the Lord Mayor.[98] It would seem that Christian's aim was to set an example to engender a spirit of generosity and care for one's fellow man among his peers. However, he noted that of the twenty-five people who had contributed, only five, including himself, were Africans. The rest were "white men and Syrians". He therefore lamented: "O ye Gods when will the Africans learn! We are so narrow in our views when it comes [to putting] our hands in our pockets that I sometimes despair ever to see my race rise, but I hope for the better."[99]

In the wake of the death of his daughter Maude in Sekondi in 1933, Christian felt the necessity to remember her life by means of donations to needy medical institutions in the Gold Coast and Dominica. About a year after her death, Christian opened an account with £100 sterling at the Bank of British West Africa in the name of the "Miss Maude Christian Memorial Fund". The purpose of this fund, which had been outlined in correspondence to the colonial secretary of the Gold Coast, was for the provision of X-ray and other equipment for the maternity ward of the African Hospital at Sekondi. The gift was to be in memory of his daughter, and a bronze plate, suitably inscribed, was to be fixed in a prominent place inside the maternity ward. This plan was eventually executed after Christian's death.[100]

Christian made a similar donation in 1936 to a hospital in Dominica in memory of Maude, via his son Peter. He sent £150 to the governor of Dominica for the purchase of an operating table and to provide other necessary alterations to the operating theatre at the Roseau Hospital. Governor H.B. Popham, in his acknowledgement, indicated that the changes effected would be of inestimable benefit to the people of Dominica at that time.[101]

Christian also recognized that there were situations where moral and financial support were inseparable. In 1937, he sent US$50, with the promise to repeat "later on", to his friend Captain Joshua Cockburn, as a contribution towards a case in which the latter was a litigant.[102] The case that was before the Supreme Court considered the question of the right of Cockburn and his wife to own property and live at "White Plains". Christian found it to be of interest and looked forward to the judgment with anticipation. He believed that the case was of historic significance and that the entire Harlem community must have followed its progress.[103] Christian realized that with the contest of this case by Cockburn in the US courts, a precedent for the benefit of the Negro race would be established. However, it would be "a costly and uphill task for [Cockburn] as a lawyer", and although others would benefit from the outcome, few people would have come forward and made a financial contribution.[104] Cockburn expressed his gratitude and considered that it was "only the honorable in heart" like Christian who he knew would make such a gesture.[105]

Christian's involvement in the life of Netelka Packwood Sam clearly illustrated the human grandeur of the man as a friend. George Packwood, an Englishman, was Christian's close friend. Six months before his death, Packwood indicated that he wanted Christian to take care of his daughter Netelka after Packwood's death. Netelka remembered that on the day her father passed away, she lay down "in front of the bungalow on the grass weeping her heart out", when she felt a tap on her shoulder and Christian said to her, "Get up, girl, get up. Don't cry anymore. From now on I am your Daddy." He took her to Dominica House and placed her in the care of his daughter Maude. Netelka continued to work at her mother's home as a dressmaker during the day, but Christian insisted that she spend her nights at Dominica House, until he handed her over to her prospective husband.[106]

Netelka met her husband, William Edu A.B. Sam, a superintendent of agriculture, while she lived with the Christian family in Sekondi.[107] In 1929, Christian received a written request from the young man for permission "to pay advances to her".[108] They were married on 2 October 1930.[109] In 1934, Netelka wrote to "Daddy Christian" and expressed excitement at the fact that they planned to be in Sekondi and looked forward to being with the Christian family again. She reflected on how much happier she would have been if "dear Auntie Maude were there".[110] Netelka reported that they kept in contact, and at the birth of each of their children, Christian presented her with a gold sovereign for the baby.[111] Christian also helped the couple in a time of need and lent them £120, for which they were extremely grateful to him.[112] In 1940, he expressed the fond hope that they would both live to see their children grow to maturity and be a source of joy and happiness to them.[113]

Christian provided monetary assistance for Leo Muss's[114] education, through his mother, towards the cost of the year's school fees and to supply him with the required textbooks and clothing.[115] Despite his financial burden of supporting his own children and grandchildren, Christian also provided more money, as requested by Muss, to buy a blazer and some white suits for his tenure at Wesley College in Kumasi.[116] Muss, who referred to Christian as "Father" and in his letters to him described himself as his "own son",[117] became a teacher at the Methodist Senior School in Anomabo and contributed to the school's overall development. On his arrival, he initiated the process of renewing the furniture and equipment at the school, and he also reformed the curriculum. He offered private tuition to his students, and as a result, he was able to raise the school's pass rate at the government's Annual Standard Seven Certificate Examination from 56 to 80 per cent.[118] In 1940, Christian sent Leo Muss a money order for twenty shillings to buy books.[119]

Christian also offered moral and financial support to Paul Munyagwa of Uganda, who had become friends with his son Ferdinand at Achimota College. Christian encouraged the friendship and invited Paul to spend holidays with the family in Sekondi in 1939, with a reminder to his son that he would also be a stranger when he went to England.[120] They subsequently kept in contact, and when Paul was assigned to the Animal Health Department in Tamale for further training, Christian sent him a gift of ten shillings and encouraged him with the words, "Be patient, plod on and you will be successful."[121] In Paul's response, he informed him of his success in the Senior Cambridge School Certificate examinations, expressed his gratitude for the words of encouragement as well as the "big gift" and described himself as "your obedient son".[122]

Christian never forgot the family, friends and associates he left in Dominica and always inquired about them. They believed that he had prospered in the Gold Coast, and his inquiries about their welfare often elicited requests for monetary assistance.[123] Generally, he was willing to help them, although he was not always able to do so according to the particular request.

One friend with whom he kept in touch throughout his life in the Gold Coast was Constance Lockhart. In 1917, Christian wanted her to join him in England in the summer, when he planned to be there. She refused to go, however, because she was afraid that it would displease his children.[124] Constance was also in contact with Christian's maternal relatives and friends in Dominica. Christian sent her remittances, especially at Christmas.[125] In 1932, when he was unable to send his usual Christmas present, he advised Peter that whatever he could manage should be sent by a cable a day or two before Christmas. Christian instructed Peter to give Constance her gift and consult with her as regards the distribution to those others to whom he usually gave, namely, "Miss Lecointe, the four daughters of Mrs Emmanuel Laudat, Matilde, Marie Jeanne, Diana, May, Melotte, and Sinne".[126] Constance also sent him home-made delicacies – guava cheese and jelly – which he appreciated and preferred to the imported version.[127] He was grateful to her for her continued interest in his son Peter.[128] Peter confided to his father in 1936: "I wish you had married her because she is my sole friend at all times in this God forsaken place of ours."[129]

Christian was obviously quite fond of Constance and was concerned about her well-being. He commiserated with her on the death of her relative Gerald, in 1938, but noted with pleasure the latter's bequest to her of £15 per annum. He indicated, however, that he would have been "more satisfied" if she had been left a lump sum which she could invest herself to earn income, because so much would depend upon how his business was managed by those left in charge.[130] Christian, who concluded his 1938 visit to Dominica in November, gave "Christmas boxes" to Constance for distribution to his friends and family in Dominica.[131] Six months later, he sent her another £5 and offered to assist her further with the remainder of the cost of painting her house.[132] In 1939, via Peter and Constance, he sent monetary Christmas gifts of £2 each to the usual relatives and friends in Dominica as follows: his uncle's daughters, Laura Lecointe, Soon Hippolyte, Sinne, Marie Jeanne's children, Vanderpool and Malotte. Constance herself received £5 and Peter £10, with an additional £1 as a contribution to Peter's Christmas dinner for the poor.[133]

Christian also gave money to other friends from Dominica who made requests of him. Clarita Potter, who had received $10 from Christian during one of his return visits, with a promise that he would do more for her when he went back to Africa, sought to collect on this agreement in 1939. She requested money owing to financial difficulty, because her daughter, who was the breadwinner, had been forbidden to work by her doctors.[134] In the same year, Mamah Alexander received a draft of £9 from him to assist her with the purchase of a sewing machine that she required to help her and her sisters earn a living. Christian, however, warned her not to publicize what he had done, because he would then be inundated with requests that he could not fulfil. He explained that times were hard on account of the decline in the price of cocoa, people could not "afford the luxury of going to Court", and as a result, there was little work for lawyers. In the four months following his return from Dominica in November 1938, he had only three cases, which earned him less than £20.[135]

Christian's financial situation in 1938 in the wake of poor returns on his investments in cocoa resulted, regrettably, in his inability to comply with a financial request made by the St George Lodge in Dominica.[136] Its members had requested £50 from him as well as the consideration money when the town council exercised the option over Christian's land and the "Pound". Christian was unable to help in this situation because of the economic atmosphere and the losses he had suffered in his business transactions.[137] Similarly, he was unable to help Royers from Dominica, who sought assistance from him in the sum of £3,500.[138] However, his refusal of this request meant that he felt under no obligation to accede to Dennis Shillingford's cabled request for Christian to "stand surety for him in the Bank". He also noted that "the folks in Dominica" appealed to him "for help not in a hundred or two but in thousands", and when he did not comply, they were displeased with him.[139] Two other requests in 1939 from people in Dominica for money to undertake house repairs and for a gift or long lease of land for a church were also denied.[140]

This discussion of Christian's experiences as a businessman and benefactor would be incomplete without any mention of the fact that he also regularly played the sweepstakes as a possible source of income.[141] As early as 1923, in the wake of severe losses with a cocoa deal, he asked a friend to invest a "fiver" in the Calcutta Sweep and such other sweeps, especially the big ones that had tickets available. He was hopeful that Fortune might smile on him.[142] Similarly, in 1924–25, he requested tickets for the Royal Colonial Institute Derby Sweep and the Cable Sweep from the firm with which he conducted business, F. Lack and Son Limited. These were bought under pseudonyms such as Merodom, Hedwig, Francois, Herbert, Harold, Frederick and Joe.[143] In 1925, Curtis, Campbell and Company also obtained six Calcutta sweepstake tickets for him.[144] In 1927, he sent postal orders for £1 10s, the 10s. to Vivian Harris, to be used to buy tickets in their joint names in the Cable Sweep or on the Baltic or Stock Exchange Derby Sweeps.[145] In a 1932 letter to his fellow West Indian friend M.D. Reece, who was domiciled in England, Christian commented on the "topsy turvy" state of the world and his hope that the "Derby Sweeps" would have changed his fortunes.[146]

Throughout the period of economic decline in the 1930s, Christian continued to invest in several sweepstakes with the "hope of recouping" his losses in business ventures.[147] He requested Horace Douglas, his friend in London, to buy a couple of tickets in both their names for the next Irish Sweep.[148] In 1935, he bought tickets in various sweepstakes from Europe as well as Africa. For example, he bought tickets in the Southern Rhodesian Sweep in a pool of twenty chances with three other friends, with the intention of sharing equally any prize or prizes that might fall to any of them under the nom de plume of the syndicate.[149] To increase his chances, he also bought joint tickets with Abbensetts, F.A. Williams and Adjuah Atta, which were to be shared fifty-fifty.[150] In 1937–38, Christian continued to participate in a variety of lotteries and sweepstakes – Accra Polo Club, Derby Sweep, and the Irish Free State Hospital's Sweepstake – all with the hope of winning big earnings.[151]

For all the years that he participated, the records indicated that he was lucky on only one occasion. In 1928, Christian won the Anchors Sweep at Sekondi, at a time at which he described himelf as broke. He greatly welcomed the prize of £15.[152]

It is evident from his final will and its three codicils that despite the ebb and flow of his financial affairs, Christian amassed a substantial estate. His will, dated 22 February 1936, as is to be expected, made endowments to his immediate family members. He also maintained his generosity of spirit with the provision of financial support through monetary bequests to his relatives and friends in the Gold Coast and the Caribbean. The codicils were dated 11 March 1938, 30 November 1938 and March 1940 [sic] respectively. He had originally appointed his son Howard, who was a student at Gray's Inn in 1936, together with George Francois, his friend of long standing, and William Plange, a merchant from Elmina in the Central Province, as executors and trustees of his real and personal estate in the Gold Coast. His son Peter was the sole executor and trustee to administer his estates in Dominica.[153] An inventory of Christian's personal property also indicated that his standard of living was high. He died possessed of marble tables, considerable silver and glassware. He also left a piano, Packard car, carpets, legal books, journals and stationery.[154] The probate was granted on 29 June 1940 by Mr Justice Doorly to George Francois and Charles William Tachie-Menson, two of the executors of the will.[155]

In his will, Christian bequeathed sums of money totalling £11,725 to several people, including his wife Mami Abba, his children, nieces, cousins and other relatives and friends in Dominica and Antigua, his grandchildren, and other close associates, for example, Mrs Leung. He left property in Dominica to his children Peter and Clara, and property in the Gold Coast to his Africa-born children. Dominica House was left to Mami Abba and her four children "absolutely as tenants in common". He also bequeathed property in Sekondi to Peter and Clara. In the first codicil, he included additional bequests in the total sum of £950 – £300 each to Dr A.E.C. Beausoleil and George Francois, and £100 to Mr C.E.M. Abbensetts and to the Wesleyan Church at Shama for renovations in memory of his "trusty deceased friend" John French. Further bequests were made of £50 each to R.U. Riley, the St Andrew's [Anglican] Church and the Roman Catholic Church, both in Sekondi.

The second codicil related to "the interest in . . . immoveable and moveable property in the Island of Bermuda", which was assigned to his daughter Clara, who was resident in Bermuda at the time. This was for Clara during her life and to her living children after her decease. The Bank of Bermuda Limited was the sole executor and trustee of the second codicil.

In the third codicil, Christian revoked William Plange's appointment as an executor and trustee of his will as well as the bequest that had been made to him, and he appointed Charles William Tachie-Menson of Sekondi in his place. He also made additional bequests in the total sum of £1,595 to some of his children – Essi, Josephine and her husband, Madam Ambah Ackun, and various friends and other people who had not been mentioned in the main will. These people included Charles Tachie-Menson and Franz Dove, Mami Abba's mother and sisters, and his maidservants and driver. He made additional bequests of property to his daughter Angela and to Mami Abba.

All of Christian's property that was not expressly disposed of was to be given to his trustee in trust to be converted into money by "sale or otherwise" and the proceeds to be divided after paying his "funeral and testamentary expenses and debts" in equal shares among Peter, Clara, Chrissie, Sarah, Joseph, Josephine, Howard, Angela, Essi, Ferdinand and Edward. Essi, Ferdinand and Edward, who were "infants" when the will was drafted, were stipulated to receive this payment when they reached the age of twenty-one; Essi, being a girl, would receive the payment if she got married before that age.

Christian in his will appointed Mami Abba to be "the guardian" of his younger children Essi, Ferdinand and Edward. He also made provision with the Atlas Assurance Company Limited for the payment of "educational annuities" for his two youngest sons, Edward and Ferdinand Christian, and his grandsons Edgar Frederick Gordon and Kenneth Clifford Montgomery Gordon. The payment was £1,700, to be paid in instalments of £150 per year for three years and £250 per annum for the following five years.[156]

SCHOOL MANAGER

Christian, whose keen interest in educational opportunities in the Gold Coast was fuelled by the size of his family and his appreciation of the role of education in the life of an individual, also undertook to manage a school, the West African Industrial Academy, in Sekondi for a few years. The Reverend R.E. and Mrs Henrietta J. Peters, "missionaries to Africa" from the American Baptist Mission, had founded the school in 1927, in response to the perceived need for a learning institution which would be devoted to the "development of youths in the Western Province of the Gold Coast", where "work among girls in particular was almost entirely neglected". The students represented "almost every district and tribe of the surrounding colonies". They were taught "a life of usefulness and appreciation of their neighbours". Mrs Peters, who was the headmistress of the school, was also a lieutenant of the Sekondi Girl Guides and vice-president of the Child Welfare and Maternity League, Gold Coast Branch, an affiliate of the Red Cross Society.[157]

Christian's experience as a school manager came in the later years of his life, during the absence in the United States of the Reverend and Mrs Peters. In 1932, while her husband was away on a visit to the United States, Mrs Peters had suffered injury from a fall. She spent a period of recuperation with the Francois family in Tafo, after which she joined her husband in the United

States. Their stay was expected to be temporary, but a series of personal and financial difficulties delayed their return to the Gold Coast.[158] Christian thought highly of Mrs Peters and the work done through the school. It was he who had recommended her to Mr Herschell, the owner of the property for which she was able to secure a rental agreement in order to establish the school.[159] He had also seen evidence of the school's positive influence in performances put on by students.[160] Furthermore, one of Christian's sons, Ferdinand (Kwamina), was also a student there.[161]

It was therefore not surprising that Christian took an active interest in the school in the absence of the Peterses. He kept up to date on its affairs and reported to the Reverend Peters on the "desperate" financial situation. Three months of arrears were owed to the Sanitary Department, and teachers' salaries had not been paid. The fact that Miss Simmons had stepped into the role of headmistress and together with the staff had kept the school functional was undoubtedly due to the positive influence of Mrs Peters. In 1933, there had been some misunderstanding among the staff, as a result of which Christian strongly suggested to the Reverend Peters that in the circumstances, he needed to be more tactful in his communication with them: "We all appreciate the usefulness of the Institution, but believe me without the presence of your wife and money to run it, it is best not to be too quick in fault finding."[162] The following year, the manager of the school, Mr Riley, submitted his resignation to the Education Department, and Christian agreed to manage the school "temporarily" to prevent its closure, although he admitted that he could hardly afford the time for this undertaking.[163] Christian kept in touch with both the Peterses and Miss Simmons, and the Education Department was informed that he was the acting manager of the school.[164] The Reverend and Mrs Peters expressed their expectation to have amassed sufficient funds by December 1934 to set sail for the Gold Coast to resume their obligations.[165]

Almost a year later, in November 1935, their financial situation had not improved. There was hope, however, as secretary of missions Dr J.H. Jackson had left on a tour of the mission stations and was due to visit the Gold Coast to report on his findings and make recommendations for further development of the work there.[166] Christian duly facilitated Dr Jackson's visit, arranged for him to be met on arrival, sent a welcome letter in which he lauded the work of the school and provided for his accommodation and meals with assistance from his West Indian lawyer friend Clarence E.M. Abbensetts. However, he seemed to have some misgivings later about Jackson, as he never received any response, feedback or "thank you" from him after the visit.[167]

In August 1936, Mrs Peters indicated that their "affairs" were "in the process of being settled". The New England Convention of the Baptist Church had agreed to assist them as soon as Dr J.H. Jackson, secretary of missions, who had visited the Gold Coast, decided what should be done. Jackson, however, had reservations. He thought that it would be costly, "thousands and thousands of dollars", to make any significant progress with the work there, and as a result, he was hesitant to commit to the project.[168] According to Mrs Peters, Jackson, like most Americans, felt that Liberia was more in need of help.[169] Christian continued to hope that the Peterses' affairs related to the school would be taken care of by the new administration.[170]

In 1936, there was a new development: the Dutch Sekondi stool had given land on the Takoradi Road to the Baptist Mission for the building of a school and college. The government then wanted to use part of the land to build a hospital, and the Peterses raised the possibility of compensation. Christian also thought that the hospital in close proximity might "enhance the suitability of the site" for the purpose of building a school.[171] He advised that they should write to the district commissioner to inform him that they had land in the vicinity of the site the government planned to acquire, and that they intended to build a school there eventually.[172] Mrs Peters expressed to Christian the hope that he would continue to manage the school and act in their best interest with regard to the sale of the land, despite the uncertainty about their return to the Gold Coast,[173] which they considered to be their "adopted home".[174]

There is evidence that the Peterses did attempt to raise funds in the United States for their work in the Gold Coast. An information flyer about the West African Industrial Academy, with details of the school and its expenses, invited donors to contribute to the work. It included photographs of the students and Mrs Peters, and details about the monthly income and expenditures as well as an endorsement from one of Christian's letters as follows:

> I wish it were possible to visit the States and in my own way give you a helping hand to make your people realise the importance of your work; the school is, no doubt suffering from your absence and from the want of funds to carry on. I paid a surprise visit there yesterday and was pleased with what I saw: the discipline, the good order and the healthy tone spoke well of the efforts that are being made, but that is not enough.[175]

Christian repeatedly commended Miss Simmons's efforts to keep the school operational despite the limitations under which she functioned. He was concerned that the work started by the Baptist Mission should be continued, especially in light of the fact that it filled a void in the society. In Christian's view, Miss Simmons was both a "wonderful teacher and a born missionary". There were approximately thirty young children, and the education and services provided were unparalleled in the country at the time. Additionally, there were another dozen or so older children, many of whom did not pay fees. The building at this stage was in constant need of repair, but with considerable arrears of rent, no recourse could be made to the owner with regard to its upkeep. Christian continued to urge that the matter be brought to the attention of the secretary of the mission.[176]

By this time, some five years had elapsed since the Peterses' initial departure from the Gold Coast, and it would seem that Christian eventually began to abandon any hope that the Reverend and Mrs Peters would return to carry on their work: "I hope that you and Reverend Peters are enjoying robust health and that one day we might yet meet again."[177] Four months later, he expressed his concern more directly: "We are all anxious to see your Mission continuing its work here. Please send me your news."[178] However, he was unwavering in his support for the school and continued to take an active interest in its affairs and to advise the Peterses accordingly. For example, the premises which the school occupied were offered for sale by the owner to one of Christian's colleagues, who had recently returned from England. Christian advised Mrs Peters that she should persuade her organization to purchase the property.[179] He continued to act on their behalf, and he passed on information about the value of the property and said they would have an advantage if they could provide the relevant amount in cash.[180]

Christian really hoped that the Peterses or their support institution would take advantage of the opportunity to buy the premises, and he communicated this several times. He had also assured the landlord that he had a proposed buyer, although he did not indicate that it was to secure a permanent place for the school.[181] He felt that the building and its location were well suited for this purpose. He was strongly of the view that the school was "the only Institution of its kind in a District where people [were] poor and unable to pay for such an institution themselves".[182] However, the Reverend and Mrs Peters were unable to raise the money to pay cash for the building, and to purchase it on credit or a mortgage was not an option.[183] Miss Simmons also made an unsuccessful attempt to raise the necessary sum of money to purchase the property.[184] Christian was committed to assist their cause, and he went a step further and offered to negotiate with the proposed buyer of the property on their behalf to secure the tenancy of the place at a cost of £6 or £7 per month, if there were multiple tenants.[185]

In the face of all these disappointments, Christian continued to offer advice and assistance to the Reverend and Mrs Peters. With regard to the land, the donors had indicated that whenever the Baptist Mission returned to Sekondi to continue the work, another portion of land would be granted.[186] Christian advised the Reverend and Mrs Peters that since the government had the power to acquire whatever land they required at a relatively low cost, they should agree to give up their portion rather than lose all of it.[187]

It is conceivable that the Reverend and Mrs Peters may have become disheartened by their inability to amass the necessary funds to facilitate their return. In a 12 April 1938 letter to Christian, the Reverend Peters indicated that they had directed "every energy" to raise funds for their school buildings and stated: "We shall return when we can build right." However, in another letter of the same date,[188] the Reverend Peters reported his observation that the government had taken the whole frontage of the property, and the remainder was only suitable for farming. It was not his intention to make money on the land, but he felt that the government should refund him his costs to survey the new site for school buildings, and to lay the boundary posts and other expenditure related to the preparation of the new deed. He intended to use the rest of the land "for school farming and perhaps a large playground".[189] Christian continued to communicate with the government on their behalf, and he prepared the necessary deeds of covenant for their execution.[190]

It would seem, however, that the Peterses' prolonged absence in the United States and their inability to settle their financial difficulties became a challenge for Christian. His interest in and commitment to the institution they had founded cost him not only his time but also his money. In 1938, the landlord, Herschell, embarked on legal action to collect the outstanding rent from the Foreign Mission Board.[191] In 1939, Christian wrote to Mrs Peters: "I am exasperated at the treatment I am receiving in this matter of Herschell's property. I am blamed by Herschell, suspected and censured by Miss Simmons and you and your people are letting me down."[192] He reported to one of his friends that when the Baptist Mission Board failed to pay the rent, he was held accountable. By January 1940, ten years' arrears of rent were due, and as the Reverend and Mrs Peters were tenants on his recommendation, he paid the municipal and other rates out of his own pocket.[193]

Christian continued to provide support and encouragement to the Peterses and their school virtually to the end of his life, although it would seem that after 1938, they ceased their communication with him. In March 1940, Christian, in a letter to C. Vaughan Charles of Washington, DC, inquired about the Peterses. His persistence is demonstrated in the following extract from his letter: "Can you tell me what has become of Revd. & Mrs Peters? Will you write and say to them or to any friend of theirs who will pass the word to them that I wrote asking them to reply to a particular question by the 31st December [1939] re the school premises."

Despite their failure to respond to his communication, he had persuaded the owner to extend the time for a further three months, on the understanding that he would dispose of the property if there was no response from them after that.[194] This was Christian's last correspondence on the subject of the West African Industrial Academy.

HONORARY CONSUL FOR THE REPUBLIC OF LIBERIA

Christian served as Liberian consul for more than twenty-five years, a position he acquired on account of his personal friendship[195] with Edwin Barclay, who was secretary of state and then president of Liberia in 1931. In this capacity, he was responsible for the welfare of Liberians, many of whom worked on ships that frequented the Sekondi seaport. In many cases, they were brought in as indentured labour and worked on the surf boats and as government employees in the Sanitary Department.[196] Christian's range of duties as consul included oversight of the charges which the Gold Coast Government made to steamship companies for tonnage and inward and outward voyages, as well as fees related to the use of the dock, harbour and lighthouse.[197]

As Liberian consul, his portfolio also included the issue of visas to Liberian citizens who wanted to travel out of the country to return to their homeland.[198] On one occasion, he was asked to assist and advise a Liberian national who had to travel to Accra for medical attention to her eyes. He was expected in his official capacity to provide information that would facilitate her arrangements for travel, accommodation, procedure for hospital admittance and the like.[199]

Christian discharged his responsibility seriously as Liberian consul and acted as required. For example, he wrote to the police officer in charge at Kumasi on behalf of ten named Liberians who lived and were employed there in different vocations. They complained that they were subjected to provocation and insults in Kumasi by people who addressed them as "Darboh", a term of contempt and ridicule. They found it difficult to ignore or have a peaceful response to these verbal attacks. Christian explained that in his capacity as Liberian consul, his action was "in the interest of good order and peace".[200] He also wrote informally to fellow West Indian Walter Callender, who was employed with the police in Ashanti, and asked him to use his influence with his staff there to ease the situation. Christian reminded him of a similar incident that was checked only when Christian caused a number of Fantes from Esikadu to be fined by the police magistrate.[201]

He kept in contact with relevant people in Liberia in order to discharge this responsibility effectively. He followed up on what feedback was sent to Liberia and questioned the veracity of the negative report of someone with whom he had unsuccessful business dealings: "I understand that Mr Glass is down your way and that he is saying very unpleasant things of me and even going so far as to say that I ridicule and treat Liberians with contempt."[202] During a period of political difficulty in Liberia, he wrote to his friend Fredericks, superintendent of Maryland County, to ask to be kept informed of all events, as he was "anxious to do all propaganda work to refute the attacks" made on the Republic of Liberia.[203]

On another occasion, his assistance was sought to collect overdue taxes and levies from Liberians who worked in the Gold Coast and had defaulted on their payments to the Rocktown Section, Maryland County, in the Republic of Liberia. According to the system, the paramount chief of the section was responsible for the collection of the taxes, and when there was a shortfall for any given period, he was held liable. The request for Christian's intervention, which included a list of forty delinquents, stated that many Liberian citizens from the Rocktown Section were employed in the Gold Coast. A committee had been sent to collect the funds from them, but they refused to cooperate, although they were aware of their indebtedness to the government. The names of six Liberians, two each from Takoradi, Tarkwa and Abosso, were also given to Christian as people who would work along with the committee.[204]

It would appear, however, that the matter of the collection of taxes gave rise to further fraudulent activity. The senior assistant superintendent of police of the Sekondi township subsequently informed Christian that monies had been collected illegally from Liberian workers by people who apparently acted on behalf of a chief who "possibly had no legal status" and not in the interest of the Liberian government.[205] Christian advised the illegal tax collectors that if the chief wanted to collect money from parties who were liable and refused to pay, the proper course of action was through the courts. He brought the matter to the attention of the secretary of state in Monrovia and indicated that the tax collectors had exercised coercion and brought pressure to bear on the employers that led to police involvement in the matter.[206]

Christian's position as consul was formally recognized by the Liberian government in due course. For example, he was invited by the Senate and House Committee of the National Legislature of Liberia to witness the inaugural ceremonies of His Excellency Edwin J. Barclay and the Honourable James S. Smith as president and vice-president of Liberia due to take place on 6 January 1936.[207] In 1937, his work as Liberian consul was "officially recognised as a knight official of the Liberian Humane Order of Africa Redemption". The award was conferred on him by the president of Liberia "as a mark of appreciation of the intense interest" he had "constantly manifested in the progress and perpetuity" of the Republic of Liberia. The diploma in testimony of the award read as follows:

REPUBLIC OF LIBERIA

To all to whom these presents shall come greeting.
Know ye that I Edwin Barclay, President of the Republic of Liberia, taking into consideration the sentiments of humanity which are displayed by you George J Christian and being aware of your sincere wishes to be a useful helper in the Christian work of civilising our brethren inhabiting the territory neighbouring to our Republic, desiring to give you a public testimony of our gratitude, using the faculties given us by the laws of our Republic, by these presents do ordain, constitute and appoint you Knight Official of the Liberian Humane Order of Africa Redemption, in virtue of which, from this day, you will be permitted to use and wear publicly the insignias of the order in the class named; and may the Omnipotent God ever guide you in your efforts for the good of our savage brothers. In Testimony whereof I have caused the Seal of the Republic to be affixed.
Given under my hand at the city of Monrovia, the 17th day of November in

the year of our Lord One thousand nine hundred and Thirty seven and of the Republic the Ninety-first."[208]

Christian regarded this accolade as not worthy of advertisement. Nevertheless, he sent it to his son Howard, for him to show his siblings and nieces, and requested that it be kept in a box and not displayed.[209] He also informed his friends Koens and the Reverend and Mrs Peters of the accolade but admitted to the former his intention to keep the matter "very quiet", because he did not want to be teased by him and his other friends.[210] Koens, who was personally aware of what Christian had done for Liberians in the twenty-five years, congratulated him on the honour and indicated that it was long overdue. Koens alluded to the shortcomings of the Liberian government and the fact that the Liberians who worked in the Gold Coast gave faithful service and left happy memories.[211]

Despite his concern about how this honour from the Liberian government might be perceived, Christian continued to give importance to his role as consul. He kept in contact with the Honourable H.D. Fredericks, Liberian consul general in Liverpool, and spent some time with him during a visit to England in 1938. He also informed Fredericks that he had been granted a licence from His Majesty the King to wear the insignia of the third class of the Order of the African Redemption.[212]

Christian attempted to pass on the portfolio of honorary consul to his son Howard. He asked Fredericks to suggest to the Liberian administration that Howard had passed his final law exams, so that "he might be appointed" Christian's assistant on his arrival in the Gold Coast.[213] Fredericks pointed out that no provision was made in the consular service for an assistant, as it carried no status. He would suggest, however, that Howard be appointed as vice-consul, "which accords consular rank".[214] There is no evidence that this ever materialized.

GEORGE JAMES CHRISTIAN AS FREEMASON

Christian also became an active participant in the Freemason movement in the Gold Coast. His entrance into the brotherhood of the Freemasons was in furtherance of a tradition passed on to him from his father and which he continued to pursue throughout his life. Christian Sr had introduced his son to the Oddfellows Society almost a decade before he left Dominica.²¹⁵ The Oddfellows, like the Freemasons, were a fraternal organization, and many men joined both.²¹⁶

As a young man, Christian clearly understood the significance of the brotherhood and kept in communication with fellow members. For example, when he left Dominica for London in 1899, they sailed first to Antigua, where they spent a day, but they did not come ashore, and so his plan to meet with "Taylor", a member of the Oddfellows there, did not materialize. They then travelled on to St Kitts, where he did meet with two brother Oddfellows, who were kind to him. Before they left St Kitts, however, he took the opportunity and "wrote to Taylor and the Secretary of the Oddfellows Lodge in Antigua".²¹⁷ During his time as a student in London, Christian continued to pursue his interest in the Freemason movement and was initiated into the Second Middlesex Artillery Lodge on 2 October 1901. After he had settled in the Gold Coast, his periodic travels to England allowed him to keep his London membership active, and in 1920, he was exalted in Second Middlesex Artillery Chapter No. 2484, EC, London.²¹⁸

According to the historical record, Masonic lodges existed in the Gold Coast at Cape Coast in 1810 and 1833 respectively, but these ceased to be formally acknowledged in 1862, when they "were struck off the roll" owing to inactivity. As a consequence, Freemasonry in the Gold Coast is linked mainly to Gold Coast Lodge No. 773, which was established in 1859 and considered "the premier Lodge of the District".²¹⁹ Tachie-Menson has reported that "although records of the early activities of this Lodge are not available, there is no doubt that some good work was done by the Founders". It was generally understood that members of this lodge played a significant role in the spread of Freemasonry throughout the Gold Coast and other parts of West Africa.²²⁰ Generally, Freemason lodges were seen as a means to provide an opportunity for men who had similar affinities or a common aim to come together for interaction and exchange of views.²²¹

According to Tachie-Menson's record, Sekondi Lodge No. 3238 was consecrated in 1908. One of its founders, who was also the consecrating officer, was W Bro. Eardly Bramwell Reece of Albion Lodge No. 196 in Barbados, past master of Accra Lodge No. 3063.²²²

Christian was obviously devoted to the craft, and he sought out fellow Masons and encouraged their participation in the establishment of a lodge in Sekondi. Records reveal that at a special meeting held on 26 November 1917, Christian was in the chair when the ways and means of "opening and consecrating" the lodge were discussed. A resolution was passed that founder members should contribute the sum of £10 each, one half of which had to be paid by the end of December and the balance by the end of January 1918. This money was to enable the purchase of furniture and other necessaries. It was also agreed that "the £10 paid by founders will be refunded as soon as the lodge shall be opened and new members enter, £5 will be for founders jewel and the other £5 may go towards contribution if so desired".[223] Christian indicated that his efforts to establish the St George's (Seccondee)[224] Lodge, No. 3851, were eventually successful "after years of trying". He was the third person to serve as master in this lodge.[225]

Tachie-Menson's history lists Bro. George James Christian, MM, Middlesex Artillery Lodge No. 2484, JW Designate, among the founders, as well as one of the "distinguished Pastmasters" of the "St George's (Seccondee) Lodge No. 3851", the seventh in the district. It was consecrated on 25 September 1918 and was destined to play a prominent role in Freemasonry in the Gold Coast.[226] Other West Indians in the Gold Coast with whom Christian associated, Clarence E.M. Abbensetts and Robert E. Dick, were also initiated into the St George's Lodge No. 3851.[227] Abbensetts, like Christian, was also noted among the distinguished past masters.[228]

Christian, who also encouraged the spread of Freemasonry in Kumasi and Cape Coast in 1921,[229] was mentioned as one of those who assisted the consecrating officer when McCarthy Lodge No. 4132, Kumasi, was established in 1920.[230] At the First Anniversary Installation Convocation of the Gold Coast Chapter No. 773, EC Cape Coast, held on 20 November 1926 at the Freemasons Hall, Ashanti Road, Christian was one of the principals elect and one of the officers for the period 1926–27, titled Ex Comp. G.J. Christian MEZ.[231]

The formation of a District Grand Lodge of the Gold Coast became the subject of consideration after the ninth lodge had been consecrated in the colony in 1922. The past masters felt that "not only had sufficient progress been made to justify such a step, but also that the expansion of the craft and the proper control of the activities of the lodges in the country depended upon the guidance provided by a District Grand Lodge". The appointment of a grand inspector for the colony was an interim measure in 1925, which lasted until the retirement and death of the initial incumbent, W Bro. Ernest Davidson,

PAGDC, in 1929. During his tenure as inspector, he had made a recommendation to Grand Lodge in favour of the establishment of a district, which would consist of the ten lodges in the Gold Coast. In 1930, Grand Lodge advised of the formation of the district and the appointment of W Bro. Daniel James Oman, OBE, VD, past master of Accra Lodge No. 3063, as first district grand master. He was well known among the brethren and a popular choice. The inauguration of the District Grand Lodge and installation of the grand master took place on 9 May 1931.[232] Christian was appointed junior warden.[233] RW Oman's tenure as grand master lasted only three years, as in 1934, "contrary to expectations, [he] found it necessary to retire from the Gold Coast earlier than anticipated".

DDGM W Bro. Major G. T. Kingsford, DSO, TD, who succeeded Oman, was installed on 30 March 1935 at a ceremony which was well attended by the brethren, and G.J. Christian, DSGW, was among the first officers appointed by him.[235] Like his predecessor, RW Bro. Major Kingsford continued to discharge his responsibilities with enthusiasm and devotion. He undertook a series of official visits to the lodges in the district, accompanied by his officers. These visits "gave great encouragement to the brethren" as evidenced by the warmth of the reception accorded to them. Under his leadership, all the lodges in the district flourished to the extent that it became possible for the District Grand Lodge to offer scholarships to the children of its members who attended technical and secondary schools.[235]

Christian's contribution to the craft was eventually recognized both in England and in the Gold Coast. In celebration of the coronation of King George VI in 1937, it was proposed by the Most Worshipful the Grand Master, HRH the Duke of Connaught, KG, that Christian be appointed to the rank of past assistant grand registrar in the Grand Lodge of England. The appointment was announced at the Especial Grand Lodge at the Royal Albert Hall in London on 30 June 1937,[236] and the news was reported to the lodge in Dominica.[237] Christian, who believed he was the only one in West Africa in such a high position in Masonry, saw it as an acknowledgement of his efforts and the good standing of his lodge, to which he had contributed. He also indicated that he was to be made grand standard bearer in the Grand Chapter in England.[238] His contribution to the founding, development, welfare and improvement of the St George's Lodge in Sekondi was recognized in 1937 with his appointment to the Grand Lodge and Supreme Grand Chapter ranks, and he was presented with a silver salver in recognition of the good work he had done for the craft for thirty-six years.[239]

It would seem that to his Masonic brothers in Dominica, Christian's receipt of these accolades was indicative of his financial prosperity. Around the same time, St George Lodge, Roseau, Dominica, made a request of Christian for a donation of £200 to pay off the mortgage of the property which the lodge occupied. In return, they offered to rename the lodge "the G.J. Christian Lodge". If he was unable to donate the money, they requested that he would "pass on to the Lodge the piece of land" which was leased to the town council.[240] Christian responded that he was unable to offer financial assistance at this time, as the economic situation was not favourable, with the result that lawyers were given an enforced holiday.[241]

Christian's thoughts on Freemasonry were articulated to his sons. When Peter became a Freemason in Dominica, his father encouraged him as much as possible and ordered the Freemason's Apron for him from London. On this occasion, he reviewed his own career to his son. He had been a junior warden of the District Grand Lodge in the previous year, was a past master of his lodge and past first principal of his chapter. As an officer of District Grand Lodge, he had visited three of the lodges in the colony in the previous month. He concluded with this advice to Peter: "If you live up to the principles of the Craft you will not go wrong in life."[242] Some months later, when Peter had attained the second degree and hoped to move to the third when he could afford to do so, his father highlighted the financial requirements of membership in the brotherhood: "You have learnt that Masonry is an expensive thing, it is all giving and no receiving, although the vulgar world thinks otherwise."[243] Some years later, Christian inquired about the progress of the lodge and whether Peter had been given any office, although he suspected that his son's lack of self-confidence would have led him to decline to hold any office.[244]

In 1937 letters to his son Howard, Christian expressed his views about Freemasonry and religion. He felt that the Catholic Church knew all there was to be known about Masonry, yet it objected to its followers being members. Consequently, he never encouraged any of his friends or associates to join unless and until they made up their own mind. He believed that many Africans joined for commercial purposes, but they were set up for disappointment, because they underestimated the sacredness of it. In his view, Masonry was about ethics, and no religion could surpass it.[245] It is to be noted, however, that his son Ebenezer Kwesi, who lived in Elmina and was raised in the Methodist Church, was a member of the Freemason lodge. His other sons, who were Roman Catholic, apparently did not embrace the craft.

Christian's contribution to and participation in the development of Freemasonry in the Gold Coast is memorialized in the St George's Lodge, Sekondi, which he co-founded. On behalf of the Christian family, his daughter Essi Forster in 1965 donated to the Worshipful Master and Members of St George's Lodge, Sekondi, the framed presentation certificate dated 11 December 1937, in which congratulations are extended to Christian on his appointment to the Grand Lodge and Supreme Chapter Ranks. It was returned to the lodge with the hope that it would be displayed as "an historical link with the past and also to honour the memory of the late George James Christian".[246]

Christian's friend Jan Koens correctly captured the essence of why Christian's life and contribution in the Gold Coast, as demonstrated by his accomplishments as Liberian consul and in Freemasonry, were worthy of recognition. He had written to congratulate Christian when he received acclaim for his work as Liberian consul. He also acknowledged the accolades showered on Christian by the local Masons, when he was presented with the silver salver in recognition of his appointment as an officer of the Grand Lodge of England. He joked as follows, "My word, dear George, we shall be having to make a great fuss of you the next time you come to England, for evidently you are becoming a very important person in the world."[247] In similar vein, Mrs Henrietta Peters, who was always profuse in her thanks for his generous assistance,[248] had predicted that Christian's "name will live on in Gold Coast history . . . through the school in some way".[249]

This survey of Christian's multifaceted life as businessman, benefactor, school manager, Liberian consul and Freemason has demonstrated that he was not only enterprising but also consistently generous with his time, abilities and resources. With regard to his finances and his philanthropy, Christian explored many possibilities and exercised his options. In the midst of the challenges, he remained hopeful and made the most of his positive and negative experiences. In the process, he lived an exemplary life. He also ensured that his responsibilities to his family and friends would be discharged after his death. It is apparent that Christian was single-minded as to the reason why he had come to the Gold Coast in the first place – "to give the benefit of his experience".[250] The repertoire of his involvement clearly demonstrated that he never lost his focus.

Figure 6.1. Angela Christian, George James Christian, Essi Christian and Netelka Packwood

Figure 6.2. Joseph, Howard and Sarah Christian (*standing*); Josephine and George James Christian (*seated*)

Figure 6.3. Clara Gordon and her six children

Figure 6.4. George James Christian in Freemason regalia, W Bro. Hon. G.J. Christian

CHAPTER 7

Christian's Contribution to the Political and Social Development of the Gold Coast

ALONGSIDE HIS LEGAL CAREER AND OTHER PURSUITS, CHRISTIAN became involved in the political life of the community within a decade of his arrival. He also contributed to the social development of the Gold Coast through his participation in a wide range of public service activities. He also maintained active membership of organizations in England. These affiliations facilitated his travel to the West Indies via London, where many of his children were students. In each case, he brought to the task commitment, passion, diligence, and where necessary, his professional training and expertise.

Christian initially served on the Sekondi Town Council from 1911 to 1915 and from 1920 to 1926.[1] In 1927, when a constitutional change granted the town representation in the Legislative Council of the Western Region/Province of the Gold Coast, this meant that candidates had to qualify for nomination according to strict criteria.[2] The conditions surrounding the Municipal Corporations Ordinance indicated that municipal members of the Legislative Council could now be elected, and Christian also served in this capacity. Reports of the 1927 election in which Christian took part shed light on the dynamics of his integration into Gold Coast society, both from an internal and external viewpoint. The two candidates contesting the election were J.E. Casely Hayford[3] and G.J. Christian. Christian, who did not have the backing of any organization, depended on his personal reputation and used his surname to advantage in his campaign rhetoric. He described himself as "Christian in name, Christian in sympathy and Christian in attitude. To whom do you turn when in trouble? Who will help you to maintain your Citadels? Whose interests are identical with yours? Vote for Mr G.J. Christian. For 15 years Liberian Consul – Approved by His Majesty King George V."[4]

This extract from Christian's election campaign material indicated that he genuinely felt he was a serious competitor for the position. He perceived himself to be someone of high moral standards who was caring and sensitive to the needs of his constituents. He felt that he had reached out to the society and made a recognizable impact. He considered his service as Liberian consul to be an endorsement from the colonial authorities.

Christian experienced a resounding defeat in the election, however, receiving less than 20 per cent of the votes – 146 votes to 25. Newspaper reports in the wake of the election indicated that he did not have the unqualified acceptance from Gold Coast society that he had been led to believe. The *Gold Coast Leader* described the results as "The Triumph of Common Sense", and according to Kimble, the newspaper offered a rebuke "to those who had tried to pitch their claims for recognition against those of such a veteran as the Honourable J.E. Casely Hayford".[5] In other words, despite indications that Christian might have been accepted in the Gold Coast legal community, acceptance by the wider community was not easily bestowed.

With time, Christian eventually achieved this goal. After the death of Casely Hayford, the Sekondi Municipal Electors' Association proposed him as nominee to succeed the deceased, and he was required to become a member of the association.[6] He responded positively to the nomination and was duly selected by a majority vote as the association's candidate for the election.[7] Christian, like all the candidates, had to meet certain qualifications to be eligible for election as a municipal member of the Legislative Council. These included nomination "in writing by three electors", who were competent to speak, read and write the English language, ownership of property "to the value of £250 sterling", and five years of normal residence in the town prior to the date of election.[8] The term of membership of a municipal member to the Legislative Council was "four years from the date of election".[9]

MEMBER OF THE LEGISLATIVE COUNCIL

Christian was elected as a municipal member of the Legislative Council for Sekondi on 24 September 1930,[10] in place of the deceased Casely Hayford.[11] He had been opposed by Nicol,[12] and in the wake of the election, Christian noted that "from jealousy some of the lawyers opposed unsuccessfully, saying that [he] was a stranger and a usurper".[13] However, he was subsequently re-elected to this position on two occasions and served continuously in the Legislative Council until his death in 1940.[14] His success was significant, as Kimble has noted that prior to Christian's appointment "the Government never nominated any other than Gold Coast Africans to the Legislative Council".[15]

Interestingly, on his election to the Legislative Council, Christian received a congratulatory letter from the general secretary of the National Congress of British West Africa, an organization which had been founded by Casely Hayford in 1920.[16] The congress felt it was their duty to commend their policies, aims and objectives for Christian's consideration, because in his capacity as a member of the Legislative Council, he would be "almost equally responsible for the good Government of the country generally". A copy of the constitution of the congress and the resolutions of the third and fourth sessions were also forwarded with the letter, with the hope that Christian would adopt the policies and contribute to the work done by the congress.[17]

Christian was apparently respected as Casely Hayford's successor, as he was given the opportunity, in his capacity as municipal member for Sekondi, along with other officials in the Legislative Council, to speak about his former political opponent, the Honourable Joseph Ephraim Casely Hayford, MBE. His contribution is reproduced in the introduction to the book titled *West African Leadership* by Magnus J. Sampson, which included the public speeches of Casely Hayford. Sampson explained that he reproduced "extracts of opinions or testimonies given . . . in the Legislative Council of the Gold Coast by men in high places and of different nationalities and spheres of life".[18] Christian, in his address, noted:

> It was some time in 1902, when I first came here as a young barrister, that I had the privilege of meeting Mr. Casely Hayford, and to me it always seemed a great gift in him that it did not matter how hard the fight, he was always calm and dispassionate. I have had cause, after a passage of words with him in Court, to go to him and say "I wish I had your gift". Mr. Casely Hayford has written books which are useful and will continue to be useful to us. We cannot forget the work he did in arousing the interest of everyone in the movement for recruiting men and collecting funds in the late war.[19]

The manifesto which Christian prepared shortly after his election to the

Legislative Council of the Gold Coast Colony was evidence of his seriousness of purpose and the breadth of his interest in the well-being of the people he was elected to serve. It detailed "ten advantages worth striving for in the immediate future" and was presented at a meeting of the Sekondi Municipal Electors' Association held on 18 October 1930.[20] These were as follows:

1. The establishment of Demonstration Stations and Nurseries, preferably between Beposo and Axim, for the benefit of the Community and in particular, for the small growers of produce.
2. Market trains to be run from the food supply centres up-country to Sekondi and Takoradi to ensure a freer and cheaper supply of food to the inhabitants.
3. Improvement in treatment at Hospitals for better class Africans and the provision of private wards for such patients as require same.
4. The appointment of African Nurses, the present staff being insufficient. So as to obtain the right type, better salaries to be paid and better treatment from the superior officers.
5. African Medical Men for Africans in the service and their dependents and incidentally for the masses.
6. The establishment of a Board of Visitors for the Hospitals and Prisons along the lines of that started by the Rev Fraser at Achimota.
7. The removal of the fifteen percent surcharge on railway fares and freights – a war measure which had outlived its usefulness or object.
8. Government subsidies for industries with a view to relieve unemployment.
9. Establishment of a water compound at Ekuasi.
10. New lay-outs to relieve the congestion at Sekondi and Esikadu.[21]

Christian's ten-point manifesto clearly demonstrated his concern for all aspects of the life and welfare of the Sekondi citizenry: food security, healthcare services, workers' benefits, employment opportunities, and public utilities such as water, traffic and transportation. He was able to draw on his own knowledge and experience in the community as well as that of his colleagues, friends and associates. He also continued to interact with the constituents he served. For example, the Rate Payers' Association and the Provincial Council of Chiefs of the Western Province at Dutch Sekondi kept him abreast of their concerns regarding rates and assessments in the light of the economic distress occasioned by the depression in the cocoa industry.[22]

Early in the following year, the Sekondi Municipal Electors' Association sent him a four-page letter with proposals for presentation to the Legislative

Council meeting at which the estimates for the 1931–32 session were to be discussed. These proposals included a call for the Medical Service and the Education Department to be spared in the government's scheme of retrenchment. They also dealt with the provision of increased educational and employment opportunities for the young and the establishment of plantations and other industries where young boys with post-primary education could earn a living while they were taught new skills.

Among the proposals was a call for a relaxation of the education rules in areas where schools were inadequate to allow parents to fill this gap with schools of their own to prevent "unfortunate children and wards from growing in ignorance".[23] Christian and the omanhene of Western Nzima did draw to the council's attention the closure of the school established by the residents of Takoradi in the absence of educational facilities there. They requested that the education rules should be relaxed until the people had the opportunity to provide the standard of building required and adequate staff. In response, the director of education indicated his willingness to accommodate this request.[24]

In another letter of the same date, the association submitted an additional proposal, related to the construction of a bridge, that was pursued to a successful conclusion. The urgent necessity to construct a bridge across the Prah River at Beposo was presented with suggestions that the work might be financed by means of a loan to be repaid by collection of a toll for use of the bridge. Apart from the fact that the construction of the bridge would ease the employment situation, it would also be "a boon to the travelling public".[25] When Christian brought this matter to the 1930–31 session, he emphasized that government would be fully justified to charge tolls for use of the bridge.[26] When it was approved in 1934, however, Christian raised questions about who would undertake the construction, because he knew from his experience in Dominica of a bridge that had not been properly constructed and washed away before it was opened by the governor. The particular engineer fled the colony and turned up as the chief engineer of the Gold Coast Railway. Christian therefore made a strong plea for "first class engineers with the best brains" to do the work.[27] When the bridge was eventually completed, the commissioner of the Ahanta–Nzima District extended an invitation to Christian to attend the ceremony to open the bridge on 1 October 1935 and indicated that "His Excellency, the Acting Governor" would be pleased if Christian could "make it convenient to attend".[28]

Christian obviously took his responsibility as a member of the Legislative Council seriously. As early as 1931, he had already visited Half Assini and various parts of Appolonia, and he had plans to go to Dunkwa and then to Akropong and Sefwi. His intention was to see places and become acquainted with the chiefs personally, so that when matters that affected them were brought up during Legislative Council meetings, his familiarity with the people and their circumstances would enable him to participate meaningfully in discussions.[29]

Christian, who was not afraid to challenge the popular opinion, made submissions to the council that were thought-provoking. He also demonstrated that uppermost in his mind were the needs and concerns of those whom he represented. In the 1932–33 session of the council, he was opposed to the proposed introduction of the Income Tax Bill and the Native Administration Revenue Ordinance. He believed that the taxpayers could not afford to pay, that there was no machinery to collect the taxes and that the proposed legislation had the potential to cause general upheaval in the community. He was aware that he did not have a consensus of support for his views, but he felt that the country was not ready for these proposed measures. He noted that the secretary of native affairs had compared the Gold Coast to Nigeria, where such proposals were enforced. Christian felt strongly that this comparison was erroneous because of the inherent differences between the societies. He explained that the people in Nigeria, with its Islamic majority, were accustomed to more autocratic rule. On the other hand, in the predominantly Christian Gold Coast, people were "loyal to the King of England" and were of "a democratic nature". Therefore, the government's plan to take pattern from the example of Nigeria was unwise. Christian further noted that according to the comptroller of customs, the increase in the customs duties would make it unnecessary to impose these measures. He also commented on the effect of the proposed measures on the community. If the people found themselves liable for duties they could not afford, the result would be either revolt or abandonment of stools. Alternatively, he suggested that the export duty on cocoa be raised from one fifth of a penny per pound to one farthing, which would bring in more revenue than the proposed taxation, and customs would be able to collect the extra duty without additional cost.[30]

Christian was severely criticized by the governor and the secretary for native affairs on account of his opposition to the legislation. The governor, in his private report to the secretary of state, described Christian's opposing view as "discordant" and thought that his intention was to cause enmity among the chiefs – who were promised a share of the taxation – and their subjects. However, Christian was willing at all costs to ensure that his actions and discussions were within the rules and boundaries of the House. As a result of this report, Christian requested assistance from his colleague Horace Douglas in England, to ascertain what his rights and privileges were in debate as a member of the Legislative Council. He also sought a copy of the rules of debates in the House in the Gold Coast as well as those of the House of Commons in England, in order to know how far he could go in debate before he exposed himself to deportation. This was a concern, because he had invested all his earnings in the Gold Coast, although he was not prepared to sacrifice the principle of honour and duty because of this concern. He was of the view that "we cannot all say yes sir, yes sir, all the time to what the Governor may choose to say".[31]

Christian recognized the long-term benefit of education to the Africans in Gold Coast society and brought his experience and knowledge to bear on his input into the discussions on this topic in the House. In one of his contributions during the Legislative Council debates, he commented on whether the Imperial College of Tropical Agriculture in Trinidad and Tobago, to which the Gold Coast government was a contributor, met the manpower needs of the Gold Coast in the area of agriculture. He referred to a recent visit to Trinidad, where he inquired about the college. He was told that it was not "the place for coloured people" and that they were "not wanted there". He further pointed out that the Gold Coast Government also sent students to California, at the same time that it was required to pay £1,000 per year to the Imperial College of Tropical Agriculture.[32] The matter was pursued, and correspondence from the acting colonial secretary in 1932 referred to the request made by Christian at the meeting of the select committee on the estimates for the financial year 1932–33 with regard to the admission of African students to the Imperial College of Tropical Agriculture. Arrangements had been made for two Gold Coast government students, Jacob O. Torto and Josiah Cofie, who had recently obtained their undergraduate degrees at the University of California, to be admitted for the associateship postgraduate course for one year from 1 October 1932.[33] The former of these two students did complete his course of study, and his thesis, titled "Detailed Examination of Cacao Fields with the Object of Determining the Influence of Soil and Age on Yields", is held at the library of the University of the West Indies at St Augustine.[34] Towards the end of his time in the Legislative Council, Christian reiterated his disagreement with sending African students to the agricultural college in Trinidad, where only a diploma, which he considered to be inadequate, was offered to them. He noted that a degree was required for the position of director of agriculture. In his view, Africans should have "the highest degree" and should aim to be "at the top and have a wider horizon".[35]

His strong support of education and its role in society was reflected in his attitude towards Achimota College and its possibilities as an agent of social change. He reported that during his travel in England, America and Europe, he had heard discussions in which Achimota was considered to be "a waste of money". He believed that it would be preferable "to have the taxpayers' money spent on education than on another reformatory".[36] In particular, as regards the implementation of the Native Administration Revenue Ordinance, he believed that if Achimota was given an opportunity to function successfully, in the next generation, there would be "men as Chiefs" who would be "able to work out that Ordinance satisfactorily". The "educated Chiefs and elders" would appreciate that it was absurd and a waste of valuable time and resources to have so many people involved in the resolution of cases or stool disputes. Instead, specific people could be assigned to act as judges, which would leave the chiefs free to engage in worthwhile occupations. Christian emphasized that his intention was not to belittle the chiefs, but he noted that when he came to the Gold Coast thirty years ago, "things like destoolments . . . were unknown". There was unrest in the communities, because the ordinance had "created a privileged class" who, rather than use their energy and their intelligence for the benefit of the community or in other productive ways, devoted their time solely to the work of the tribunals. Christian believed these men should direct their energy otherwise.[37]

He also raised the subject of education from the perspective of available facilities as well as remuneration for teachers. In essence, his ultimate concern was for the creation of the next generation of leaders. He suggested the establishment of a college where people "could be taught . . . by having the instruction from the nursery stage right up to the shipping stage of any particular product. They would see and learn better than being told things by a European through an African interpreter. It would be money well spent in view of the significant role of agriculture in the prosperity of the country." He envisaged the longer-term benefits of a school and farms where old men could go and learn and where boys could be apprenticed, as being beneficial to solve "the greatest problem facing this country".[38]

With regard to schoolmasters and teachers, he highlighted the fact that they should be paid a wage that would make them take an interest in their work and "keep the best of them at their profession rather than leave it to those who are not qualified or who have been failures elsewhere to fill the gap". He argued that with an attractive wage, the profession would appeal to the "best men", who would in turn be responsible for the education of the next generation.[39]

In the same year, 1935, Christian raised the concern about the medical facilities available to non-Europeans, another issue he described as "very dear to [his] heart". He explained that

> whereas we have a pretty fine European hospital at Takoradi, men of my type and better types of Africans have no such accommodation. There is an open ward and be you a sanitary boy or a long service man who has just been granted the Order of Merit you are put side by side with him in that place; the fact that you have a different culture and different habits of life is immaterial.

Christian sought to bring such issues to the notice of the governor and hoped that a site would be selected between Sekondi and Takoradi and a hospital built or alterations made to the present hospital so as to accommodate his suggestion. He also sought from the governor the provision of more doctors in the Medical Department and the establishment of an examining board to oversee native herbalists.[40]

The following year, Christian recorded the appreciation of his constituents for the action taken by the governor to allocate monies in the estimates for the erection of a hospital at Sekondi which would provide a better standard of health care for a wider cross-section of Africans. Christian also proposed that provision be made for a maternity ward, even if this required the conversion of the upper storey of the building which housed the clinic to make it suitable for the purpose. He estimated that it would cost £600 and believed that "the public would be willing to contribute to make it a reality".[41] When Korsah submitted Christian's request with respect to the establishment of a maternity hospital at Sekondi, he also included Cape Coast. This submission was done, after the issue was raised in select committee by the acting commissioner of the Western Province. The omanhene of Assin Atandasu supported Korsah's request on behalf of the inhabitants of Cape Coast, and the colonial secretary stated "that the matter would receive full consideration".[42]

Christian also demonstrated his willingness to make suggestions for a change in the status quo to allow for wider representation in the decision-making process or an increase in salaries and other retirement benefits for faithful service. In one of his contributions he noted as follows: "We look forward, Sir to the day when not only will there be more unofficial members representing the various sections of the community, but, Sir when the privilege will be extended to them to participate in the deliberations of the Executive Council and to assist Your Excellency (the Governor) in arriving at conclusions for the benefit of the country."[43]

At that same session, he also proposed that people who had worked in institutions such as the railway should not only receive a compassionate allowance when they left the service, but where they had served for a sufficiently long time, they should be adequately rewarded and some provision made for them by way of pensions or other remuneration.[44]

Christian took care to attend every session as required, and if ill health prevented him, as happened early in 1936, he would send written opinions and proposals on behalf of his constituencies to be brought to the notice of the governor at the council meeting.[45] In such a case, it was apparent that for Christian every issue was significant, once the needs and rights of the ordinary citizen were involved. He brought to the table the danger of a particular railroad crossing in 1935, "near Effia Nkwanta going to Takoradi", where an accident had happened that brought about death and injury to private citizens as a result of an absentee gatekeeper in an inefficient railway system. A goods train had passed when there was "no light at the point of the crossing". Christian, who had witnessed the resulting carnage – men and women lying dead and dying on the ground – drew attention to the fact that with the bridging of the river Prah, traffic on the road from Sekondi to Takoradi had increased. He proposed that "a gate and electric light" should be erected at the crossing to remove the possibility of human error.[46] Shortly afterwards, it was reported that the issue of "lights at level crossings" had already engaged the attention of the railway authorities and that "a new system to warn of approaching traffic" was being considered.[47]

When Christian received letters from the colonial secretary's office that requested his opinion on issues being considered by the governor, he left no stone unturned in dealing with them. In one instance, he was asked whether he agreed with the proposed expenditure for the formation of a "mine-sweeping unit" for use in the approaches to Takoradi Harbour in the event of war. The tug *Sir Gordon* was to be equipped for "mine-sweeping and to make provision for uniforms and training allowances to personnel" at an estimated initial expenditure of around £1,000 and "annual recurrent expenditure" not exceeding £100.[48] Christian had no objection to the proposed project and expenditure. His response showed the expected concern that competent personnel be engaged to "maintain a good standard of efficiency". However, he also kept in view employment possibilities for his constituents and added that "later, competent local men might be trained to assist".[49]

On another occasion, when the governor, through the colonial secretary, also sought his opinion, Christian gave his constituents an opportunity to participate in the decision making. The proposals related to the erection of a public hall in Accra as a memorial to His late Majesty King George V as well as the establishment of a memorial fund. The latter was to be organized by an influential public committee and the government would undertake to contribute "an amount equal to that derived from public subscriptions".[50] Christian sent the proposals to the Rate Payers' Association for its consideration.[51] He was therefore able to advise the colonial secretary that he and his constituency were in support of the proposals put forward by the governor.[52]

Similarly, Christian referred to his constituents a letter from the colonial secretary on the subject of surplus revenue intended for transfer to the Sinking Fund.[53] These included the omanhene of Dutch Sekondi, omanhin of British Sekondi and the Municipal Electors' Association. They in turn offered suggestions on how the surplus revenue should be expended.[54] Christian was diligent in forwarding the letter addressed from his constituents to the provincial commissioner of Sekondi.[55] The governor considered the proposals and directed the colonial secretary to inform Christian that provided nothing unforeseen occurred, it would be possible "to erect a new African hospital, including a maternity ward, at Sekondi during the financial year 1937–38".[56] This was in fact one of the suggestions put forward by the constituents.

In another request, his responses demonstrated that not only did he have the welfare of his constituents at heart, but also he was progressive in his ideas. On the subject of the proposed construction of aerodromes at Accra and Takoradi, Christian expressed "the fond hope that in erecting these Aerodromes conditions will be studied so as to avoid the possibility of introducing disease" in the community by "those travellers arriving at the Aerodromes".[57]

A 1937 letter from the Colonial Secretary's Office revealed the extent to which Christian's contribution was valued in the Legislative Council. In March 1937, he supported a discussion and proposal for the legislation "to provide for the licensing and control of pawnbrokers", and although much thought had been given to the subject, no satisfactory action had been taken. The Colonial Secretary's Office requested that Christian prepare a document to detail the main points relevant to the subject and to formulate suggestions for specific legislative clauses. This was a subject in which it was not feasible to draw on legislation enacted in other jurisdictions. It was felt that Christian's personal knowledge of local affairs would enable him to make a valuable contribution towards the solution of the problem.[58]

Christian's response demonstrated that he understood the fundamental motivation of groups within Gold Coast society and suggested a bilateral approach to enact the necessary legislation. His investigations had led him to conclude that the majority of people who suffered at the hands of pawnbrokers and moneylenders were African government officials. He discerned that the moneylender was secure in the knowledge that the officer had a regular salary and that legal action to recover payment might endanger his position. Christian therefore felt that measures to deal with the problem should include action which would put African government officials on a more satisfactory financial footing. He pointed out that "the initial salaries, and the length of time taken in attaining maximum rates in the various divisions, or promotion to higher divisions, are far from satisfactory, and both in the case of younger officers, as well as of family men with heavy responsibilities, there can be no adequate margin for thrift or provision for emergency".

He made reference to the position of second-division and daily paid clerks that called for urgent attention. Given the importance of the subject, he felt that a committee that would include members of council, merchants and others should be convened to look at restrictive measures to deal with pawnbrokers and moneylenders and the enactment of legislation.[59]

The extent to which his contribution on this subject was valued was further supported by the fact that the colonial secretary subsequently asked him to prepare draft legislation to regulate the practice of moneylending and pawnbroking in the Gold Coast. Christian sought advice on this assignment from his fellow West Indian George Francois.⁶⁰ He recognized that it would be wise to confer with this friend, who was actively involved in the business sector and could provide valuable input from that perspective. Christian believed that the colony was "being ruined by money lending", and he wished "the time would come when it would be made a criminal offence to borrow money at all". He felt that there should be some means to regulate it, so that young men would not be stuck in debt and unable to "discharge their obligations to their families and be useful members of the community".⁶¹

Christian also took a holistic view of the problem. He had observed the changes in how moneylenders operated during the three decades he had lived in the Gold Coast. Initially, the rate was 50 per cent, and the moneylender would exercise patience until the money was repaid. Things had changed, however, and once the due date had passed, the security was sold, which caused further hardship to the borrower. Christian felt strongly that rather than focus on the race of the moneylenders, legislation should regulate transactions and limit the rate of interest. It would be applicable to anyone who lent money, whether they were Lebanese, Fante or any African who came from abroad.⁶²

On another occasion, when he was invited to draft legislation in an area in which he was inexperienced, Christian sought advice from a colleague in England. In 1940, he was involved in drafting the Workman's Compensation Ordinance and sent a copy to Mr Douglas to have him advise on the scope of the bill and how it differed from the English statute. This was necessary, because there was no previous workman's compensation legislation in the Gold Coast, and the bill was based on the old common law.⁶³

As regards the general issue of salaries, the discrepancy between the earnings of European medical officers and their African counterparts also held Christian's attention. He had written a letter to his son-in-law Dr J.E. Armah on the subject and made reference to an analysis of the salaries in various departments.⁶⁴ He was also in contact with Dr Agnes Savage of the maternity hospital at Korle Bu, to whom he made it abundantly clear that African medical officers should be rated and treated along lines similar to those laid down for Europeans. In particular, their quarters and allowances should be the same.⁶⁵ He also wrote to the colonial secretary in 1937 to request the appointment of a female doctor for Sekondi, a matter in which he had the support of the senior health officer.⁶⁶ Christian eventually wrote a letter dated 10 March 1938 to the governor on the subject of the "salary scales for the African staff" and was informed by the colonial secretary that his proposals would be "kept in mind when any revision of the salaries of African officers was undertaken".[67]

He offered practical solutions that took the local situation into consideration, as was the case during discussions on the efficiency of the postal service and the implementation of the Post Office Bill. Owing to shortage of funds and economic depression, the postal service in Sekondi was reduced from three times to twice per week. It therefore took two days for a letter posted in Sekondi to reach Accra. Christian proposed that the government make use of the lorry service, so that there could be delivery every day. He pointed out that the *African Morning Post* newspaper reached Sekondi between the hours of four and five every morning. He felt that similarly, the delivery of mail was of sufficient importance to businessmen and others that the government should "serve the public" instead of "trying to put an embargo upon lorries and others who transported letters". He believed that every facility that improved the delivery of mail should be encouraged, rather than curtailed, by the proposed ordinance. Christian recommended a reduction in the telephone rates in order to increase the number of subscribers. He also questioned why one should have to pay the high rates which were charged for trunk calls.[68] He noted that in England and other parts of the world, trunk calls had been reduced, and that in some parts of the West Indies, a trunk call was treated as an ordinary call without any charge.[69]

Christian was an advocate for reforestation and also offered a realistic resolution in this regard. He noted that it was important to protect the future of the timber industry of the colony, which was affected by the mining industry. His suggestion was that "if we insist on every tree that is cut being replaced, every area that is deforested will soon be full of timber again". He also felt that reforestation should be made compulsory and that it was necessary not only to control the industry but also to ensure that regulations were enforced.[70]

His knowledge of the law always informed his opinions. For example, Christian spoke against an amendment by which "natives" suspected of being in possession of gold had to prove the source from which they had obtained it. He believed that the amendment went against the "very fundamental principle" of British law and procedure of a man being innocent until he is proven guilty. He believed that the excuse that people had come to the Gold Coast and invested money in "winning gold" and that there was "leakage" in the industry was not sufficient to strike against a principle that had "distinguished British administration of justice". According to Christian, there was a possibility of leakage "as much on the part of African workers as on the part of European employees", and it was the responsibility of those who invested in the gold industry to be able to "prove gold to be specific from that which is won by the women who go to the rivers . . . and use their pans". If their experts were not able to do so, the "onus of proof" should not be thrown "upon the native whose every stream has gold". He believed that the true intentions of those who proposed the amendment were to facilitate the situation that "when a Police Officer or the Mines Authority suspected any person . . . in possession of gold, they take advantage of the law and put that man to Court".[71]

In a discussion related to the cocoa industry, an important pillar of the Gold Coast economy, Christian did extensive research in preparation for a motion to be raised. He was mainly concerned for the disadvantaged, and his "suggested questions" included consideration of related issues, such as who should control local purchases, what was the composition of the Cocoa Central Control in the United Kingdom and whether the allocation of quotas was a retrograde step. He felt that the system proposed should carefully consider the control of procedures to buy and ship cocoa that involved European firms and African brokers and shippers. In his view, it was necessary to ensure that the African brokers who had previously made a living in their role as middlemen were not disadvantaged.[72]

At the session on 19 March 1940, Christian addressed the Legislative Council on the motion moved by Nana Sir Ofori Atta regarding the decision of His Majesty's Government to purchase the whole cocoa crop of the year 1939–40. It was felt that the control now exercised from England was inequitable, especially towards the African community and small shippers. It was proposed that for the 1940–41 crop, the central committee in England should not include representatives of the companies or firms buying cocoa in the Gold Coast and that the control of local purchases should be left in the hands of the Gold Coast government assisted by a representative committee with the power to make regulations for the control of these purchases. Such a motion obviously took the locals into consideration. Christian, always a supporter of the downtrodden, voted in favour of the motion. However, the motion was lost.[73]

Throughout his terms in the Legislative Council, a consistent position that Christian espoused was that Africans should be trained to provide the manpower for the society in various spheres of activity. In 1937, he quoted from "a progressive programme of African appointments in the Government Service" for a twenty-year period, 1925–26 to 1945–46, outlined by Governor Guggisberg, which had been presented to the 1926–27 session of the Legislative Council. This plan envisaged that "the number of Europeans employed in the particular appointments shown in the programme will be decreased by 162 in the next twenty years, while the number of African employed will increase by 201". It allowed for the rate of replacement of Europeans by Africans to be less than the retirement rate of the former and anticipated staff increases in every department as might be necessary for the development of the country. It was perceived that although new European appointments would always be essential, they should be fewer in number as Africans became qualified to fill positions. He further pointed out, however, that the programme had not been effectively implemented, and ten years later, the number of Europeans employed had increased significantly, from 481 to 685, while the number of Africans had remained the same. Christian also drew attention to the fact that only 5 per cent of the revenue was devoted to education and repeated his warning that if 80 per cent of the school-age children did not attend schools, owing to an inadequate number of learning institutions, there would be a need for reformatories.[74]

In 1938, he continued to emphasize his position and commiserated with the governor as follows: "One cannot help feeling sorry for Your Excellency – your ears must be falling deaf at times with a continual ding, ding, ding of more appointments for African officials. Promises have been made. Those promises we hope and look forward to you to bring them to fruition."[75]

Christian, the pragmatist, called for an end to the practice where an African remained in a particular post for over twenty years, "with the result that no two men in one office could do the work of the other". He contrasted it with the experience of a young cadet from overseas who came to the colony and was expected to be able, sooner or later, to take charge of a station. Unlike his local counterpart, he was rotated throughout the organization and eventually became proficient in the work of every department.[76]

Christian remained consistent in his call for change in employment practices. In 1939, he made a point of expressing gratitude to the administration for the passage of a new bill which allowed people to hold office as cadets and other higher ranks "irrespective of creed or race". This bill was in response to a call made in 1936 in the council for Africans to be given the same considerations as other races serving in the army.[77] In a 1940 discussion on the work being done by the Health Department to maintain healthy children, Christian drew attention to the shortage of dentists. He advocated for more Africans to be trained in Europe as dentists, to meet the need for schoolchildren to have their teeth examined. Similarly, in the field of agriculture he called for Africans to be trained to the "highest possible degree", which would make them eligible for any position.[78]

OTHER GOLD COAST ACTIVITIES

Christian was a man of varied interests, and throughout his life, his professionalism and leadership role in the community was also evident through the variety of organizations with which he was associated or actively involved. Some activities resulted from his membership in the Legislative Council. In other instances, he either volunteered or was invited to participate in an activity or organization, and he became involved out of interest, goodwill, or because his expertise was relevant to the cause. In some instances, the activity or the organization served a purpose that was relevant or beneficial to him or his children.

At the outbreak of the First World War, Christian volunteered his services to assist with recruitment of additional manpower needed for the Gold Coast Regiment. Christian, along with J.E. Casely Hayford, F.S. Arkhust, James Mercer and Chief Krakue of Elmina, undertook to tour the districts between Sekondi and Kumasi to inform the people about the necessity for able-bodied men to join the Gold Coast Regiment. It was reported that their efforts were successful, especially at Dunkwa and Kumasi.[79]

Some years later, in 1924, Christian played a prominent role as part of a deputation of the "African gentlemen, property owners and residents of Sekondi" who met with Frederick Palmer, who had been appointed by the secretary of state for the colonies to inquire into matters related to the proposed deep-water harbour at Takoradi. The Gold Coast Aborigines' Rights Protection Society was also present at the meeting, where both groups had the opportunity to present statements of their point of view. Christian featured prominently in that he read the statements on behalf of both groups. They agreed that the cost of construction of the Takoradi Harbour was too great for the resources of the colony. It would impose a loan debt which was out of proportion to the country's financial strength and would result in the "impoverishment of the Colony". They felt that the scheme would also result in the closure and consequent ruin of Cape Coast, Sekondi and other ports. Christian's deputation presented a counter-proposal for an upgrade of the facilities at Sekondi. Palmer was of the view that the counter-proposal was as costly if not more so and did not see how the development of Takoradi would have a negative effect on the colony as a whole, although he acknowledged that Sekondi would be affected.[80]

Christian, who had funded his legal studies from sales of the produce of his land in Dominica, transported his keen interest in agriculture and its possibilities for commercial purposes to the Gold Coast. In 1924, he was invited to serve as a judge for the Gold Coast Agricultural Society in several classes at its annual show.[81] Ten years later, as a member of the Ahanta Agricultural Committee, he lauded the virtues of agricultural shows as a means to encourage the development of local industries and was part of a subcommittee to explore this matter.[82]

Christian was also a patron of the Society of African Herbalists. Established on the premise that the knowledge and practice of African medical herbalists had been handed down by their forebears and was still in existence, the Society of African Herbalists, with headquarters in Sekondi, was instituted on 12 December 1931. Its portfolio included the preservation of the knowledge of the healing powers of native plants, the conduct of experiments and research to improve the local practice of medical herbalism and the documentation of herbal medical practice for the guidance of new practitioners. The society was also intended to foster unity among African herbal practitioners.[83]

Another area in which Christian gave active and efficient service was that of prison oversight. In 1931, he served on the Visiting Committee for the Prisons at Sekondi. The director of prisons was required to call together such a committee once every six months to inspect prisons where prisoners with long-term sentences were kept.[84] In 1931, the commissioner of the Western Province invited Christian "in conjunction with" the district commissioner of Sekondi to inspect and report on the Sekondi prisons, in accordance with the prison regulations of 1923.[85] Less than a week later, the two reports on the Central Prison and Fort Orange Prison were submitted.[86] Both reports were for the most part positive.

Some years later, Christian raised the question as to who was eligible to be appointed "Visitor of Prisons". He was advised that every member of the Legislative Council, justices of the peace and "some other officers were eligible".[87] In July 1939, he was duly appointed a "Visitor to the Prisons of the Gold Coast". Notice of the appointment was published in the *Gold Coast Gazette*, no. 49, of 22 July 1939, and he was advised by letter from the director of prisons in Accra. According to the prison regulations, a visitor could inspect the prison at any time between 6 a.m. and 6 p.m., once reasonable notice had been given to the officer in charge or to the gaoler. Christian was also free to visit any prisoner and hear or receive any representation from the prisoner as regards the treatment received. On the basis of a visit, Christian could then report to the director of prisons, or to the colonial secretary, or to the chief commissioner in Ashanti or the Northern Territories.[88]

In June 1932, Christian had been invited first via a telegram, followed by letter, to join the central committee of the Gold Coast Branch of the Red Cross Society and to attend its first meeting.[89] Christian cabled his acceptance but warned, and subsequently confirmed, that he was unable to attend owing to ill health.[90] The Gold Coast Branch of the British Red Cross was originally founded to offer and provide assistance with maternal- and child-welfare activities provided by the government and for the other objects set forth in the charter and supplemental charter of the British Red Cross Society.[91] It was run by an executive committee that met in Accra. Divisions were established in Sekondi, Cape Coast and Kumasi.[92]

In August of the same year, Christian attended the inaugural meeting of the Sekondi Branch of the British Red Cross Society and was duly elected deputy president. Among the others listed as present was Mrs H. Peters, who ran the West African Industrial Academy on behalf of the American Baptist Missionary Society.[93] At subsequent meetings of the society later that year and the next, Christian was recorded as chairman of the proceedings.[94] In January 1934, he was officially appointed vice-president of the Sekondi (Western Province) Division of the society.[95] At a meeting held immediately after his appointment, it was agreed to recommend to the president that the appointment should be for the year.[96]

Christian's involvement in the Sekondi Branch of the British Red Cross Society provided additional opportunities for him to be more deeply involved in Gold Coast society. When Dr D. Lennox, the medical officer of health and secretary of the Sekondi Red Cross, gave a public lecture on welfare work to the Optimum Club, Christian, who was a patron of the latter organization, served as chairman of the proceedings.[97] Christian also wrote letters to prospective donors to solicit funds for the Red Cross Society. As a result of these appeals, responses were received from the catechist of the Presbyterian Church,[98] the African Methodist Episcopal Zion Church in Sekondi and the superintendent of the Sekondi Methodist Church.[99] In December 1933, Christian received a commendatory greeting from the president of the British Red Cross Society, Gold Coast Branch, that had been sent to those who had "worked in the Gold Coast for the advancement of the spirit of service", which the Red Cross represented. The president commented on the "enthusiastic support" which the society had gained from "a strikingly large section of the community" in the brief period since its founding. It was now positioned to develop into an organization with a "far-reaching and beneficent influence".[100]

Christian was one of the vice-presidents of the Empire Day Celebrations Committee for the Empire Day Celebrations of 24 May 1935. The celebrations, on the cricket ground, included a parade in the morning by the children of the Sekondi schools and a ceremony of saluting the flag. In the afternoon, there were sporting events for the children of the Sekondi schools, while some events were open to anyone willing to participate. These events included a cross-country run, high jump, hundred-yard race, tug of war, climbing the greasy pole and wheelbarrow race.[101]

It is not surprising that Christian, who had several children at school in England, agreed to serve on the Gold Coast Advisory Committee for Students Proceeding to the United Kingdom for the Purposes of Study. This committee was intended to provide supervision in the United Kingdom for students from the Gold Coast who desired this intervention in their life. It had the sanction of the Colonial Secretary's Office in Accra, and notice about its formation had been published in the *Gazette*, the *Gold Coast News* and the local press. Expenses incidental to this supervision were to be borne by the Gold Coast government and not by the students or their parents. The acting secretary for native affairs sought Christian's approval on the appointment of Mr P.H. Ezechiel, director of colonial scholars, who was to fulfil this role of supervisor.[102] The fact that Christian was consulted on the choice of the person who was appointed to fulfil the director's role is further evidence of the high esteem in which he was held in Gold Coast society.

In 1932, he served as the leader of the Western Province Bar Association of Sekondi. In this capacity, he and his colleagues were commended for their assistance to the Provincial Commissioner's Office and the maintenance of congenial and happy relationships.[103] In 1938, the Methodist Mission of Sekondi had "unqualified praise" for the "very able and efficient manner" in which he conducted affairs at the annual missionary meeting, when he made a donation of £6 to the church.[104] The following year, Christian applied to the director of public works on behalf of the Sekondi Dramatic Society for permission to use the King George V Memorial Hall in Accra, which included the gallery, stage and stage effects.[105]

In the aftermath of the relatively severe earthquake in the Gold Coast in 1939, the Central Committee of Accra Earthquake Relief Fund was established in response to the call for relief in Accra, where considerable damage had been reported. Christian was a member of the committee, undoubtedly on account of his membership in the Legislative Council. Dr J.H. Murrell, another West Indian, was also a co-opted member of the central committee. The aim of the committee was to collect funds and administer them, as well as any other funds collected by sympathizers, locally or otherwise.[106]

In the Sekondi community, Christian exercised his initiative, and with assistance from "some other gentlemen", they launched the Accra Earthquake Relief Fund, Western Province (Sekondi) Branch. Christian served as chairman, and he also gave a generous donation. By August 1939, there was the sum of £315 in the fund and the hope that the amount would be doubled when all contributions were accepted. At a meeting held at his residence some months after the earthquake, a resolution was passed that the fund be wound up and the bank instructed to transfer the amount collected to the central committee in Accra.[107] As a result of the earthquake, Christian went a step further and advocated for the "employment of an expert" who had visited places like San Francisco, Sicily, Japan and Quetta, and who would be qualified to recommend what type of buildings should be erected in the new Accra.[108]

UNITED KINGDOM ACTIVITIES

From his home in the Gold Coast, Christian retained membership of the West Indian Club Limited in England, which brought together people who were interested in the West Indies and related mainland colonies to promote discussion and consideration of pertinent issues. Those desiring membership in the club would submit an application, signed also by a seconder, and members were elected by ballot by the management committee.[109] Members paid a subscription fee, which was less for those who were resident abroad. Christian stayed at the West Indian Club Limited for periods of up to a month when he travelled through England en route to and from America and the West Indies, and he used the club as his address when he visited London.[110] He also actively supported its ventures. For example, he participated in the club's various sweepstakes, which were popular among the members.[111] On one occasion, when there was a special appeal for funds, the club's treasurer acknowledged Christian's "generous contribution" of £10 10s. and the fact that he also promised to send "a further contribution if necessary".[112]

He obviously felt very much a part of this club and appreciated the services membership offered. He took the opportunity to record his sorrow at the news of the death of one of the club members (Mr Hunn), whose "genial face welcomed" him every time he visited. Christian had read about it in the *West India Committee Circular* and was sure that there would be many like himself who would miss the deceased.[113] This gesture demonstrates that Christian was the kind of person who took advantage of an opportunity to say a kind word or express positive sentiments.

Evidence also suggests that Christian was involved with the West India Committee. This organization, which was described as "the oldest Colonial Body in the Empire", was incorporated by royal charter in 1904 "to promote the interests of the Agricultural and Manufacturing industries and the trade of The British West Indian Islands, British Guiana, British Honduras, The Bahama Islands, and Bermuda, and thus increase the general welfare of those colonies".[114] Christian received an invitation to contribute to the purchase of a suitable gift for the king and queen on the occasion of the silver jubilee.[115] Christian responded favourably and enclosed a cheque for £1 to the Royal Jubilee Gift Fund.[116]

Christian also became a member of the League of Coloured Peoples,[117] an organization founded early in 1931 by Dr Harold A. Moody, a Jamaican physician who had studied medicine at London University and was unable to secure a hospital post on account of racial discrimination. He was also actively involved with the Congregational Church and the Colonial Missionary Society. The League of Coloured Peoples was intended "to promote the welfare of coloured peoples in all parts of the world, to improve the relations between the races and to collaborate with other organizations of like interests". Its membership consisted of students from the British Empire and white people with religious affiliations. Moody was also associated with the plans of the Colonial Office to establish a student hostel in London, known as Aggrey House.[118] One of Christian's sons who was a student in England had met with Dr Moody and shared information about the other family members who were in England at the time. Moody and Christian subsequently corresponded on the subject of his granddaughters. Moody offered advice on their education,[119] and Christian requested his assistance to secure apprentice positions for them in a hospital. He also hoped to meet with Moody during his 1938 summer visit to London.[120] There is evidence that in 1939 Christian was a member of the executive committee of the League of Coloured Peoples.[121]

Other organizations in England sought Christian's membership and patronage. For example, in 1934, he received a request from the council of the Royal Society of Arts, London, for permission to add his name to its list of its supporters. This society, founded in 1754, was well known for its interest in "the development of the commercial, industrial and artistic resources of the Empire". It had evolved into a forum for experts in scientific and technical fields to discuss their findings on the applications of their work in industry and commerce and to share their common interests.[122] The receipt of such a request, which came in a lengthy letter from its secretary, G.K. Menzies, was a clear indication that Christian's reputation was widely known at this stage of his life. In order to continue its work "on as broad and influential a basis as possible", the council wanted to add residents to its long and distinguished list of fellows in all parts of the world.[123]

Similarly, in 1936, Christian was invited to "become a Patron" of the National Union of Empire Africans. Founded two years earlier, this organization, which had its headquarters in Liverpool, England, was meant "to promote Anglo-African cooperation and ensure the unity of the British Empire in Africa". Membership was open to Africans of British nationality, while others sympathetic to the cause would be admitted as associate members. The secretary indicated that the union hoped to "benefit from Christian's long and varied experience in a distinguished career".[124]

Early in his first term as a member of the Legislative Council, Christian expressed the view that it was an unrewarding task which took a lot of one's time and money.[125] It is evident, however, that he was not to be deterred even by negative circumstances, whether real or perceived. In 1932, for example, he felt that he was victimized because of his contributions. He claimed that his opposition to the Native Revenue Bill had resulted in loss of jobs for two of his children. His son Joe had been retrenched from the Agricultural Department, and Maude had lost her job as nurse-midwife.[126] "God bless them", was his sarcastic comment on the matter.[127] In 1934, he noted that he had "put [his] hand to the plough", and he had no intention to renege on his decision to serve his constituents.[128]

Christian served two four-year terms, and in 1938, he was "returned unopposed . . . for a third term of office as member of the Legislative Council". Even then, he admitted that there was "so much to do, so very little appreciation", and he sometimes felt "like throwing up [sic] the sponge". Generally the members of the Legislative Council were not paid for their services, except an allowance for travelling expenses, but gave the administration their services free for the betterment of the community.[129] However, he considered himself to be responsible for "his children and his African friends". He did not want them to be made "wage earners and landless while a foreign master reaped the benefit of their labour".[130]

In 1939, Christian reported to his son Howard on negative feedback in one of the local newspapers about his performance in the Legislative Council. The author of the article, who used the pseudonym "Lobster", was of the view that Christian was "too old to be useful as Member of the Council" and that he did not "speak up" as he should about his municipality. Christian considered the article as merely giving him "a cheap advertisement" and that people in the community who knew better thought differently.[131] As has been demonstrated, however, official records of the Legislative Council sessions do not support this criticism.

This survey of Christian's performance during his lengthy service as a member of the Legislative Council and his involvement in other aspects of public and cultural life validates his outstanding contribution to the political and social development of Gold Coast society. He was outspoken in his contributions during meetings, seemingly without fear of possible repercussions. He also proved that he was a person of integrity and remained committed even in the face of adverse consequences. His reach and influence in the council were certainly noticed by his colleagues. The colonial secretary observed that no one who had the privilege of listening to Christian "could fail to observe the keen enthusiasm, the conviction and the deep sincerity that marked all his public work".[132] Others described him as "a wise and experienced Councillor", whose speeches were "outspoken", and who was a "trenchant but constructive critic".[133] Christian exploited his knowledge, experience, training and interests to inform his presentations to the council on a wide range of subjects that affected his constituents. His performance in the Legislative Council and his active involvement in the wider society also underscored his initial commitment to his cause in this part of the "fatherland", which he had made his home.[134]

Figure 7.1. George James Christian, member of the Legislative Council, Accra, Gold Coast

CHAPTER 8

Christian and His Compatriots in the Gold Coast
Community, Identity and Heritage

UNLIKE THE EARLIER GROUPS OF MIGRANTS TO THE Gold Coast mentioned in chapter 1, Christian and the other West Indians who settled there in the first four decades of the twentieth century were mainly professionals.[1] They came to offer their skills and to make a better life for themselves. There was an engine fitter employed in the Railway Department in Sekondi from 1908 to 1924,[2] and a teacher,[3] as well as an assistant commissioner of police from Barbados, who worked in Kumasi, Ashanti, in the 1920s.[4] There were three lawyers from British Guiana, Dominica and Trinidad, four doctors (two from Trinidad, and one each from St Lucia and British Guiana respectively),[5] a sanitary inspector who came from Trinidad in 1910[6] and two St Lucian businessmen.[7] There was also at least one West Indian each employed as follows: in the Prison Department in the 1920s,[8] and the diamond mines in Akwatia[9] and as a licensed auctioneer in Abosso.[10] There were also West Indian teachers at a school in Cape Coast in the 1920s.[11]

The West Indians gravitated to each other, and ties of family, friendship and professional solidarity played a significant role in their lives. Leonard Muss, the West Indian who had heard about Christian "by accident" and offered assistance and accommodation on his initial arrival in the Gold Coast, was a senior officer in the Customs Department.[12] Within a year of his arrival, Christian had established a legal firm with Francis Stanislaus Leung, who was originally from British Guiana.[13] As was mentioned earlier, Christian had letters of introduction to two men from Trinidad, Maurice D. Reece and Dr Simmonds,[14] and he would most likely have met them fairly soon after his arrival in the Gold Coast.

ISSUES RELATED TO THE MIGRATION PROCESS

Correspondence with a young agricultural professional resident in British Guiana who wanted to work in the Gold Coast has provided some insight into the issues with which the West Indian migrants to the Gold Coast had to contend. H. Dudley Huggins, an assistant field manager at the Sugar Planters Experiment Station in Sophia, British Guiana, made inquiries and sought advice, via correspondence with Christian and another West Indian, George Francois, about a position in agriculture in the Gold Coast in the mid-1920s.[15] Their replies indicated that preference was generally given to white colonials who applied for any available positions. Francois advised Huggins that in practice, a West Indian, being also of African descent racially, could be appointed as "native", and this carried with it "the stigma of inferiority". He should therefore ensure that he was being employed under the same regulations that applied to Europeans. This included provisions for leave and an allowance for travel.[16]

Christian conferred with Reece, who provided useful information based on his experience in the Agricultural Department. According to the person's area of expertise, the only possible employer would be the government, as was the case for positions in agriculture. Private companies, particularly in the cocoa industry, were competitive and "always subject to bankruptcy".[17] Huggins was advised that "to get on at all as a coloured man one will have to be very tactful". Furthermore, the cost of living was high.[18] Mobility within the professional ranks could also be hampered for West Indians. They could expect to receive annual salary increments, but it was unlikely that they would be promoted to the level of head of a department.[19] Christian shared with Huggins that Reece of Trinidad, who worked as a curator in the Agricultural Department[20] and was considered an "expert", never secured an upper-level position, "because he was not white".[21] Reece himself wrote to Christian about Huggins and noted that he was well qualified for the position, except for the fact that he was "West Indian, and coloured at that".[22] The indication was that colonial policy did not treat West Indians the same as other, white colonials. Huggins remained in British Guiana at that time and was appointed assistant superintendent in the Department of Agriculture, Georgetown.[23]

In 1924, when conditions in the Gold Coast were adverse, Christian was cautious and realistic in the advice he gave to Alex R. Cools-Lartigue, a young lawyer from Dominica who sought his opinion as to whether he should come to the Gold Coast to practise. Despite the fact that Christian was successful, he was aware that working as a lawyer was not always financially viable. He pointed out to Cools-Lartigue the extent to which things had changed for the worse since he first migrated and noted that fat retainers were no longer obtainable and the struggle for existence was strenuous. He described the Gold Coast as a "soul killing" country and advised that unless one had strength of character, one might easily go to extremes to the detriment of one's health.[24] Christian was willing to assist Cools-Lartigue, however, if he chose to migrate.[25]

WEST INDIAN PROFESSIONALS IN THE GOLD COAST

Trinidad and Tobago

Among Christian's circle of friends and associates were two lawyers, one of whom, Richard Emmanuel Phipps, was from Trinidad, although he also had connections in St Lucia.[26] Phipps, who was called to the Bar in London on 27 June 1900,[27] had served as "Secretary for the West Indies" on the 1900 Pan-African Conference committee and had also attended the conference.[28] After the conference, he had returned to Trinidad, where he practised as a barrister for some ten years and was also involved in the Trinidad branch of the Pan-African Association.[29] He reportedly left Trinidad shortly afterwards, following the death of Henry Sylvester Williams there in 1911, and migrated to the Gold Coast.[30] In the Gold Coast, he and Christian maintained contact. Phipps practised in the Eastern Province in Accra and helped Christian in legal matters. For example, on an occasion when Christian was unable to attend to the case of one Mr London, Phipps "wrote the opinion" on which the case succeeded.[31] On another occasion, Christian sought Phipps's advice and assistance in the case of Mr Mansour, a client seeking unpaid rent from the firm of Dayaram Brothers, who had leased one of Mansour's business premises.[32] Phipps, described by Christian as "a Barrister friend", attended his

1938 New Year's gathering, together with Francois, Lewis, Beausoleil, Hoyte, Auguste and Busby.[33] Christian also invited Phipps, by letter, to participate in the fundraising event of the West Indian group for the Accra Earthquake Relief Fund.[34] Phipps was also solicitor for George Francois, and apart from that, the two were friends.[35] Phipps lived at Castle Road, Christiansborg, in Accra, and sources indicate that by 15 April 1949, he had passed away.[36]

In the late 1930s, mention is made of another legal professional, also from Trinidad, a judge in Sekondi, Mr Savary, and his wife, who was from Antigua.[37] They had invited Christian to a gathering at their home, but he was unable to attend.[38] On 28 January 1938, members of the Bar entertained Mr Justice Savary, a "very sound Lawyer" who was going home on leave, at a farewell luncheon at Dominica House.[39] Christian reported that the luncheon was a pleasant occasion. He enjoyed himself and was pleased to have had the opportunity to meet Savary socially.[40]

Among the group of professionals who also migrated to the Gold Coast during Christian's earlier years there were two brothers who went to the Gold Coast from Trinidad, in 1910 and 1923 respectively. Cunliffe Malcolm Gustave (C.M.G.) Hoyte was "sent out" to the Gold Coast, and he invited his younger brother, Dr Ralph Allen Sergeant Hoyte Sr, who "went out on his own as a doctor", in 1923.[41] C.M.G. Hoyte was originally appointed to the Gold Coast government Service as a first-grade sanitary inspector in April 1910. He was largely responsible for the training of subordinate public health officers, not only from the Gold Coast but also from Nigeria, Gambia and Sierra Leone. In 1916 and 1923, he received the Certificate of Appreciation of Government for services rendered as organizer of the Red Cross movement in Ashanti during the outbreak of relapsing fever in Accra. Mr Hoyte also served, with success, as joint honorary secretary of the Gold Coast Central Council's Branch of the British Red Cross Society, and his selfless contribution in this regard was publicly recognized. His particular interest in horticulture was well known, and he donated the proceeds of his successful flower shows to the Red Cross Movement. Mr Hoyte gave "twenty four years of trustworthy and efficient service", and his conduct was "always exemplary and a model to others". He was awarded the Member of the Order of the British Empire not for his work as a sanitary inspector but for his hobby, the Grow More Food Campaign that he organized in the vicinity of Accra during the First World War.[42]

Dr Ralph Hoyte Sr, like his brother, gave more than forty years of distinguished service to the Gold Coast, in the medical profession. He went there in 1923, was joined by his wife and children three years later and remained there until his death in 1967. He worked first in Accra and eventually settled in Nsawam. Initially he worked in a partnership with Dr Simmonds that also included Drs Beausoleil and Auguste from St Lucia. Dr Simmonds was known to have been in the Gold Coast when Christian arrived there in 1902.[43] Dr Hoyte Sr withdrew from the collaboration with Simmonds in 1928 and continued to work on his own in Nsawam.[44] Hoyte Sr was in turn responsible for the migration to the Gold Coast of Dr George Busby of Trinidad, who arrived to assist him in his medical practice. They had a joint practice at Nsawam.[45]

In 1949, Dr Hoyte's son, also named Ralph, who grew up mainly in England and Trinidad, went back to the Gold Coast at the age of twenty-nine after qualifying as a doctor at McGill University in Canada. He worked there for a year and a half with his father. Dr Hoyte Jr indicated that there were few doctors, and he described the conditions under which his father worked, assisted by an interpreter and two clerks:

> On Monday, my father worked in his dispensary . . . there were no pharmacies and doctors had to do their own dispensing. He imported all his mixtures, all his tablets, everything and dispensed it himself. . . . On Tuesday, he drove a few miles to Adesu to our friend. . . . Mr Banfu was a cocoa merchant . . . and we set up shop on Tuesday in his cocoa shed, and we saw our patients there. On Wednesday, we drove much further to Asamankese. Again we set up shop in a cocoa shed, and then drove back, this time at night.[46]

In the early 1920s, Julian C. Roberts, railway engineer and native of Trinidad and Tobago, came with his wife Carmen and two sons from London to the Gold Coast via Panama, where he had worked previously on the construction of the Panama Canal. He was recruited by the Colonial Office to work on the building of railways, and the family settled first in Takoradi, where he was involved in the railroad tracks at Takoradi Harbour and outward to other planned destinations, including Tarkwa, Kumasi and Accra. He and his family eventually moved to Accra. After this contract ended, he was engaged in the export of cocoa on two occasions, but he was charged for illegal trading and that resulted in costly litigation. He therefore had to abandon plans for his two sons, J.C. Roberts and L.W. Roberts, to study law and medicine in the United Kingdom. It is possible that at this juncture in his life, Christian stepped in to help him.[47]

Correspondence between the two men demonstrated the extent to which Christian was willing to assist a fellow West Indian. In 1924, J.C. Roberts, a licensed auctioneer, wanted to establish himself as a trader. Christian not only introduced him to the agent of a firm but also made a request that he be supplied with goods to be sold on commission in three locations – Sekondi, Prestea and Dunkwa. Roberts indicated to Christian that he would be stationed at Dunkwa, his older son at Prestea and his younger son at Sekondi.[48] Christian sent the letter to Roberts at three locations just to ensure that he met with the agent. Christian went further and gave a commitment "to guarantee the payment of the goods supplied".[49] Roberts expressed his gratitude on behalf of himself and his family for the assistance and promised to give account of all sales and receipts to avoid deception.[50]

In the early to mid-1930s, J.C. Roberts left the Gold Coast and travelled to Nigeria with one of his sons, J.C. Roberts Jr, and the two were never heard from again.[51] His second son, L.W. Roberts, remained in the Gold Coast with his mother and became a chartered accountant. His mother was later joined by a sister, Adil, from Trinidad and Tobago, and the family spent the rest of their days in the Otekpelu/Agomeda area of the Gold Coast.[52]

St Lucia

Dr Amédée Edwin Charles Beausoleil and Dr E.L. Auguste were two other doctors, both from St Lucia. They practised in Tafo and Koforidua respectively.[53] A patient who had been treated by Dr Beausoleil for an "unusual" disease went for further treatment in Boston, United States, and the doctors there confirmed that the diagnosis and treatment of the condition were correct.[54] A newspaper report indicated that Drs Beausoleil and Auguste, together with Drs Busby, Hoyte and Murrell, "were responsible for much valuable pioneering medical work in the rural areas of Ghana".[55] During the illness of his daughter Maude in 1932, Christian commented that the experience showed him that he had friends in the community, because "all the West Indian Doctors six in number were in attendance night and day besides Nurses from the Hospital".[56] Dr Beausoleil was Christian's personal physician.[57]

There were other St Lucians, George Joseph Francois and George Stanley Lewis, both of whom seemed to have come to the Gold Coast to engage in business. Francois, who left St Lucia to join the British Army, came to the Gold Coast at the end of the First World War on the invitation of Franz Dove, a lawyer from Sierra Leone who was also a businessman in Accra. Together they started the Anglo African Corporation, which was engaged in the preparation of cocoa for export. Francois was based in New Tafo and was a friend of Christian.[58] He married Mercy Awuah from Akropong, Akwapim, and they had four children. He became a successful businessman. His home included "a garden of fruit trees where there were antelopes and deer, turkeys, ducks and rabbits". There were also facilities for tennis[59] and cricket. Francois also established a small private school which was attended by his children, their cousins and the progeny of other West Indians.[60]

George Stanley Lewis (1906–1999),[61] the last surviving West Indian from that wave of migrants to the Gold Coast in the earlier decades of the twentieth century, was the eldest of a family of five sons[62] born to George and Ida Lewis. When George Lewis died in the 1920s, leaving Stanley and his four younger brothers, Francois, who was the godfather of Stanley Lewis, encouraged Ida to send him to the Gold Coast to be trained in the business there. Stanley left for the Gold Coast several years after the death of his father.[63] He arrived in August 1929, to work with the company of which Francois was the managing director. Franz Dove was also a close friend of Christian, and Lewis reportedly met Christian at Dove's house in 1930.[64] Lewis worked in the cocoa-farming industry in Suhum in the Eastern Region for seventeen years. When disease spelled the demise of the cocoa industry in the late 1940s, Lewis moved to the capital, Accra, where he helped to found another company with Francois, the Cheapside Syndicate Limited, which specialized in imports. However, the relationship between the two businessmen deteriorated significantly over the issue of Lewis's remuneration from the proceeds of the company.[65] In 1950, Lewis set up his own company, Lewis and Company, which went on to become one of the foremost non-European commercial firms in Ghana.

Lewis was also an active member of his church community and both young and old turned to him for counsel on family matters. This tribute, which was paid to Lewis on his ninetieth birthday, indicated that the contribution he made to society was widely recognized: "You may little have realized that, over the years you have become an outstanding example and leader, without any show of professional pomp. You have achieved this by example of integrity, compassion and humane attitude towards all with whom you associated. Accordingly you have become for West Indian/Ghanaian citizens their reference of integrity, an unassuming personality, above reproach, and one whose advice was always sought."[66]

British Guiana

The other lawyer who was a friend and colleague of Christian was Clarence Edmund Maxwell Abbensetts, originally from British Guiana, who was called to the Bar on 16 April 1913.[67] He had also served as a solicitor of the Supreme Court of Nigeria and the Gold Coast Colony, and he was the solicitor for the executors of Christian's estate.

Mr Percy Roberts and his wife Ingeretha Roberts from British Guiana had also lived and worked in the Gold Coast. Roberts died on 21 October 1937, after their return to British Guiana, and his widow sought Christian's assistance to obtain three months of her husband's salary and an allowance which was to be continued until her death. Mrs Roberts requested this of Christian, as he was "in the Court" and she felt that his "influence" was "high".[68] The Murrells, together with a three-year-old granddaughter, Louise Jean Murrell, had arrived in the Gold Coast in 1930. Dr Murrell was a "highly respected doctor" and operated a clinic in Accra near the Princess Marie Louise Hospital at Korle Wokon.[69]

Barbados

At least three of the professionals among the West Indians in the Gold Coast were from the island of Barbados. One of them, George Campbell Deane (1873–1948), was a colonial official. He was appointed the chief justice of the Gold Coast from 1929 to 1935.[70] The son of a sugar planter, he was educated at Harrison College, Barbados, and St John's College, Oxford, England, and called to the Bar at Inner Temple in 1898. He practised law in British Guiana from 1898 to 1903. He then moved to Trinidad, where he worked as a stipendiary magistrate before being appointed puisne judge in 1920. He also served as chief justice of the Leeward Islands in 1923, and as puisne judge, Straits Settlements, based in Singapore, from 1924 to 1929. In 1930, during his stint in the Gold Coast Colony, he was given a knighthood in the King George V Birthday Honours list. From 1936, he served as chief justice in the Windward Islands, based in Grenada, and a year later, he was appointed by the governor of Barbados, Sir Mark Young, as chairman of the commission to inquire into the 1937 riots in Barbados.[71]

Another Barbadian, Mr Alleyne, went to the Gold Coast as a teacher for the Grammar School of the Society for the Propagation of the Gospel in Cape Coast. He died in 1933 after a second attack of blackwater fever. He had been treated by two of the West Indian doctors, Drs Murrell and Hoyte, but he was eventually hospitalized and passed away. On this occasion, the sense of community and caring that existed among the West Indians was evident. Christian wrote to the Callenders, another family from Barbados who had returned home from the Gold Coast, with a request that they pass on the news to Alleyne's relatives.[72] Dr Murrell, who had sent a cable to the mother of the deceased,[73] formulated a plan to collect the £20 7s. required for the funeral expenses and erection of a concrete tombstone. He requested donations from members of the West Indian community, including C.M.G. Hoyte, Stanley Lewis, R.E. Phipps, Abbensetts and Riley. He collected the sum of £8 4s. 6d., and it was agreed that the remainder should be made up by Francois, Beausoleil, Auguste, Dr Hoyte, Murrell and Christian.[74]

The third Barbadian family mentioned was that of Walter Callender, who served as assistant commissioner of police in Kumasi, Ashanti, in the 1920s. Unlike many of the other migrants, he had his wife, Eva, with him. They had no children, and on their return to Barbados in 1928, they adopted a little girl from the Gold Coast, Margaret, age seven.[75] Her father, lawyer Francis Stanislaus Leung, had entrusted the child to their care. Margaret had become attached to Mrs Callender, and before his death, Leung had indicated that she should remain with them and be raised as their own. Her mother, a local woman, was torn between whether to keep her child on the advice of her relatives or to relinquish her so that Margaret might have a better opportunity at life with the Callenders.

Christian advised the Callenders on the relevant documents. He gave the child's mother the assurance that Margaret would be returned to the Gold Coast after she had grown up and was educated. Margaret eventually accompanied the Callenders to Barbados and also had the opportunity to visit British Guiana to meet her father's relatives. The Callenders kept in contact with

Margaret's mother until the latter's death in 1933.[76] Eva Callender reported to Christian in 1939 that Margaret had grown into a fine young woman. She wrote that Mr Callender had taken her out of school earlier than she had anticipated, and she regretted this, because she had planned to have Margaret trained as a teacher. However, at the age of eighteen, Margaret had learned to sew and was able to make her own clothes. She was being courted by a young man from British Guiana, and Mrs Callender had taken a "wait and see" stance on the matter. She considered Margaret to be young, but at the same time, the young man seemed personable, and Margaret's relatives were also from British Guiana.[77] Later that year, Christian wrote and enclosed a monetary Christmas gift for Margaret and Mrs Callender and inquired whether Margaret had married and gone to British Guiana.[78] It is not known what became of her.

Dominica

The Reverend Joseph Oliver Bowers

It is relevant to include in this discussion the story of another West Indian from the island of Dominica, the Reverend Joseph Oliver Bowers, who also migrated to the Gold Coast and made a valuable contribution to society there. Christian, who knew of Bowers, was aware of his impending migration to the Gold Coast in 1940.[79] Born on 28 March 1910, Bowers was the son of Mary and Sheriff Montague Bowers, a head teacher who had been Christian's roommate at the Mico Institution in the 1890s. Christian and the young Bowers had met on one occasion in 1922,[80] during one of the former's return visits to Dominica, when Bowers's father had introduced them to each other. Bowers arrived in the Gold Coast for the first time in January 1940, but Christian died before they had the opportunity to meet.[81] However, Christian's son Ferdinand met Bowers, then a young priest, and because of the relationship between their fathers, the two of them developed a close relationship "like brothers".[82]

The young Bowers, who was Dominica's first native priest, had shown an interest in the priesthood from an early age and became a legend in his lifetime. His cousin, with whom he lived during his childhood days as a student at Dominica Grammar School, recalled that as a young boy, he always decorated a table with flowers and played the role of priest at an altar.[83] On completion of his secondary education at the age of eighteen, he entered St Augustine's Seminary at Bay St Louis, Mississippi, which at that time was the only Roman Catholic seminary in the United States that would accept students of African descent. While there, Bowers joined the Society of the Divine Word, a Catholic missionary congregation.[84] His studies also took him to Wisconsin, and to Rome, where he was ordained, after which he went to Accra in 1940 as a missionary assigned to the Catholic mission.[85] He spent twelve years there, during which Bowers undertook the task of increasing the size of the church numerically, and in the process, he learned three of the local languages.[86] When he was appointed bishop of Accra in 1953, his consecration service was held in the United States at the Church of Our Lady of the Gulf in Bay St Louis, the town where he had trained. This event placed him "in the annals of black history in the United States" as "the first black bishop" to be ordained in that country.[87]

Although Christian and the Reverend Bowers never met in the Gold Coast, there was a brief but significant exchange of correspondence between them. A couple of months after his arrival, the Reverend Bowers heard that Christian was ill and sent him a note, in which he introduced himself and extended Easter greetings with a wish for a speedy recovery:

Dear Mr Christian

I am taking the liberty of sending you an Easter Card. Though I suppose you will not remember me, I have had the pleasure of meeting you in Dominica, and I am well acquainted with your son who is a dentist at home, and who has given me a letter of introduction to you, which, however, I have had no occasion of using since I am living here in Accra. My father and yourself are fellow countrymen and used to be roommates in the Mico Training College in Antigua. I have often heard him speak about you.

Having heard from one Mr. Hutchinson that you are not in the best of health at present, I take this opportunity of wishing you a speedy and complete recovery.

Hoping that our Divine Savior will fill you with the joy of His Resurrection this Eastertide.

Yours Sincerely
In the charity of the H.G.
Joseph O Bowers S.V.D.
Catholic Mission,
P.O. Box, Accra

March 21st 1940[88]

Bowers never received a response to his note but was informed that a letter addressed to him was found on Christian's desk after his death.[89]

Christian's letter to the Reverend Bowers poignantly described the experience of enslaved Africans during the Atlantic crossing. In addition, it articulated the reason for his migration and summarized his experience in the Gold Coast. He also offered words of encouragement to the young priest:

> 6th April 1940
> My Dear Revd. Father Bowers
> Fancy two Dominicans (and two Antiguans) both associated with the Mico College should meet in Africa. You to labour in the Masters Vineyard, I to plead on the seat of mercy as too often happens on behalf of our race and people. Truly the ways of Providence are beyond our comprehension. To think of the suffering that our people went through when being taken from Africa to the West Indies, packed as herrings in a ship which if chased by a man-of-war, and finding it was being overhauled would dump its human cargo into the sea and so when overtaken there would be none on board to prove the traffic that was being engaged in. Providence has ordained it that we the descendants of those unfortunate exiles should return to the father-land and give the benefit of our experience to the descendants of those who were responsible for the cruelty inflicted upon our ancestors.
> Little did Joseph's brethren realise what the future of their brother held in store for them. Well it is our privilege to be here. We have got a duty to perform by our fellows even though at times they may sneer at us as returned exiles – enough of this.
> Let me hope that I shall have the pleasure of seeing you either here or at your end. Meanwhile may the Great Architect of the Universe protect and help you to discharge your duty by those you are destined to enlighten.
> Sincerely yours.[90]

Bowers's involvement in the Gold Coast/Ghana is unique in terms of the length of time he served there and his impact on Catholicism in Ghana in the twentieth century. His contribution to the development of the Catholic Church there was outstanding. He was credited in 1957 with having completed the building of the Cathedral of the Holy Spirit and with founding the congregation of the Sisters of the Handmaids of the Divine Redeemer, who undertook to provide care and comfort for the poor in society. The substantial increase (300 per cent) of the Catholic population and parishes in Ghana and the growth in size of the priesthood and laity are also attributed to his "visionary and dynamic" leadership. He was also responsible for founding many schools and other training institutions as well as health facilities.[91]

Unlike Christian, Bishop Bowers did return to serve in the Caribbean and also to live in his native Dominica. In 1971, he was appointed the first bishop for the newly constituted Diocese of St John's–Basseterre in the West Indies, which comprised the islands of Antigua–Barbuda, St Kitts–Nevis, Montserrat, Anguilla and the British Virgin Islands, and he was the chief pastor in Antigua until his retirement in 1981. He subsequently returned to his home in Dominica and lived "humbly and without fanfare" in the village of Mahaut, being cared for by his sister.[92]

The indelible mark which Bowers left on Catholicism in Ghana is evidenced by the fact that he migrated there a second time in 1997, at the age of eighty-seven, on the invitation of the Congregation of Sisters of the Handmaids of the Divine Redeemer, who had kept in contact and offered to care for him in his last days. At the age of ninety, he was still serving as their spiritual director.[93] He celebrated his centenary on 28 March 2010 on the Agomanya Convent grounds, where he was still being cared for by the Handmaids of the Divine Redeemer.

Bowers's long life permitted ample opportunity for his sterling contribution to be recognized in both countries. In 2008, he received Dominica's second highest award, the Sisserou Award of Honour for meritorious service. And in 2011, Ghana's prestigious Companion of the Order of the Volta for "devoted" service was conferred on him for his service to the country. Although he was bedridden in his later years, Bishop Bowers reportedly remained mentally alert and read in order to keep abreast of events in Ghana and the world. He died in Ghana at the age of 102 on 5 November 2012 and was buried in the Holy Spirit Cathedral in Accra. At the time of his death, he was the oldest bishop in the world.[94]

Other West Indian Professionals

Although it would appear that most of the West Indians in the Gold Coast led successful lives, there were exceptions. Mr R.E. Dick was an engine fitter for the Gold Coast's Railway Department, which he joined in 1908 on a three-year agreement, which was periodically renewed.[95] Dick became ill two weeks before his death with bleeding from the gums and subsequently died after suffering a stroke.[96] Despite the fact that he had been a "confirmed officer" on the pensionable establishment, on his death he left his widow "penniless". After Dick's death, Christian demonstrated his commitment to help the West Indians and their families in the Gold Coast, although in this case, it was reinforced by the fact that Dick was also a Freemason. Christian not only drafted a letter on behalf of Dick's widow to the chief mechanical engineer of the Railway Department to request a pension and gratuity from the railway, but he also enlisted the assistance of the colonial secretary in Accra in the matter.[97] The government refused to grant a pension to Mrs Dick, and Christian continued to inquire further through "Brother Thompson" of the treasury whether there were previous cases of widows of Africans or West Indians on the list of pensionable public servants being granted a pension.[98] Christian went even further to organize a raffle of Dick's car, selling tickets to other West Indian friends and his brothers of the Gold Coast Lodge to make money to help Dick's widow.[99] She eventually returned to Barbados and later died there.[100]

Christian also assisted a Mr Riley, a West Indian who was ill and seemed to have fallen on hard times. He helped Riley to secure medical attention and find employment. Dr Beausoleil eventually hired Riley, and Christian urged Beausoleil to "inject into [Riley] some practical ideas". Riley, he felt, "was kinder to the African than to himself" and as a result was unable to secure adequate remuneration for his labour.[101]

ISSUES OF COMMUNITY, IDENTITY AND HERITAGE

The development of a sense of community seems to have been characteristic of the migration experience generally. These twentieth-century migrants to the Gold Coast were generally identified as "West Indian", and the different islands from which they originated were not usually mentioned. Lewis, who outlived his West Indian peers in the Gold Coast, noted that very few of them were accompanied by wives. They therefore married local women and seldom returned to the West Indies.[102] They participated in society, raised their families, educated their children and were fully integrated into the host society.

The West Indian community in the Gold Coast was homogeneous in the provision of services, social life and support to one another throughout the many and varied circumstances of life. The evidence suggests that they kept in touch with each other by post. The way in which advice was given to Huggins and the fact that Christian referred him to others and followed up with correspondence supports this view. When Mr C.M.G. Hoyte first moved to the Gold Coast in 1922 and wanted to establish business relationships, Christian made the necessary introductions by letter to Henry Dietrich and others.[103] When Mr and Mrs Roberts, the former employed in the Prison Department, returned to their home in British Guiana on leave, they took back with them a little boy related to Abbensetts.[104]

Christian, willingly but regrettably unsuccessfully in the long run, used his legal training and expertise to assist Dick's widow in her efforts to secure his pension.[105] When Mrs Hoyte, wife of Dr Hoyte, died in 1930, Christian reported that "the whole West Indian crowd mourned the loss".[106] Dr Busby also reported to Christian on the condition of Dr Hoyte and Lewis, when they were laid up on account of a neuralgic attack and a lorry accident respectively.[107] Years later, when C.M.G. Hoyte was awarded the Member of the Order of the British Empire, the West Indian clan, namely Dr Hoyte, R.E. Phipps, C.E.M. Abbensetts, Drs Auguste and Busby, R.E. Riley and Christian, hosted him at Koforidua and celebrated his achievement.[108]

Christian maintained his friendship with Maurice D. Reece, the Trinidadian who retired to England, and they kept in contact. On Reece's retirement from government service in the Gold Coast in 1924, Christian requested a favour of L.A. Smart in England to assist Reece, whom he considered "a worthy and deserving brother", to secure another appointment.[109] In 1939, Reece wrote to Christian when he read the news that Christian's son Howard had been called to the Bar. He enclosed the clipping of the article, offered congratulations on Howard's success and expressed the hope that as a good son, he would brighten his father's "autumn days".[110]

Christian played a major role in the creation of a West Indian community in the Gold Coast and organized periodic gatherings of his compatriots. During the Christmas and Easter holidays, Dominica House was the venue for many annual gatherings of the West Indian community in Sekondi and the surrounding areas. Christian himself reported to his son Peter on one reunion, that "on New Year's Day the West Indian clan gathers at Dominica House and brings joy and happy recollections of home and distant ones".[111] Those who couldn't fit in Dominica House were accommodated at "[a] beautiful bungalow on the farm" situated between Sekondi and Takoradi.[112]

Lewis, who attended an Old Year's Night gathering in 1931, also reported that other members of the West Indian community hosted similar get-togethers at other holiday periods. For example, Lewis reported that the Guyanese lawyer Abbensetts, who also lived in Sekondi, had the gathering at his house for lunch on New Year's Day. He also gave details of another occasion at Easter, during which the group of West Indians met in the Eastern Province, instead of at Sekondi in the west. As Lewis described it: "They first put up with Dr Hoyte at Nsawam where we all gathered on Good Friday for lunch. Then the following day, they proceeded to Tafo and were the guests of Mr Francois, Dr Beausoleil at Tafo, and Dr Auguste at Korforidua. On Easter Monday we might go out for an outing. I recall once an outing to Aburi and indeed we had a jolly time."[113] Lewis was of the view that these get-togethers did much to knit the small group of West Indians together.[114] Christian kept up this tradition to the end of his life.[115]

Lewis, who spent a brief holiday with Christian at Dominica House in 1934, provided an insight into the life of Christian, this larger-than-life West Indian in the Gold Coast who was well known for his hospitality and whose home was the venue for much social activity. Lewis's observations summarize well the fact that Christian was someone whose personal and private life exuded order and success.

> He was a very well ordered man. He rose early, went for a stroll and on his return had a bath and dressed, breakfasted and went to court. On return from court, if there were no business or legal callers, he would go to his office and do some work before lunch. After lunch he had a siesta, but was again in his office dictating letters from about four o'clock. Around sunset he would go to the billiard room, have a game or two of billiards and then have dinner. After dinner [he would] return to the billiard room for a chat and turned in early – by nine o'clock he had gone to rest – maybe to read before actually retiring.[116]

A visitor to the home, Dr M.C.F. Easmon of Sierra Leone, mentioned happy recollections of his brief stay at Sekondi and in particular the hospitality enjoyed at Christian's home, which included a game of billiards.[117] Rosamund Quist, a close family friend, confirmed that there were many overseas visitors, dinners, concerts and other social gatherings at Dominica House. She remembered Christian, who was known as "GJ" to his friends, as someone who was "bright, jovial, likeable and sociable".[118]

The evidence indicates that the West Indians in the Gold Coast kept in touch with their relatives and friends in the islands. Both Christian and Francois had left children in the West Indies. As was discussed earlier, Christian corresponded with his West Indian family and took responsibility for educating his three West Indian children and his nieces. Francois also had a daughter in St Lucia and supported his family there.[119] In his letters to his son Peter, Christian consistently sent messages and affectionate wishes to a close friend, Constance Lockhart, with whom he maintained contact.[120] Relatives and friends in the West Indies also recognized that Christian had prospered and looked to him for assistance. They sent requests either directly or through friends and relatives who corresponded with him.[121] In his communication with relatives and friends in Dominica, Antigua and the surrounding islands, Christian generally reminisced, kept in touch and sent money and gifts. In this way, he demonstrated that he continued to value his West Indian upbringing and heritage.[122]

There seems to have been a correlation between one's family situation and the likelihood of return to the West Indies, and few of the migrants resettled in the West Indies. The Callenders from Barbados and the Murrells from British Guiana were two West Indian couples among the group of professionals in the Gold Coast. As was mentioned, the Callenders did return to Barbados with a child they had adopted. Dr Murrell died in Accra in 1939 while still in active service, and his wife remained in the Gold Coast. C.M.G. Hoyte went to the Gold Coast without his wife and his children, but they never joined him. His children were educated in England. He did have a second family in the Gold Coast, and he remained there. His brother, Dr Ralph Hoyte Sr, who initially went to the Gold Coast alone, returned to the West Indies three years later and brought back his wife and three children. The children were then sent to England for their education. His wife died six years later, and he remarried a Nigerian of Brazilian descent named Ribeiro, with whom he had two more children, who were raised in the Gold Coast. He indicated that he could not return to a small island after he had lived in a large country such as the Gold Coast, and he spent the remainder of his life there. However, his wish that his remains should be returned to his native Trinidad was carried out by his son after his death.¹²³ Dr Busby married one of Christian's daughters. Generally the children of the migrants were educated in England and returned to the Gold Coast/Ghana as trained professionals, thus perpetuating the contribution of West Indians to that society.

It is evident that the West Indians were eager to maintain their identity and to leave a reminder of their presence on the host society which had become their home. Abbensetts's law firm in the Gold Coast was named Berbice Chambers after a well-known river in Guyana. As was mentioned earlier, Christian's home in Sekondi, Dominica House, was a constant recollection of his West Indian heritage.¹²⁴ Similarly, two of the properties that Christian acquired in Dominica, named "Sekondi House" and "Secondom House" respectively,¹²⁵ were obvious tributes to the relative who had migrated to the Gold Coast. Interestingly, too, when the Callenders returned to Barbados, they named their home in Marchfield, St Philip, "Kumasi Cot", in celebration of their sojourn in the Ashanti region of the Gold Coast.¹²⁶

Christian received many expressions of condolence and support from the West Indian community on the death of his daughter Maude and sought advice from his friends and others on how to perpetuate her memory. Dr Hoyte strongly suggested that any memorial to her should make reference to her life's profession, which was midwifery, and proposed that a furnished ward in the Maternity and Child Welfare Department in her honour would be appropriate and at the same time useful.¹²⁷ Christian did act on Hoyte's recommendation and wrote to both Dr Duff of the Medical Department in Accra and Dr Clarke, director of the British Red Cross Society.¹²⁸ Maude Mary Christian's contribution to the Gold Coast community is memorialized in a wall plaque in the Effia Nkwanta Hospital in Sekondi, Ghana. The inscription, which also serves as a reminder of her West Indian heritage, reads as follows: "Maude Mary Christian Memorial. These rooms were furnished to perpetuate the memory of Maude Mary Christian, a midwife and native of Dominica, British West Indies and a benefactor to this institution. Born 24-12-1899; Died 28-6-1933."¹²⁹

Generally Christian and the other West Indians participated actively in life in the Gold Coast. Four West Indians were among the sixty-plus people listed as members of the Accra Turf Club in 1938: Dr E.L. Auguste¹³⁰ (1935); Dr G.A. Busby (1930); G.J. Christian (1927); Dr R.A. Hoyte (1925). As mentioned earlier, Christian was also responsible for the formation of the St George's Lodge,

Sekondi, No. 3851, in 1918, and he encouraged the spread of Freemasonry in Kumasi and Cape Coast in 1921.[131] Clarence E.M. Abbensetts and Robert Ebenezer Dick were also initiated into the Sekondi Lodge. Both Christian and Abbensetts served in leadership roles.[132]

There is some evidence, however, to suggest that despite their professional success and their participation in society, the West Indians in the Gold Coast, being of African descent, were not accepted as social equals in the country by the white colonials. A 1906 letter to the press "by a native resident" commented on the fact that "no native or coloured person" had been invited to participate in the activities surrounding the visit of the acting governor to the town of Sekondi. The newspaper correspondent cited "Christian, Leung, Ribeiro" as being "fit and proper" and noted that there "was absolutely nothing against these gentlemen except their colour".[133] Years later, Christian commented that praiseworthy achievements of West Indians were never reported in the press, because they were "so unpopular".[134]

This was obviously a matter about which he felt strongly. Christian had made several attempts to have his son Peter, who had trained as a dentist in the United States, join him in the Gold Coast. This never materialized, mainly because Peter's US qualifications were not recognized there. In 1934, he confessed that after being in the Gold Coast for more than thirty years and with his sister and other near relatives in Dominica all dead, he was hesitant to encourage Peter to leave home and join him in the Gold Coast. He felt that Peter should not be "lost to our dear Island home" and become, like his father, "an exile in Africa" who sometimes felt that he was an unwelcome stranger.[135] He certainly did not want "all the Christians to be in Africa where one is perpetually looked upon as a stranger".[136]

CHRISTIAN'S ILLNESS, DEATH AND ACCOLADES

Christian's accomplishments are even more outstanding when considered in light of the fact that he was plagued with ill health throughout his adult life. As early as 1899, while in his early thirties and shortly after his arrival in London, he recorded certain ailments – a fresh cold, painful boil over his left eye, constipation, influenza and fever.[137] In the Gold Coast, he was plagued mainly with bouts of rheumatism that occasionally laid him up for lengthy periods and at times with other disorders such as malarial fever and gastric indigestion. He was treated there mainly by his friend and fellow West Indian Dr Beausoleil.

During one of his periodic visits to London, in 1922, Christian was unwell for "nearly a month". The diagnosis was "gout and rheumatic fever". He could scarcely use his right arm, and the joint at his shoulder was almost fixed. On that occasion, he seriously considered a suggestion that he should go to Germany for treatment.[138] In the course of his return journey to the Gold Coast, his condition flared up, and he attributed it to possible overexertion on the London-to-Liverpool leg of the journey. His "ankle and knee again re-asserted themselves", and when he arrived in Sierra Leone, he was forced to remain in his cabin. He felt that the warm weather was a contributor to his recovery, but he requested his friend L.A. Smart to follow up on a prescription with the doctor.[139] Smart, in his response, impressed upon Christian that he had been seriously ill and that his life was undoubtedly saved because he had sought attention "in Devonshire Street", which "considerably lengthened [his] life", although it "probably shortened" his bank account.[140]

Christian reported to another friend on this episode that he had been "laid up in a nursing home in London for twelve weeks" and eventually sailed from London in January, but it was some months before he was physically on his feet. In March 1923, he was being treated by Dr Calder, who had travelled with him on the same steamer. He said that "the heart and water" were all right but was in doubt as to the cause of the swelling. He had prescribed a French preparation, Urodonal. Christian did not know whether the swelling of the ankles was due to the after-effects of the injections or Bright's disease from bad kidneys. He felt that doctors made "such a mystery of these things".[142]

Christian continued to use various medications and treatments, with uncertain results. In 1925, for example, he ordered from Curtis, Campbell and Company two dozen bottles of Urodonal, an item which he described as being urgently required.[143] A year later, one of his doctors recommended a new medicine for rheumatism, Atophan, which was available in London, and he asked his son Peter to arrange for the purchase of two or three bottles so that he could try it.[144] In 1926, he planned to go to Europe in the summer "to take the waters at Vichy in France".[145] One of his business partners noted that this trip to Europe had made no positive impact on Christian's health and that it did not augur well for the continuance of his involvement in the cocoa business.[146] In 1927, he experimented with an "embrocation or ointment" as a treatment on his knee, but it did not ease the pain,[147] and the rheumatism persisted.[148]

In 1928, he took a further drastic step, which proved to be ineffective. He "sacrificed all [his] teeth . . . in the hope of shaking off the enemy forever". However, a year later his right shoulder and the joints in the right hand were still painful, and he requested treatment from Dr Beausoleil.[149] He attributed his attacks of rheumatism, which confined him to the house and kept him away from business, to the "very bad" rainy season.[150] His temporary dentures were not satisfactory, although he hoped to consult with another dentist to rectify this.[151] In 1931, he was fitted with a complete set of dentures. Initially he suffered a great deal, as they felt like a "mouth full", but after a while, they were acceptable.[152]

Christian's friend Vivian Harris, a medical student, shared verbatim the medical opinion of "the rising surgeon" of the day, Affleck Greeves, on the subject of teeth extraction: "Gentlemen, in my view and that of an increasing number of intelligent surgeons, the recently fashionable practise of dragging out a man's perfectly good teeth on any excuse or none, as a panacea for anything from diphtheria and small pox to arthritis, the habit, I say, gentlemen, is dangerously testicular."[153] Harris empathized with Christian on the fact that he was "still being troubled by the enemy". Christian agreed with Harris that "those people who drag out a man's perfectly good teeth are fools and ought to be prosecuted". He conceded that he had derived no benefit from such a course of action, and instead he was greatly inconvenienced.[154]

In the latter part of 1929, Christian spent some time with Dr Beausoleil at Tafo, and the treatment he received for his arthritis brought some relief. He reported to Francois that his joints were easier, and he anticipated further relief when he began "the douche treatment". He asked Francois to remind Beausoleil to order another supply of the gonococcal vaccine, which, together with prostatic massage and irrigation, seemed to agree with him. He wrote that he could not remain longer with Beausoleil, even though he was not certain that the government doctor at Sekondi would continue the treatment.[155]

It would seem, however, that with the arthritis under control, other ailments showed up. In February 1930, Christian was troubled with periodic fever and headache. Dr Beausoleil made a diagnosis of "malaria and migraine" as the basic trouble. He sent Christian a letter with a prescription for a few capsules of quinine and phenozonum "to charm it away" and, in the event that he needed medication, to relieve the symptoms.[156] A month later, Christian developed earache that hindered his massage treatments.[157]

Christian continued to be plagued with his rheumatic condition, however, which sometimes prevented his attendance at Legislative Council meetings for lengthy periods. In 1931, he wrote to the colonial secretary to request a leave of absence and was granted permission to be away from council meetings for four months, on the grounds that he had been ordered to go away for a change on account of his health.[158] Three years later, he recorded his inability to attend the meeting of Council of 23 November 1934 due to the fact that he was suffering from an attack of rheumatism.[159] This bout seemingly persisted so much that in December 1934, Christian was still "not feeling well" from rheumatism and proposed to "leave Sekondi for the interior" to be treated by one of his "West Indian doctor friends" who lived at Tafo.[160] In April 1935, he happily reported to his son Peter that he was much better and able to walk about the house freely and hoped soon to be able to go out.[161]

Throughout his 1935 summer vacation, Christian was once again very ill in England from the end of June to mid-September.[162] This rheumatic attack had been preceded by a bout of malarial fever.[163] During his stay, he was laid up in the Great Western Hotel in Paddington,[164] and throughout the return voyage, he was suffering so much that he landed on a stretcher.[165] Fortunately his son Peter accompanied him on the voyage in order to look after him.[166] After his arrival in the Gold Coast, he continued to be confined to bed owing to his inability to move about.[167] Three weeks after his return from England, however, the pain decreased and his mobility returned.[168]

Following this bout of his illness, Dr Beausoleil, in consultation with a colleague in England who had studied Christian's case, kept him at Tafo in November 1935, where he underwent a trial of special injections for his rheumatoid arthritis.[169] After one injection, however, there may have been a flare-up of the old complaint on its own, or a reaction to the injection.[170] By 30 December 1935, Christian was back in bed with a sprained ankle along with the rheumatism. He remained at Tafo, where he continued to receive medical treatment,[171] and almost a month later, he was still unable to walk. Dr Beausoleil refused to discharge him until he was in good health.[172]

Eventually, in February 1936, Christian was in recovery from this attack of rheumatoid arthritis. In reports to his friends and family overseas about this episode, Christian related that it was a severe attack that had kept him in bed a long time, and he had suffered terribly. The "gold cerium" with which he had been injected "did not prove satisfactory", and he had suffered a relapse.[173]

Mami Abba had nursed him night and day under the instructions of Dr Beausoleil.[174] He eventually returned home in February, feeling better to the extent that he could walk about in the bedroom, although he still experienced some pain in his knees.[175] He anticipated that he would be completely pain-free within a month's time.[176] By June, apart from residual pain in his left knee, his health was considerably improved, and he looked forward to a game of billiards.[177] At this point, he acknowledged to one of his friends that good health was the best asset to possess.[178]

The "see-saw" existence with his arthritic condition and other ailments persisted throughout the remainder of the 1930s. Early in 1937, he reported that at nights, he had to wear light woollen bedsocks stretched to his knees.[179] In 1938, he had a nasty cold, a touch of lumbago with pains at the elbow and he felt "very rotten".[180] In 1939, he wanted an instrument to massage his joints and sought the medical knowledge of Josephine's husband, Dr Armah.[181] He concluded that an attack in his right shoulder, from which he had recovered, was caused by the "rum punch and champagne" he had consumed at the farewell party for Judge Barton. He had also noted that in Dr Beausoleil's absence, he was treated by another doctor, who felt his condition was gout rather than arthritis. After Christian received no relief from the two bottles of medication prescribed, the doctor conceded that it might be arthritis, and not gout as he had first thought.

Thereafter, Christian was no longer willing to take anything without the approval of Dr Beausoleil and Dr Dudley Stone of Harley Street, both of whom had treated him for years.[182] In July 1939, he was so ill for two days after an overdose of cascara that he had to get a colleague to handle his cases for him.[183] The following month, after being bedridden with a bout of arthritis which followed "a chill" he had caught, Christian compared arthritis to Hitler in that "it listens to no one and resents being interfered with". On this occasion, he concluded that he had to confine himself with "copious draughts of vichy water instead of a jolly good whiskey and soda".[184] Towards the end of 1939, he again spent seven weeks in Tafo under treatment for arthritis and reported that he was feeling much better except for slight pains in the toes.[185]

M.D. Reece's letter to Christian in December 1939 expressed concerns about his health and suggested a local remedy which would not "interfere with any doctor's medicine – a small quantity of yeast in a cup of milk" and also Elasto for the rheumatic attack.[186] Christian's response a month later was optimistic but cautious: he was "still suffering from gastric indigestion and arthritis, but ... getting over same slowly". He was afraid to try anything without consulting his doctor, due to the fact that the attack came on so easily.[187]

The 1939/40 Christmas holiday season was pleasant for Christian, although at the start of 1940, once again, he was not in the best of health. Apart from Dr Beausoleil, the other West Indian friends did not turn up for the New Year holiday gathering, which was fortunate, as Christian conceded that he was not well enough to entertain them.[188] In the ensuing days, he wrote several letters to his children, grandchildren and associates, in which the state of his health was documented. He complained about pain between the pylorus and pelvis near the front left abdomen, insomnia and loss of appetite.[189]

As January 1940 progressed, Christian reported to his friend Reece on attacks of arthritis, which were easily triggered during that time.[190] He kept in touch with Dr Beausoleil and reported that he had repeated his prescription, as his stomach wanted attention.[191] He also wrote to Mrs Leung about his gastric indigestion caused "by eating slices of oranges and smoking immediately", which resulted in stomach pain and severe loss of weight and appetite.[192] A few days later, he confined himself to porridge and milk for breakfast, barley or vermicelli soup for lunch, and Ovaltine or toast for dinner. He also took a slice of bread with coffee at six in the morning but had no oranges, and neither did he smoke.[193]

At times, Christian tended to be optimistic about his recovery. In February, he told his granddaughter Barbara Gordon that he was happy that his health was much improved, and he hoped to return to work, having been absent since the summer.[194] He also reported to his doctor that he was holding his own against the enemy and anticipated his attendance at the Legislative Council meeting in Accra the next month.[195]

In 1939, when Christian was seventy, he expressed the hope that his life would be spared until Howard's return.[196] Two years earlier, he had noted that "in the tropics", people did not usually live beyond that age.[197] With the passage of time and the effects of his prolonged illness on his activities and responsibilities, however, he expressed covertly concerns about his own mortality. For example, when his children returned to school after the Christmas holiday in January 1940, he commented that the parting was sad, especially as he was unwell.[198]

At that same time, Christian seemed to be acutely conscious of the economic effects of his ill health. He commented on his inability to attend court and admitted to another friend that were it not for the rent he received from his properties, he would have been "very much inconvenienced".[199] He also gave consideration to one of his properties in Dominica, which was being looked after by Laura Lecointe, and felt it was necessary to take action. He discussed it with Peter and pointed out that the property had not been "given away", and it was his wish that it should remain in the family and be of benefit to them.[200] Christian therefore wrote to Laura Lecointe with reference to the "uncertain" nature of life and their "advancing in years" and instructed her to hand over the responsibility for the land at Place-a-Will to his son Peter. He reasoned that owing to economic difficulties in Dominica and Bermuda, and his lengthy illness, it was "only fair" that his son and family should receive whatever benefit could be got from the land. She could continue "to look after the house at Coulibistrie".[201] In early March, shortly after his seventy-first birthday, he lamented the fact that his persistent illness had reduced his income-earning ability, "with the result that finance is low". He hoped to regain his health, especially as he still had "obligations" to "children and three grandchildren in England".[202]

DEATH OF GEORGE JAMES CHRISTIAN

In late March 1940, Dr Beausoleil's diagnosis of Christian's state of health was cause for concern. He had examined him at Tafo and confirmed that Christian's condition had deteriorated. He advised him that his heart was weakened and did not have "the vitality and resilience of youth". He had explained that in order to conserve his failing strength, Christian needed to "go slow".[203]

In Dr Beausoleil's words to Howard three weeks later, Christian's death "took place with dramatic suddenness". He described Christian's last hours and noted:

> It is curious that that very morning he had just written in a letter that he had never felt better during the last nine months and he was about going [*sic*] to court on behalf of a client for the first time for all those months. That letter remained unposted and was handed to me the next morning. . . . It appears that he was seated in a chair, interviewing . . . the surveyor, when he collapsed with a seizure

at 9 a.m. Two Sekondi doctors, Dr. John . . . who was in charge of the Sekondi Hospital . . . and Dr. Chilpps, a young African doctor . . . [came to attend to him]. I believe they did all that was possible to do to save his life. He collapsed at 9 a.m. and lingered till 7 p.m. never regaining consciousness to the end. I arrived on the scene from Tafo just a few minutes too late to help my old friend.[204]

Christian died at his residence, Dominica House, Poassi Road, Sekondi, on 17 April 1940. The interment ceremony commenced with a brief service the next day, 18 April, at St Andrew's Anglican Church at 3:30 p.m.[205] and then on to the European Cemetery at Shama Road.[206] He was buried alongside his daughter Maude, and an identical tombstone was ordered for his grave.[207] The "final obsequies" a month later took the form of "wake-keeping" on 17 May 1940, from 8 p.m. to midnight, and a thanksgiving service at St Andrew's Church on 19 May 1940, at 9 a.m.[208]

On the anniversary of Christian's birthday in 1943, Howard reported to Essi that Mami Abba was still mourning the loss, as the customary three-year period had not yet come to an end.[209] Mami Abba died on 2 January 1964.[210]

ACCOLADES

The tributes from Christian's colleagues in the Legislative Council truthfully summarize his life of service and his outstanding contribution to Gold Coast society.

> COLONIAL SECRETARY: Your Excellency, I rise to move that this Council expresses its profound regret at the death of the Honourable George James Christian, and its sense of the loss sustained thereby by this Colony. In particular this Council desires to record its appreciation of the services rendered by Mr. Christian as a member of this Council for nearly ten years. Lastly all members of this Council desire to offer their deep sympathy to Mr. Christian's relatives in their bereavement.
>
> George Christian was born in 1869 in the West Indian island of Dominica. He was educated in Antigua and began his career as a schoolmaster in the Government Service of his native island.
>
> Forsaking this field in favour of the profession of the law . . . he went to England in 1899 and entered Gray's Inn. After being called to the Bar in 1902 he came to Cape Coast where he set up a legal practice and entered upon his long and honourable connection of 38 years with this Colony.

Shortly afterwards he moved to Sekondi which he made his permanent home. Here he enjoyed a large practice and quickly established an enviable reputation at the Bar, becoming in due course the legal luminary of the Western Province and one of its most outstanding figures.

Though a busy man he found time to take a deep interest in public affairs, and he served two terms as an unofficial member of the Sekondi Town Council. At a later stage, he widened the sphere of his activities and stood as a candidate for this Council, to which he was elected as Municipal Member for Sekondi in 1930. He was re-elected twice and served continuously as a Legislative Councillor until his death, last April, at the ripe age of 71.

No one who had the privilege of listening to Mr Christian, in Council or elsewhere, could fail to observe the keen enthusiasm, the conviction and the deep sincerity that marked all his public work. In private life Mr. Christian was the soul of kindness and hospitality; his good deeds and generosity were proverbial, while his great charm of manner, his ready wit and dry humour endeared him to all who knew him.

By his passing, the Gold Coast lost a striking character, Sekondi a notable citizen, and we a wise and experienced Councillor. Yet great though our loss is, those who were nearer to him by ties of blood and relationship have suffered a still more grievous and poignant loss. To his family, this Council – in all sincerity and with deep sympathy – desires to convey its condolences.

Sir I beg to move the resolution.

MR. KORSAH: Your Excellency, in seconding this motion, I take this opportunity to place on record how deeply the whole community outside this Council mourn the sad loss of our late lamented member. Ever since the late Mr. Christian arrived in this country he identified himself with the people of this country. He shared in our sorrows and rejoiced with us. He had taken part in all matters affecting the development of this country politically, socially and economically. Mr. Christian was interested in the education of this country not only in the Western Province where he lived but also in the whole of the Colony. He had travelled far and wide to support any cause which he thought would assist in the development of the country. He would long be remembered for his outspoken speeches in this Council. One man said to me: "He was a trenchant but constructive critic."

In his private practice as a barrister, Mr. Christian acted with promptitude and consideration for all his clients; he felt it was his duty to do his best for all those who consulted him on legal matters. In Court he always presented the case of his clients fairly, honestly and conscientiously. Whether in public or private life Mr. Christian's sense of duty was so high that he never spared any effort he believed would enable him to discharge his duty to the community at large, or to achieve for his clients what he believed was their just due. He felt that sense of duty so keenly that, as some members now know, he actually collapsed when he was getting ready to go to Court. He knew he was not well but felt that his clients' duty must be discharged. And although he had had a warning, he got up in the morning and actually prepared to leave for Court when he collapsed. Mr Christian died in harness and I am sure that those of us who live after him will copy his example. Mr. Christian was a staunch friend of the majority of Chiefs of the Western Province and they had always found in him a stalwart supporter in all their laudable undertakings. The Chiefs of the Western Province will be able to give better evidence of that, if necessary. I am sure that those of us who live after him will ever remember his life of sacrifice and copy all the good characteristics which he exhibited whilst he was alive.[211]

Another business colleague wrote the following letter to the colonial secretary:

It is with extreme satisfaction that one heard the message of His Excellency the Governor on the local radio in his eulogy of the late George Christian, Esq., barrister-at-law and member of the Legislative Council.

As H.E. remarked . . . the loss of Mr. Christian is well nigh irretrievable.

As Mr. Justice Doorly said from the bench last week, the strange part was that Mr. Christian, although neither European nor African, entered in to the life of both, with such commanding success and understanding.

To me who had known Mr. Christian for the past 27 years, it was always apparent that this indeed was the strength and genius of his character, that of being able to understand both the African and the European so well.

Christian will be remembered by the Africans in Sekondi for many a year and there are many Europeans now scattered elsewhere who have good cause to remember him with gratitude. Men, whose own colour turned on them in time of distress, yet Christian helped them. To my mind, here is a splendid opportunity for government to assist and do the right thing.

The opportunity occurs to commemorate his memory and I would suggest that Government release, for the purpose of a public park, the plot of ground adjacent to the Sekondi High Court and opposite Christian house, so that the Sekondi people could find a pleasant oasis in a rather crowded area.

. . . I would suggest that the park contain seats made in ferro-concrete in the same way as the French colonies in public places. A small band stand might even be put in so that on occasions music might be given.

I feel that this would be a very satisfactory manner in which to commemorate

Mr. Christian's memory amongst the people he loved and those who had such affection for him.²¹²

GEORGE JAMES CHRISTIAN: RETURNED EXILE

Generally, the unveiling of the lives of Christian and these migrants, who successfully went back to Africa and may be considered as heroes in the Caribbean, is of importance in these emerging societies for identity, heritage and nation-building. Gordon Rohlehr defined "a sense of heritage" as "the shadow and substance of passing and current lifestyles, as well as the inter-linkages between them".²¹³ In other words, it is the traditions people live by – their activities and attitudes, values and viewpoints, symbolic expressions of culture, their legacy, everything that will be handed down from them through the generations, both tangible and intangible.

This expression of heritage was generally applicable to the experience of the West Indians who made the Gold Coast their home. Indeed, the fact that the personal histories of Christian, Bowers, the Hoytes and the other West Indians discussed in this chapter can be interrogated is a direct result of Christian's "sense of heritage". This was expressed in his clear understanding that it was important and imperative to document his experience and to pass on the information to the next generation, who subsequently ensured that his papers were preserved and made available for research and scholarship.²¹⁴ As a group, the migrants might be considered West Indian patriots on account of their identification with one another, the activities and values which they continued to practise, their symbolic acts to remind themselves of their homeland and other expressions of their West Indian heritage.

Christian himself is unique and complex. He clearly had pan-Africanist leanings, as he had been involved with the early adherents of the movement and attended the first conference in London in 1900. He was also knowledgeable about Africa and fulfilled his desire to make his home there. As someone who achieved fame in another part of the world, where his accomplishments brought attention to his native Dominica, George James Christian and similarly Bishop Joseph O. Bowers, as a result of their experiences, meet the criteria articulated in 1990 by Dame Eugenia Charles, former Prime Minister, for helping to build Dominica's reputation as a proud and hard-working people and making a contribution to its nationhood.[215]

Christian had accomplished what he set out to do when he decided to make his home in the Gold Coast. He considered it a privilege to have had the opportunity to return to the homeland of his African ancestors and make a contribution there. In many ways, his transition from his island home in the Caribbean to the African continent was seamless. He persevered despite chronic illness and other challenges and lived a full life in every respect. He had an outstanding legal career and extended himself beyond the confines of his profession to make a formidable and lasting impact on the wider society in many and varied spheres of activity. He played a leadership role and was a person of influence among his West Indian peers. He also went to great lengths to ensure that he left progeny who would continue his legacy of professionalism and devoted service to the society. At the same time, he maintained his relationships with his family and friends in Dominica and the Caribbean.

As has been shown here, however, the fact that Christian fulfilled his dream to return to Africa and make a contribution to society there did not mean that he was impervious to the manner in which West Indians in the Gold Coast were viewed. In his April 1940 letter to the Reverend Bowers, Christian compared common elements of the experience of their West Indian forebears, whom he described as "descendants of those unfortunate exiles", with those of his own life in the Gold Coast. In the final analysis, he was of the view that his return to Africa was an act of divine providence, and throughout his thirty-eight years of service there, he was motivated by a sense of destiny and duty in all that he did. He was not deterred by the fact that the involvement and impact of West Indians were generally not received with approval or admiration by the host society.[216] Indeed, the inscription on his tombstone, "In ever loving memory of George James Christian of Roseau, Dominica, British West Indies, Barrister-at-Law, who died at Sekondi, April 17, 1940", was Christian's final public acknowledgement of his identification with his West Indian homeland. His life in the Gold Coast was characterized by absolute dedication and service, without any rancour or self-absorption, but with a deeply felt understanding that he was indeed a "returned exile" in Africa.

Figure 8.1. George Francois, formerly of St Lucia, and his family. *Reproduced with permission of the Francois family of Accra, Ghana.*

Figure 8.2. George Stanley Lewis, formerly of St Lucia, Accra, Ghana, 1994. *Photograph by Estelle M. Appiah.*

Figure 8.3. George James Christian

Figure 8.4. Graves of Maude Mary Christian and George James Christian, European Cemetery, Sekondi. *Photograph by Margaret D. Rouse-Jones.*

APPENDIX 1

List of Oral History Interviews Related to George James Christian

Appiah, Estelle. Interview with Margaret D. Rouse-Jones, London, England, 9 July 1991. Estelle Appiah, barrister-at-law, is the daughter of Essi Forster and the granddaughter of George James Christian.

Bowers, SVD, Bishop Joseph Oliver. Interview with Margaret D. Rouse-Jones, Roseau, Dominica, 6 August 1993. Bishop Bowers went to the Gold Coast in 1940, shortly before George James Christian died. Bowers's father and Christian were roommates at the Mico Institution in Antigua.

Burke, Chrissie. Interview with Elizabeth Felix, Roseau, Dominica, August 1992.

———. Interview with Margaret D. Rouse-Jones, Roseau, Dominica, 5 August 1993. Chrissie Burke was over eighty-six and blind at the time of the interview. She was a niece of George James Christian.

Busby, Sarah H. Interviews with Margaret Busby, Abidjan, Ivory Coast, 9 March 1978, and in London, England, 14 April 1989. Sarah Busby, nurse and midwife, was the daughter of George James Christian. She married Dr George Busby of Trinidad, who had migrated to the Gold Coast at the invitation of Dr Ralph Hoyte Sr.

Chinbuah, A.B. Interview with Margaret D. Rouse-Jones, Tema, Ghana, 9 August 2007. A.B. Chinbuah, barrister-at-law, also conducts historical research for his series of newspaper articles on Ghanaian personalities.

Christian, Ferdinand Francisco. Interview with Estelle Appiah, Accra, Ghana, 19 April 1992. Dr Ferdinand Christian was the son of George James Christian, the third of the four children he had with Abba Lucy French.

Christian, Grace. Interview with Margaret D. Rouse-Jones, Accra, Ghana, 8 August 2007. Grace Christian, widow of Ferdinand Christian, was the daughter-in-law of George James Christian.

Christian, Mary (May) Eudora. Interview with Margaret D. Rouse-Jones, Roseau, Dominica, 5 August 1993. May Christian, retired teacher, was the niece of George James Christian.

Forster, Essi Matilda. Interview with Estelle Appiah, Accra, Ghana, 13 June 1992. Essi Matilda Forster was the daughter of George James Christian. She was the first woman to be called to the Ghana Bar and served for many years as the legal adviser to Mobil Oil.

Francois, Edward. Interview with Margaret D. Rouse-Jones, Accra, Ghana, 14 August 2007. Edward Francois was the son of George James Francois who came originally from St Lucia. George Francois was an associate of George James Christian.

Hoyte, Dr Ralph Jr. Interview with Margaret D. Rouse-Jones and Estelle M. Appiah, Port of Spain, Trinidad and Tobago, 28 June 2005. Dr Ralph Allen Hoyte Jr, a doctor, served briefly in the Gold Coast alongside his father, who was a contemporary of George James Christian.

Lewis, George Stanley. Interview with Estelle Appiah, Accra, Ghana, 24 June 1992. George Stanley Lewis, one of the celebrated Lewis brothers from St Lucia, went to the Gold Coast in 1929 and was involved in the cocoa-exporting industry. He became a personal friend of George James Christian.

Quist, Rosamund. Interview with Margaret D. Rouse-Jones, Accra, Ghana, 21 May 1994. Mrs Rosamund Quist, age eighty at the time of the interview, was the daughter of a Scottish businessman who was an associate of George James Christian. She knew the family well.

Sam, Netelka. Interview with Estelle Appiah, Accra, Ghana, 5 May 1992. Netelka Sam was eighty-three years of age at the time of the interview. She was the daughter of George Henry Packwood, an Englishman. Her mother was from Somanya. When her father died, George Christian took her to live with his family and took care of her until she got married and left his home.

APPENDIX 2

Published Articles and Conference and Lecture Presentations on George James Christian

2012

Margaret D. Rouse-Jones. "Of Heroes and Heritage: The Contribution of George James Christian of Dominica to the Social, Political, and Legal Landscape of the Gold Coast (Ghana), c. 1900–1940". Seventh annual Dame Eugenia Charles Distinguished Lecture, organized by the University of the West Indies, Open Campus, and Fort Young Hotel. Fort Young Hotel, Roseau, Dominica, 29 November 2012.

Margaret D. Rouse-Jones. "History at the Personal Level: Tesserae in the Mosaic of Caribbean Social History". *Caribbean Quarterly: A Journal of Caribbean Culture* 58, no. 1 (March 2012): 65–86. This essay is an adaptation of the second Kenneth E. Ingram Memorial Lecture delivered at the University of the West Indies, Mona, Jamaica, 3 March 2011.

Margaret D. Rouse-Jones and Estelle M. Appiah. "West Indian Patriot in West Africa: A Study of George James Christian of Dominica and the Gold Coast". In *Caribbean Heritage*, edited by Basil A. Reid, 195–206. Kingston: University of the West Indies Press and the Reed Foundation, 2012.

Margaret D. Rouse-Jones and Estelle M. Appiah. "West Indian Returnees and Their Communities: Examples from the Gold Coast in the Nineteenth and Twentieth Centuries". In *Back to Africa*, volume 2, *The Ideology and Practice of the African Returnee Phenomenon from the Caribbean and North-America to Africa,* edited by Kwesi Kwaa Prah, 380–406. Cape Town: Centre for Advanced Studies of African Society, 2012.

2010

Margaret D. Rouse-Jones and Estelle M. Appiah. "West Indian Returnees and Their Communities: Examples from the Gold Coast". Paper presented to the workshop Back to Africa: African-American and West Indian Returnees and Their Communities (18th–21st Century), organized by the Centre for Advanced Studies of African Society (CASAS). Johannesburg, South Africa, 15–16 November 2010.

2007–2008

Margaret D. Rouse-Jones. "Unveiling Hidden Treasures: An Exploration of our Caribbean Heritage Materials". Inaugural professorial lecture, University of the West Indies, St Augustine, Trinidad and Tobago, 29 November 2007. Also delivered at the University of the West Indies, Mona, Jamaica, 23 January 2008 and Cave Hill, Barbados, 22 May 2008.

2007

Margaret D. Rouse-Jones and Estelle Appiah. "West Indian Patriot in West Africa: A Case Study of George James Christian of Dominica and the Gold Coast". Panel theme: Pan-Africanism as Lived Experience. Paper presented to the Fourth Conference of the Association for the Study of the Worldwide African Diaspora in commemoration of the bicentennial of the British and American abolition of the transatlantic slave trade. Conference theme: Interrogations of Freedom: Memories, Meanings, Migrations. Hosted by the University of the West Indies, Cave Hill, Barbados, with co-sponsorship from New York University, 9–12 October 2007.

Margaret D. Rouse-Jones (with Estelle Appiah as co-discussant). "George James Christian of Dominica and the Gold Coast: West Indian Patriot and Pan-Africanist". Open lecture, Institute of African Studies, Accra, Ghana, 16 August 2007.

2006

Margaret D. Rouse-Jones. "Reverse Caribbean-African Migration: The Case of George James Christian of Dominica and the Gold Coast". Paper presented at the Seminar on the Acquisition of Latin American Library Materials 51, Crossing Borders, Latin American Migrations: Collections and Services for/from New Library Users for panel theme: Representations of Migration and Diasporic Movements in the Special Collections at the University of the West Indies, St Augustine. Santo Domingo, Dominican Republic, 19–22 March 2006.

2001

Margaret D. Rouse-Jones. "George James Christian of Dominica and the Gold Coast". Paper presented to the conference on Henry Sylvester-Williams and Pan-Africanism: A Retrospection and Projection. University of the West Indies, St Augustine, and Oberlin College, Ohio, 4–13 January 2001.

Notes

CHAPTER 1. MIGRATION AND DOCUMENTARY HERITAGE

1. [George James Christian to Joseph O. Bowers] 6 April 1940, GJC Papers, Folder 64. This letter is quoted in its entirety in chapter 8.
2. Ibid.
3. Kwesi Kwaa Prah, introduction to *Back to Africa*, vol. 2, *The Ideology and Practice of the African Returnee Phenomenon from the Caribbean and North-America to Africa*, ed. Kwesi Kwaa Prah (Cape Town: Centre for Advanced Studies of African Society, 2012), 1.
4. Fitzroy André Baptiste, "Developments in African History and the African Diaspora at the University of the West Indies (UWI), 1968–1998: A Personal Odyssey", in *Caribbean Perspectives on African History and Culture,* ed. Richard Goodridge, 3–4 (Cave Hill, Barbados: Department of History and Philosophy, University of the West Indies, 2004).
5. Waibinte Wariboko, *Ruined by "Race": Afro-Caribbean Missionaries and the Evangelization of Southern Nigeria, 1895–1925* (Trenton, NJ: Africa World Press, 2007), 198.
6. Brian L. Moore, foreword to *Ruined by "Race": Afro-Caribbean Missionaries and the Evangelization of Southern Nigeria, 1895–1925*, by Waibinte Wariboko (Trenton, NJ: Africa World Press, 2007), xiii–xiv.
7. Prah, introduction, 5–6. The second tradition referred to "emerged among people who, from the beginning, felt that Africans in the diaspora should make permanent homes and integrate into American society. Frederick Douglass is the first-in-line in this tradition".
8. Bela Vassady Jr, "The Role of the Black West Indian Missionary in West Africa, 1840–1890" (PhD diss., Temple University, 1972), 1–4, 191. See also Horace O. Russell, *The Missionary Outreach of the West Indian Church; Jamaican Baptist Missions to West Africa in the Nineteenth Century,* Research in Religion and Family, vol. 3 (New York: Peter Lang, 2000).
9. Maureen Warner-Lewis, "The West Indian Anglican Mission to West Africa" (typescript, 2010), 2.

10. [Peter Hall] *Autobiography of Rev. Peter Hall, First Moderator of the Presbyterian Church of Ghana* (Accra: Waterville Publishing House, 1965), 5–6. See also Margaret D. Rouse-Jones and Estelle M. Appiah, "West Indian Returnees and Their Communities: Examples from the Gold Coast in the Nineteenth and Twentieth Centuries", in *Back to Africa,* vol. 2, *The Ideology and Practice of the African Returnee,* 380–406.
11. Samuel Boadi-Siaw, "The Afro-Brazilian Returnees in Ghana", in *Back to Africa,* vol. 1, *Afro-Brazilian Returnees and Their Communities,* ed. Kwesi Kwaa Prah (Cape Town: Centre for Advanced Studies of African Society, 2009), 145–48.
12. Ray Jenkins, "'West Indian' and 'Brazilian' Influences in the Gold Coast-Ghana, c. 1807–1914: A Review and Reappraisal of Continuities in the Post-Abolition Links between West Africa and the Caribbean and Brazil" (paper presented to the Twelfth Annual Conference of the Society for Caribbean Studies, Hoddesdon, Hertfordshire, UK, 12–14 July 1988). See also cited in Jenkins: J. Green, "Caribbean Influence in the Gold Coast Administration in the 1900s", *Ghana Studies Bulletin* 2 (1984): 10–16.
13. Obiagele Lake, "Toward a Pan-African Identity: Diaspora African Repatriates in Ghana", *Anthropological Quarterly* 68, no. 1 (January 1995): 21–36.
14. Rita Marley with Hettie Jones, *No Woman No Cry: My Life with Bob Marley* (New York: Hyperion, 2004), 197–98.
15. Rita Marley, http://www.thetalkingdrum.com/marley.html (accessed 5 November 2010); Rita Marley in Ghana, http://www.info-ghana.com/Rita%20Marley%20in%20Ghana.htm (accessed 5 November 2010).
16. Elizabeth Thomas-Hope, "Globalisation and the Development of a Caribbean Migration Culture", in *Caribbean Migration,* ed. Mary Chamberlain, 188–91 (London: Routledge, 1998). For a detailed discussion of this subject, see also Lloyd Braithwaite, *Colonial West Indian Students in Britain* (Kingston: University of the West Indies Press, 2001). In the context of this book, it is to be noted that the main subject, George James Christian, went to Great Britain as a student. Many of his children and grandchildren were also educated there.
17. See, for example, GJC to Peter, 15 August 1932, GJC Papers, Folder 147.
18. See, for example, GJC to Peter, 2 September 1932, GJC Papers, Folder 147 and other correspondence in Folders 146 and 147.
19. A.W. Cardinall, *The Gold Coast 1931* (n.p., 1931), chapter 7, "Non-African Population", 255.
20. *Gold Coast Handbook 1937* (n.p.: Gold Coast Government, 1937), 402.
21. One of the later migrants, George Stanley Lewis, was interviewed in 1994, as were two relatives of other West Indians who were part of the small group. George Stanley Lewis, one of the celebrated Lewis brothers from St Lucia,

went to the Gold Coast in 1929. He became a personal friend of George James Christian. Copies of the tapes and transcripts of the oral-history interviews which were collected as part of this research are held in the Oral and Pictorial Records Programme (OPReP) at the Alma Jordan Library, University of the West Indies, St Augustine, Trinidad and Tobago (hereafter, OPReP Collection).
22. John-Baptiste Charles, manuscript autobiography, unpublished, Eugenia Charles Fonds, University of the West Indies, Cave Hill, Barbados. The authors are grateful to the late Dr Cheryl King for drawing this information to our attention.
23. The West African Industrial Academy, Sekondi, Gold Coast Colony, West Africa. American Address: 44 Pliny Street, Hartford, Conn. [Information flyer, [1937?], GJC Papers, Folder 271.
24. Mrs Hen[rietta Peters] to GJC, 4 October 1934, GJC Papers, Folder 63.
25. GJC to Colonial Secretary, 14 May 1935, GJC Papers, Folder 194.
26. Mr Wood to GJC, 19 May 1936, GJC Papers, Folder 195.
27. "National Pride", speech by the Hon. M. Eugenia Charles, Prime Minister of Dominica, on the occasion of the twelfth anniversary of independence, 3 November 1990. Eugenia Charles Fonds, University of the West Indies, Cave Hill, Barbados. The authors are grateful to the late Dr Cheryl King of the library at the University of the West Indies, Cave Hill, for her assistance in locating this information.

CHAPTER 2. ANTECEDENTS AND EARLY YEARS IN DOMINICA, ENGLAND AND THE GOLD COAST

1. This information was provided by May Christian, niece of Christian, in an interview with a research assistant, Elizabeth Felix, Roseau, Dominica, in August 1993.
2. This date of birth is given on the tombstone of his grave in the European Cemetery, Sekondi.
3. May Christian, interview with Margaret D. Rouse-Jones, Roseau, Dominica, 5 August 1993, transcript, OPReP Collection. May Christian was the niece of Christian, the daughter of his younger brother, William Nathaniel Alexander Christian. Christian also made reference to May Christian's father in correspondence with her, GJC to Miss May Christian, 7 April 1936, GJC Papers, Folder 28. See also GJC to Peter and GJC to Florrie Giraud, both on 8 December 1931, where he refers to William, who doubted the paternity of his daughter May, GJC Papers, Folder 147. May refers to the death of her father in Jamaica in 1942, May Christian to Mammie Abba, 12 May 1946, GJC Papers, Folder 50.

4. *Who Do You Think You Are?*, with Moira Stuart (video from BBC2, Family History Series [London: BBC, 2004]), GJC Papers, Folder 245. Moira Stuart is the great-granddaughter of George James Christian and the first black woman newsreader in Britain. See: http://www.bbc.co.uk/pressoffice/pressreleases/stories/2004/09_september/24/who.shtml and http://www.bbc.co.uk/pressoffice/pressreleases/stories/2004/09_september/24/who_stuart.shtml (accessed 26 September 2013).
5. Laudat, a French aristocrat, allegedly fled to Dominica to escape the French Revolution. He owned extensive plantations and had children with a local woman (information from an unconfirmed source). In a 1930 letter, Christian refers to cousins Emmanuel and Marijenne, to whom he sent monetary gifts at Christmas. See GJC to Peter, 15 October 1930, GJC Papers, Folder 147. A 1934 letter with monetary Christmas gifts for friends and relatives confirms the Laudat relationship. GJC sends £2 to be divided "amongst the daughters of my late uncle Emmanuel Laudat". GJC to "My dear Lecointe", 29 October 1934, GJC Papers, Folder 35.
6. The names of Christian's mother and grandmother were provided by his niece Chrissie Burke in an interview with a research assistant, Elizabeth Felix, Roseau, Dominica, August 1992.
7. *Collins' Gentleman's Diary for 1899 Showing One Page for Each Day* (London, Glasgow: William Collins). See entry for 25 August, where Christian refers to his sister, GJC Papers, Folder 172.
8. May Christian, interview with Margaret D. Rouse-Jones, 5 August 1993, transcript, OPReP Collection.
9. Jeanvillia Romain, Portsmouth, Dominica, to Mr Christian, 11 August 1938, GJC Papers, Folder 79. Later in life, she wrote to Christian with a request for financial assistance.
10. Sarah Duguid, "Moira's Roots", *Mail on Sunday*, 3 October 2004, 38. http://sarahduguid.com/pdf/Newspapers/roots.pdf (accessed 22 November 2014).
11. This was confirmed through his correspondence with the Colonial Office. CO 71/129 3478/64: Lieutenant Governor T. Price to His Excellency Colonel Hill, Governor in Chief of Antigua, 10 March 1864.
12. G.G. Oliver Maynard, *A History of the Moravian Church, Eastern West Indies Province* (Trinidad: Printed by Yuille's Printerie, 1968), 47–48; Olva Flax, *The Influence of Church and School upon the Antiguan Society* ([Antigua]: Antigua Archives Committee, [1984?]), 9.
13. May Christian, interview with Margaret D. Rouse-Jones, 5 August 1993, transcript, OPReP Collection.
14. *Who Do You Think You Are?*, with Moira Stuart.

15. May Christian, interview with Margaret D. Rouse-Jones, 5 August 1993, transcript, OPReP Collection.
16. The authors are extremely grateful to Dr Susan Craig-James, who drew our attention to the information about George James Christian Sr.
17. CO 71/129 3478/64: Lieutenant Governor T. Price to His Excellency Colonel Hill, Governor in Chief of Antigua, 10 March 1864.
18. CO 71/134: No. 1 Longden to Carnarvon, 12 January 1867, transmitting letter from Chief Justice Pemberton to Lieutenant Governor T. Price, 26 December 1866.
19. CO 71/130: Chief Justice Sholto Pemberton to His Excellency the Lieutenant Governor, 22 April 1864.
20. CO 71/132: George James Christian, Sworn Statement in the Court of the Queen's Bench and Grand Sessions of the Peace, 18 February 1864.
21. In the context of the Caribbean during this period, the term "coloured" referred to people of mixed European and African descent.
22. Lennox Honychurch, *The Dominica Story: A History of the Island* (Roseau: Dominica Institute, 1984), 98.
23. CO 71/127: Lieutenant Governor Price to Colonel Stephen Hill, Governor in Chief, Antigua, 8 June 1863.
24. CO 71/127: Colonial Secretary to Chief Justice, 1 June 1863
25. CO 71/ 127: Lieutenant Governor Price to Colonel Stephen Hill, Governor in Chief, Antigua, 8 June 1863.
26. CO 71/133: No. 11502/66 GJC Sr to the Secretary of State, 20 October 1866, Annexure B, *Antigua Weekly Register*, 2 October 1866.
27. CO 71/129 3478/64: Lieutenant Governor T. Price to His Excellency Colonel Hill, Governor in Chief, Antigua, 10 March 1864.
28. CO 71/130 7279/65: Chief Justice Sholto Pemberton to His Excellency Governor Hill, 24 June 1865.
29. CO 71/132 2104/66: GJC to Her Majesty, 8 May 1865.
30. Ibid.
31. CO 71/132: Sholto Pemberton, Chief Justice, to His Excellency the Governor, 24 January 1866.
32. CO 71/130 7279/65: Chief Justice Sholto Pemberton to His Excellency Governor Hill, 24 June 1865.
33. CO 71/133: Bo. 11502/66 GJC Sr to the Secretary of State, 20 October 1866.
34. CO 71/133: Lieutenant Governor Longden to the Rt Hon. the Earl of Carnarvon, 5 November 1866.
35. CO 71/134 47: Governor Hill to Buckingham and Chandos, 18 June 1867; CO 71/134: No. 5 Administrator Bulwer to Governor Hill to dispatch the petition

of Christian Sr and Doyle to the Duke of Buckingham for placement before the House of Commons, 18 January 1868; CO 71/136 14: Forwards petition from Christian and also joint petition from Thomas Doyle and G. James Christian, 26 February 1868.

36. CO 71/136 14: Forwards petition from Christian and also joint petition from Thomas Doyle and G. James Christian, 26 February 1868.
37. CO 71/130 7279/65: Chief Justice Sholto Pemberton to His Excellency Governor Hill, 24 June 1865.
38. Officers Administering the Government of Dominica, http://presidentoffice.gov.dm/administering-officers (accessed 22 September 2013).
39. In 1869, Governor Benjamin Pine was assigned to organize a federation of Antigua–Barbuda, Dominica, Montserrat, Nevis, St Kitts, Anguilla and the British Virgin Islands. St Kitts and Nevis opposed sharing their government funds with Antigua and Montserrat, which were bankrupt. Governor Pine told the Colonial Office that the scheme had failed owing to "local prejudice and self-interest". His only achievement was to give the Leeward Islands a single governor. All laws and ordinances, however, had to be approved by each island council. http://en.wikipedia.org/wiki/British_West_Indies (accessed 22 September 2013).
40. CO 71/140: Governor Freeling to Governor Pine, 9 April 1870.
41. CO 71/140: GJC Sr to His Excellency Sanford Freeling, the Lieutenant Governor, 15 February 1869.
42. CO 71/140: Governor Freeling to Governor Pine, 9 April 1870.
43. CO 71/140: Governor Pine to Governor Freeling, 16 April 1870.
44. CO 71/133 4639/66: Christian to Longden, 23 April 1866.
45. Despite its sixty-one-year existence until 1899, the school is reported to have been of limited benefit to education in Antigua. See Brian Dyde, *A History of Antigua: The Unsuspected Isle* (London: Macmillan, 2000), 152.
46. [Testimonial] from Vivian Grell, District Magistrate for District E Acting as Registrar General of Births, Deaths and Marriages, Dominica, 9 September 1899, GJC Papers, Folder number not recorded. This information was also mentioned in reports at the time of his death. See, for example, "Hon. George James Christian, 'Defender of Poor Criminals', Passes Away at Sekondi", in the *African Morning Post*, 19 April 1940, 1. It was also confirmed by other sources, viz., Angela Christian, one of his daughters. Personal correspondence: Estelle Appiah to Margaret Rouse-Jones, 14 June 1992.
47. Geo. J. Christian and Sheriff M. Bowers to [the Revd Chas. W. Farquhar], Roseau, Dominica, 29 March 1890, GJC Papers, Folder 49.
48. See, for example, exchange of correspondence between Geo. J. Christian and

Sheriff M. Bowers and [the Revd Chas. W. Farquhar], both dated at Roseau, Dominica, 29 March 1890, GJC Papers, Folder 49. See also exchange of correspondence between GJC and the son of his roommate the Revd Joseph O. Bowers fifty years later: Joseph O. Bowers, SVD to Mr Christian, 21 March 1940, GJC Papers, Folder 50; [George James Christian to Joseph O. Bowers] 6 April 1940, GJC Papers, Folder 64; George James Christian to the Revd Charles W. Farquhar, All Saints Parsonage, Conakry, Guinea, 29 October 1924, GJC Papers, Folder 18.

49. A.H. Barrow, *Fifty Years in Western Africa: Being a Record of the Work of the West Indian Church on the Banks of the Rio Pongo* (1900; reprint New York: Negro Universities Press, 1969), 133–34. The Revd Charles W. Farquhar was the father of Canon Max Eric Farquhar of Trinidad, who was stationed for years at the St Paul's Anglican Church in San Fernando. Canon Farquhar was also a regular columnist in the *Guardian*. See Maureen Warner-Lewis, "The West Indian Anglican Mission to West Africa" (typescript, 2010), 4.

50. Exchange of correspondence between Geo. J. Christian and Sheriff M. Bowers and [the Revd Chas. W. Farquhar], both dated at Roseau, Dominica, 29 March 1890, Folder 49. See also exchange of correspondence between George James Christian and the son of his roommate the Revd Joseph O. Bowers fifty years later: Joseph O. Bowers, SVD, to Mr Christian, 21 March 1940, GJC Papers, Folder 50; [George James Christian to Joseph O. Bowers] 6 April 1940, GJC Papers, Folder 64.

51. Geo. J. Christian and Sheriff M. Bowers to [the Revd Chas. W. Farquhar], Roseau, Dominica, 29 March 1890, GJC Papers, Folder 49.

52. Ibid. See also exchange of correspondence between George James Christian and the son of his roommate the Revd Joseph O. Bowers fifty years later: Joseph O. Bowers, SVD, to Mr Christian, 21 March 1940, GJC Papers, Folder 50; [George James Christian to Joseph O. Bowers] 6 April 1940, GJC Papers, Folder 64.

53. The Revd Chas. W. Farquhar to [Geo. J. Christian and Sheriff M. Bowers], Roseau, Dominica, 29 March 1890, GJC Papers, Folder 49.

54. Barrow, *Fifty Years in Western Africa*, 133–34, 139. Farquhar "immediately threw himself . . . into the work of preparation and organization". Farquhar was the first archdeacon of the Pongas. His devoted service is confirmed in another source in the GJC Papers which also makes reference to the fact that he persevered under difficulties and in the face of many discouragements. He died in 1929, "in his thirty-ninth year of active service in the great cause". He was succeeded by the Revd De Jean McEwen, who was given an honorary canonry and appointed to the position by the Lord Bishop of Sierra Leone. (See the Revd Canon De Jean S. McEwen, "The Pongas Mission". Reprinted from "The

Mission Field", September 1929, 3–4; see also the Honorary Secretary of the Pongas Mission, "Notes on the Pongas Mission, 1929", GJC Papers, Folder 294. The Revd De Jean Baptist McEwen, "apparently a Grenadian, was posted to Fallanghia" and worked in the Rio Pongas Mission from 1871 to 1901. His son, Canon De Jean Sigismund McEwen, who was born in Fallanghia in 1880 and educated in England, followed in his father's footsteps and became archdeacon of Conakry in 1929. See Warner-Lewis, "West Indian Anglican Mission", 3. See also Warner-Lewis, "West Indian Memories of Life in West Africa as Agents of the British Colonial Enterprise" (paper presented at Heritage: Its Management and Preservation, Eighth Symposium, Social History Project, Department of History and Archaeology, University of the West Indies, Mona, 2008), 4.

55. *Collins' Gentleman's Diary for 1899*, GJC Papers, Folder 172.
56. Ibid., entry for 5 January, GJC Papers, Folder 172.
57. Ibid., entries for 28 February, 6 March, 13 March, GJC Papers, Folder 172.
58. Ibid., entries for 2 April, 28 April, 4 May, GJC Papers, Folder 172.
59. Ibid., entries for 1 May, 20 June, 8 August, 2 September, GJC Papers, Folder 172.
60. Ibid., entries for 6, 7 January, GJC Papers, Folder 172.
61. Ibid., entries for 1 March, 22 June, GJC Papers, Folder 172.
62. Ibid., entries for 20 April, 15, 16 June, GJC Papers, Folder 172.
63. Surname confirmed from another source: John-Baptiste Charles, manuscript autobiography, unpublished, Eugenia Charles Fonds, University of the West Indies, Cave Hill, Barbados.
64. *Collins' Gentleman's Diary for 1899*, entries for 14, 15, 27 April, 12 May, GJC Papers, Folder 172.
65. Ibid., entry for 19 June, GJC Papers, Folder 172.
66. Ibid., entry for 12 May, GJC Papers, Folder 172.
67. Ibid., entries for 1 January, 2 April, GJC Papers, Folder 172.
68. Ibid., entries for 2 January, 3 April, May 22, GJC Papers, Folder 172.
69. Ibid., entries for 4, 5 September, GJC Papers, Folder 172.
70. Ibid., entry for 12 September 1899, GJC Papers, Folder 172.
71. Ibid., entry for 22 September 1899, GJC Papers, Folder 172.
72. Ibid., entry for 25 September 1899, GJC Papers, Folder 172.
73. Ibid., entries for 26–30 September 1899, GJC Papers, Folder 172.
74. Ibid., entry for 14 September 1899, GJC Papers, Folder 172.
75. [Testimonial] from William Everard, Rector of St George's, St Kitts, WI, 12 September 1899, GJC Papers, folder not known; see also entry in 1899 Diary for 14 September 1899, GJC Papers, Folder 172.
76. Hilton Pierre (St Jos, Dominica) to Mr Christian, 14 March 1900, GJC Papers, Folder 33.

77. Tim Shuttleworth, "The Way We Were", *Graya (House Magazine of Gray's Inn)*, 119: 52.
78. Francis Cowper, *A Prospect of Gray's Inn*, 2nd rev. ed. (London: GRAYA on behalf of Gray's Inn, 1985), 117–18.
79. *Collins' Gentleman's Diary for 1899*, entries for 1–3 October 1899, GJC Papers, Folder 172.
80. *Collins' Gentleman's Diary for 1899*, entries for 9–25 October 1899, GJC Papers, Folder 172. The people to whom he referred are Dennis Douthwaite, steward of Gray's Inn, and fellow students Henry Sylvester Williams, from Trinidad, and Francis Stanislaus Leung, from British Guiana, who became his legal associate.
81. Dennis Douthwaite, Steward, Gray's Inn, to G.J. Christian Esq., 25 October 1899, GJC Papers, Folder 49.
82. Pension Book, vol. 20: 95, 8 November 1899, Gray's Inn Library, London.
83. Pension Book, vol. 20: 102–3, 15 November 1899, Gray's Inn Library, London.
84. *Collins' Gentleman's Diary for 1899*, entries for 9–25 October 1899, GJC Papers, Folder 172.
85. Gray's Inn admission document, 5 October 1899, Gray's Inn Library, London.
86. *Collins' Gentleman's Diary for 1899*, entries for 26 October to 20 November 20 1899, GJC Papers, Folder 172; see also Reference 1 and Reference 2 in Gray's Inn Admissions Files and Calls Register, 1625–1945, Gray's Inn Library, London.
87. J. Leonard Crouch to GJC, 28 July 1937, and GJC to J. Leonard Crouch, 3 September 1937, GJC Papers, Folder 85.
88. *Collins' Gentleman's Diary for 1899*, entries for 9–25 October 1899, GJC Papers, Folder 172.
89. Ibid., entry for 7 December 1899, GJC Papers, Folder 172.
90. Ibid., entries for 21 November to 16 December 1899, GJC Papers, Folder 172.
91. T.H. Shillingford, Roseau, to GJC ("My dear George"), 6 December 1900, GJC Papers, Folder 49.
92. *Collins' Gentleman's Diary for 1899*, entries for 11, 12 and 21 December 1899, GJC Papers, Folder 172.
93. Ibid., 24 to 30 December 1899, GJC Papers, Folder 172.
94. Owen Charles Mathurin, *Henry Sylvester Williams and the Origins of the Pan-African Movement, 1969–1911* (Westport, CT: Greenwood, 1976), 35.
95. Mathurin, *Henry Sylvester Williams*, 41.
96. Ibid., 49–53.
97. Ibid., 35, 44, 53.
98. *Anti-Slavery Reporter* (March–May 1899): 112. Quoted in Mathurin, *Henry Sylvester Williams*, 49, 58.
99. *Report of the Pan-African Conference* (London: Pan-African Association,

1900), 2, quoted in Mathurin, *Henry Sylvester Williams*, 49, 58; see also Marika Sherwood, *Origins of Pan-Africanism: Henry Sylvester Williams, Africa, and the African Diaspora* (London: Routledge, 2011), 75–97. Sherwood has reported that she secured a copy of the lone typescript of the proceedings of the Pan-African Conference, which is held at the W.E.B. DuBois Library, University of Massachusetts. This document makes no mention of the speeches given at the conference. Her work therefore relies on newspaper accounts (78).

100. Mathurin, *Henry Sylvester Williams*, 37, 67–68.
101. Christian's contribution to the conference is in the Report of the Pan-African Conference 1900 and quoted by Sherwood, *Origins of Pan-Africanism*, 90.
102. Ibid.
103. Mathurin, *Henry Sylvester Williams*, 74.
104. Ibid., 68.
105. George Christian to the Secretary, Pan-African Association, 15 September 1900, GJC Papers, Folder 33.
106. GJC to Howard Christian, 6 November 1937, GJC Papers, Folder 115. It is interesting to note that nine of the seventeen students who were called to the Bar at Gray's Inn with Christian were originally from India; "Gray's Inn, Trinity Term, 1902, List of Students Desirous of being called to the Bar this Term", Gray's Inn Library, London.
107. Dennis W. Douthwaite, Steward and Under Treasurer of Gray's Inn, 13 June 1901, GJC Papers, Folder 32.
108. Gray's Inn, 10 June 1902, Received of G.J. Christian Esq. . . . /sgd/ S.W. Bunning, Chf. Clerk, GJC Papers, Folder 32.
109. Admissions and Calls Register, 1625–1945; see also Pension Book, vol. 20: 572, 11 June 1902, Gray's Inn Library, London.
110. "Gray's Inn, Trinity Term, 1902, List of Students Desirous of being called to the Bar this Term", Gray's Inn Library, London.
111. Ernest Cockle, Great Ormond Street, to the Secretary of State, Colonial Office, 13 June 1901, Manuscript, GJC Papers, Folder 49.
112. Colonial Office, Downing Street (E. Marsh) to George J. Christian, Esq., 21 June 1901, GJC Papers, Folder 32.
113. The farewell function took place on 17 August 1929; see GJC to Horace Douglas, 30 August 1929, GJC Papers, Folder 119.
114. His Honour Philip Crampton Smyly, LLD, a member of the Irish Bar, was also one of those listed on the "Gray's Inn, Trinity Term, 1902, List of Students Desirous of being called to the Bar this Term", Gray's Inn Library, London.
115. Speech by GJC [on the occasion of a farewell function for Chief Justice Sir Philip Crampton Smyly], GJC Papers, Folders 23 and 33.

116. http://en.wikipedia.org/wiki/List_of_British_coronations (accessed 27 May 2013).
117. Peter Fraser, "Africans and Caribbeans in London", in *The Peopling of London: Fifteen Thousand Years of Settlement from Overseas*, ed. Nick Merriman, 55–56 (London: Museum of London, 1993).
118. Mathurin, *Henry Sylvester Williams*, 44–45.
119. Sherwood, *Origins of Pan-Africanism*, 73, 78.
120. H.S. Williams to Maurice Reece, 21 July 1902, GJC Papers, Folder 119.
121. H.S. Williams to Dr Simmonds, 21 July 1902, GJC Papers, Folder 119.
122. Ronald Courtney Noel, "Henry Sylvester-Williams: A New Inquiry into an Old Hero" (MPhil thesis, University of the West Indies, St Augustine, Trinidad, 2006), 69.
123. Williams to Reece, 21 July 1902, GJC Papers, Folder 119. Both letters from H.S. Williams to Maurice Reece and Dr Simmonds were written on Gray's Inn Common Room stationery. The signature does not obviously look like Williams's as seen on 1904 correspondence from South Africa in Noel's thesis, but the content of the letters leaves no doubt that the author was Henry Sylvester Williams.
124. Crampton Smyly to GJC, Switzerland, 12 July 1902, GJC Papers, Folder 119.
125. George James Christian to Horace Douglas, 21 August 1929, GJC Papers, Folders 22, 119.
126. George James Christian to Joe Christian, 8 June 1937, GJC Papers, Folder 118. See also George James Christian to Mr Broadhurst, Vice Consul for Liberia, 5 January 1940, GJC Papers, Folder 70.
127. GJC to Joe Christian, 8 June 1937, GJC Papers, Folder 118.
128. [George James Christian] to . . . Vice Consul for Liberia, 5 January 1940.
129. Sekondi was also spelled "Seccondee" in the colonial period. This version is retained only when used in quotations and titles of documents.
130. *Gold Coast Leader,* 18 April 1903, 2
131. Joe Isaac Haizel, "Sekondi: The Sleeping Giant", Takoradi, *Daily Graphic*, 28 September 2002, 13.
132. Lease agreement between GJC and Gottlob Siegfried Rottmann, 12 April 1908, GJC Papers, Folder 203.
133. African Union Company to George James Christian, 14 April 1915, GJC Papers, Folder 14. Charles Ward Chappelle (1872–1941) was an architect, electrical engineer, aviation pioneer and businessman with interest in the Gold Coast. He eventually became president of the African Union Company. See https://en.wikipedia.org/wiki/Charles W. Chappelle and http://m.famousfix.com/p33685897/charles-w-chappelle/ (accessed 14 July 2015).

134. General News, Seccondee, *Gold Coast Leader*, 7 August 1915, 2, centre column, GJC Papers, Folder 4.
135. J.E. Kwegyir Aggrey to "Lawyer Christian", 28 May 1926, GJC Papers, Folder 31. More information on Dr James Emmanuel Kwegyir is in chapter 4.
136. GJC to Sarah Christian, 31 May 1937, GJC Papers, Folder 81.
137. Geo. Padmore to GJC, 30 August 1939, GJC Papers, Folder 273.
138. K.W. Todd to Mr Christian, 1 February 1931, GJC Papers, Folder 56.
139. See, for example, Minutes of Proceedings of the Meeting of the Bar Association held at Dominica House on the 12th day of July 1930, GJC Papers, Folder 49.
140. GJC to George Francois, 28 January 1938, GJC Papers, Folder 98.
141. [GJC] to Dr Peter Christian, 15 January 1938, GJC Papers, Folder 83.
142. Monty Morphy to GJC, 29 February 1940, GJC Papers, Folder 64.
143. Mrs Leung to GJC, 28 September 1925, GJC Papers, Folder 12; Copies of postcards of Dominica House also in GJC Papers, Folders 33 and 231.
144. Edward Francois, interview with Margaret Rouse-Jones, Accra, Ghana, 14 August 2007; Edward Francois lived at Dominica House for six months in 1945 while he was enrolled as a student of civil engineering at Achimota College. He was the son of George Francois, formerly of St Lucia, who had also migrated to the Gold Coast and was a friend of Christian.
145. "Fire at Dominica House – 7 July 1949" [Report by Howard Christian], GJC Papers, Folder 157.
146. An agreement between George James Christian and Contractors Zeph Demetrow and Alec Zalanos, 10 November 1927, GJC Papers, Folder 61.
147. Grace Christian, interview with Margaret D. Rouse-Jones, Accra, Ghana, 8 August 2007, OPReP Collection. Mrs Grace Christian, originally from Nigeria and daughter-in-law of Mami Abba, was the wife of G.J. Christian's son Ferdinand, whom she married in 1954. She lived with Mami Abba at Dominica House for three years while her husband, who was a radiologist, completed his studies in England.
148. "Fire at Dominica House", GJC Papers, Folder 157.
149. Several spellings of her name occur throughout the records, as may be observed in the notes. The authors have chosen to use "Mami Abba" in the main text of the book.
150. Grace Christian, interview with Margaret D. Rouse-Jones, 8 August 2007, OPReP Collection.
151. "Fire at Dominica House", GJC Papers, Folder 157.
152. [Essi Forster] to Mamie Abba, 9 September 1962, GJC Papers, Folder 70; Secretary to the Regional Commissioner to F.F. Christian, 8 September 1964.

CHAPTER 3. CHRISTIAN AS FATHER AND FAMILY MAN

1. These include interviews with four of his children – Sarah Busby, Essi Forster, Ferdinand Christian and Edward Christian.
2. Ira P. Philip, *HAKIM, Son of Mazumbo: The Extraordinary Life of Hakim Gordon* (Warwick, Bermuda: Writers' Machine, 1995), Photocopy, GJC Papers, Folder 1. Another source, the BBC2 programme *Who Do You Think You Are?*, featuring Moira Stuart, gives 1893 as Clara's date of birth.
3. There is conflicting information on Peter's age. His father in a 1925 letter indicated that Peter was in his twenty-ninth year. See GJC to Dr Akinwande Savage, Nigeria, 20 November 1925, GJC Papers, Folder 39. In another source, Immigration Officer's Certificate, Takoradi, 1 October 1935, GJC Papers, Folder 26, Peter's age is given as thirty-six. An obituary in a local newspaper on his death in 1945 gives his age as fifty. Obituary: Doctor Peter Christian, *Dominica Chronicle*, 3 November 1945, 5, GJC Papers, Folder 104. Two of the three sources mentioned would suggest that Peter was born in 1895.
4. Conrad R. Cole, MD, MPH, MSc, professor of pediatrics, University of Cincinnati, and clinical director, Division of Gastroenterology, Hepatology and Nutrition, Cincinnati Children's Hospital Medical Center, has suggested that Ulric may have suffered from persistent gastroenteritis and probably died of dehydration, which was a common occurrence at the time.
5. *Collins' Gentleman's Diary for 1899*, notes on Memoranda page at front of diary, GJC Papers, Folder 172.
6. GJC to "Dear Mr Hypolite", 29 October 1934, GJC Papers, Folder 35.
7. This date of birth is given on the headstone on Maude's grave in the European Cemetery in Sekondi, Ghana.
8. *Collins' Gentleman's Diary for 1899*, entries for 19 March and 3 September 1899, GJC Papers, Folder 172.
9. Coumere refers to a co-godparent of the same child.
10. See GJC to Miss Laura Lecointe, Coulibistrie, Dominica, 5 March 1925, GJC Papers, Folder 127. See also [GJC] to Dr P.C. Christian, 27 October 1939, in which he sent £2 for Miss Laura Lecointe, GJC Papers, Folder 144.
11. There is no mention of the name Virginia Boland in records, which are also silent as to the names of the mother(s) of his Dominica-born daughters, Clara and Maude.
12. May Christian, interview with Margaret D. Rouse-Jones, 5 August 1993, OPReP Collection.
13. See GJC to Peter, 19 February 1934, GJC Papers, Folder 147, where GJC mentions to Peter the hope that "Miss Mena Serrant" had recovered her health. See

also May Christian to Mamie Abba, 12 May 1946, GJC Papers, Folder 50, where May Christian mentions George Serrant as Peter's half-brother, thus confirming Peter's relationship as the son of Felina Serrant.
14. *Collins' Gentleman's Diary for 1899*, entries for 5 and 6 September, GJC Papers, Folder 172.
15. GJC to Peter, 19 February 1934, GJC Papers, Folder 147. See also Peter Christian to GJC, 17 June 1937, GJC Papers, Folder 143; Peter Christian to GJC, 21 June 1937; Peter Christian to GJC, 28 May 1939, GJC Papers, Folders 116 and 81; Peter Christian to GJC, 8 July 1939, GJC Papers, Folder 143.
16. In the Gold Coast/Ghana, three types of marriage exist, but they cannot be mixed. There is Muslim marriage, customary marriage and marriage under the ordinance, the latter being civil marriage as it is known elsewhere. Marriage by customary law is potentially polygamous. A customary marriage can be converted into a civil marriage if the parties to the marriage are the same. A civil marriage cannot, however, be converted into a customary marriage unless the parties divorce. Estelle Appiah, interview with Margaret D. Rouse-Jones, London, England, 9 July 1991, OPReP Collection.
17. GJC to C. Hodgett, GJC Papers, n.d. [1937?], Folder 85. GJC is responding to a letter from Hodgett dated 11 July and is writing sometime after 28 September. The year is believed to be 1937 as are all the letters in that folder.
18. "Memorial and Thanksgiving Service for the Late Mary Aba Ackon Who Died on 28 December 1978", GJC Papers, Folder 19.
19. [Ebenezer Kwesi Christian: Brief Biography, 1906–1969] July 2015. Typescript prepared by his daughter and granddaughter, Veronica McNeil and Aileen Ewuradwoa Conteh, in response to a request from Margaret Rouse-Jones and Estelle Appiah, GJC Papers, Folder 302.
20. This version of the name has been used consistently in the GJC Papers and has been retained. It is currently spelled "Ekua".
21. Mami Abba is first mentioned in chapter 2.
22. "Biography of the Late Angela Christian", in "Burial and Thanksgiving Mass for the Late Angela Christian (Aged 83) at the Christ the King Catholic Church on 18 March 2000, Committal at Osu Cemetery", [booklet], 5, GJC Papers, Folder 301.
23. In 1915, Christian asked Mrs Annie Porter to make inquiries in Freetown about the sailing of a boat commanded by "Captain Pooley", as he wanted to send Kwesi away during "the first week of January, DV". See [GJC] to Mrs Annie H. Porter, Freetown, Sierra Leone, 6 December 1915, GJC Papers, Folder 24. In 1924, Christian's friend T.H. Wellington reported and commented on a conversation with Mrs Annie Porter about this boy, who had died. There is a suggestion that

she may have been his mother. T.H. Wellington, Sierra Leone to GJC, 18 May 1924, GJC Papers, Folder 53.
24. His surname is given as Mansour in the oral records, but when he was born, it was evident that he was "an African child". See Sarah Busby, interview with Margaret Busby, Abidjan, Ivory Coast, 9 March 1978, OPReP Collection. Margaret Busby, OBE, is the daughter of Sarah Busby. We are grateful to Margaret Busby, granddaughter of George James Christian, for making copies of these interviews available to us. See also Estelle Appiah, interview with Margaret Rouse-Jones, 9 July 1991, OPReP Collection. See also John Mansour's letter to GJC, in which he extends congratulations on "the new baby" he had and which may be cause for speculation. John Mansour to GJC, 23 February 1931, GJC Papers, Folder 188.
25. This is a distance of more than 100 miles, or 190 kilometres.
26. A passbook enabled a trader to obtain goods on credit to sell.
27. "Thanksgiving Service in Ever-loving Memory of the Late Madam Mary Aba Ackon at the African Methodist Episcopal Church, Sekondi, on 25 February 1979 at 9:30 a.m. Officiating Minister Revd Sir George A. Zormelo", GJC Papers, Folder 19, 5.
28. GJC to T.H. Wellington, Freetown, Sierra Leone, 21 July 1923, GJC Papers, Folder 53.
29. Ibid.
30. GJC to Mrs Josephine Armah, 16 November 1937, GJC Papers, Folder 115.
31. [Ebenezer Kwesi Christian: Brief Biography, 1906–1969] July 2015, GJC Papers, Folder 302.
32. Mrs Grace Christian, interview with Margaret Rouse-Jones, 8 August 2007, OPReP Collection. See also correspondence in response to a request for information about Mami Abba's tombstone; her dates of birth and death are given as 23 February 1899 and 2 January 1964 respectively. J. Bart-Plange, Kumasi-Ashanti, to Essi Christian, "From the Family Record", 8 February 1967, GJC Papers, Folder 171.
33. Mrs Grace Christian, interview with Margaret Rouse-Jones, 8 August 2007, OPReP Collection.
34. J.E. Kwegyir Aggrey to "Lawyer Christian", 28 May 1926, GJC Papers, Folder 31.
35. GJC to Howard Christian, 25 October 1935, GJC Papers, Folder 26.
36. GJC to Howard Christian, 22 November 1935, GJC Papers, Folder 26.
37. GJC to Howard Christian, 13 March 1936, and GJC to Peter Christian, 13 March 1936, GJC Papers, Folder 26.
38. GJC to Peter Christian, 8 April 1936, GJC Papers, Folder 37.

39. GJC to Mrs Leung, 27 March 1936, GJC Papers, Folder 156.
40. GJC to Clara Gordon, 14 November 1939, GJC Papers, Folder 144.
41. These are the children of his oldest daughter Clara, who was married to Edgar Gordon.
42. GJC to Peter Christian, 8 April 1936, GJC Papers, Folder 37.
43. GJC to Mrs Leung, 27 March 1936, GJC Papers, Folder 156.
44. GJC to George Francois, 21 January 1938, GJC Papers, Folder 98.
45. GJC to George Francois, 25 January 1938, GJC Papers, Folder 98. George Francois had migrated from St Lucia and had set up in the business of coco trading in the Gold Coast.
46. GJC to George Francois, 11 November 1937, GJC Papers, Folder 99.
47. GJC to Clara Gordon, 15 January 1938, GJC Papers, Folder 82.
48. GJC to Clara Gordon, 12 February 1938, GJC Papers, Folder 82.
49. Sierra Leone, which became the home of various groups of Africans who returned to the continent in the nineteenth and twentieth centuries, played a leading role in the promotion of western education in West Africa. Among these African returnees were slaves who were rescued after the slave trade had been abolished, as well as groups of settlers who returned from the New World: "the black poor from England, the Nova Scotians from Halifax, Canada, and the maroons from Jamaica . . . and liberated Africans . . . from along the Atlantic coast". It has been noted that "because Sierra Leone's repatriates were from England and the Americas, they valued Western culture and education". Their desire, combined with the commitment of the missionaries to education as a means of civilizing Africans, led to the founding of Fourah Bay College by the Church Missionary Society in 1826. The establishment of a connection between Fourah Bay College and Durham University in 1876 resulted in the availability of university education to students in Sierra Leone and across British West Africa. As the repatriates migrated to other parts of West Africa in search of their families, or business opportunities, or to share their faith, "they took with them aspects of Western education and culture". Akintola J.G. Wyse, "The Sierra Leone Krios: A reappraisal from the Perspective of the African Diaspora" in *Global Dimensions of the African Diaspora*, ed. Joseph E. Harris (Washington, DC: Howard University Press, 1993), 339. See also Joseph E. Harris, "Return Movements to West and East Africa: A Comparative Approach", in *Global Dimensions of the African Diaspora*, 52–53.
50. GJC to T.H. Wellington, Freetown, Sierra Leone, 21 July 1923, Folder 53.
51. GJC to Clara Gordon, 15 January 1938, GJC Papers, Folder 82.
52. GJC to Clara Gordon, 12 February 1938, GJC Papers, Folder 82.
53. GJC to Clara Gordon, 15 January 1938, GJC Papers, Folder 82.

54. Peter Christian to George James Christian, 21 June 1937, GJC Papers, Folder 81. Peter also bequeathed his share of the Dominica House, Sekondi property to Mami Abba. See in the Supreme Court of the Windward Islands and Leeward Islands, Colony of Dominica, Probate Re Peter Charles Christian (Deceased) Grant of Probate of Will, Recorded in Book of Probate Folios 65–67, Dated 29 November 1945. Official Copy of "the Last Will and Testament of me Peter Charles Christian . . . 5 April 1945", GJC Papers, Folder 50.
55. GJC to Peter Christian, 26 November 1937, GJC Papers, Folder 81.
56. See, for example, [GJC] to Mrs Leung, 1 October 1927, GJC Papers, Folder 10.
57. GJC to Miss Angela Christian, 3 June 1935, GJC Papers, Folder 29.
58. GJC to Mrs Peters, 2 May 1936, GJC Papers, Folder 65.
59. Sarah Duguid, "Moira's Roots", *Mail on Sunday*, 3 October 2004, 38. http://sarahduguid.com/pdf/Newspapers/roots.pdf (accessed 22 November 2014).
60. GJC to Capt. Joshua Cockburn, 20 July 1925, GJC Papers, Folder 60.
61. Duguid, "Moira's Roots", 38.
62. GJC to Capt. Joshua Cockburn, 20 July 1925, GJC Papers, Folder 60.
63. Edgar Gordon's admission of the "manly and timely help" he received from Christian, in a 1920 letter to GJC, indicated that there was some truth in this assertion. See Edgar [Gordon] to "My dear Lawyer", 29 August [19]20, GJC Papers, Folder 74.
64. GJC to Clara Gordon, 14 November 1939, GJC Papers, Folder 144.
65. GJC to Clara Gordon, 27 November 1939, GJC Papers, Folder 144.
66. Edgar [Gordon] to "My dear Lawyer", 29 August [19]20, GJC Papers, Folder 74.
67. Duguid, "Moira's Roots". See also Margaret Busby, [unpublished obituary of] "Kenneth Clifford Montgomery Gordon (13 February 1927–2 November 2013)" [November 2013]. Kenneth, the youngest, was born in Bermuda on 13 February 1927 and died in London on 2 November 2013.
68. Philip, *HAKIM, Son of Mazumbo*, 3.
69. George James Christian to Dr Akinwande Savage, 20 November 1925, GJC Papers, Folder 39.
70. Emmett J. Scott, Secretary Treasurer, Howard University, to GJC, 13 February 1925, GJC Papers, Folder 149.
71. Vice-Dean Collins Marshall to Emmett Scott, 17 September 1925. See also Dean Edward Ballock to Dr Emmett Scott, 27 October 1925, GJC Papers, Folder 149.
72. GJC to Emmett Scott, 25 September 1925, GJC Papers, Folder 149. See also Ag. Director, Medical and Sanitary Services, to GJC, 23 September 1927, GJC Papers, Folder 146, in which he cites the latest edition of a "Report as to the conditions under which Medical and Dental Practitioners registered or legally qualified in their own country may practice abroad – 6th Edition 1927", which

does not indicate that the DDS of [Howard] University, Washington, will entitle Peter to practise in the Gold Coast.
73. Emmett Scott to Mr George Christian, 12 October 1925, GJC Papers, Folder 149.
74. GJC to the Private Secretary to His Excellency the Governor, Sekondi, 12 November 1927, GJC Papers, Folder 146.
75. Bruce Crabb for Acting Colonial Secretary to GJC, 3 December 1927, GJC Papers, Folder 146.
76. Liberian Consul General, Liverpool, to Dr Peter Christian, 12 November 1925, GJC Papers, Folder 145.
77. Frederic G. Hallett, Director of Examinations, London, to Dr Christian, 10 November 1925, GJC Papers, Folder 145.
78. GJC to Dr Selwyn-Clarke, 17 December 1936, GJC Papers, Folder 76. Christian was of the view that Peter had got in with the wrong crowd of people during this stint in London. He described them as "impecunious and probably insignificant West African wasters ... [not] that better class of Fanti men, but rather ... that class who having no money to support themselves in London, earn a precarious living by ... their wits and by imposing on less experienced ones who they may be able to fool to lend them money ... the man he is now living with in North London is of that type". See GJC to Mrs Leung, 20 November 1925, GJC Papers, Folder 12.
79. Acting Governor T.R. St Johnston, Dominica, 15 September 1926, GJC Papers, Folder 80.
80. GJC to Dr P.C. Christian, 13 December 1926, and 18 February 1928, GJC Papers, Folder 146.
81. Dr Selwyn-Clarke to "My dear Mr Christian", 20 July 1937, with copies of correspondence from the director of Medical Services, Lagos, to Mr Geo. Christian, 19 July 1937, and Temporary Licence to Practise Dentistry granted to Peter Charles Christian, Lagos 19 July 1937. See also Director of Medical Services to GJC, 31 August 1937, GJC Papers, Folder 81.
82. Peter to "My dear Papa", 21 June 1937, GJC Papers, Folder 81. Peter felt that Maude's death was not due to natural causes.
83. GJC to "My dear Peter", 23 July 1937, GJC Papers, Folder 81.
84. Payments for sundry items for Maude Christian, Marjorie Burke and Christiane Burke between 1913 and 1915, GJC Papers, Folder 24.
85. Education Institute of Scotland, Hugh Cameron, Registrar, to the Board of Examiners [Report], GJC Papers, Folder 49. See also "Story of the Life and Death of a Noble Woman: Miss Maude Christian's Example of Public Service and Duty", *Times of West Africa*, 5 July 1933, GJC Papers, Folder 151.

86. GJC to Emmett Scott, 17 January 1925, GJC Papers, Folder 148. See also "Story of the Life and Death of a Noble Woman", *Times of West Africa*, 5 July 1933, GJC Papers, Folder 151.
87. GJC to Mrs R.H. Ribeiro, 10 September 1924, GJC Papers, Folder 77.
88. GJC to Peter C. Christian, 13 September 1924, GJC Papers, Folder 145.
89. GJC to Peter C. Christian, 23 October 1924, GJC Papers, Folder 145.
90. GJC to Mrs Heroine Ribeiro, 25 October 1924, GJC Papers, Folder 77.
91. GJC to Peter Christian, 6 December 1924, and GJC to Peter Christian, 17 January 1925, GJC Papers, Folder 145; GJC to Emmett Scott, Secretary Treasurer, Howard University, 14 February 1925, GJC Papers, Folder 149
92. Emmett Scott to Mr George Christian, 26 March 1925; GJC to Emmett Scott, 12 April 1925, GJC Papers, Folder 149.
93. GJC to Mrs Leung, 10 and 21 January 1928, GJC Papers, Folder 11. GJC's concern was also expressed in GJC to Peter Christian, 18 February 1928, GJC Papers, Folder 146.
94. GJC to Mrs Leung, 10 March 1928 and 5 May 1928, GJC Papers, Folder 11.
95. GJC to T.H. Wellington, Freetown, Sierra Leone, 21 July 1923, GJC Papers, Folder 53.
96. GJC to Mrs Leung, 6 August 1927, [GJC] to Mrs Leung, 1 October 1927, GJC Papers, Folder 10.
97. GJC to Mrs H. Leung, 6 March 1929, GJC Papers, Folder 16.
98. See correspondence from GJC to Mrs H. Leung, 10 January 1928, 10 March 1928, 17 March 1928, GJC Papers, Folder 11.
99. GJC to Mrs H. Leung, 18 February 1928, GJC Papers, Folder 11.
100. GJC to Vivian Harris, 3 September 1927, GJC Papers, Folder 40.
101. GJC to Mrs H. Leung, 7 April 1928, GJC Papers, Folder 11.
102. GJC to Vivian Harris, 19 November 1927, GJC Papers, Folder 40.
103. GJC to P.C. Christian, 18 February 1928, GJC Papers, Folder 146.
104. GJC to Mrs H. Leung, 16 November 1928, GJC Papers, Folder 11.
105. GJC to Mrs Eva Callender, 9 July 1930, GJC Papers, Folder 54.
106. Seale-Hayne Agricultural College, Terminal Report, Spring 1929, GJC Papers, Folder 150.
107. GJC to T.H. Wellington, Sierra Leone, 15 January 1924, GJC Papers, Folder 53. See also GJC to Frans Dove, 23 December 1926, GJC Papers, Folder 71. (Note that Dove's first name appears as "Frans" or "Franz" interchangeably throughout the documents. The authors have opted to use Franz in the main text of the book.) See GJC to Mrs Eva Callender, 20 February 1933, GJC Papers, Folder 54, which mentions Mrs Dick's death in Barbados, to which she returned as a widow.

108. Essi Matilda Forster (née Christian), interview with Estelle Appiah, Accra, Ghana, 13 June 1992, OPReP Collection. Estelle Appiah is the daughter of Essi Matilda Forster.
109. GJC to Mrs H. Leung, 16 July 1927, GJC Papers, Folder 10.
110. GJC to Mrs H. Leung, 29 January 1928, GJC Papers, Folder 11.
111. GJC to Mrs Leung, 17 June 1937, GJC Papers, Folder 25.
112. GJC to Mrs Leung, 22 May 1937, GJC Papers, Folder 25.
113. GJC to Dr P.C. Christian, 10 March 1928, GJC Papers, Folder 146.
114. GJC to Mrs Leung, 16 February 1929, GJC Papers, Folder 16.
115. GJC to Mrs Leung, 6 February 1929, GJC Papers, Folder 16.
116. GJC to the Revd Charles W. Farquhar, Conakry, Guinea, 29 October 1924, GJC Papers, Folder 18.
117. GJC to Peter, 27 June 1932, GJC Papers, Folder 147.
118. GJC to Peter, 8 September 1932, GJC Papers, Folder 147.
119. Howard Christian to GJC, 30 August 1939, GJC Papers, Folder 142.
120. Howard Christian to GJC, 15 June 1939, GJC Papers, Folder 129.
121. "Tribute to the Late Angela Christian by the Family", in "Burial and Thanksgiving Mass for the Late Angela Christian (Aged 83) at the Christ the King Catholic Church on 18 March 2000. Committal at Osu Cemetery", 8, GJC Papers, Folder 19.
122. GJC to Peter C. Christian, 14 March 1925, GJC Papers, Folder 145.
123. GJC to Howard, 30 September 1939, GJC Papers, Folder 143.
124. GJC to Essie, 14 February 1940, GJC Papers, Folder 156.
125. See, for example, GJC to Essie, 4 January 1940, GJC Papers, Folder 152.
126. GJC to Essie, 18 January 1940, GJC Papers, Folders 28 and 152.
127. His precise words were "University drawl or side", GJC to Mrs Leung, 27 February 1935, GJC Papers, Folder 155.
128. GJC to Mrs Leung, 27 February 1935, GJC Papers, Folder 155.
129. GJC to Sarah Christian, 9 December 1937, GJC Papers, Folder 81; GJC to Howard Christian, 9 December 1937, GJC Papers, Folder 115.
130. GJC to Howard Christian, 9 December 1937, GJC Papers, Folder 115.
131. Ibid.
132. This was a reference to Stanley Lewis's brother, Sir Arthur Lewis, who later became Nobel laureate.
133. GJC to Howard Christian, 9 December 1937, GJC Papers, Folder 115.
134. GJC to Sarah Christian, 9 December 1937, GJC Papers, Folder 81; GJC to Howard Christian, 9 December 1937, GJC Papers, Folder 115.
135. Sarah (Christian) Busby, interview with Margaret Busby, London, England, 14 April 1989, OPReP Collection.

136. GJC to Essie, 1 July 1939, GJC Papers, Folder 152.
137. GJC to Essie, 29 August 1939, GJC Papers, Folder 152.
138. Essi to "Papa and Mother", 5 September 1939 and 22 September 1939, GJC Papers, Folder 152.
139. GJC to Essi, 7 November 1939, GJC Papers, Folder 152.
140. GJC to Howard Christian, 29 August 1939, GJC Papers, Folder 59.
141. GJC to Howard Christian, 2 February 1940, GJC Papers, Folder 53.
142. Howard Christian to GJC, 21 February 1940, GJC Papers, Folder 124.
143. GJC to Howard, 11 January 1940, GJC Papers, Folder 55. Christian substituted the word "affection" in this quotation from William Shakespeare's *Hamlet*, 1.2, where the word "adoption" is used.
144. Howard Christian to GJC, 11 January 1939, GJC Papers, Folder 114.
145. GJC to Howard Christian, 29 January 1939, GJC Papers, Folder 115.
146. GJC to Peter Christian, 6 December 1924 and 28 March [1925], GJC Papers, Folder 145; GJC to Howell Shillingford, 10 December 1924 and 13 February 1926, GJC Papers, Folder 39. See also GJC correspondence with Peter during 1929 to 1930 and especially GJC to Peter, 5 March 1930, GJC Papers, Folder 146.
147. GJC to Peter, 15 August 1932, GJC Papers, Folder 147.
148. Chrissie to "My darling uncle", 7 June 1932 (aboard the *Monarch of Bermuda*), GJC Papers, Folder 34.
149. GJC to Miss Chrissie Burke, 10 August 1934, GJC Papers, Folder 34.
150. GJC to Chrissie Burke, 6 December 1938, GJC Papers, Folder 78.
151. GJC to Miss Chrissie Burke, 11 April 1935, GJC Papers, Folder 29.
152. Ibid.
153. GJC to Mrs Clara Menders, Bermuda, 8 April 1936, GJC Papers, Folder 138.
154. GJC to Peter Christian, 3 April 1937, GJC Papers, Folder 80.
155. Chrissie to GJC, 29 August 1939, GJC Papers, Folder 273.
156. GJC to Chrissie Burke, 29 March 1940, GJC Papers, Folder 64.
157. GJC to Miss May Christian, 23 September 1934, GJC Papers, Folder 34.
158. GJC to Miss May Christian, 8 November 1934, GJC Papers, Folder 35.
159. May Christian to: "My dear Uncle", 16 December 1934, GJC Papers, Folder 35
160. GJC to Miss May Christian, 7 April 1936, GJC Papers, Folder 28.
161. GJC to Dr J.E.K. Aggrey, 4 June 1927, GJC Papers, Folder 57.
162. GJC to Mrs Peters, 10 April 1935, GJC Papers, Folder 58.
163. GJC to Mrs H. Peters, 5 January 1[9]35, GJC Papers, Folder 58.
164. GJC to Mrs Peters, 4 February 1935, GJC Papers, Folder 58.
165. GJC to Mrs Peters, 2 May 1936, and Henrietta Peters to GJC, 14 August 1936, GJC Papers, Folder 65.
166. GJC to Mrs H. Leung, 4 March 1937, GJC Papers, Folder 50.

167. GJC to Horace Douglas, 27 February 1935, GJC Papers, Folder 50.
168. GJC to Horace Douglas, 17 January 1937, GJC Papers, Folder 50.
169. GJC to Horace Douglas, 22 January 1940, GJC Papers, Folder 50.
170. GJC to Capt. Joshua Cockburn, 20 July 1925, GJC Papers, Folder 60.
171. Ibid.
172. GJC to Mrs H. Leung, 26 November 1927, GJC Papers, Folder 10.
173. GJC to Howard Christian, 19 May 1935, GJC Papers, Folder 29.
174. GJC to Hollis Hallet, Barrister-at-Law, Bermuda, 15 January 1938, GJC Papers, Folder 79.
175. GJC to Peter Christian, 8 April 1936, GJC Papers, Folder 37.
176. GJC to Mrs Clara Manders, Bermuda, 8 April 1936, GJC Papers, Folder 138.
177. GJC to Peter Christian, 22 November 1935 and 13 February 1936, GJC Papers, Folder 26; GJC to Mrs M. Savage, Edinburgh, 14 February 1936, GJC Papers, Folder 138.
178. GJC to Marjorie Gordon, 13 February 1936, GJC Papers, Folder 26.
179. GJC to Mrs Clara Manders, Bermuda, 8 April 1936, GJC Papers, Folder 138.
180. GJC to Mrs M. Savage, Edinburgh, 25 April 1936, GJC Papers, Folder 138. The content of the letter suggests that Mrs Savage had oversight of Clara's children, who were being educated in England.
181. Clara Gordon to GJC, 25 February 1938, GJC Papers, Folder 82.
182. Edgar [Gordon] to "My dear Christian", 2 August 1938, GJC Papers, Folder 78.
183. GJC to Clara Gordon, 27 November 1939, GJC Papers, Folder 144.
184. http://www.bbc.co.uk/whodoyouthinkyouare/past-stories/moira-stuart.shtml (accessed 18 August 2013).
185. Philip, *HAKIM, Son of Mazumbo*, 10–13, GJC Papers, Folder 1. "Mazumbo", the "singular ethnonym for Zoombo, a Koongo sub-group", was also the popular name appropriated by Emmanuel Lazare (1864–1929), a famous Trinidadian lawyer with African/pan-African connections. He was the son of African parents who had migrated from Guadeloupe. See Maureen Warner-Lewis, *Central Africa in the Caribbean: Transcending Time, Transforming Cultures* (Kingston: University of the West Indies Press, 2003), 80.
186. GJC to Mrs Leung, 20 November 1925 and 4 December 1925, GJC Papers, Folder 12. See also GJC to Dr Peter Christian, 17 June 1937, GJC Papers, Folder 81.
187. GJC to Peter, 19 November 1927 and 12 February 1928, GJC Papers, Folder 146.
188. GJC to Dr P.C. Christian, 30 April 1929, GJC Papers, Folder 146; Dr Beausoleil also expressed the same view; see GJC to Peter, 13 November 1929, GJC Papers, Folder 146. Dr O.C. Arthur, a dental surgeon based in Kumasi, attended to Christian's family.
189. He also felt that the increased earnings would allow Peter to afford medical

treatment in Washington. GJC to Peter, 13 November 1929, GJC Papers, Folder 146.
190. GJC to Peter, 23 November 1929, GJC Papers, Folder 146.
191. GJC to Peter, 5 March 1930, GJC Papers, Folder 146.
192. For example, see GJC to Peter ("My dear Percy"), 11 November 1932, and GJC to Peter, 10 March 1934, GJC Papers, Folder 147.
193. Peter to GJC, 21 July 1932, GJC Papers, Folder 147.
194. GJC to Peter, 23 July 1932, GJC Papers, Folder 147.
195. GJC to Dr Peter Christian, 12 April 1940, GJC Papers, Folder 144.
196. See, for example, GJC to Peter ("My dear Percy"), 11 November 1932, GJC Papers, Folder 147; Peter [Christian] to "My dear Dad", 22 April 1934, GJC Papers, Folder 34; GJC to Peter Christian, 29 January 1938, GJC Papers, Folder 143; GJC to Dr Peter Christian, 12 April 1940, GJC Papers, Folder 144.
197. GJC to Peter, 12 April 1940, GJC Papers, Folder 144.
198. GJC to Dr Peter Christian, 2 September 1934, GJC Papers, Folder 34. See also GJC to Mrs Peters, 15 September 1934, GJC Papers, Folder 63.
199. Ibid. See also GJC to "My dear Cockburn", 25 August 1934, GJC Papers, Folder 34.
200. GJC to Dr Selwyn-Clarke, 17 December 1936, GJC Papers, Folder 76.
201. GJC to Dr P.C. Christian, 6 May 1928, GJC Papers, Folder 146.
202. Peter to "My dear Papa", 2 March 1929, GJC Papers, Folder 146.
203. GJC to "My dear Peter", 8 June 1929, GJC Papers, Folder 146.
204. GJC to Dr P.C. Christian, 20 July 1929, GJC Papers, Folder 146.
205. GJC to Dr P.C. Christian, 18 September 1929, GJC Papers, Folder 146.
206. See GJC letter to Peter, 14 February 1930, GJC Papers, Folder 146; GJC to Peter, 10 May 1930 and 20 August 1930, GJC Papers, Folder 147.
207. GJC to Peter, 2 December 1932, GJC Papers, Folder 147.
208. GJC to Peter, 29 October 1933, GJC Papers, Folder 147.
209. Peter [Christian] to "My dear Dad", 22 April 1934, GJC Papers, Folder 34.
210. GJC to Reginald J.R. Brett, 11 November 1938, and GJC to the Hon. H.D. Fredericks, 22 November 1938, GJC Papers, Folder 78.
211. Dr C. Belfield Clarke to GJC, 10 January 1939, GJC Papers, Folder 114.
212. GJC to Peter Christian, 3 January, 1939, GJC Papers, Folder 114.
213. Dr C. Belfield Clarke to GJC, 10 January 1939, GJC Papers, Folder 114.
214. Howard Christian to GJC, 16 December 1938, and Dr C. Belfield Clarke to GJC, 10 January 1939, GJC Papers, Folder 114.
215. Peter Christian to GJC, 20 December 1938, GJC Papers, Folder 120; Dr C. Belfield Clarke to GJC, 10 January 1939, GJC Papers, Folder 114.
216. Peter Christian to GJC, 20 December 1938, GJC Papers, Folder 120.

217. GJC to Dr S.B. Jones, 28 July 1939, GJC Papers, Folder 273.
218. See, for example, A.M. MacRae to GJC, 1 February 1931, GJC Papers, Folder 150; Resident Medical Officer, Gold Coast Hospital, to George James Christian, 7 January 1933, GJC Papers, Folder 151; Joe Christian to GJC, 5 February 1934, GJC Papers, Folder 151; GJC to Sarah Christian, 9 December 1937, GJC Papers, Folder 81; GJC to Clara Gordon, 20 February 1939, GJC Papers, Folder 84; GJC to Howard Christian, 28 February 1939, GJC Papers, Folder 114.
219. GJC to Harold Fredericks, Liberia, 25 June 1932, GJC Papers, Folder 23; GJC to T.I. Brett, 17 August 1932, GJC Papers, Folder 42; see also GJC to Peter, 23 July 1932, GJC Papers, Folder 147, and GJC to Dr O.C. Arthur, 15 May 1933, GJC Papers, Folder 69.
220. GJC to Dr O.C. Arthur, 15 May 1933, GJC Papers, Folder 69.
221. GJC to Peter, 8 July 1933, GJC Papers, Folder 147.
222. GJC to Peter, 2 February 1934, GJC Papers, Folder 147.
223. GJC to George Francois, 23 February 1934, GJC Papers, Folder 42.
224. Joe Christian to GJC, 2 October 1939, GJC Papers, Folder 142.
225. Joe Christian to GJC, 8 October 1939, GJC Papers, Folder 142.
226. Anne Marie Dwyer, "Parents Burying Children is Unnatural", http://annmariedwyer.hubpages.com/hub/Parents-Burying-Children-is-Unnatural (accessed 28 January 2015). This writer has noted that when a husband or wife dies, the remaining spouse is a widow or widower, when parents die they leave orphans, but "there is no word or name for the parent whose child dies. Parents burying children is unnatural."
227. Sarah Busby, interview with Margaret Busby, 9 March 1978, OPReP Collection.
228. R.S. Dyer, Richmond College, Cape Coast Castle, to George J. Christian, Esq., 23 January 1922, GJC Papers, Folder 32.
229. Address delivered at the Jubilee Memorial Chapel, 23 January 1922, on the occasion of the death of George Kwesi Christian, GJC Papers, Folder 32.
230. GJC to Howard Christian, 9 January 1938, GJC Papers, Folder 115. Unfortunately, this photograph is not in the GJC Papers.
231. GJC to Prof. J.E.K. Aggrey, 10 January 1927, GJC Papers, Folder 54.
232. GJC to J.W. French, Esq., 12 December 1924, GJC Papers, Folder 18.
233. GJC to Mrs Dick, 14 August 1925, GJC Papers, Folder 18.
234. GJC to J.W. French, Esq., 16 September 1925, GJC Papers, Folder 18.
235. Document listing George James Christian and family attendance to Dr Maclean from September 1926 to March 1927, 21 March 1927, GJC Papers, Folder 69.
236. Ibid.: See also GJC to Prof. J.E.K. Aggrey, 10 January 1927, GJC Papers, Folder 54.
237. GJC to Aggrey, 10 January 1927, GJC Papers, Folder 54.

238. GJC to Peter, 7 May 1927, GJC Papers, Folder 146.
239. GJC to Mrs Leung, 10 and 21 January 1928, GJC Papers, Folder 11. GJC's concern was also expressed in GJC to Peter Christian, 18 February 1928, GJC Papers, Folder 146.
240. GJC to Mrs Leung, 10 March 1928 and 5 May 1928, GJC Papers, Folder 11.
241. GJC to Harold Fredericks, Liberia, 25 June 1932, GJC Papers, Folder 23.
242. GJC to M.D. Reece, 25 June 1932, GJC Papers, Folder 62.
243. GJC to Dr O.C. Arthur, Kumasi, 2 July 1932, GJC Papers, Folder 62.
244. GJC to Peter, 2 September 1932, GJC Papers, Folder 147.
245. GJC to T.I. Brett, 17 August 1932, GJC Papers, Folder 42.
246. GJC to Maude Christian, London, 20 August, 3 September, 12 September, 1 October 1932, GJC Papers, Folder 51.
247. GJC to M.D. Reece, 8 October 1932, and GJC to Dr O.C. Arthur, Kumasi, 18 November 1932, GJC Papers, Folder 62.
248. "Story of the Life and Death of a Noble Woman", *Times of West Africa*, 5 July 1933, GJC Papers, Folder 151.
249. GJC to Peter, 25 June 1933, GJC Papers, Folder 147.
250. GJC to Howell Shillingford, Roseau, Dominica, 8 July 1933, GJC Papers, Folder 42; see also GJC to Peter, 8 July 1933, GJC Papers, Folder 147.
251. "Story of the Life and Death of a Noble Woman", *Times of West Africa*, 5 July 1933, GJC Papers, Folder 151.
252. GJC to Howell Shillingford, Roseau, Dominica, 8 July 1933, GJC Papers, Folder 42; see also GJC to Peter, 8 July 1933, GJC Papers, Folder 147.
253. GJC to C.W. Chappelle, 10 April 1934, GJC Papers, Folder 123.
254. GJC to Capt. Cockburn, 9 July 1933, GJC Papers, Folder 151.
255. Ibid.
256. GJC to Mrs H. Leung, 9 June 1934, GJC Papers, Folder 121.
257. "Story of the Life and Death of a Noble Woman", *Times of West Africa*, 5 July 1933, GJC Papers, Folder 151.
258. GJC to Peter Christian, 15 January 1938, GJC Papers, Folder 83. The family normally celebrated New Year's Day with the West Indian community, and this gathering is described in chapter 8.
259. GJC to Howard Christian, 2 January 1939, GJC Papers, Folder 114.
260. GJC to Clara Gordon, 15 January 1938, GJC Papers, Folder 82.
261. Howard Christian [to GJC], 11 January 1939, GJC Papers, Folder 114.
262. GJC to Howard Christian, 31 January 1939, GJC Papers, Folder 114.
263. GJC to Angela Christian, 24 February 1939, GJC Papers, Folder 123.
264. GJC to Howard Christian, 28 February 1939, GJC Papers, Folder 114.
265. GJC to C. Vaughan Charles, 6 March 1940, GJC Papers, Folder 64.

266. Ibid.
267. GJC to Peter, 8 April 1927, GJC Papers, Folder 146.
268. GJC to Howard Christian, 27 October 1939, GJC Papers, Folder 144.
269. GJC to Howard, 21 November 1939, GJC Papers, Folder 33.
270. GJC to Howard Christian, 7 December 1939, GJC Papers, Folder 59.
271. GJC to Peter Christian, 12 April 1940, GJC Papers, Folder 144.
272. [Dr Beausoleil] to Howard Christian, 19 April 1940, GJC Papers, Folder 277. The letter was addressed at Tafo, where Dr Amédée Edwin Charles Beausoleil, Christian's personal physician, had his practice.
273. Howard Christian to GJC, 25 January 1939, GJC Papers, Folder 124.
274. GJC to Howard, 21 August 1939, GJC Papers, Folder 59.
275. Peter [Christian] to "My dear Dad", 22 April 1934, GJC Papers, Folder 34.
276. GJC to Joyce Gordon, 2 February 1939, GJC Papers, Folder 84.
277. Sarah Busby, interview with Margaret Busby, 9 March 1978, OPReP Collection.
278. Essie Christian to Howard Christian, 31 May 1943, GJC Papers, Folder 131; Duguid, "Moira's Roots", 38.
279. Margaret Busby, [Obituary for] Kenneth Clifford Montgomery Gordon.
280. Philip, *HAKIM, Son of Mazumbo*, 10–13, GJC Papers, Folder 1.
281. Howard Christian to Essi Christian, 8 May 1941, GJC Papers, Folder 128.
282. Peter to Howard, 4 January 1941, GJC Papers, Folder 104.
283. Peter to Howard, 9 February 1942, GJC Papers, Folder 104.
284. [George] Francois to Howard Christian, 29 June 1943, GJC Papers, Folder 278.
285. Obituary: Doctor Peter Christian, *Dominica Chronicle,* 3 November 1945, 5, GJC Papers, Folder 104; May Christian to Mami Abba, 14 December 1945, indicated that Peter was ill for six months after he received a burn on his feet, which would have crippled him if he had lived, GJC Papers, Folder 104.
286. In the Supreme Court of the Windward Islands and Leeward Islands, Colony of Dominica, Probate re Peter Charles Christian (Deceased) Grant of Probate of Will, Recorded in Book of Probate Folios 65–67, Dated 29th November 1945. Official Copy of "the Last Will and Testament of me Peter Charles Christian ... 5th April 1945", GJC Papers, Folder 50. Correspondence from May Christian indicates that Chrissie Burke may have persuaded Peter to change his earlier will and that there was disagreement about the content of his final will. See May Christian to Howard Christian, 5 June 1946, GJC Papers, Folder 103.
287. GJC to Essie Christian, 31 January 1939, GJC Papers, Folder 129.
288. GJC to Clara Gordon, 20 February 1939, GJC Papers, Folder 84. See also Sarah H. Busby, interview with Margaret Busby, 9 March 1978, OPReP Collection.
289. Howard Christian to Essie Christian, 8 May 1941, GJC Papers, Folder 128.

290. [Ebenezer Kwesi Christian: Brief Biography, 1906–1969] July 2015, GJC Papers, Folder 302.
291. Seale-Hayne Agricultural College, Terminal Report, Spring 1929, GJC Papers, Folder 150.
292. GJC to Joseph Christian, 11 November 1930, GJC Papers, Folder 150.
293. GJC to Capt. Joshua Cockburn, 8 June 1932, GJC Papers, Folder 150.
294. Mr Brett to Messrs T. and R. Tennents, Limited, 23 February 1934, GJC Papers, Folder 151.
295. GJC to W. Minta-Jacobs, 22 January 1935, GJC Papers, Folder 30.
296. GJC to Mrs Leung, 9 December 1926, GJC Papers, Folder 69.
297. GJC to Howard Christian, 21 June 1939, GJC Papers, Folder 61.
298. Howard Christian to GJC, 5 December 1939, GJC Papers, Folder 124.
299. Joe Christian to GJC, 8 October 1939, GJC Papers, Folder 142.
300. Howard Christian to Essie Christian, 31 January 1942, GJC Papers, Folder 126. The details of Joe's family life were provided by his daughter Nana.
301. It has been suggested that Joe may have practised as a dentist or optician, but there is no data to support this.
302. GJC to Mrs Leung, 22 May 1937, GJC Papers, Folder 25.
303. GJC to Mrs Leung, 9 December 1936, GJC Papers, Folder 69.
304. His full name is given as a witness to the third codicil of George James Christian's will.
305. GJC to Mrs Peters, 16 January 1937, GJC Papers, Folder 65; GJC to Mrs Leung, 14 January 1937, GJC Papers, Folder 27.
306. Howard Christian to GJC, 5 October 1939, GJC Papers, Folder 142.
307. GJC to Howard Christian, 12 April 1940, GJC Papers, Folder 156.
308. GJC to Howard Christian, 28 November 1939, GJC Papers, Folder 59.
309. Howard Christian to GJC, 9 November 1939, GJC Papers, Folder 144.
310. Howard Christian to GJC, 22 November 1939, GJC Papers, Folder 124.
311. Howard Christian to GJC, 5 December 1939, GJC Papers, Folder 124.
312. GJC to Edu Sam, 10 February 1940, GJC Papers, Folder 64.
313. Howard Christian to Essie Christian, 31 January 1942, GJC Papers, Folder 126.
314. Ibid.
315. Howard Christian, "An Address about His Experience in London as an Air Raid Protection Services Warden [Sekondi, Gold Coast]", n.d., GJC Papers, Folder 154.
316. Howard Christian to Ferdinand Christian, 5 November 1942, GJC Papers, Folder 277.
317. Howard Christian to Essie Christian, 23 April 1942, GJC Papers, Folder 126.
318. Howard Christian to Josephine Armah, 18 April 1943, GJC Papers, Folder 70.

319. Howard Christian to Essie Christian, 6 September 1943, GJC Papers, Folder 131.
320. C.R.E. Russell, Solicitor, London, to Howard Christian, 13 January 1956, enclosing a copy of Beausoleil's last will, dated 16 September 1953, GJC Papers, Folder 33.
321. Angela Christian to GJC, 3 August 1937, GJC Papers, Folder 123.
322. Angela Christian to GJC, 10 September 1937, GJC Papers, Folder 123.
323. GJC to Howard Christian, 14 February 1940, GJC Papers, Folder 53.
324. "Biography of the Late Angela Christian", in "Burial and Thanksgiving Mass for the Late Angela Christian (Aged 83) at the Christ the King Catholic Church on 18 March 2000, Committal at Osu Cemetery", 5, GJC Papers, Folder 301. The date of this assignment has not been verified, but it was most likely in the late 1950s.
325. Ibid., 5–7.
326. The Ceres Medal, inspired by the Roman goddess of agriculture, is the highest award given by FAO to women who have made an important contribution to food security and sustainable development.http://www.fao.org/news/story/en/item/48443/icode/ (accessed 23 July 2012). See also "FAO Ceres Medals – Angela Christian", Food and Agricultural Organization of the United Nations, GJC Papers, Folder 113.
327. "Tribute to the Late Angela Christian by the Family", in "Burial and Thanksgiving Mass for the Late Angela Christian (Aged 83) at the Christ the King Catholic Church on 18 March 2000, Committal at Osu Cemetery", 8–9, GJC Papers, Folder 301.
328. Essi to "Papa and Mother", 4 January 1939, GJC Papers, Folder 152.
329. Essie to "Papa and Mother", 17 and 24 January 1940, GJC Papers, Folder 152.
330. Essie Christian to Howard Christian, 18 May 1940, GJC Papers, Folder 131.
331. Howard Christian to Essie Christian, 23 April 1942, GJC Papers, Folder 126.
332. Essie Christian to Howard Christian, 8 July 1942, GJC Papers, Folder 126.
333. Howard Christian to Essi Christian, 7 September 1942, GJC Papers, Folder 126.
334. The first African woman lawyer was Stella Thomas, who was appointed stipendiary magistrate in Lagos, Nigeria. Frances Wright from Sierra Leone, who also attended Gray's Inn, was the second woman. See Aba Sagoe, "Essi Matilda: A Woman among Pace-Setters", *Africa Woman* 7 (November–December 1976): 10, GJC Papers, Folder 214.
335. Howard Christian to Essie Christian, 23 April 1942, GJC Papers, Folder 126.
336. Howard Christian to Essi Christian, 7 September 1942, GJC Papers, Folder 126.
337. Howard to Mrs L. Murrell, 25 February 1947, GJC Papers, Folder 157.
338. Essi Matilda Forster, [résumé, n.d] typescript with handwritten corrections, 3, GJC Papers, Folder 214.

339. Ibid. FIDA is also known as the International Federation of Women Lawyers.
340. Sagoe, "Essi Matilda", GJC Papers, Folder 214.
341. "Burial and Thanksgiving Service for the Late Mrs Essi Matilda Forster on 14 August 1998, at 10 a.m. at the Ridge Church, Accra", GJC Papers, Folder 301.
342. GJC to Mrs Leung, 17 February 1935, GJC Papers, Folder 155.
343. GJC to Mrs H. Peters, 5 January 1[9]35, GJC Papers, Folder 58.
344. "Burial and Thanksgiving Service for the Late Dr Ferdinand Francisco Christian at the Christ the King Catholic Church on 16 August 2002, at 8 a.m., Committal at Osu Cemetery", 6–7, GJC Papers, Folder 7.
345. Dr Ferdinand Francisco Christian, interview with Estelle Appiah, Accra, Ghana, 19 April 1992, OPReP Collection.
346. "Burial and Thanksgiving Service for the Late Dr Ferdinand Francisco Christian . . .", 6–7, GJC Papers, Folder 7.
347. Ibid., 8–10.
348. Ibid., 8.
349. Their mother was Mercy Ayettey.
350. "Biography of Professor Edward Clifford Christian, 27 November 1930–23 November 2002", in "Burial and Thanksgiving Service for the Late Prof. Edward Clifford Christian at the Cathedral Church of the Most Holy Trinity, Accra on 31 May 2003", [programme], printed by Ghana Publishing Corporation Assembly Press, Accra, [2003], GJC Papers, Folder 50.

CHAPTER 4. ACHIMOTA COLLEGE, DR J.K. AGGREY, CHRISTIAN AND HIS FAMILY EXPERIENCES

1. C. Kingsley Williams, *Achimota: The Early Years* (Accra, Ghana: Longmans of Ghana, 1962), 4. Williams served as assistant vice-principal of Achimota College from 1927 to 1938.
2. K.B. Asante, "Achimota: A Heritage to Cherish", *Daily Graphic,* June 25, 2001, 7, GJC Papers, Folder 31. As noted in the foreword, in 1948, Achimota College became three separate institutions: the University College of the Gold Coast (which was subsequently moved to a separate campus at Legon and is now known as the University of Ghana), the Achimota Teacher Training College, and Achimota School. Achimota College still operates today as Achimota School under the oversight of the Ghana Education Service, providing a senior high school education to young women and men. The Kwame Nkrumah University of Science and Technology also had its roots in Achimota College's Engineering School. See BlackPast.org, "Remembered and Reclaimed: An Online Reference Guide to African American History", http://www.blackpast.org/gah/achimota

-college-achimota-school-1924#sthash.wDZYIaBN.dpuf (accessed 11 September 2014). See also "87th Achimota School Founders Day Celebration: Celebrating Our Founders", *Daily Graphic*, 1 March 2014, 14.
3. Edwin W. Smith, *Aggrey of Africa: A Study in Black and White* (New York: Richard R. Smith, 1930). See chapter 14, "The Genesis of Achimota", 225–26.
4. Williams, *Achimota*, 6, 16.
5. Smith, *Aggrey of Africa*, 225–26.
6. Williams, *Achimota*, 18.
7. Ibid., 10.
8. [Statement entitled] "The Death of James Emman Kwegyir Aggrey Assistant Vice-Principal of Prince of Wales College Gold Coast, West Africa", undated typescript, GJC Papers, Folder 57, [1].
9. Smith, *Aggrey of Africa*, 144–52.
10. Williams, *Achimota*, 13, 16.
11. [Statement entitled] "The Death of James Emman Kwegyir Aggrey Assistant Vice-Principal . . .", GJC Papers, Folder 57.
12. Dr Emmanuel Evans-Anfom, [personal reflections, January 2015], GJC Papers, Folder 86. Dr Evans-Anfom, born 1919, attended Achimota College from 1935, "when he was admitted to Form Three of the secondary department". He remembered Sarah, Angela and Ferdinand Christian. He also served as vice-chancellor of the Kwame Nkrumah University of Science and Technology. See more at http://www.graphic.com.gh/features/features/10680-dr-evans-anfom-one-of-ghana-s-talented-surgeons.html (accessed 28 April 2015).
13. Williams, *Achimota*, 14, 18; see also Smith, *Aggrey of Africa,* chapter 14, "The Genesis of Achimota", 225–45, [statement entitled] "The Death of James Emman Kwegyir Aggrey Assistant Vice-Principal . . .", GJC Papers, Folder 57.
14. Legislative Council Papers [1928], [photocopy, no bib. ref.], "The Construction of Achimota", Description of Achimota, para. 139, item (iv) and (v), 143, GJC Papers, Folder 130.
15. The foundation stone for the new buildings was laid in March 1924. Just over a year later (April 1925), His Royal Highness the Prince of Wales ceremonially authorized the college and school to be called by his name and unveiled a brass plate in the main entrance. In January 1926, a small class of "six little Twi-speaking boys" was started in a staff bungalow as the nucleus of the kindergarten, which was to be opened the following year. In March 1926, staff quarters were complete and occupied. In September, there was a change of contractor, which resulted in an increase in the rate of progress of the building work. It was therefore decided that the kindergarten would open in January 1927. Williams, *Achimota*, 20–21. A photocopy of this book is in the GJC Papers, Folder 54.

16. Legislative Council Papers [1928], [photocopy, no bib. ref.], para. 138, 140–42, GJC Papers, Folder 130.
17. Headmistress of Prince of Wales School, Achimota College, to GJC, 29 December 1926, GJC Papers, Folder 54.
18. Smith, *Aggrey of Africa*, 146, 151.
19. Christian made reference to this in a letter he wrote to Aggrey on his departure in 1927. "This is to wish you bon voyage and to repeat my wishes and hope when I wrote you whilst in port here on the occasion of your first visit", GJC to Prof. J.E.K. Aggrey, 8 May, 1927, GJC Papers, Folder 57.
20. Smith, *Aggrey of Africa*, 149–52.
21. According to Aggrey's biographer, "Aggrey's work was also marked out. It was for him to introduce Mr Fraser and his colleagues to the people, to expound the principles on which Achimota was to be run, and to win for them the enthusiastic support of his fellow-countrymen. His origin and position made him, of course, the ideal person for this task." Smith, *Aggrey of Africa*, 235. 22. Smith, *Aggrey of Africa*, 241–42.
23. "Story of the Life and Death of a Noble Woman", *Times of West Africa*, 5 July 1933, GJC Papers, Folder 151.
24. J.E. Kwegyir Aggrey to "Lawyer Christian", 28 May 1926, GJC Papers, Folder 31.
25. The spelling of the name has changed over the years, and "Ekua" is the modern spelling. "Eccuah", as it appears in the original documents, has been retained.
26. GJC to Dr J.E.K. Aggrey, Achimota College, 14 December 1926, GJC Papers, Folder 54.
27. Headmistress of Prince of Wales School, Achimota College, to GJC, 29 December 1926, GJC Papers, Folder 54.
28. GJC to Prof. J.E.K. Aggrey, 10 January 1927, GJC Papers, Folder 54.
29. "The wearing of cloths" in this context refers to the wearing of traditional apparel and is applicable to men and women.
30. A "single sleeping cloth" refers to a bedsheet.
31. GJC to Prof. J.E.K. Aggrey, 18 February 1927, GJC Papers, Folder 54.
32. Headmistress A. Mary Witten, the Kindergarten, Achimota College, to Miss Christian, 4 March 1927, GJC Papers, Folder 57.
33. Telegraph from Achicoll to Christian, referred to a letter of 19 March [1927], "admitting children", GJC Papers, Folder 57.
34. GJC to Prof. J.E.K. Aggrey, 30 March 1927, GJC Papers, Folder 57.
35. GJC to Prof. J.E.K. Aggrey, 8 May, 1927, GJC Papers, Folder 57.
36. J.E. Kwegyir Aggrey to GJC, 10 May 1927, GJC papers, Folder 57.
37. GJC to Dr J.E.K. Aggrey, 4 June 1927, GJC Papers, Folder 57.

38. [Statement entitled] "The Death of James Emman Kwegyir Aggrey Assistant Vice-Principal . . .", GJC Papers, Folder 57.
39. Ibid. See also Smith, *Aggrey of Africa*, 271–79.
40. Invitation card dated 5 August 1927, addressed to Miss Maude Christian, Order of Service inserted, GJC Papers, Folder 47.
41. Thomas Jesse Jones, [Statement from the] Phelps Stokes Fund, New York, 19 September 1927, GJC Papers, Folder 56.
42. [George James Christian]. Untitled manuscript, in pencil, n.d. The opening sentence reads, "What one could feebly add to the many and varied testimony of the late Dr J.E. Aggrey was . . .", GJC Papers, Folder 57.
43. Dr Aggrey Memorial High School, Sekondi. *School Prospectus 1936*, Sekondi, December 1935, A.W.E. Appiah, Principal. [It contains pencilled amendments to information intended for the 1939 edition], GJC Papers, Folder 83.
44. The principal reported that Teddy had "fallen in love with his school". He was an enthusiastic student who was able to repeat the letters of the alphabet in order, and the principal held out "great hopes" for him in the next term. Dr Aggrey Memorial High School, Sekondi, Report: June Term 1935, Edward Clifford Christian, GJC Papers, Folder 29.
45. Aggrey College, Sekondi, Report: Christmas Term 1938, [for] E.C. Christian, U. Prep One B, GJC Papers, Folder 83.
46. Honorary Secretary [of committee] to the Hon. G.J. Christian, 23 February 1935; J. Henley Coussey to GJC, 23 February 1935. The committee consisted of the Hon. Dr F.V. Nanka Bruce, MLC; Mr John Buckman, MBE; Dr J.H. Murrell, and Messrs S.E. Odamtten, E.C. Quist, H.F. Ribeiro and Akilagpa Sawyer, GJC Papers, Folders 31 and 194.
47. GJC to J. Henley Coussey, 23 February 1935, GJC Papers, Folder 194.
48. GJC to Chief Kwesi Andoh II, 27 February 1935, GJC Papers, Folder 31.
49. GJC to J. Henley Coussey, 23 February 1935, GJC Papers, Folder 194.
50. GJC to F. Awoonor-Williams, 28 February 1935, GJC Papers, Folder 194.
51. GJC to [unknown], 4 March 1935, GJC Papers, Folder 194.
52. GJC to J. Henley Coussey, 12 March 1935, GJC Papers, Folder 194.
53. The various European powers – starting with the Portuguese in 1471, and subsequently the British, Dutch, Danish, Swedish and Prussian – had trading interests in the Gold Coast until 1901, when it became a British colony. The Dutch and British presence in Sekondi was marked by their respective forts. See https://en.wikipedia.org/wiki/Sekondi-Takoradi and https://em.wikipedia.org/Gold_Coast (British_Colony) (accessed 15 March 2016).
54. Letter to the Revd A.G. Fraser [1935], signed by twelve people including the Omanhene of English and Dutch Sekondi; Christian; C.E.M. Abbensetts; F.

Awoonor-Williams; P. Carlis Paittoo, President "Optimism" Club, Sekondi; R. Crowther Nicol and others, GJC Papers, Folder 31.
55. Seale-Hayne Agricultural College, Terminal Report, Spring 1929, GJC Papers, Folder 150.
56. Principal A.G. Fraser to G.[J]. Christian, Dominica House, 1 September 1930, GJC Papers, Folder 57.
57. Principal A.G. Fraser to G.[J]. Christian, Dominica House, 11 September 1930, GJC Papers, Folder 56.
58. Principal A.G. Fraser to G.[J]. Christian, 3 October 1930, GJC Papers, Folder 56.
59. Principal A.G. Fraser to G.[J]. Christian, Dominica House, 16 December 1930, GJC Papers, Folder 56.
60. GJC to Mrs Leung, 15 October 1930, GJC Papers, Folder 13.
61. Principal A.G. Fraser to G.[J]. Christian, Dominica House, 16 December 1930, GJC Papers, Folder 56.
62. Geo. J. Christian to the Revd A.G. Fraser, 5 January 1931, GJC Papers, Folder 56.
63. Principal A.G. Fraser to G.[J]. Christian, 9 January 1931, GJC Papers, Folder 56.
64. GJC to Mrs Leung, 4 February 1931, GJC Papers, Folder 13.
65. Exchange of correspondence between E.A. Binks, Acting Bursar, Achimota College, and G.J. Christian, 22 April 1931, 28 April 1931, 13 May 1931, and enclosed receipt of 4 May 1931; GJC to the Revd A.G. Fraser, 18 August 1934, GJC Papers, Folder 56.
66. GJC to F.H. Derriman, c/o Bank of British West Africa Ltd, 37 Gracechurch Street, London E.C. 5, 4 February 1932, GJC Papers, Folder 51.
67. GJC to the Revd A.G. Fraser, 18 August 1934, GJC Papers, Folder 31.
68. See GJC to Miss Simons, 4 September 1934, GJC Papers, Folder 63, and GJC to Mrs H. Peters, 5 January 1[9]35, GJC Papers, Folder 58.
69. GJC to Miss Simons, 3 January 1934, GJC Papers, Folder 63.
70. Evans-Anfom, [Personal Reflections, January 2015], 2, GJC Papers, Folder 86.
71. See correspondence from Ferdinand Christian to "Father and Mother" throughout 1939, GJC Papers, Folder 152.
72. Ferdinand Christian to "Father", 30 June [1939], GJC Papers, Folder 152.
73. Gari is a popular West African food made from grated cassava, from which the moisture has been extracted and which is lightly toasted or fried. It may be prepared in different ways, mixed with hot or cold water.
74. Ferdinand Christian to "Mother", 23 September 1939, GJC Papers, Folder 152.
75. Ferdinand Christian to "Father", 25 October 1939, GJC Papers, Folder 152.
76. Ferdinand Christian to "My dear brother" [Howard], 19 March 1940, GJC Papers, Folder 105.

77. Ferdinand Christian to "Dear Brother" [Howard], 10 July 1940, GJC Papers, Folder 105.
78. Ferdinand Christian to "Dear Howard", 5 July 1942, GJC Papers, Folder 105.
79. Ferdinand to "Dear Howard", 6 September 1942, GJC Papers, Folder 105.
80. Howard] to "My dear Ferdinand", 9 September 1942, GJC Papers, Folder 105.
81. See correspondence mainly between Ferdinand Christian and his brother Howard, 1934–1942, GJC Papers, Folder 105.
82. "Burial and Thanksgiving Service for the Late Prof. Edward Clifford Christian on 31 May 2003", GJC Papers, Folder 50.
83. Teddy to Howard, 23 February 1947, GJC Papers, Folder 157.
84. Teddy to Howard, 2 March 1947, GJC Papers, Folder 157.
85. "Burial and Thanksgiving Service for the Late Prof. Edward Clifford Christian on Saturday, 31 May 2003", GJC Papers, Folder 50.
86. GJC to T.I. Brett, c/o Bank of British West Africa, London, 7 June 1930, GJC Papers, Folder 41.
87. S.H. Christian to Mr Grace, 2 December 1936, GJC Papers, Folder 76.
88. Copy of Agreement between the Council . . . of the Prince of Wales College and School of Achimota . . . and S.H. Christian, 30 May 1932, GJC Papers, Folder 80.
89. Principal A.G. Fraser to G.W. Christian, Dominica House, 11 September 1930, GJC Papers, Folder 56.
90. GJC to Mrs Leung, 26 August 1930, GJC Papers, Folder 13.
91. Evans-Anfom, [Personal Reflections, January 2015], 1, GJC Papers, Folder 86.
92. C. Kingsley Williams, Acting Principal, Achimota College, to G.J. Christian, 16 June 1932, GJC Papers, Folder 56.
93. George Francois to "My dear Christian", 2 February 1934, GJC Papers, Folder 42.
94. Sarah to "My dear Papa", 2 December 1936, GJC Papers, Folder 76.
95. S.H. Christian to Mr Grace, 2 December 1936, GJC Papers, Folder 76.
96. Sarah to "My dear Papa", 2 December 1936, GJC Papers, Folder 76.
97. Francois to "My dear G.J.", Tafo, 8 December 1936, GJC Papers, Folder 76
98. GJC to Frans Dove, Barrister-at-Law, 11 December 1936; GJC to E.C. Quist, Barrister-at-Law, 11 December 1936; GJC to L.E.V. McCarthy, Solicitor General, 11 December 1936; GJC to Canon Grace, Principal of Achimota College, 11 December 1936, GJC Papers, Folder 76.
99. GJC to Quist, 11 December 1936, GJC Papers, Folder 76.
100. GJC to McCarthy, 11 December 1936, GJC Papers, Folder 76.
101. GJC to Quist, 11 December 1936, GJC Papers, Folder 76.
102. H.M. Grace, Principal, Achimota College, to Geo. J. Christian, Esq., 15 December 1936, GJC Papers, Folder 76.

103. GJC to Canon Grace, 11 December 1936, GJC Papers, Folder 76.
104. Sarah to "My dearest Papa", 12 January 1937, GJC Papers, Folder 80.
105. GJC to Sarah at the Royal Infirmary, Scotland, 29 January 1938, GJC Papers, Folder 83.
106. GJC to Sarah, 25 May 1938, GJC Papers, Folder 83.
107. Principal, Achimota, to Mrs C.M. Gordon, Somerset, Bermuda, 3 May 1937, GJC Papers, Folder 33.
108. Clara Gordon to the Revd H.W. Grace, Principal Achimota College, 13 August 1937, GJC Papers, Folder 33.
109. "Burial and Thanksgiving Mass for the Late Angela Christian (Aged 83) at the Christ the King Catholic Church on Saturday, 18 March 2000, Committal at Osu Cemetery", 5, GJC Papers, Folder 19.
110. GJC to Essie, 4 January 1940, GJC Papers, Folder 33.
111. Evans-Anfom, [Personal Reflections, January 2015], 2, GJC Papers, Folder 86.
112. Angela Christian to GJC, 23 November 1938, GJC Papers, Folder 123.
113. Howard Christian to Essie Christian, 23 April 1942, GJC Papers, Folder 298.
114. Ibid.
115. Howard Christian to "My dearest Essie", 18 June 1942, GJC Papers, Folder 126.
116. Dr Evans-Anfom has indicated that "the problem of the non-Europeans not receiving the same remuneration and conditions of service was one which needed proper resolution" and that "it was not solved adequately until the time of the transition to independence". Evans-Anfom, [Personal Reflections, January 2015], 1–2, GJC Papers, Folder 86.

CHAPTER 5. "LAWYER CHRISTIAN"

1. David Kimble, *A Political History of Ghana: The Rise of Gold Coast Nationalism, 1850–1928* (Oxford: Oxford University Press, 1963), 68.
2. A.B. Chinbuah, "John Mensah Sarbah: First Gold Coast Barrister", *Daily Graphic*, 22 April 2005, 17, and 29 April 2005, 11, GJC Papers, Folder 130. See also Roger Gocking, "The Adjudication of Homicide in Colonial Ghana: The Impact of the Knowles Murder Case", *Journal of African History*, 52 (2011): 85–104.
3. Gocking, "Adjudication of Homicide", 88.
4. *Gold Coast Leader*, 21 March 1903, 2
5. Francis Stanislaus Leung died on 15 May 1916. [Document] "In the Estate of Francis Stanislaus Leung". Supreme Court Records, Western Province, Gold Coast Colony. Will dated 21 August 1910. G.J. Christian was one of the witnesses of the will.

6. Douglas, Grant and Dold to the Hon. Geo. J. Christian, 30 December 1931, GJC Papers, Folder 121; GJC to Horace Douglas, 6 January 1932, GJC Papers, Folder 121.
7. *Gold Coast Leader*, 21 March 1903, 2.
8. See Wanted [advertisement], *Gold Coast Leader*, 29 September, 6 October and 13 October 1906, Cape Coast Archives.
9. Essi Matilda Forster, interview with Estelle Appiah, Accra, Ghana, 13 June 1992, OPReP Collection.
10. *Gold Coast Leader*, 7 and 14 February 1903, 2, GJC Papers, Folder 32.
11. Ibid.
12. *Gold Coast Leader*, 21 March 1903, 2, GJC Papers, Folder 32.
13. *Gold Coast Leader*, 11 May 1907, 4, British Library Newspapers.
14. GJC to the Commissioner of Stamps, District Treasury, 11 December 1924, GJC Papers, Folder 72.
15. George James Christian to Mr Stockfeld, 8 November 1913, GJC Papers, Folder 74.
16. R.H. Ribeiro to George J. Christian, 8 December 1924, GJC Papers, Folder 72.
17. George James Christian to J.R. Cardew Smith, 5 July 1923, GJC Papers, Folder 2.
18. George James Christian to J.R. Cardew Smith, 1 March 1924, GJC Papers, Folder 2.
19. GJC to J.R. Cardew Smith, 5 July 1923, GJC Papers, Folder 4.
20. GJC to L.A. Smart, 13 February 1921, GJC Papers, Folder 8.
21. GJC to L.A. Smart, 2 March 1923, GJC Papers, Folder 8.
22. Amanful Compensation Document, GJC Papers, Folder 6.
23. GJC to J.R. Cardew Smith, 26 October 1923 and 5 July 1923, GJC Papers, Folder 4.
24. GJC to J.R. Cardew Smith, 2 August 1923, GJC Papers, Folder 4.
25. GJC to L.A. Smart, 1 September 1923, GJC Papers, Folder 6.
26. GJC to J.R. Cardew Smith, 18 July 1924, GJC Papers, Folder 2.
27. GJC to L.A. Smart, 5 July 1924, GJC Papers, Folder 9.
28. GJC to L.A. Smart, 2 August 1924, GJC Papers, Folder 9.
29. L.A. Smart to George James Christian, 26 July 1921, GJC Papers, Folder 3.
30. GJC to J.R. Cardew Smith, 24 November 1923, GJC Papers, Folder 4.
31. GJC to J.R. Cardew Smith, 27 September 1924, GJC Papers, Folder 2.
32. GJC to L.A. Smart, 19 January 1924, GJC Papers, Folder 9.
33. GJC to L.A. Smart, 13 September 1924, GJC Papers, Folder 9.
34. "Stool" means the institution of chieftaincy under the leadership of a traditional ruler who is nominated, elected and enstooled in accordance with the relevant

customary law. "Stool lands" refers to the area administered by the chief for the stool on behalf of the people in a particular place.
35. In the Supreme Court of the Gold Coast Colony Western Province Divisional Court Sekondi, *Odikro Kwaw Koom* v. *Odikro Kojo Awortwi*, Motion filed by Counsel for the Plaintiff, 9 December 1927, GJC Papers, Folder 173.
36. In the Supreme Court of the Gold Coast Colony, Eastern Province, at the Full Court held at Victoriaborg, Accra, *Odikro Kwaw Koom of Jombo* v. *Odikro Kojo Awortwi*, 25 March 1929, GJC Papers, Folder 173.
37. Affidavit of Robert John Hayfron in support of Motion of Review of Judgment, In the Supreme Court of the Gold Coast Colony Eastern Province, Full Court-Accra, *Odikro Kwaw Koom of Jombo* v. *Odikro Kojo Awortwi*, 11 May 1929, GJC Papers, Folder 173.
38. GJC to R.J. Hayfron, 1 June 1929, GJC Papers, Folder 173.
39. GJC to the Manager, Bank of British West Africa, Ltd, 20 November 1929, GJC Papers, Folder 31.
40. GJC to Douglas, 24 September 1914, GJC Papers, Folder 14.
41. Henry Dietrich to German Consulate, Accra, West Africa, Gold Coast, 14 December 1935, GJC Papers, Folder 140.
42. GJC to the Manager, Bank of British West Africa, Ltd, 20 November, 1929, GJC Papers, Folder 31; Power of Attorney, Henry Dietrich to George James Christian, December 1914, GJC Papers, Folder 113.
43. Henry Dietrich to German Consulate, Accra, West Africa, Gold Coast, 14 December 1935, GJC Papers, Folder 140.
44. Mr Henry Dietrich to Mrs Leung, 6 June 1933, GJC Papers, Folder 140.
45. Mrs H. Leung to Mr Dietrich, 24 July 1932, GJC Papers, Folder 140.
46. GJC to Mrs H. Leung, 12 February 1936, GJC Papers, Folder 140.
47. Mrs Leung to Mr Dietrich, 2 March 1932, GJC Papers, Folder 141.
48. GJC to Horace Douglas, 13 May 1932, GJC Papers, Folder 141.
49. GJC to Henry Dietrich, 15 September 1933, GJC Papers, Folder 140.
50. Mrs H. Leung to George James Christian, 20 September 1932, GJC Papers, Folder 140.
51. Mrs H. Leung to Miss Grimm, 15 January 1932, GJC Papers, Folder 141.
52. Mrs Leung to Mr Dietrich, 2 March 1932, GJC Papers, Folder 141.
53. The Humble Memorial of John Mansour for Permission to Naturalise as a British Subject, 8 August 1936, GJC Papers, Folder 210.
54. GJC to Provincial Commissioner, West Province, Sekondi, 19 December 1927, GJC Papers, Folder 183.
55. Ag. Commissioner, West Province, 24 December 1927, GJC Papers, Folder 183.

56. GJC to Provincial Commissioner, West Province, Sekondi, 27 February 1928, GJC Papers, Folder 184.
57. John Mansour to GJC, 4 February 1929, GJC Papers, Folder 186.
58. GJC to John Mansour, 5 February 1929, GJC Papers, Folder 186.
59. GJC to Immigration Officer of Takoradi, 9 April 1931, and GJC to John Mansour, 16 April 1931, GJC Papers, Folder 188.
60. John Mansour to GJC, 19 December 1931, GJC Papers, Folder 188.
61. See correspondence between GJC and John Mansour during the period 31 March 1932 to 1 June 1934, GJC Papers, Folders 191, 192 and 193.
62. See the following correspondence: John Mansour to GJC, 21 February 1933, GJC Papers, Folder 192; John Mansour to GJC, 18 July 1933, GJC Papers, Folder 192; GJC to John Mansour, 8 March 1934, GJC Papers, Folder 193.
63. GJC to John Mansour, 3 March 1933, GJC Papers, Folder 192; John Mansour to GJC, 4 March 1933, GJC Papers, Folder 193.
64. John W. Daw to Mr Richards, 30 November 1925, and George James Christian to Mr Richards, 5 December 1925. GJC Papers, Folder 12.
65. GJC to Mrs Leung, 4 December 1925, GJC Papers, Folder 12.
66. GJC to Innes Browne and Company, 23 April 1926, GJC Papers, Folder 12.
67. GJC to Mrs Leung, 4 December 1925, GJC Papers, Folder 12.
68. GJC to Mrs Leung, 3 November 1926, GJC Papers, Folder 12.
69. Giles Hunt and Co. to G.J. Christian, 30 October 1926, GJC to Giles Hunt and Co., 2 November 1926, GJC to Mrs Leung, 3 November 1926, GJC Papers, Folder 12; Giles Hunt and Co. to G.J. Christian, 12 May 1927, G.J. Christian to Giles Hunt and Co., 13 May 1927, GJC Papers, Folder 10.
70. See Formal Notices from attorney for and on Behalf of Barclays Bank (Dominion, Colonial and Overseas) to Hedwig Leung and to George James Christian, her true and lawful Attorney, dated 30 October 1926 and 20 October 1928, GJC Papers, Folders 11 and 12; see also GJC to Mrs Leung, 30 April 1927, GJC Papers, Folder 10.
71. Giles Hunt and Co. to G.J. Christian, 22 October 1928, 25 October 1928, 29 October 1928, GJC Papers, Folder 11; GJC to Mrs Leung, 19 October 1928, 3 November 1928; GJC to Giles Hunt and Co., 24 October 1928, 26 October, 1928.
72. GJC to Giles Hunt and Co., 7 November 1928; Giles Hunt and Co. to G.J. Christian, 10 November 1928, enclosing copy of lease dated 20 October 1928; GJC to Mrs Leung, 16 November 1928, GJC Papers, Folder 11.
73. GJC to Howard Christian, 23 February 1940, GJC Papers, Folder 53.
74. Ibid.
75. Acting Chief Commissioner of Ashanti to Franz Dove, 22 June 1927, GJC Papers, Folder 127.

76. GJC to L.S. Gruchy, 17 January 1929, GJC Papers, Folder 89.
77. GJC to L.S. Gruchy, 22 January 1929, GJC Papers, Folder 89.
78. GJC to L.S. Gruchy, 11 June 1929, GJC Papers, Folder 92.
79. GJC to W.I. Shepley-Taylor, 6 December 1929, GJC Papers, Folder 186.
80. GJC to the District Commissioner of Sekondi, 4 January 1931, GJC Papers, Folder 188; Kojo Edwin to the District Commissioner of Sekondi, 2 February 1932, GJC Papers, Folder 191.
81. GJC to the Manager of Barclays Bank in Sekondi, 23 March 1932, GJC Papers, Folder 191.
82. Secretary of the Western Province Teachers' Union to GJC, 16 February 1933, GJC Papers, Folder 299
83. GJC to the Manager of Abbontiakoon Mines Limited, 11 February 1928, GJC Papers, Folder 184.
84. GJC to Chief Kwamina Faibill II, Ohene of Apintoe, 11 February 1928, GJC Papers, Folder 184.
85. Power of Attorney given to George James Christian by Central Wassau Gold Mines Limited, 21 February 1929, GJC Papers, Folder 175.
86. GJC to C.W. Chappelle, 23 January 1932, GJC Papers, Folder 122.
87. Chairman, Aristan Gold Mines (1929) Ltd, to GJC, 29 May 1934, GJC Papers, Folder 123.
88. GJC to C.W. Chappelle, 2 February 1932, GJC Papers, Folder 122.
89. GJC to C.W. Chappelle, 4 February 1932, GJC Papers, Folder 122.
90. GJC to Howard Christian, 26 February 1940, GJC Papers, Folder 124.
91. Howard Christian to GJC, 27 February 1940, GJC Papers, Folder 124.
92. GJC to Howard Christian, 1 March 1940, GJC Papers, Folder 124.
93. Howard Christian to GJC, 7 February 1940, GJC Papers, Folder 124.
94. GJC to Howard Christian, 20 February 1940, GJC Papers, Folder 124.
95. "Destool" or "destoolment" refers to the removal of a chief.
96. "Enstoolment" means the installation of a chief as a traditional ruler.
97. GJC to the Colonial Secretary in Accra, 19 February 1935, GJC Papers, Folder 194.
98. GJC to Howard Christian, 29 January 1938, GJC Papers, Folder 115.
99. GJC to Howard Christian, 12 February 1938, GJC Papers, Folder 115.
100. GJC to Howard Christian, 2 October 1937, GJC Papers, Folder 118.
101. GJC to Howard Christian, 28 October 1937, GJC Papers, Folder 118.
102. GJC to Howard Christian, 6 November 1937, GJC Papers, Folder 118.
103. GJC to A.I. Zaitzeff, 10 May 1932, GJC Papers, Folder 18.
104. GJC to Viscount Greenwood, 14 October 1938, GJC Papers, Folder 120.
105. GJC to Mrs Leung, 4 September 1936, GJC Papers, Folder 156.

106. GJC to Mrs Clara Gordon, Hamilton and New York, 3 June 1935, GJC Papers, Folder 29; see also GJC to Mrs Peters, 10 April 1935, GJC Papers, Folder 58.
107. GJC to Viscount Greenwood, 14 October 1938, GJC Papers, Folder 120.
108. GJC to Horace Douglas, 22 January 1940, GJC Papers, Folder 50.
109. Gocking, "Adjudication of Homicide".
110. No. 12 Statement of Accused on Investigation before Commitment in the Supreme Court of the Gold Coast, GJC Papers, Folder 168.
111. See, for example, *Daily Express*, 27 November 1928; *Daily Telegraph*, 27 November 1928; *West Africa*, 22 December 1928; *West Africa*, 8 December 1929; and *Daily Mail*, 27 November 1928 among others.
112. CO 96/686/6: Privy Council Proceedings on Appeal from the Chief Commissioner's Court of Ashanti, Eastern Province, 18 November 1929, Volume 1.
113. CO 96/705/2 7272: Administration of Gold Coast, Ashanti and Northern Territories.
114. An Ordinance to provide for the Administration of the Government of Ashanti, No. 1, 1902, National Archives, Accra, Ghana.
115. CO 96/691/1: Extract from the Truth publication dated 29 January 1929 entitled "Judicial Administration in Ashanti".
116. CO 96/691/1: Supplement to *African World*, 29 December 1928,
117. In the Privy Council, on Appeal from the Circuit of Ashanti, *Rex* v. *Benjamin Knowles*. Date unknown. GJC Papers, Folder 168.
118. CO 96/686/3: Acting Circuit Court Judge McDowell in correspondence dated 24 November 1928 addressed to His Excellency the Governor in the matter of *Rex* v. *Dr Benjamin Knowles*, Notes on the Case.
119. CO 96/682/16: Draft letter from Mr L.S. Amery, Downing Street, 28 January 1929, to Sir Ransford Slater, KCMG, CBE. The Case of Dr B. Knowles.
120. Albert Lieck, ed., *Trial of Benjamin Knowles* (Edinburgh: William Hodge, 1933), 129, GJC Papers, Folder 5.
121. CO 96/682/16: Notes of the case reported in the *Daily Express* of 24 November 1928. The Case of Dr B. Knowles.
122. Lieck, *Trial of Benjamin Knowles*, 126–27.
123. An Ordinance to provide for the Administration of the Government of Ashanti, No.1, 1902, National Archives, Accra, Ghana.
124. Lieck, *Trial of Benjamin Knowles*, 127.
125. CO 96/682/16: Correspondence dated 29 November 1928. The Case of Dr B. Knowles.
126. "Dr. Knowles Reprieved", *Daily Mail*, 3 December 1928, 19.
127. Central News, "Dr. Knowles", *Daily Mail*, London, 27 November 1928, 5; *Daily Mail* Historical Web Archive, Colindale Library (accessed 25 July 2013).

128. An Ordinance to provide for the Administration of the Government of Ashanti, No.1, 1902, 3, Sections 9, 13 and 16. See also, "Sentence on Dr. Knowles", *Daily Mail*, 28 November 1928, 5.
129. CO 96/682/16: This was reported in the *Daily Mail*, 28 November 1928, captioned "Sentence on Dr. Knowles". The Case of Dr B. Knowles.
130. Ibid.
131. CO 96/691: Ashanti Judicial Systems, Northern Territories Judicial System.
132. CO 96/691/1: This was reported in *West Africa*, 22 December 1928, 1748, "Administrators' Courts in West Africa".
133. GJC to the Treasurer and Masters of the Bench of Gray's Inn, 8 May 1906, ADM 12/1/28, National Archives, Accra, Ghana. This is also cited in SMarika Sherwood, *Origins of Pan-Africanism: Henry Sylvester Williams, Africa, and the African Diaspora* (London: Routledge, 2011) 88.
134. D.W. Douthwaite to Earl of Elgin, 23 May 1906 and 10 June 1906, ADM 12/1/28, Ghana Archives.
135. CO 96/693/11: R.L. Antrobus to D.W. Douthwaite, Steward and Under Treasurer, Gray's Inn, 27 March 1907.
136. An Ordinance to provide for the Administration of the Government of Ashanti, No. 1, 1902, National Archives, Accra, Ghana
137. GJC to Horace Douglas, 24 November 1928, GJC Papers, Folder 168.
138. Two Afghan wars between 1839 and 1879 helped the British to consolidate their power in Balochistan. Sir Robert Sandeman, who later became the Chief Commissioner of Balochistan, was the architect of British strategy in the region, and he negotiated a number of treaties with the khan of Kalat during 1854 to 1901. Through these treaties, the British government gained control over the leased territory of Chaghi, Bolan Pass, Quetta and other areas. The princely states of Mekran, Kharan, Lasbela and a little later Kalat state acceded to Pakistan after it came into being in 1947. In 1955, Balochistan was merged into one unit of West Pakistan. After the dissolution of one unit, Balochistan emerged as one of the four new provinces of Pakistan. http://www.balochistan.gov.pk/index.php?option=com content&view=article&id=38&Itemid=784. (accessed 13 May 2013).
139. GJC to Horace Douglas, 24 November 1928, GJC Papers, Folder 168.
140. "Murder Trial and No Jury: English Doctor's Plight", *Daily Mail*, 15 November 1928, 7, included G.J. Christian's letter.
141. GJC to Horace Douglas, 24 November 1928, GJC Papers, Folder 168. See Black's *Law Dictionary*, 5th ed. "Justice is neither to be denied or delayed". http://constitutionalgov.us/Blacks5th.htm (accessed 13 May 2013).

142. "Writer to the Signet" is a senior Scots solicitor and a member of an ancient society of solicitors. http://www.collinsdictionary.com/dictionary/english/writer-to-the-signet.
143. GJC to Horace Douglas, 24 November 1928, GJC Papers, Folder 168.
144. GJC to Messrs Wynne-Baxter and Keeble, 2 April 1929, GJC Papers, Folder 169.
145. GJC to Horace Douglas, 1 May 1929, GJC Papers, Folder 119.
146. GJC to Mrs Leung, 24 November 1928, GJC Papers, Folder 16; GJC to Horace Douglas, 30 April 1930, GJC Papers, Folder 121.
147. Authorization Note from Benjamin Knowles, 28 November 1928; B. Knowles to Senior Supt of Prisons, 28 November 1928, GJC Papers, Folder 168.
148. GJC to Frans Dove, 29 November 1928, GJC Papers, Folder 168.
149. GJC to Frans Dove, 28 December 1928, GJC Papers, Folder 68.
150. GJC to Mrs H. Leung, 2 December 1928, GJC Papers, Folder 16.
151. GJC to Horace Douglas, 10 December 1928, GJC Papers, Folder 168. Christian's involvement is also recorded in "Dr. Knowles Reprieved", *Daily Mail*, 3 December 1928, 19.
152. GJC to Horace Douglas, 19 January 1929, GJC Papers, Folder 169.
153. Wynne-Baxter and Keeble to GJC, 13 March 1929, GJC Papers, Folder 169.
154. CO 96/686/6: Privy Council Proceedings of Knowles trial, vol. 1, 1.
155. Wynne-Baxter and Keeble to GJC, 19 April 1929, GJC Papers, Folder 169.
156. "Woman's Aid for Dr. Knowles: Letter to the King/Friends Signing Petition", GJC Papers, Folder 246.
157. "Dr. Knowles's Move: Judge Reviewing Case", *Daily Mail*, GJC Papers, Folder 246. See also, "Dr. Knowles Reprieved", *Daily Mail*, 3 December 1928, 19.
158. "Dr Knowles's Appeal Fund to Pay Costs", newspaper clipping [*Daily Mail*], 16 January 1929, GJC Papers, Folder 169.
159. Aid for Dr B. Knowles, newspaper clipping, n.d., GJC Papers, Folder 169.
160. "Dr B. Knowles's Appeal Delayed by Lack of Funds", newspaper clipping, n.d., GJC Papers, Folder 169.
161. "Aid for Dr. B. Knowles", newspaper clipping, n.d., GJC Papers, Folder 169.
162. Douglas Crawford to Messrs Wynne-Baxter and Keeble, 6 December 1928, GJC Papers, Folder 168.
163. GJC to Horace Douglas, 2 December 1928, GJC Papers, Folder 168.
164. GJC to Horace Douglas, 10 December 1928, GJC Papers, Folder 168.
165. CO 96/686/6: Correspondence between Burchells and the Colonial Office enclosing account of charges, 24 March 1930; J.E.W. Flood to Crown Agts for the colonies, 10 April 1930.
166. GJC to Mrs H. Leung, 2 December 1928, GJC Papers, Folder 16.
167. See reports "Dr. Knowles on Way Home", *Daily Mail*, 25 March 1929, 7; "Dr.

Knowles Arrives", *Daily Mail*, 2 April 1929, 9; "Dr. Knowles Ill", *Daily Mail*, 15 November 1929, 7.
168. CO 96/686/4: Dr B. Knowles. Appeal to the Privy Council at the Court of St James, 7th day of May 1929, by M.P.A. Hankey.
169. CO 96/686/4: Dr B. Knowles. Appeal to the Privy Council, Draft from L.S. Amery, 26 March 1929.
170. GJC to Horace Douglas, 1 May 1929, GJC Papers, Folder 119.
171. GJC to Frans Dove, 6 December 1928, GJC Papers, Folder 68.
172. GJC to Frank N. Hillier, 5 January 1938, GJC Papers, Folder 79.
173. Lieck, *Trial of Benjamin Knowles*, 183.
174. GJC to George Francois, 21 November 1929, GJC Papers, Folder 41.
175. Cable from GJC to Ambaah, Kumasi, 20 November 1929, and E.H. Ambaah to GJC, 22 November 1929, GJC Papers, Folder 23.
176. GJC to Vivian Harris, 7 December 1929, GJC Papers, Folder 41.
177. GJC to Horace Douglas, 30 April 1930, GJC Papers, Folder 121.
178. GJC to George Francois, 5 December 1929; GJC to Vivian Harris, 18 February 1930, GJC Papers, Folder 41.
179. GJC to Horace Douglas, 23 November 1929, GJC Papers, Folder 121.
180. GJC to Horace Douglas, 14 March 1930, GJC Papers, Folder 121.
181. GJC to Horace Douglas, 10 April 1930, GJC Papers, Folder 121.
182. GJC to John Angus, 10 April 1930, GJC Papers, Folder 121.
183. Casely Hayford, Vice-President of the Gold Coast Bar Association, to Sir John Simons, c/o the Secretary, the General Council of the Bar, London, 17 August 1929, GJC Papers, Folder 68.
184. Gocking, "Adjudication of Homicide", 93.
185. Ibid., 94.
186. Ibid., 98.
187. See CO 96/705/1 7271: Ashanti and Northern Territories; admission of lawyers, jury system.
188. See discussion of George James Christian Sr in chapter 2.
189. GJC to Frank N. Hillier of the *Daily Mail*, 5 January 1938, GJC Papers, Folder 79.
190. For a detailed discussion of the steps to this development, see Gocking, "Adjudication of Homicide", 94–104.
191. "Mr. Clyne's Order", *Daily Mail*, 21 November 1929, 11.
192. Fred Agyemang, *Accused in the Gold Coast*, 2nd ed. (Ghana: Waterville, 1972), 129.
193. George James Christian to John Angus, 20 March 1930, GJC Papers, Folder 22.
194. Agyemang, *Accused in the Gold Coast*, 129.

276 Notes to pages 131–135

195. CO 96/705/5: Barry Higgins to Secretary of State for the Colonies, 18 May 1832.
196. Agyemang, *Accused in the Gold Coast*, 130. See also "Death of Dr. Knowles: Gold Coast Drama Recalled", *Daily Mail*, 30 October 1933, 8.
197. The guinea was the original gold coin and was worth twenty shillings. Its increase in value was parallel with the value of gold until it was officially fixed at twenty-one shillings. It was originally minted in the United Kingdom between 1663 and 1814 and named after the Guinea region in West Africa from which the gold was derived. Similarly, the sovereign is a gold coin with a nominal value of one pound sterling used as a bullion coin. It was minted in the United Kingdom from 1817 to 1917, and has continued from 1957 to the present time. http://en.wikipedia.org/wiki/Guinea_%28British_coin%29 and http://en.wikipedia.org/wiki/Sovereign_%28British_coin%29 (accessed 6 January 2015).
198. GJC to Mar. Bannerman, 1 August 1939, GJC Papers, Folder 273.
199. Jno. M. Sarbah to G.J. Christian, June 1910, GJC Papers, Folder 32.
200. George James Christian to Sir Phillip Smyly, 22 August 1929, GBR/0115/RCMS 137/2, Gold Coast Letters and Papers, 1921–1953, Correspondence and Papers of Sir Philip Smyly, Cambridge University Library, Cambridge, United Kingdom. We are grateful to Simone Charles for assistance with research conducted at Cambridge University Library.
201. "Hon. George James Christian, Defender of Poor Criminals, Passes Away at Sekondi", *African Morning Post*, 19 April 1940, 1–2.
202. "Justice Strother-Stewart and Crown Counsel Ainsley Speak Highly of Late Barrister Christian", *Daily Echo*, 24 April 1940.
203. Gold Coast, Legislative Council Debates, Session 1940, 5–6.
204. This is discussed in chapter 2.
205. For a discussion of this subject in the context of the particular case, see Gocking, "Adjudication of Homicide".

CHAPTER 6. CHRISTIAN'S MULTIFACETED LIFE

1. Deed of settlement recorded 27 March 1913, Dominica, relating to a mortgage executed on 15 October 1894 in favour of George James Christian. See also "Gordon v. Burke", *West Indian Reports*, 16 (1970): 204–15 [photocopies].
2. GJC to Howell Shillingford, 16 February 1924, GJC Papers, Folder 39.
3. GJC to Howell Shillingford, 13 December 1926, GJC Papers, Folder 39.
4. GJC to Howell Shillingford, 19 November 1925, GJC Papers, Folder 39.
5. GJC to Peter, 8 April 1927, GJC Papers, Folder 146; see also GJC to Alex R. Cools-Lartigue, 24 March 1927, GJC Papers, Folder 127, and Alex R. Cools-Lartigue to GJC, 8 June 1927, GJC Papers, Folder 127.

6. GJC to Peter, 8 April 1927, GJC Papers, Folder 146.
7. GJC to Peter, 13 August 1927, 31 October 1927, GJC Papers, Folder 146. The title of the "Pound" being in Thomas Howard Shillingford's name was rectified by a deed of conveyance in Mr Christian's favour drawn up by Mr Alex R. Cools-Lartigue and executed by Mary Eliza Shillingford and Howell Donald Shillingford. This was dated 25 April 1928 and recorded at the Registrar's Office in Dominica in Book of Deeds Liber M, No. 7, folio 198, and was in Peter Christian's possession. See Alex R. Cools-Lartigue to GJC, 9 October 1929, GJC Papers, Folder 127.
8. GJC to Peter, 8 April 1927, GJC Papers, Folder 146.
9. Cecil E.A. Rawle to George James Christian, 17 June 1935, GJC Papers, Folder 135.
10. Chrissie Burke, interview with Margaret D. Rouse-Jones, Roseau, Dominica, August 1993, OPReP Collection. See also in the Supreme Court of the Windward Islands and Leeward Islands Colony of Dominica Probate, 29 November 1945, Last Will and Testament of Peter Charles Christian, 5 April 1945.
11. Peter Christian to GJC, 5 March 1939, GJC Papers, Folder 116.
12. GJC to Peter Christian, 6 March 1939, GJC Papers, Folder 116.
13. GJC to Peter Christian, 17 May 1939, GJC Papers, Folder 116.
14. Peter Christian to GJC, 30 April 1939, GJC Papers, Folder 116.
15. Ibid.
16. Document of conveyance entitled "This Indenture", 29 February 1904, GJC Papers, Folder 252.
17. African Union Company (Chas. W. Chappelle) to Geo. J. Christian, 7 July 1919, GJC Papers, Folder 134.
18. "Mr. Christian's Properties and Rents", 2 July 1920, GJC Papers, Folder 109.
19. GJC to G.H. Garford, 1 November 1923, GJC Papers, Folder 110.
20. George James Christian to Messrs Robinson and Watt, 4 December 1924, GJC Papers, Folder 72.
21. GJC to L.S. Gruchy, 29 May 1922, GJC Papers, Folder 87.
22. GJC to L.S. Gruchy, 31 May 1922, GJC Papers, Folder 87.
23. GJC to L.A. Smart, 27 September 1924, GJC Papers, Folder 9.
24. GJC to L.A. Smart, 21 June 1924, GJC Papers, Folder 9.
25. Property Owners and Residents of Secondee to the Officer appointed by the Principal Secretary of State for the Colonies to enquire into the proposed Deep Sea Harbour, April 1924, GJC Papers, Folder 47.
26. GJC to L.A. Smart, 21 June 1924, GJC Papers, Folder 9.
27. Report of a meeting with Mr Fred Palmer at Secondee, 25 April 1924, GJC Papers, Folder 47.

28. GJC to J.R. Cardew Smith, 5 July 1924, GJC Papers, Folder 2.
29. GJC to L.S. Gruchy, 12 November 1928, GJC Papers, Folder 88.
30. GJC to L.S. Gruchy, 2 and 24 November 1928, GJC Papers, Folder 88.
31. George James Christian to J.P. Allen, 10 and 13 February 1930, GJC Papers, Folder 91.
32. GJC to J.P. Allen, 20 February 1930, GJC Papers, Folder 91.
33. George James Christian to L.S. Gruchy, 13 February 1930, GJC Papers, Folder 91.
34. J.P. Allen to George James Christian, 18 February 1930, GJC Papers, Folder 91.
35. GJC to L.S. Gruchy, 9 April 1930 and 14 March 1930, GJC Papers, Folder 91.
36. GJC to Capt. Joshua Cockburn, 1 October 1929, GJC Papers, Folder 60.
37. GJC to Capt. Joshua Cockburn, 1 October 1929, GJC Papers, Folder 60.
38. Arthur Puls to George J. Christian, 19 March 1921, GJC Papers, Folder 74.
39. Walker R. Gess to George J. Christian, 8 December 1921, GJC Papers, Folder 74.
40. Paul Splettstoesser to GJC, 9 April 1922, GJC Papers, Folder 74.
41. Curtis, Campbell and Co. to George James Christian, c/o Messrs Scrutton, Sons and Co., 1 September 1920, GJC Papers, Folder 109.
42. Ibid.
43. Ibid.; Curtis, Campbell and Co. to George James Christian, 4 September 1923, GJC Papers, Folder 110.
44. GJC to L.S. Gruchy, 2 August 1923, GJC Papers, Folder 94.
45. GJC to L.S. Gruchy, 18 August 1923, GJC Papers, Folder 94.
46. George James Christian to Messrs Curtis, Campbell and Co., 18 November 1923, GJC Papers, Folder 110.
47. Curtis, Campbell and Co. to George James Christian, 27 October 1923; George James Christian to G.H. Garford, 29 October 1923, GJC Papers, Folder 110.
48. GJC to G.H. Garford, 9 November 1923, GJC Papers, Folder 110.
49. Ibid.
50. Curtis, Campbell and Co., to George J. Christian, 4 December 1923, GJC Papers, Folder 73.
51. George J. Christian to G.H. Garford, 8 December 1923, GJC Papers, Folder 73.
52. Ibid.
53. G.R. Garnett to GJC, 5 February 1924, GJC Papers, Folder 182.
54. George James Christian to G.H. Garford, 25 February 1926, GJC Papers, Folder 97.
55. GJC to Curtis, Campbell and Co., 25 February 1926, GJC Papers, Folder 97.
56. J.W. French to GJC, 25 August 1924; GJC to J.W. French, 2 November 1928, GJC Papers, Folder 18. Christian noted that the actual debt was £2,000, but

"for peace sake" he accepted Otoo's figure of £1,146. He also did not claim the costs of his attendance or Abbensetts's.
57. See exchange of correspondence between GJC and George Francois, August–October 1932, GJC Papers, Folder 42.
58. Goods and Cash Taken Over by Cheapside Syndicate Ltd, 1 July 1937, GJC Papers, Folder 100.
59. George Francois to George James Christian and G. Stanley Lewis, 24 April 1937, GJC Papers, Folder 102.
60. Circular of Cheapside Syndicate Ltd, 14 January 1938, GJC Papers, Folder 98.
61. GJC to Constance, 14 January 1938, GJC Papers, Folder 270; GJC to Clara Gordon, 15 January 1938, GJC Papers, Folder 82.
62. GJC to W.P. Allen, 16 January 1938, GJC Papers, Folder 82.
63. GJC to Mrs Ribeiro, 9 February 1925, GJC Papers, Folder 72.
64. GJC to the Registrar, Divisional Court, Sekondi, 10 November 1924, GJC Papers, Folder 72.
65. GJC to Mrs Leung, 9 December 1926, GJC Papers, Folder 69.
66. GJC to Mrs Leung, 28 September 1928, GJC Papers, Folder 16.
67. GJC to Capt. Joshua Cockburn, 3 September 1932, GJC Papers, Folder 150.
68. GJC to M.D. Reece, 9 June 1932, GJC Papers, Folder 62.
69. GJC to Mrs Leung, 15 October 1930, GJC Papers, Folder 13.
70. GJC to Peter, 15 October 1930, GJC Papers, Folder 147.
71. GJC to Peter, 19 December 1930, GJC Papers, Folder 147.
72. GJC to Peter, 4 January 1931, GJC Papers, Folder 147.
73. See exchange of correspondence, Capt. Joshua Cockburn to GJC, 1 June 1927, and GJC to Capt. Cockburn, 13 August 1927, GJC Papers, Folder 60.
74. GJC to Joseph Christian, 15 March 1930, GJC Papers, Folder 150.
75. GJC to E.H. Ambaah, Kumasi, 17 December 1931; 23 March 1932; 18 October 1932, GJC Papers, Folder 23. See also GJC to A.I. Zaitzeff, 7 September 1932 and 11 November 1932, GJC Papers, Folder 20; GJC to Capt. Joshua Cockburn, 8 June 1932, GJC Papers, Folder 150.
76. GJC to M.D. Reece, 8 October 1932, GJC Papers, Folder 62.
77. Bank of British West Africa Limited to George James Christian, 28 October 1935, GJC Papers, Folder 26; GJC to the Manager of the Bank of British West Africa, 8 August 1936, GJC Papers, Folder 17.
78. GJC to Peter Christian, 15 January 1938, GJC Papers, Folder 83.
79. Ibid.
80. GJC to Vivian Harris, 3 September 1927, GJC Papers, Folder 40.
81. GJC to Vivian Harris, 24 March 1927, GJC Papers, Folder 39.
82. GJC to Vivian Harris, 18 March 1928, GJC Papers, Folder 40.

83. GJC to Vivian Harris, 5 May 1928; GJC to Vivian Harris, 3 November 1928, GJC Papers, Folder 40.
84. GJC to Vivian Harris, 16 November 1928; GJC to Vivian Harris, 2 December 1928, GJC Papers, Folder 40.
85. GJC to Vivian Harris, 7 December 1929; Vivian Harris to GJC, 1 January 1930, GJC Papers, Folder 41.
86. GJC to Harris, 21 March 1932; GJC to Vivian Harris, 4 April 1932, GJC Papers, Folder, 41.
87. GJC to the Under Secretary of Middle Temple, 27 April 1939, GJC Papers, Folder 273.
88. GJC to unknown, 9 May 1939, GJC Papers, Folder 273.
89. GJC to Howard Christian, 5 May 1939, GJC Papers, Folder 61.
90. GJC to Emmett Scott, 26 April 1924, GJC Papers, Folder 149.
91. GJC to Peter Christian, 26 April 1924, GJC Papers, Folder 145.
92. Emmett Scott to GJC, 31 May 1924, GJC Papers, Folder 148.
93. House Governor of the Middlesex Hospital, London, 23 September 1927; Secretary of the All Help League to George James Christian, 24 September 1927, GJC Papers, Folder 61.
94. Acting Administrator, Dominica, to George James Christian, 15 December 1930, GJC Papers, Folder 61.
95. [Extract from Diary of J.W. French of Elmina, 27] French Ebiradze Royal Family, Nyankrom, Family Archives, Accra, Ghana.
96. A.J. Newman, Principal of Mico Training College, to GJC, 15 September 1937, GJC Papers, Folder 85.
97. The HMS *Thetis* was a submarine of the British Royal Navy which sank off North Wales during trials on 1 June 1939. Ninety-nine lives were lost in the tragedy. See "The Tragic Story of the HMS *Thetis*", https://sites.google.com/site/francisscalpell/Home/story-of-the-thetis-submarine (accessed 3 March 2015).
98. GJC to Howard Christian, 16 August 1939, GJC Papers, Folder 59.
99. GJC to R.U. Riley, 23 June 1939, GJC Papers, Folder 273.
100. Christian died before paying the money to the Colonial government as he had indicated, and there was no mention of the Maude Christian Memorial Fund in his will or in any of the three codicils. The court ordered that the executors of the will should be entitled to withdraw the money – the sum was over £830 – for payment to the government. See High Court, Western Judicial Division, Divisional Court (Acolatse J, 3 July 1958) *Francois and Others* v. *Bank of Africa West Africa Ltd*, *West African Law Reports* [1958?], 439–41. See chapter 8 for further details of the bronze plate.
101. H.B. Popham, Government House, Dominica, to Mr Christian, 7 January 1936,

GJC Papers, Folder 33; see also *Dominica Official Gazette* 59, no. 42 (20 July 1936), item no. 200, 227, GJC Papers, Folder 83.
102. GJC to Joshua Cockburn, 9 October 1937, GJC Papers, Folder 264.
103. GJC to Joshua Cockburn, 9 April 1937, GJC Papers, Folder 264.
104. GJC to Joshua Cockburn, 9 October 1937, GJC Papers, Folder 264.
105. Joshua Cockburn to Honorable GJC, 11 December 1937, GJC Papers, Folder 264.
106. Netelka Sam, interview with Estelle Appiah, Accra, Ghana, 5 May 1992, OPReP Collection. Netelka Sam, who was eighty-three years at the time of the interview, was the daughter of George Henry Packwood, an Englishman. Her mother was from Somanya.
107. "Burial, Memorial and Thanksgiving Service for the Late Mrs Netelka Theresa Edu-Sam, aged 93, at the Christ the King Catholic Church, Accra, 22 August 2002 at 10 a.m., followed by Interment at the Osu Cemetery", 2, GJC Papers, Folder 7.
108. To GJC, 11 September 1929, GJC Papers, Folder 69.
109. "Burial, Memorial and Thanksgiving Service for the Late Mrs Netelka Theresa Edu-Sam", 2, GJC Papers, Folder 7.
110. Netelka to GJC, 6 May 1934, GJC Papers, Folder 193.
111. Netelka Sam, interview with Estelle Appiah, 5 May 1992, OPReP Collection.
112. Edu Sam to GJC, 5 May 1938; Netelka to GJC, 7 May 1938, GJC Papers, Folder 287.
113. GJC to Edu Sam, 10 February 1940, GJC Papers, Folder 64.
114. Leo Muss was the son of a West Indian of the same name who assisted Christian when he first arrived in the Gold Coast. This is mentioned in chapter 2. See also GJC to Joe Christian, 8 June 1937, GJC Papers, Folder 118.
115. Leo J. Muss to GJC, 3 February 1938, GJC Papers, Folder 270.
116. GJC to Leo J. Muss, 16 February 1938, GJC Papers, Folder 270.
117. Leo Muss to George James Christian, 22 January 1940, GJC Papers, Folder 67.
118. Ibid.
119. GJC to Leo Muss, 31 January 1940, GJC Papers, Folder 67.
120. Paul N. Munyagwa to Mr Christian, 3 July 1939, GJC Papers, Folder 152; GJC to Ferdinand, 18 July 1939, GJC Papers, Folder 152.
121. GJC to "My dear Paul", 26 February 1940, GJC Papers, Folder 64.
122. Paul N. Munyagwa to GJC, 11 March 1940, GJC Papers, Folder 64. Paul continued to keep in touch with the family after Christian's death. In 1944, he was part of the West Africa Artillery serving with other Ugandans in India; see Paul Munyagwa to Howard Christian, 5 December 1944, GJC Papers, Folder 157.

123. See, for example, Lewdena Germain to [GJC], 2 September 1928; Matoute Daniel to the Hon. G.J. Christian, 16 October 1938, GJC Papers, Folder 78.
124. Constance to GJC, 31 October 1916, GJC Papers, Folder 154.
125. See, for example, GJC to the Manager, Bank of British West Africa, Sekondi, 13 April 1935, GJC Papers, Folder 29.
126. GJC to Peter, 31 October 1932, GJC Papers, Folder 147.
127. GJC to Constance, 14 January 1938, GJC Papers, Folder 270.
128. GJC to Constance Lockhart, 13 February 1936, GJC Papers, Folder 138.
129. Peter to "My dear Papa", 14 June 1936, GJC Papers, Folder 104.
130. GJC to Constance Lockhart, 27 April 1938, GJC Papers, Folder 270.
131. GJC to Constance Lockhart, 24 February 1939, GJC Papers, Folder 273. His closing words in this letter were: "Now Darling, I send you my love with the best of good wishes to you, to Maggie and the family. Affectionately yours."
132. GJC to Constance Lockhart, 13 June 1939, GJC Papers, Folder 273.
133. GJC to Peter Christian, 27 October 1939, GJC Papers, Folder 144.
134. Clarita Potter to GJC, 1 February 1939, GJC Papers, Folder 273.
135. GJC to Miss Mamah Alexander, 13 June 1939, GJC Papers, Folder 273.
136. GJC to the Secretary, St George's Lodge, Roseau, Dominica, 29 January 1938, GJC Papers, Folder 83.
137. GJC to Peter Christian, 29 January 1938, GJC Papers, Folder 143.
138. GJC to Constance, 14 January 1938, GJC Papers, Folder 270.
139. GJC to C.W. Winston, 27 July 1939, GJC Papers, Folder 273.
140. See GJC to Peter Christian, 26 May 1939; A.E. Hempel to GJC, 31 May 1939; GJC to Peter Christian, 5 July 1939, GJC Papers, Folder 116.
141. One writer has noted that in Britain, "gambling as a proportion of consumer spending rose from 1.3% in 1920 to 5% in 1938". The prizes for the Stock Exchange, Baltic and Calcutta sweepstakes in the 1920s and the Irish Hospital Sweepstakes in the 1930s were "huge", and the winners were published in the *Times* and other leading newspapers. See Mike Huggins, "BBC Radio and Sport 1922 to 1939", *Contemporary British History* 21, no. 4 (December 2007): 502. https://www.academia.edu/2080003/BBC_Radio_and_Sport_1922_39 (accessed 8 March 2015).
142. GJC to L.A. Smart, 8 November 1923, GJC Papers, Folder 6.
143. GJC to F. Lack and Son Ltd, 18 January 1924, GJC Papers, Folder 125.
144. Curtis, Campbell and Co. to George James Christian, 28 April 1925, GJC Papers, Folder 96.
145. GJC to Vivian Harris, 24 March 1927, GJC Papers, Folder 39.
146. GJC to M.D. Reece, 9 June 1932, GJC Papers, Folder 62.
147. GJC to Capt. Joshua Cockburn, 14 May 1932, GJC Papers, Folder 150.

148. GJC to Horace Douglas, 6 August 1932, GJC Papers, Folder 113.
149. GJC to Mrs Savage, 27 October 1935, GJC Papers, Folder 136.
150. GJC to W Bro. Montague, 26 October 1935, GJC Papers, Folder 136.
151. See, for example, Southern Rhodesia Lottery Tickets, 10/- Rhodesian Currency, The Derby to be run at Epsom on 2 June 1937 and Grand National Sweepstake, 1938, Limited, to members of the West Indian Club, GJC Papers, Folder 50. See also Accra Polo Derby Sweepstake, 1939, Irish Free State Hospital's Sweepstake, the Derby 1938, and the Grand National 1938, GJC Papers, Folder 119.
152. GJC to L.S. Gruchy, 16 October 1928, GJC Papers, Folder 88.
153. Probate in the Supreme Court of the Gold Coast Western Province, 29 June 1940. The Last Will with three codicils of George James Christian of Dominica, British West Indies, and of Dominica House, Sekondi, in the Western Region of the Gold Coast, 22 February 1936, GJC Papers, Folders 157.
154. Declaration of the Personal Property of a Testator in the Supreme Court of the Gold Coast Colony . . . Personal Property of George James Christian, May 1940. National Archives of Ghana, Sekondi, Ghana.
155. Letter to Probate Court, Sekondi, 1 March 1946, GJC Papers, Folder 157.
156. The details are summarized from Copy of Probate and Will and Codicils of George James Christian Deceased. Certified True Copy, GJC Papers, Folder 157.
157. Information flyer, the West African Industrial Academy, Sekondi, Gold Coast Colony, West Africa. American Address: 44 Pliny Street, Hartford, Conn. [1937?], GJC Papers, Folder 271.
158. See exchange of correspondence between Christian and George Francois: GJC to George Francois, 7 October 1932, and George Francois to GJC, 15 December 1932, GJC Papers, Folder 42. See also R.E.P. to G.J., 4 June 1934, GJC Papers, Folder 34.
159. GJC to Mrs H. Peters, 13 November 1938, GJC Papers, Folder 66.
160. GJC to Mrs Peters, New York City, 20 December 1937, GJC Papers, Folder 63.
161. GJC to Miss Simmons, 3 January 1934, GJC Papers, Folder 63.
162. GJC to the Revd R.E. Peters, Philadelphia, 9 December 1933, GJC Papers, Folder 63.
162. GJC to the Revd R.E. Peters, 22 July 1934, GJC Papers, Folder 63.
164. See the following exchange of letters: GJC to Mrs Peters, 5 August 1934; GJC to Miss Simmons, 28 August 1934; GJC to Mrs Peters, 29 August 1934; Miss Simmons (Headmistress) to GJC, Ag. Manager, 4 September 1934; Henrietta Peters to GJC, 12 September 1934, GJC Papers, Folder 63.
165. [The Revd] Peters to GJC, 12 September 1934, GJC Papers, Folder 63.
166. Mrs Peters to the Hon. G.J. Christian, 13 November 1935, GJC Papers, Folder 58.

167. GJC to Mrs H. Peters, 9 January 1936; GJC to Mrs Peters, 18 September 1936, GJC Papers, Folder 65.
168. Mrs Peters to GJC, 14 August 1936, GJC Papers, Folder 65.
169. Mrs Peters to GJC, 16 June 1936, GJC Papers, Folder 65.
170. GJC to Mrs Peters, 18 September 1936, Folder 65.
171. Ibid.
172. GJC to the Revd Peters, 18 January 1937, GJC Papers, Folder 65.
173. Mrs Peters to "Lawyer" [Christian], 10 December 1936, GJC Papers, Folder 65.
174. The Revd Peters to the Hon. G.J. Christian, 21 December 1936, GJC Papers, Folder 65.
175. GJC to Mrs Peters, 10 April 1935, GJC Papers, Folder 58.
176. GJC to Mrs Peters, 16 January 1937, GJC Papers, Folder 65.
177. Ibid.
178. GJC to Mrs Peters, 9 April 1937, GJC Papers, Folder 65.
179. Ibid.
180. GJC to the Revd Peters and Mrs Peters, [Letters] dated 3 June 1937, 4 June 1937; [cablegram of] 5 June 1937; 12 June 1937, GJC Papers, Folder 65.
181. See, for example, letters from GJC to Mrs H. Peters, 27 June 1937, 24 July 1937 and 7 August 1937, GJC Papers, Folder 65.
182. GJC to Mrs H. Peters, 23 June 1937, GJC Papers, Folder 65.
183. Henrietta Peters to "Lawyer" Christian, 4 August 1937, GJC Papers, Folder 65.
184. GJC to Mrs Peters, 2 April 1938; GJC to Mrs Peters, 24 April 1938, GJC Papers, Folder 66.
185. GJC to Mrs Peters, 4 September 1937, GJC Papers, Folder 65.
186. F. Awoonor-Williams, Solicitor for Omanhene Bekyire Yankeh II, to Mrs Peters, 14 April 1938; F. Awoonor-Williams to the Revd Peters, 20 April 1938, GJC Papers, Folder 66.
187. GJC to Mrs Peters, 24 April 1938, GJC Papers, Folder 66.
188. Interestingly, both letters were written on the verso of copies of the information flyer.
189. R.E. Peters to GJC, 21 April 1938, GJC Papers, Folder 271.
190. GJC to the Revd R.E. Peters, 3 June 1938, GJC Papers, Folder 66.
191. GJC to Mrs Peters, 2 April 1938; GJC to Mrs H. Peters, 13 November 1938, GJC Papers, Folder 66.
192. GJC to Mrs H. Peters, 24 January 1939, GJC Papers, Folder 199.
193. GJC to Capt. Joshua Cockburn, 9 January 1940, GJC Papers, Folder 70.
194. GJC to Mr C. Vaughan Charles, Washington, USA, 6 March 1940 (typescript), GJC Papers, Folder 64.

195. Essi Matilda Forster, interview with Estelle Appiah, 13 June 1992, OPReP Collection.
196. Raymond Leslie Buell, *Liberia: A Century of Survival, 1847–1947* (Philadelphia: University of Pennsylvania Press, 1947), 36.
197. Walter F. Walker, Secretary to the Liberian President, to George James Christian, 1 July 1914, GJC Papers, Folder 74.
198. George Stanley Lewis, interview with Estelle Appiah, Accra, Ghana, 24 June 1992.
199. Harold [F.?] Harper, Cape Palmas, Liberia, to GJC, Liberian Consulate, 8 June 1936, GJC Papers, Folder 37.
200. GJC to Police in Charge, Kumasi, Ashanti, 15 March 1928, GJC Papers, Folder 54. The names were listed in a separate note dated 6 March 1928.
201. GJC to Callender, 15 March 1928, GJC Papers, Folder 54.
202. GJC to Harold Fredericks, Cape Palmas, Liberia, 5 February 1926, GJC Papers, Folder 24.
203. GJC to Harold Fredericks, Liberia, 25 June 1932, GJC Papers, Folder 23.
204. Office of the Paramount Chief, Rocktown Section, Maryland County, to the Honourable Consul General of Liberia, Gold Coast Colony, 22 November 1938, GJC Papers, Folders 198 199.
205. Senior Asst Sup. of Police, Sekondi District, to G.J. Christian, Consul to the Liberian Gov't, 21 April 1939, GJC Papers, Folder 199.
206. GJC to the Secretary of State, Republic of Liberia, 24 April, 1939, GJC Papers, Folder 199.
207. Formal invitation dated at Monrovia, 16 December 1935 (includes photographs of Barclay and Smith as well as the Liberian national anthem and song entitled "The Lone Star Forever"), GJC Papers, Folder 163.
208. Secretary to the President of Liberia to Mr George J. Christian, Liberian Consul, 22 November 1937, GJC Papers, Folder 254. [Diploma from] Edwin Barclay, President of the Republic of Liberia . . . to George J. Christian . . . appoint you Knight Official of the Liberian Humane Order of African Redemption . . . 17 November 1937, GJC Papers, Folder 254.
209. GJC to Howard Christian, 9 December 1937, GCJ Papers, Folder 115.
210. GJC to J.H. Koens, 10 December 1937, GJC Papers, Folder 85; GJC to Mrs Peters, New York City, 20 December 1937, GJC Papers, Folder 63.
211. Jan H. Koens to the Hon. George Christian, 18 January 1938, GJC Papers, Folder 79.
212. GJC to the Hon. H.D. Fredericks, Liberian Consul General, Liverpool, 22 November 1938, GJC Papers, Folder 78.
213. GJC to Harold D. Fredericks, 8 November 1939, GJC Papers, Folder 273.

214. Harold D. Fredericks to GJC, 17 November 1939, GJC Papers, Folder 273.
215. Geo. J. Christian to [the Revd Chas. W. Farquhar], Dominica, 29 March 1890, GJC Papers, Folder 49.
216. Mark A. Tabbert, 2003, "Masonic Papers: The Odd Fellows", http://www.freemasons-freemasonry.com/tabbert5.html (accessed 5 November 2010); C.W. Tachie-Menson, *Freemasonry in the Gold Coast* [pamphlet] (n.p., 1953), 1, GJC Papers, Folder 158. The author made the point that little or no information is available on the early activities of the lodges in the Gold Coast. The information in the pamphlet was compiled from sources at Freemasons' Hall, London.
217. Entries in Diary for 11 and 12 September 1899, GJC Papers, Folder 172.
218. W Bro. C.W. Tachie-Menson, *Brief History of the St. George's (Seccondee) Lodge No. 3851 of Ancient, Free and Accepted Masons, English Constitution 1918–1939* (Sekondi: Hope Press, 31 March 1939), 37, GJC Papers, Folder 32.
219. Tachie-Menson, *Freemasonry in the Gold Coast*, 1.
220. Ibid., 2.
221. Tachie-Menson, *Brief History*, [11].
222. It is interesting to note that no mention was made of George James Christian in the founding of this lodge, although many of its founding members had practised Freemasonry in other parts of the world, namely, England, Barbados, Perak, Malaya, Queensland, the Channel Islands, Canada, India, Scotland and Australia.
223. Letter addressed to "Sir and Brother" from the Hon. Secretary, 11 December 1917, GJC Papers, Folder 260.
224. This is how the name is spelled in the history of the lodge. See note 219, above.
225. [GJC] to Worshipful Master, St George's Lodge, Sekondi, 30 May 1927, GJC Papers, Folder 71.
226. Tachie-Menson, *Freemasonry in the Gold Coast*, 9–10; Tachie-Menson, *Brief History*, 11.
227. Tachie-Menson, *Brief History*, 12, 16–17, 41.
228. Tachie-Menson, *Freemasonry in the Gold Coast*, 9–10.
229. [GJC] to Worshipful Master, St George's Lodge Sekondi, 30 May 1927, GJC Papers, Folder 71; "Hon. George James Christian, Defender of Poor Criminals, Passes Away at Sekondi", *African Morning Post*, 19 April 1940, 2.
230. Tachie-Menson, *Freemasonry in the Gold Coast*, 11.
231. Programme for the First Anniversary Installation Convention of the Gold Coast Chapter, GJC Papers, Folder 23.
232. Tachie-Menson, *Freemasonry in the Gold Coast*, 20.
233. GJC to L.S. Gruchy, 5 May 1931, GJC Papers, Folder 90.
234. Tachie-Menson, *Freemasonry in the Gold Coast*, 20–21.

235. Ibid., 21.
236. Grand Secretary of the United Grand Lodge at England to GJC, June 1937, GJC Papers, Folder 269.
237. B. Marcus Green, Secretary of St George Lodge, No. 3421, EC, to GJC, 18 December 1937, GJC Papers, Folder 124.
238. GJC to Peter Christian, 23 July 1937, GJC Papers, Folder 81.
239. St George's (Seccondee) Lodge, No. 3851, Citation to George James Christian... on appointment to Grand Lodge and Supreme Grand Chapter Ranks, Presented 11 December 1937, GJC Papers, Folder 153.
240. B. Marcus Green, secretary of St George Lodge, No. 3421, EC, to GJC, 18 December 1937, GJC Papers, Folder 124.
241. GJC to the Secretary of St George Lodge, No. 3421, Roseau, Dominica, 29 January 1938, GJC Papers, Folder 83.
242. GJC to Peter, 15 August 1932, GJC Papers, Folder 147.
243. GJC to Peter, 2 September 1932, GJC Papers, Folder 147.
244. GJC to Dr Peter Christian, 23 July 1937, GJC Papers, Folder 81.
245. GJC to Howard Christian, 28 October 1937 and 6 November 1937, GJC Papers, Folder 118.
246. Essi Matilda Forster to the Worshipful Master and Members of St George's [Lodge], Sekondi, 25 March 1965, GJC Papers, Folder 214.
247. Jan H. Koens to the Hon. George Christian, 18 January 1938, GJC Papers, Folder 79.
248. See, for example, Henrietta Peters, Hartford, Conn., to GJC, 7 February 1934; Henrietta Peters to GJC, 12 September 1934; GJC Papers, Folder 63.
249. Mrs Hen[rietta Peters] to GJC, 4 October 1934, GJC Papers, Folder 63.
250. [GJC to Joseph O. Bowers] 6 April 1940, GJC Papers, Folder 64.

CHAPTER 7. CHRISTIAN'S CONTRIBUTION TO THE POLITICAL AND SOCIAL DEVELOPMENT OF THE GOLD COAST

1. This detail appears in one of the accounts reporting his death: "Hon. George James Christian, Defender of Poor Criminals, Passes Away at Sekondi", *African Morning Post*, 19 April 1940, 1.
2. Sir Frederick Gordon Guggisberg, *The Gold Coast: A Review of the Events of 1920–1926 and the Prospects of 1927–1928* (Accra: C. Fairweather, Government Printer, 1927), 7.
3. Joseph Ephraim Casely Hayford was "a teacher, author, lawyer, politician, pan-Africanist, and founder of the National Congress of British West Africa (one of the continent's first Pan-African organizations)". http://africanhistory.about

.com/od/panafricanists/a/JECasely Hayford.htm (accessed 11 November 2014).
4. Quoted in David Kimble, *A Political History of Ghana: The Rise of Gold Coast Nationalism, 1850–1928* (Oxford: Oxford University Press, 1963), 453.
5. *Gold Coast Leader*, 3 and 10 September 1927, quoted ibid.
6. Assistant Secretary, Sekondi Municipal Electors' Association, to G.J. Christian, Esq., Sekondi, 16 August 1930, GJC Papers, Folder 52.
7. Assistant Secretary, Sekondi Municipal Electors' Association, to G.J. Christian, Esq., Sekondi, 22 August 1930, GJC Papers, Folder 52.
8. *Gold Coast Gazette*, no. 61, 23 August 1930, 1587–1588.
9. Ibid., 1588.
10. Notice from the Acting Colonial Secretary, Accra, 29 September 1930, GJC Papers, Folder 36; *Gold Coast Gazette*, October 4, 1930, 1786.
11. GJC to Horace Douglas, 26 September 1939, GJC Papers, Folder 119.
12. GJC to Mrs Leung, 26 September 1930, GJC Papers, Folder 13.
13. GJC to Capt. Joshua Cockburn, 1 October 1930, GJC Papers, Folder 60.
14. Colonial Secretary's motion expressing regret at the death of the Honourable George James Christian, Legislative Council Debates, Session 1940, 1 October 1940, 5, National Archives of Ghana, Accra.
15. Kimble, *Political History of Ghana*, 429n1.
16. The National Congress of British West Africa was patterned in part on the formation of the Indian National Congress, which sought independence from Britain through national self-determination. The leadership of the National Congress of British West Africa broadened the concept of nationalism to encompass all West African colonies under British rule. Thus Sierra Leone, Liberia, Nigeria and ultimately the Gold Coast (Ghana) were brought under the nationalist rubric of the congress. http://diaspora.northwestern.edu/mbin/WebObjects/DiasporaX.woa/wa/displayArticle?atomid=620 (accessed 5 June 2014).
17. General Secretary of the National Congress of British West Africa to GJC, 28 October 1930, GJC Papers, Folder 263.
18. Magnus J. Sampson, *West African Leadership: Public Speeches delivered by J.E. Casely Hayford* (London: Frank Cass, 1969), 27. The other officers whose contributions were recorded were as follows: Colonial Secretary (the Honourable G.A.S. Northcote, CMG); Provincial Member for the Akan Section of the Eastern Province (the Honourable Nana Sir Ofori Atta, KBE, Omanhene of Akyim Abuakwa); the Acting Commissioner, Central Province; the Mining Member (the Honourable J.D. M'ckay, OBE); Municipal Member for Accra (the Honourable J. Glover-Addo, OBE); Provincial Member for the Central Province (the Honourable Nana Ayirebi Acquah III, KMAC, Omanhene of

Effutu (Winneba) State; Municipal Member for Cape Coast (the Honourable K.A. Korsah), and His Excellency the Governor (Sir Ransford Slater, KCMG, OBE, 27–30. (Photocopy of extract in GJC Papers, Folder 86.)
19. Sampson, *West African Leadership*, 32.
20. Sekondi Municipal Electors' Association, Public Meeting at the "Optimism" Club, Sekondi, on Saturday, 18 October 1930 at 6 p.m., Programme, GJC Papers, Folder 53; Frank Krakue to the Honourable G.J. Christian, enclosing the Manifesto, 18 October 1930, to the President, Officers and Members of the Sekondi Municipal Electors' Association, Sekondi, the Humble Manifesto of George James Christian of Dominica House, in the town of Sekondi, elected Municipal Member for Sekondi to the Legislative Council of the Gold Coast Colony, 1930–1934, GJC Papers, Folder 52.
21. The... Manifesto of George James Christian..., GJC Papers, Folder 52.
22. GJC to Frank Krakue, Registrar, Provincial Council of Chiefs' Court, enclosing Minutes of the Executive Committee of the Provincial Council of Chiefs of the Western Province held at the Ahinfie at Dutch-Sekondi on 23 December 1930; GJC to Samuel Morgue-Duncan, Assistant Secretary, Rate Payers' Association, 27 December 1930; GJC forwarding Petition of the Rate Payers of Sekondi to His Excellency Sir Alexander Ransford Slater... Governor and Commander in Chief of the Gold Coast Colony, 29 December 1930, GJC Papers, Folder 52.
23. Sekondi Muncipal Electors' Association to the Honourable G.J. Christian, Municipal Member for Sekondi, 20 February 1931, GJC Papers, Folder 51.
24. Minutes of the Legislative Council and Sessional Papers [1930–31], 9, National Archives of Ghana, Accra.
25. Sekondi Muncipal Electors' Association to the Honourable G.J. Christian, Municipal Member for Sekondi, 20 February 1931, GJC Papers, Folder 51.
26. Minutes of the Legislative Council and Sessional Papers [1930–31], 15, National Archives of Ghana, Accra.
27. Gold Coast, Legislative Council Debates, Session 1934, 22–23 (Accra, Ghana: Government Printery).
28. District Commissioner, Ahanta-Nzima District, Sekondi, to the Honourable G.J. Christian, 25 September 1935, GJC Papers, Folder 51.
29. GJC to the Revd A.G. Fraser, Principal, Prince of Wales College, Achimota, 23 January 1931, GJC Papers, Folder 56.
30. Gold Coast, Legislative Council Debates, Sessions 1932–1933, 215–17.
31. GJC to Horace Douglas, 28 November 1932, GJC Papers, Folder 121.
32. Gold Coast, Legislative Council Debates, Sessions 1932–1933, 127–34; 214–20.
33. Colonial Secretary's Office, Accra, to the Honourable G.J. Christian, Sekondi, 6 September 1932, GJC Papers, Folder 36.

34. Seen by the authors at the West Indiana and Special Collections Division, Alma Jordan Library, University of the West Indies, St Augustine, Trinidad and Tobago, on 9 July 2010.
35. Gold Coast, Legislative Council Debates, Session 1940, 20 March 1940, 143–44, National Archives of Ghana, Accra.
36. Gold Coast, Legislative Council Debates, Sessions 1932–1933, 218.
37. Gold Coast, Legislative Council Debates, First Session, 29 March 1933, 110.
38. Gold Coast, Legislative Council Debates, Session 1935, No. 1, 28 March 1935, 129, GJC Papers, Folder 86.
39. Ibid., 131–2, GJC Papers, Folder 86.
40. Ibid.
41. GJC to K.A. Korsah, 18 February 1936, GJC Papers, Folder 195.
42. Acting Commissioner, Western Province, to GJC, 3 March 1936, GJC Papers, Folder 195.
43. Gold Coast, Legislative Council Debates, Session 1935, No. 1, 28 March 1935, 127, GJC Papers, Folder 86.
44. Ibid., 132, GJC Papers, Folder 86.
45. GJC to K.A. Korsah, 18 February 1936, GJC Papers, Folder 195.
46. Ibid.
47. Acting Commissioner, Western Province, to GJC, 3 March 1936, GJC Papers, Folder 195.
48. G.C. du Boulay, Acting Colonial Secretary, to GJC, 4 April 1935, GJC Papers, Folder 194.
49. GJC to G.C. du Boulay, Acting Colonial Secretary, 11 April 1935, GJC Papers, Folder 194.
50. Colonial Secretary to GJC, 9 April 1936, GJC Papers, Folder 195.
51. GJC to the President of the Rate Payers' Association, 17 April 1936, GJC Papers, Folder 195.
52. GJC to the Colonial Secretary, 22 April 1936, GJC Papers, Folder 195.
53. This fund was kept "primarily for the redemption of the Public Debt" but was also available for "use in any grave emergency", Colonial Secretary to GJC, 19 March 1936, GJC Papers, Folder 195.
54. Omanhene of Dutch Sekondi, the Omanhin of British Sekondi, Kwesi Andoh, and others to GJC, 26 March 1936, GJC Papers, Folder 195.
55. GJC to the Provincial Commissioner in Sekondi, 30 March 1936, GJC Papers, Folder 195.
56. Colonial Secretary to GJC, 12 May 1936, GJC Papers, Folder 195.
57. Colonial Secretary to GJC, 20 April 1936, and GJC to Colonial Secretary, 7 May 1936, GJC Papers, Folder 195.

58. G.E London, Colonial Secretary, Gold Coast, to "Dear Mr Christian", 28 August 1937, GJC Papers, Folder 48.
59. GJC to "Dear Mr London", 13 September 1937, GJC Papers, Folder 48.
60. GJC to George Francois, 20 January 1938, GJC Papers, Folder 98.
61. Gold Coast, Legislative Council Debates, Session 1940, 20 March 1940, 145.
62. Extracts from the Legislative Council Debates relating to the meetings held on 15, 16, 17, 21 and 23 March 1938, of statements made by George James Christian, GJC Papers, Folder 215.
63. GJC to Howard Christian, 26 January 1940, GJC Papers, Folder 55.
64. GJC to "Dear Armah", 7 September 1937, GJC Papers, Folder 48.
65. GJC to Dr A. Savage, 13 September 1937, GJC Papers, Folder 48.
66. GJC to Dr H.P. Fowler, 29 November 1937; H.P. Fowler to the Hon. George J. Christian, 30 November 1937, GJC Papers, Folder 166.
67. Colonial Secretary to GJC, 17 March 1938, GJC Papers, Folder 156.
68. A "trunk call" is a long-distance phone call made within the same country.
69. GJC to K.A. Korsah, 18 February 1936, GJC Papers, Folder 195.
70. Attached extracts of the Legislative Council Debates related to remarks made by GJC at meetings held on 20–23 March 1939; Clerk of Legislative Council, Accra, to GJC, 29 April 1939, 1–3, GJC Papers, Folder 280.
71. Extracts from the Legislative Council Debates relating to the meetings held on 15, 16, 17, 21 and 23 March 1938, of statements made by George James Christian, GJC Papers, Folder 215.
72. Suggested Questions, [n.d.], GJC Papers, Folder 162.
73. Minutes of the meeting of the Legislative Council held in the Supreme Court (Court C) Accra, at 10 a.m., on 19 March 1940, GJC Papers, Folder 163.
74. Gold Coast, Legislative Council Debates, Session 1937, 23 March 1937, 115, National Archives, Accra, Ghana.
75. Gold Coast, Legislative Council Debates, Session 1938, 23 March 1938, 89, National Archives, Accra, Ghana.
76. Ibid.
77. Gold Coast, Legislative Council Debates, Session 1939, 21 March 1939, 93, National Archives, Accra, Ghana.
78. Gold Coast, Legislative Council Debates, Session 1940, 19 March 1940, 143–44, National Archives, Accra, Ghana.
79. Isaac S. Ephson, *Gallery of Gold Coast Celebrities 1632–1958* (Accra, Ghana: Ilen, 1970), 1:176–77, GJC Papers, Folder 86.
80. Gold Coast Aborigines' Rights Protection Society to Frederick Palmer, Esq., 24 April 1924; see also, We the undersigned, property owners and residents of the town of Sekondi, [List of] matters relating to the proposed Deep Sea Harbour at

Takoradi, April 1924; Report of a Meeting with Mr Fred Palmer at Seccondee, 25 April 1924, sgd Geo. J. Christian for self and other of the Seccondee deputation, GJC Papers, Folder 47.
81. "Ag Hon. Sec.", Gold Coast Agricultural and Commercial Society, to GJC, 3 November 1924 and 9 October 1925, GJC Papers, Folder 24.
82. Ahanta Agricultural Committee, Minutes of the 15th Meeting held in Sekondi on 6 February 1935, at 2:30 p.m. in the District Commissioner's Court, GJC Papers, Folder 266.
83. Memorial of the Society of African Herbalists to His Excellency the Governor-in-Council, through the Aman-Ahinfu of Dutch and British Sekondi and the Honourable the Municipal Member of the Legislative Council for the Western Province, 15 February 1935, GJC Papers, Folder 31.
84. Colonial Secretary, Accra, to the Hon. G.J. Christian, 26 April 1933, GJC Papers, Folder 35.
85. Commissioner, Western Province, to the Hon. G.J. Christian, 15 April 1931, GJC Papers, Folder 36.
86. Report of a Visiting Committee to the Prisons at Sekondi . . . on Saturday, 18 April 1931, Central Prison; Report of a Visiting Committee . . . on 20 April 1931, Fort Orange Prison, 20 April 1931, GJC Papers, Folder 36.
87. Colonial Secretary, Accra, to the Hon. G.J. Christian, 26 April 1933, GJC Papers, Folder 35.
88. Director of Prisons, Accra, to the Hon. G.J. Christian, Barrister-at-Law, 25 July 1939, GJC Papers, Folder 21.
89. Selwyn-Clarke to the Hon. G. J. Christian, Gold Coast Government Telegram, 4 June 1932; Selwyn-Clarke to Christian, [letter] 10 June 1932, MS Folder 46.
90. GJC to Dr Selwyn-Clarke, Accra, Gold Cost Government Telegrams, 5 June 1932 and 10 June 1932, MS Folder 46.
91. "Draft Rules", Gold Coast Branch, British Red Cross Society (n.d), cyclostyled. See also booklet titled *The Origin, Objects and Organisation of the British Red Cross Society, Founded 1870. Incorporated by Royal Charter, 1908* (London, n.d.), GJC Papers, Folder 45.
92. See Cape Coast Local Red Cross Committee, Statement of Account . . . Jan. 1, 1933 to June 30, 1933; British Red Cross Society Kumasi Division, Statements of Receipts and Disbursements for the period ended 30 June 1933, MS Folder 45.
93. Inaugural Meeting of the Sekondi Branch of the British Red Cross Society held on 8 August 1932, MS Folder 46.
94. Monthly Meeting of the Sekondi Branch of the British Red Cross Society held in the Town Council Chambers at 2:15 p.m. on 3 October 1932, GJC Papers, Folder 46; Meeting of the Sekondi Branch of the British Red Cross Society held on

11 January 1933, GJC Papers, Folder 46; Minutes of the Meeting of the Sekondi Branch of the British Red Cross Society held on 4 April 1933, GJC Papers, Folder 46.
95. President, Gold Coast Branch, British Red Cross Society [to GJC], 6 January 1934, GJC Papers, Folder 45.
96. Minutes of a Meeting of the Sekondi (Western Province) Division of the Gold Coast Branch of the British Red Cross Society, held at the office of the Senior Health Officer on 8 January 1934, GJC Papers, Folder 45.
97. Ibid.; P. Carlis Paittoo, Honorary Secretary of the Optimism Club, to the Hon. George James Christian, 17 August 1932, GJC Papers, Folder 46.
98. GJC to A. Akrofi-Nnam, Esq., Catechist, Presbyterian Church, Sekondi, 28 April 1933; GJC to the Revd Isaac S. Cole, 16 May 1933, GJC Papers, Folder 46.
99. Superintendent, Methodist Mission, Sekondi, to the Hon. George J. Christian, 20 November 1933, GJC Papers, Folder 45.
100. [Message from the] President, Gold Coast Branch, British Red Cross Society, At the approach of the Christmas season . . . greeting . . . to all who have worked in the Gold Coast for the advancement of the spirit of service . . ., Accra, December 1933, GJC Papers, Folder 45.
101. Empire Day, 24 May 1935, Celebration Programme, GJC Papers, Folder 135.
102. Acting Secretary for Native Affairs, Colonial Secretary's Office, Accra, to the Hon. G.J. Christian, 10 September 1934, GJC Papers, Folder 170.
103. Provincial Commissioner's Office, Sekondi, to GJC, 22 December 1932, GJC Papers, Folder 62.
104. F.E. Ekuban to the Hon. G.J. Christian, 11 April 1938, and 21 December 1938, GJC Papers, Folder 78.
105. Director of Public Works, Accra, to the SDS, c/o the Hon. J.G. Christian at Accra [sic], 14 March 1939, GJC Papers, Folder 21.
106. Accra Earthquake Relief Fund (Central Committee), *General Appeal* (Accra: Government Printer, 1939), GJC Papers, Folder 50. It is recorded that in 1862 and 1906, there were two significant earthquakes in the Gold Coast. The 1939 earthquake was less severe than in 1862 but more severe than the one in 1906. See N.R. Junner, *Preliminary Report on the Earthquake of 22 June 1939* (Accra, Gold Coast Colony, 1939), 1–3, GJC Papers, Folder 200.
107. GJC to Essie, 1 July 1939, GJC Papers, Folder 152. See also GJC to Howard Christian, 16 August 1939, GJC Papers, Folder 59. See also Minutes of a meeting of the Committee for the Accra Earthquake Relief Fund, Western Province (Sekondi) Branch, held at the residence of the Honourable George J. Christian on Wednesday, 15 November 1939, GJC Papers, Folder 28.
108. GJC to Howard Christian, 5 July 1939, GJC Papers, Folder 129.

109. The West Indian Club Ltd, 4 Whitehall Court, London SW 1. Leaflet and application form. GJC Papers, Folder 44. See also David Clover, "The West Indian Club Ltd: An Early 20th Century West Indian Interest in London", in *The Society for Caribbean Studies Annual Conference Papers*, ed. Sandra Courtman, vol. 8 (2007). http://sas-space.sas.ac.uk/3119/1/Clover%2007.pdf (accessed 1 October 2014).
110. GJC to Secretary West Indian Club, 9 April 1938, GJC Papers, Folder 43. See also, for example, GJC to RW Bro. Dr Gray, 25 May 1938, GJC Papers, Folder 78.
111. Letters between West Indian Club and GJC re purchase of tickets, 5 June 1934 and 6 July 1934, 3 and 24 March 1936; Hon. Secretary, West Indian Club, to GJC, 31 August 1937, GJC Papers, Folders 43 and 44.
112. The Hon. Treasurer, West Indian Club Ltd, to the Hon. G.J. Christian, 19 November 1934, GJC Papers, Folder 44.
113. GJC to Honorary Secretary, West Indian Club, 17 June 1936, GJC Papers, Folder 43.
114. See West India Committee form of application for membership, verso, GJC Papers, Folder 44.
115. West India Committee [to GJC], 7 March 1935, GJC Papers, Folder 44.
116. GJC to the Hon. Secretary, West India Committee, 10 April 1935. See also official receipt from the West India Committee, 29 Apr 1935, GJC Papers, Folder 44.
117. GJC to Secretary, 10 March 1938, acknowledging receipt for subscription for 1938 and membership card, GJC Papers, Folder 43.
118. Hakim Adi and Marika Sherwood, *Pan-African History: Political Figures from Africa and the Diaspora since 1787* (London: Routledge, 2003), 134–37, 175. See also *WASU Protests Aggrey House: The Truth* [pamphlet] (London: West African Students' Union at the African Hostel, March 1934), [4]. It appeared that Dr Moody was acting on behalf of the British government, GJC Papers, Folder 32.
119. Harold A. Moody, Founder and President of the League of Coloured Peoples, to GJC, 5 February 1938, GJC Papers, Folder 43.
120. GJC to Doctor Moody, 10 March 1938, GJC Papers, Folder 43.
121. "G.J. Christian, Gold Coast" is listed among the "HONORARY OFFICERS AND EXECUTIVE COMMITTEE" on the letterhead of the League of Coloured Peoples. See, for example, Harold A. Moody to Sir John Harris, 11 February 1939. The authors are grateful to Philip Janzen, PhD candidate at University of Wisconsin-Madison, US, for sharing this document.
122. Secretary, Royal Society of Arts, to GJC, 22 September 1934, GJC Papers, Folder 44.
123. Ibid.

124. Secretary, National Union of Empire Africans, to G.J. Christian, Esq., MLC, 17 August 1936. Statement of objective and application form also attached, GJC Papers, Folder 4.
125. GJC to Horace Douglas, 29 October 1930, GJC Papers, Folder 121.
126. GJC to Howell Shillingford, Roseau, Dominica, 21 March 1932, GJC Papers, Folder 41.
127. GJC to M.D. Reece, 21 March 1932, GJC Papers, Folder 62.
128. GJC to Mrs H. Leung, 9 June 1934, GJC Papers, Folder 121.
129. GJC to Harold D. Fredericks, 8 November 1939, GJC Papers, Folder 273.
130. GJC to Chas. W. Chappelle, 1 December 1938, GJC Papers, Folder 270.
131. GJC to Howard Christian, 11 April 1939, GJC Papers, Folder 129. Howard's response was that if he could "get such a person into a boxing ring", he would "flay the life out of him"; Howard Christian to GJC, 20 April 1939, GJC Papers, Folder 129.
132. Gold Coast, Legislative Council Debates, Session 1940, 1 October 1940, 5–6, National Archives of Ghana, Accra.
133. Ibid.
134. [George James Christian to Joseph O. Bowers], 6 April 1940, GJC Papers, Folder 64.

CHAPTER 8. CHRISTIAN AND HIS COMPATRIOTS IN THE GOLD COAST: COMMUNITY, IDENTITY AND HERITAGE

1. Some of the information in this chapter appeared previously in the following articles: Margaret D. Rouse-Jones, and Estelle M. Appiah, "West Indian Patriot in West Africa: A Study of George James Christian of Dominica and the Gold Coast", in *Caribbean Heritage,* ed. Basil A. Reid (Kingston: University of the West Indies Press and the Reed Foundation, 2012), 195–206; Margaret D. Rouse-Jones, and Estelle M. Appiah, "West Indian Returnees and Their Communities, Examples from the Gold Coast in the Nineteenth and Twentieth Centuries", in *Back to Africa,* vol. 2, *The Ideology and Practice of the African Returnee Phenomenon from the Caribbean and North-America to Africa,* ed. Kwesi Kwaa Prah (Cape Town: Centre for Advanced Studies of African Society, 2012), 380–406; Margaret D. Rouse-Jones, "History at the Personal Level: Tesserae in the Mosaic of Caribbean Social History", *Caribbean Quarterly* 58, no. 1 (March 2012): 65–86.
2. George J. Christian to Frank J. Ribeiro, Colonial Secretary, 14 January 1925, GJC Papers, Folder 72.

3. [GJC] to Eva Callender, 30 April 1933, and Eva Callender to [GJC], 28 May 1933, GJC Papers, Folder 54.
4. Correspondence between George J. Christian and Walter and Eva Callender, 16 October 1927 to 6 January 1928, GJC Papers, Folder 54; [GJC] to Mrs Leung, 21 January 1928, GJC Papers, Folder 10.
5. Ferdinand Francisco Christian, interview with Estelle Appiah, 19 April 1992, OPReP Collection.
6. Dr Ralph Hoyte Jr, interview with Margaret Rouse-Jones and Estelle Appiah, Port of Spain, Trinidad and Tobago, 28 June 2005, OPReP Collection. Dr Hoyte first joined his father in the Gold Coast at the age of six.
7. George Stanley Lewis, interview with Estelle Appiah, 24 June 1992, OPReP Collection.
8. GJC to Mrs Leung, 4 June 1927, GJC Papers, Folder 10.
9. Edward Francois, interview with Margaret Rouse-Jones, 14 August 2007, OPReP Collection.
10. Correspondence between GJC and J.C. Roberts, Licensed Auctioneer, 7 June 1924 et seq., GJC Papers, Folder 77.
11. Dr Ralph Hoyte Jr, interview with Margaret Rouse-Jones and Estelle Appiah, 28 June 2005, OPReP Collection.
12. George James Christian to Joe Christian, 8 June 1937, GJC Papers, Folder 118; see also George James Christian to Mr Broadhurst, vice consul for Liberia, 5 January 1940, GJC Papers, Folder 70.
13. Francis Stanislaus Leung died on 15 May 1916. [Document] "In the Estate of Francis Stanislaus Leung", Supreme Court Records, Western Province, Gold Coast Colony. Will dated 21 August 1910. G.J. Christian was one of the witnesses of the will.
14. See chapter 2.
15. Three letters from George James Christian, one containing an attachment, were found among the H. Dudley Huggins Papers, which are also held at the University of the West Indies, St Augustine (hereafter Huggins Papers). H. Dudley Huggins had a long association with the University of the West Indies. He graduated from the Imperial College of Tropical Agriculture in 1926, after which he took up the position in British Guiana. The college was the forerunner to the University of the West Indies, St Augustine, in Trinidad and Tobago. He became the director of the Institute of Social and Economic Research, University of the West Indies, Mona, Jamaica, from 1948 to 1963, and principal of the St Augustine campus of the University of the West Indies from 1963 to 1969. For further details of Huggins's early life, see also Anne Huggins Leaver,

Dudley Huggins: Memoir of a West Indian's Journey (Milton Keynes: Author House, 2010), 16–25.
16. George Francois to Mr [Dudley] Huggins, 25 August 1926, Huggins Papers.
17. M.D. Reece to Mr Christian, 13 September 1927, Huggins Papers.
18. Geo. J. Christian to H.D. Huggins, 2 September 1927, Huggins Papers.
19. George Francois to Mr [Dudley] Huggins, 25 August 1926, Huggins Papers.
20. [GJC] to Mrs Leung, n.d., GJC Papers, Folder 12.
21. George James Christian to H.D. Huggins, 2 September 1927, Huggins Papers.
22. M.D. Reece to "Mr Christian", 13 September 1927, Huggins Papers.
23. Huggins was appointed as assistant superintendent in the Agriculture Department in British Guiana. Geo. J. Christian to H.D. Huggins, 17 October 1928, Huggins Papers.
24. GJC to A.R. Cools-Lartigue, 9 October 1924, GJC Papers, Folder 127.
25. GJC to A.R. Cools-Lartigue, 12 September 1925, GJC Papers, Folder 127.
26. George Stanley Lewis, interview with Estelle Appiah, 24 June 1992, OPReP Collection; GJC to Clara Gordon, 3 January 1938, GJC Papers, Folder 82.
27. List of Legal Practitioners and Dates of Call, n.d. GBR/0115/RCMS 137/2, Gold Coast Letters and Papers, 1921–1953 Correspondence and papers of Sir Philip Smyly, Cambridge University Library, Cambridge, United Kingdom.
28. Mathurin, *Henry Sylvester Williams*, 35, 44, 53.
29. Ibid., 96, 97.
30. Ibid., 154, 167.
31. GJC to B.S. London, 3 November, 1933, GJC Papers, Folder 296.
32. GJC to R.E. Phipps, 16 March 1933, GJC Papers, Folder 296.
33. GJC to Clara Gordon, 3 January 1938, GJC Papers, Folder 82.
34. GJC to R.E. Phipps, Barrister-at-Law, Accra, 15 September 1939, GJC Papers, Folder 273.
35. Edward Francois, interview with Margaret Rouse-Jones, 14 August 2007, OPReP Collection.
36. Secretary of Cheapside Syndicate Ltd to GJC, 15 April 1949.
37. GJC to Peter Christian, 29 January 1938, GJC Papers, Folder 143.
38. GJC to Peter Christian, 26 November 1937, GJC Papers, Folder 81.
39. GJC to Joe Christian, 28 January 1938, GJC Papers, Folder 115; GJC to Howard Christian, 29 January 1938, GJC Papers, Folder 115.
40. GCJ to Howard Christian, 29 January 1938, GJC Papers, Folder 115.
41. According to his nephew, when the British colonies in West Africa were being opened up, West Indians were "sent out, taken out, or went out on their own". Dr Ralph Hoyte Jr, interview with Margaret Rouse-Jones and Estelle Appiah, 28 June 2005, OPReP Collection.

42. Information taken from document entitled "Notes for Certificate of Honor and Badge", owned by Dr Ralph Hoyte Jr, and consulted and documented in the interview with Dr Ralph Hoyte Jr, 28 June 2005.
43. [Henry Sylvester Williams] to Dr Simmonds, 21 July 1902, GJC Papers, Folder 119. It is likely that Dr Simmonds was also from Trinidad.
44. GJC to Vivian Harris, 18 March 1928, GJC Papers, Folder 40. Vivian Harris was a medical student whom Christian had assisted. In this correspondence, he also advised Harris, who had completed his studies, to contact Dr Hoyte in the event that he needed to hire another assistant.
45. Evidence of this is their letterhead stationery, which also gives the telegram address as HOYTIBUS, NSAWAM. Busby to [Chris]tian, 9 December 1938, GJC Papers, Folder 78.
46. Dr Ralph Hoyte Jr, interview with Margaret Rouse-Jones and Estelle Appiah, 28 June 2005, OPReP Collection.
47. Julian Coffie Roberts, a pharmacist resident in Atlanta, Georgia, US, grandson of J.C. Roberts, gave this background information to Estelle Appiah in Accra, Ghana. See email correspondence from Julian Coffie Roberts to Estelle Appiah and Margaret Rouse-Jones, 22 January 2015 and 14 May 2015.
48. J.C. Roberts to Mr Christian, 1 July 1924, GJC Papers, Folder 77.
49. GJC to E.J. Metcalf, Esq., Provincial Agent, Messrs Millers Ltd, 9 July 1924, GJC Papers, Folder 77.
50. J.C. Roberts to Mr Christian, 11 July 1924, GJC Papers, Folder 77. Correspondence between J.C. Roberts and GJC between 7 June 1924 and 11 July 1924, GJC Papers, Folder 77.
51. There are two pieces of correspondence in the GJC Papers – J[?] Roberts, Abidjan, Ivory Coast to Mr Christian, 24 January 1940 and J[?] Roberts c/o Coker, Sekondi, to the Hon. G.J. Christian, 10 February 1940, GJC Papers, Folder 67. The writer knew Christian in "the old cable days" and had been travelling for "many years" and decided to return to Sekondi. He was seeking Christian's assistance for a letter of introduction in order to find employment. However, it has not been possible for the authors to verify that these documents refer to the same J.C. Roberts referred to here.
52. Julian Coffie Roberts . . . email correspondence to Estelle Appiah and Margaret Rouse-Jones, 22 January 2015 and 14 May 2015.
53. Edward Francois, interview with Margaret Rouse-Jones, 14 August 2007, OPReP Collection.
54. Sister Hen[rietta] Peters to "Lawyer Christian", 3 January 1935; GJC to Mrs Peters, 4 February 1935, GJC Papers, Folder 58.
55. "Dr Busby Dies", *News Extra*, [photocopy, source not given].

56. GJC to Peter, 23 July 1932, GJC Papers, Folder 147.
57. Ferdinand Francisco Christian, interview with Estelle Appiah, 19 April 1992, OPReP Collection.
58. Edward Francois, interview with Margaret Rouse-Jones, 14 August 2007, OPReP Collection.
59. According to another source, the lawn-tennis court at the Francois home in New Tafo was "the only one in the country at the time". "Biography of Justice George Richard McVane François", in "Burial and Thanksgiving Service for the Late Justice George Richard McVane François", GJC Papers, Folder 301.
60. "Tribute to Justice George Richard McVane François" in "Burial and Thanksgiving Service for the Late Justice George Richard McVane François", GJC Papers, Folder 301.
61. "Burial and Thanksgiving Service for the Life of George Stanley Lewis, Friday 14 January 2000", [booklet] front cover, GJC Papers, Folder 19.
62. Stanley outlived his four younger brothers, each of whom was distinguished in his own right: Professor Sir W. Arthur Lewis, 1979 Nobel laureate, world-renowned economist and development strategist for Ghana and fifteen Commonwealth countries; His Excellency Sir Allen Lewis, governor general of St Lucia, chancellor of the University of the West Indies and chief justice of the West Indies Associated States Supreme Court; Dr Earl Lewis, chief psychiatrist, Government of Trinidad and Tobago; Mr Victor Lewis, legal counsellor in London and St Lucia. "Burial and Thanksgiving Service for the Life of George Stanley Lewis, Friday 14 January 2000", 9.
63. Information from Angela Hudson-Phillips, neé Lewis, niece of Stanley, to Maureen Warner-Lewis, Kingston, Jamaica, 2015.
64. George Stanley Lewis, interview with Estelle Appiah, 24 June 1992, OPReP Collection.
65. See correspondence between George Francois and G.S. Lewis, dated 6, 9 and 15 October 1948, GJC Papers, Folder 289.
66. "Biography of the Late George Stanley Lewis", and "A Tribute to the Late Mr. Stanley Lewis", in "Burial and Thanksgiving Service for the Life of George Stanley Lewis, Friday 14 January 2000", 4–5 and 8–9.
67. List of Legal Practitioners and Dates of Call, n.d. GBR/0115/RCMS 137/2, Gold Coast Letters and Papers, 1921–1953, Correspondence and Papers of Sir Philip Smyly, Cambridge University Library, Cambridge, United Kingdom.
68. Mrs Ingeretha Roberts, 25 October 1937, and GJC to Mrs Ingeretha Roberts, 28 October 1937, GCJ Papers, Folder 85.
69. "Biography" and "Louise Remembered by Frances Ademola", in "Order of Service for the Funeral of Mrs Louise Jean Olympio (neé Murrell), 19 November

1927–2 May 2015 on Wednesday 27 May 2015 at Lashibi Funeral Homes at 10:30 a.m.", 5, 12 (photocopy of selected pages), GJC Papers, Folder 301. The Olympio family name can be traced to Francisco Olympio Silva, who had migrated from Brazil to eastern Gold Coast/Togo in 1850. Francisco's grandson, Sylvanus Olympio (1902–1963), became president of Togo in 1960. See Alcione M. Amos, "The History of the Afro-Brazilian Community in Togo: With Special Emphasis on the Olympio Family", in Prah, *Back to Africa*, vol. 1, *Afro-Brazilian Returnees and their Communities*, 121, 136–37.

70. George James Christian to Mrs Leung, 27 November 1929, GJC Papers, Folder 15.
71. Peter Leyel, "A Distinguished Barbadian: The Story of My Grandfather, Sir George Campbell Deane, Kt", *Journal of the Barbados Museum and Historical Society* 58 (2012): 79–89. We are grateful to librarians in Barbados, Joan Brathwaite, Christine Matthews-Rocheford and Harriet Pierce (Barbados Museum and Historical Society), who located information on George Campbell Deane of Barbados. See also [George Campbell Deane] Biography. http://www.wikitree.com/wiki/Deane-478 (accessed 20 February 2014).
72. [GJC] to Eva Callender, 30 April 1933, GJC Papers, Folder 54.
73. Eva Callender to [GJC], 28 May 1933, GJC Papers, Folder 54.
74. J.H. Murrell to "Dear G.J.", 19 November 1933, GJC Papers, Folder 48.
75. Eva Callender cites Margaret's date of birth as 6 June 1921. Eva Callender to [GJC], 28 May 1933, GJC Papers, Folder 54.
76. Correspondence between George J. Christian and Walter and Eva Callender, 16 October 1927 to 9 April 1934, GJC Papers, Folder 54; GJC to Mrs Leung, 21 January 1928, GJC Papers, Folder 10.
77. Eva Callender to Mr Christian, 10 July 1939, GJC Papers, Folder 273.
78. GJC to Mrs Walter Callender, 2 December 1939, GJC Papers, Folder 273.
79. Peter Christian to GJC, 4 September 1939, GJC Papers, Folder 142.
80. Bishop Joseph O. Bowers, conversation with Margaret D. Rouse-Jones, Roseau, Dominica, 6 August 1993, OPReP Collection. The year 1922 is mentioned in conversation, but not in the taped interview.
81. Bishop Joseph O. Bowers, interview with Margaret D. Rouse-Jones, Roseau, Dominica, 6 August 1993, transcript, OPReP Collection. See GJC to Dr Peter Christian, 12 April 1940, GJC Papers, Folder 144, where he expressed the hope to meet "soon" with the Revd Bowers.
82. Dr Ferdinand Francisco Christian, interview with Estelle Appiah, 19 April 1992, OPReP Collection.
83. Mary Ursula Dominique, *From a Small Beginning: Autobiography of Ma Baba*, transcribed and written by Natalie Charles Andrew, illustrations by Ronald

Deschamps (n.p., 1983; repr. Roseau, Dominica: Tropical Printers, 2007), 45–47.
84. Wendell Lawrence, "Bishop Joseph Oliver Bowers", article contributed to the Dominica Academy of Arts and Science July 2007. http://www.da-academy.org/daas_honorees_bowers.html. (accessed 27 August 2014).
85. Bishop Joseph O. Bowers, interview with Margaret D. Rouse-Jones, Roseau, Dominica, 6 August 1993.
86. "Religion: St Augustine's Firsts", *Time*, 4 May 1953. http://content.time.com/time/magazine/article/0,9171,818393,00.html?promoid=googlep (accessed 20 August 2014).
87. Thomson Fontaine, "Bishop Joseph Oliver Bowers: The World's Earliest Ordained Bishop", *Dominican Net*, 21 June 2009, http://www.thedominican.net/2009/06/bishop-joseph-oliver-bowers-worlds.html (accessed 10 October 2010).
88. Joseph O. Bowers, SVD, to Mr Christian, 21 March 1940, GJC Papers, Folder 50. See also Margaret D. Rouse-Jones, "History at the Personal Level", *Caribbean Quarterly* 58, no. 1 (March 2012): 65–86, which includes the correspondence quoted in this section of the chapter and a comparison of Christian's and Bowers's experience in the Gold Coast/Ghana, in the context of why they went back to Africa. The essay is an adaptation of the second Kenneth E. Ingram Memorial Lecture delivered by the author on 3 March 2011 at the University of the West Indies, Mona, Jamaica. See also Thomson Fontaine, "The Catholic Community Celebrates the 100th Birthday of Bishop Joseph Oliver Bowers of Dominica", *Dominican Net*, 5 April 2010. http://www.thedominican.net/2010/04/catholic-community-celebrates-100th.html (accessed 27 August 2014).
89. Bowers, interview with Margaret D. Rouse-Jones, 6 August 1993, OPReP Collection.
90. [George James Christian to Joseph O. Bowers] 6 April 1940, GJC Papers, Folder 64. See also Rouse-Jones, "History at the Personal Level", 79.
91. Damian Avevor, "Bishop Bowers, Gone but not forgotten: His legacies still live on among Ghanaians". [2012]. The author is the editor of the *Catholic Standard Newspaper*, Ghana.
92. Dominica Academy of Arts and Science, "DAAS Honors Dominican Stalwarts" Bishop Joseph Oliver Bowers http://www.da-academy.org/daas_honorees_boers.html (accessed 20 August 2014).
93. Joseph Bowers SVD, DW, to Margaret Rouse[-Jones], 22 January 2000, personal correspondence.
94. Avevor, "Bishop Bowers, Gone but Not Forgotten . . .", 10. See also Ghana Catholic Conference, "Reverend Joseph Oliver Bowers, SVD", *Daily Graphic* [Ghana], 10 November 2012 [newspaper clipping].
95. GJC to Frank J. Ribeiro, Colonial Secretary, Accra, 14 January 1925, GJC Papers,

Folder 72. A report dated 16 January 1925 by J.E. Moffatt, MO Sekondi, on R.E. Dick's death at the African Hospital, indicated that when Dick "suddenly had a seizure and became paralysed and unconscious" on the evening of 25 December 1924, his wife sent for two of his friends, George Christian and Mr Brett. Christian was present at the bedside when Moffatt arrived. Dick's wife and two of her friends remained with him until he passed away. The authors are grateful to Philip Janzen, PhD candidate at University of Wisconsin-Madison, for sharing this information.

96. GJC to Percy Roberts, 13 January 1925, GJC Papers, Folder 72.
97. George J. Christian to Frank J. Ribeiro, Colonial Secretary, 14 January 1925, GJC Papers, Folder 72.
98. GJC to Percy Roberts, 19 February 1925, GJC Papers, Folder 72.
99. GJC to Percy Roberts, 13 January, 1925, and Percy Roberts to George James Christian, 23 January 1925, GJC Papers, Folder 72.
100. GJC to Mrs Eva Callender, 20 February 1933, GJC Papers, Folder 54.
101. GJC to [Dr Beausoleil], 15 January 1940, GJC Papers, Folder 67.
102. George Stanley Lewis, interview with Estelle Appiah, 24 June 1992, OPReP Collection.
103. GJC to Henry Dietrich, 13 May 1922, GJC Papers, Folder 141.
104. GJC to Mrs Leung, 4 June 1927, GJC Papers, Folder 10.
105. George J. Christian to Frank J. Ribeiro, Colonial Secretary, 14 January 1925, GJC Papers, Folder 72.
106. GJC to Mrs Leung, 26 September 1930, GJC Papers, Folder 13.
107. Busby to [Chris]tian, 8 December 1938, GJC Papers, Folder 78.
108. GJC to Miss Cath Ladoo, St John's, Antigua, 27 March 1940, GJC Papers, Folder 64.
109. GJC to L.A. Smart, 13 September 1924, GJC Papers, Folder 71.
110. M.D. Reece, Hayward Heath, to GJC, 19 November 1939, GJC Papers, Folder 273.
111. [GJC] to Dr Peter Christian, 15 January 1938, GJC Papers, Folder 83.
112. Ferdinand Francisco Christian, interview with Estelle Appiah, 19 April 1992, OPReP Collection.
113. George Stanley Lewis, interview with Estelle Appiah, 24 June 1992, OPReP Collection.
114. Ibid.
115. For example, the gathering in celebration of C.M.G. Hoyte's receipt of the Member of the Order of the British Empire took place a month before Christian's death. See GJC to Miss Cath Ladoo, St John's, Antigua, 27 March 1940, typescript, Folder 64.

116. George Stanley Lewis, interview with Estelle Appiah, Accra, Ghana, 24 June 1992, OPReP Collection.
117. N.C.F. Easmon to Mr Christian, 3 March 1938, GJC Papers, Folder 78.
118. Rosamund Quist, interview with Margaret D. Rouse-Jones, Accra, Ghana, 21 May 1994, OPReP Collection. Mrs Rosamund Quist, aged eighty at the time of the interview, was the daughter of a Scottish businessman who was an associate of George James Christian. She knew the family well. See also George Stanley Lewis, interview with Estelle Appiah, Accra, Ghana, 24 June 1992, OPReP Collection.
119. Edward Francois, interview with Margaret Rouse-Jones, 14 August 2007, OPReP Collection.
120. See, for example, GJC's letters to Peter in 1928–1930 and 1934, GJC Papers, Folders 146 and 147.
121. Constance (Roseau, Dominica) to GJC, "Dear Christian", 9 November 1939, manuscript, Folder 62, GJC Papers, Folder 62; Maynard M. Prosper (Coulibistrie, Dominica) to GJC, "My dear cousin", 8 December 1939, manuscript, GJC Papers, Folder 62.
122. See, for example, note on file headed "Money Orders Required" and 1934 correspondence to Laura Lecointe, Constance Lockhart, Alice Burton, Elizabeth Halliday, Kate Ladoo and others, GJC Papers, Folder 35 and Folder 138.
123. Dr Ralph Hoyte Jr, interview with Margaret Rouse-Jones and Estelle Appiah, 28 June 2005, OPReP Collection.
124. See discussion of Dominica House in chapter 2.
125. See discussion of the acquisition and naming of these properties in chapter 6. Sekondi House, with its name intact, still exists in Roseau, Dominica, although it has changed owners.
126. Eva Callender to Mr Christian, 10 July 1939, GJC Papers, Folder 273.
127. Hoyte to "My dear Mr Christian", 19 November 1933, GJC Papers, Folder 48.
128. GJC to Dr D. Duff, 23 November 1933; GJC to Dr Selwyn-Clarke, 2 December 1933, GJC Papers, Folder 48.
129. Photograph of memorial plaque in GJC Papers, Folder 231.
130. Accra Turf Club, List of Members 1938, GJC Papers, Folder 62.
131. [GJC] to Worshipful Master, St George's Lodge, Sekondi, 30 May 1927, GJC Papers, Folder 71; "Hon. George James Christian, Defender of Poor Criminals, passes away at Sekondi", *African Morning Post*, 19 April 1940, 2.
132. W Bro. C.W. Tachie-Menson, *Brief History of the St. George's (Seccondee) Lodge No. 3851 of Ancient, Free and Accepted Masons, English Constitution 1918–1939* (Sekondi: Hope Press, 31 March 1939), 12, 16–17, 41.

133. [Letter] by a native resident, *Gold Coast Leader*, 18 August 1906, 6, Cape Coast Archives.
134. [GJC] to Vivian Harris, 7 December 1929, GJC Papers, Folder 41.
135. GJC to Mrs Peters, 15 September 1934, GJC Papers, Folder 63.
136. GJC to the Revd R.E. Peters, 31 October 1934, GJC Papers, Folder 63.
137. *Collins' Gentleman's Diary for 1899 . . .*, entries for 9 October to 27 October 1899, GJC Papers, Folder 172.
138. GJC to Herrn Rundé, Hamburg, 13 November 1922, GJC Papers, Folder 154.
139. GJC to L.A. Smart, London, 16 February 1923, GJC Papers, Folder 71.
140. Lewis Smart, London, to GJC, 20 February 1923, GJC Papers, Folder 71. Devonshire Street is the location of several hospitals and outpatient centres which offer a range of specialist medical services. Among them is the Harley Street Clinic Diagnostic Centre, http://theharleystreetclinic.com/diagnostic/contact (accessed 2 April 2015). Christian later indicated that Dr Dudley Stone of Harley Street had treated him for years. GJC to R.U. Riley, 23 June 1939, GJC Papers, Folder 273.
141. GJC to the Revd Charles W. Farquhar, All Saints Parsonage, Conakry, Guinea, 29 October 1924, GJC Papers, Folder 18.
142. GJC to L.A. Smart, London, 3 March 1923, GJC Papers, Folder 71.
143. GJC to Messrs Curtis, Campbell and Co., 4 July 1925, GJC Papers, Folder 69.
144. GJC to Dr Peter Christian, London, 27 February 1926, GJC Papers, Folder 145.
145. GJC to Harold D. Fredericks, Cape Palmas, Liberia, 5 February 1926, GJC Papers, Folder 24.
146. Wilfred Arthur to GJC, 28 October 1926, GJC Papers, Folder 24.
147. GJC to Dr K.A. Maclean, 20 December 1927, GJC Papers, Folder 69.
148. See, for example, GJC to Mrs Leung, 28 September 1928, GJC Papers, Folder 16.
149. GJC to George Francois, 19 July 1929, GJC Papers, Folder 41.
150. GJC to Capt. Joshua Cockburn, 1 October 1929, GJC Papers, Folder 60.
151. GJC to Dr R. A. Hoyte, 16 October 1928, GJC Papers, Folder 68.
152. GJC to Reece, 5 July 1939, GJC Papers, Folder 273.
153. Vivian Harris to GJC, 1 January 1930, GJC Papers, Folder 41. Harris also reported that this pronouncement produced "loud sobs of suppressed laughter" from the audience.
154. GJC to Vivian Harris, 18 February 1930, GJC Papers, Folder 41.
155. GJC to George Francois, 12 November 1929; 21 November 1929, GJC Papers, Folder 41; GJC to Vivian Harris, 18 February 1930, GJC Papers, Folder 41.
156. Dr A.E.C. Beausoleil to GJC, 19 February 1930, GJC Papers, Folder 41.
157. [George] Francois to GJC, 10 March 1930, and GJC to Beausoleil, 22 March 1930, GJC Papers, Folder 41.

158. GJC to the Colonial Secretary, 21 May 1931; Colonial Secretary to GJC, 29 May 1931, GJC Papers, Folder 36.
159. GJC to the Acting Colonial Secretary in Accra, 20 November 1934, GJC Papers, Folder 193.
160. GJC to Capt. Joshua Cockburn, 8 December 1934, GJC Papers, Folder 264.
161. GJC to Peter Christian, 8 April 1935, GJC Papers, Folder 37.
162. GJC to Montague Temple Morphy, 26 October 1935, GJC Papers, Folder 136.
163. GJC to Dr F. Ribeiro, 14 October, 1935, GJC Papers, Folder 136.
164. Manager of Westminster Bank Limited, Temple Bar Branch, to George James Christian, 17 September 1935, GJC Papers, Folder 135.
165. GJC to Mr and Mrs Edu Sam, 13 October 1935, GJC Papers, Folder 136.
166. GJC to Miss Alice Burton, 17 October 1935, GJC Papers, Folder 136.
167. GJC to Dr F. Ribeiro, 14 October, 1935, GJC Papers, Folder 136.
168. GJC to Mrs Savage, 27 October, 1935, GJC Papers, Folder 136.
169. GJC to Peter Christian, 22 November 1935; GJC to Constance Lockhart, 22 November 1935, GJC Papers, Folder 26.
170. GJC to Dr R.A. Hoyte, 30 November 1935, GJC Papers, Folder 137.
171. GJC to C. Hodgett, 30 December 1935, GJC Papers, Folder 137.
172. GJC to C. Hodgett, 27 January 1936, GJC Papers, Folder 137.
173. GJC to Dr O.C. Arthur, Freetown, 13 February 1936, GJC Papers, Folder 138.
174. GJC to Clara Gordon, 13 February 1936, GJC Papers, Folder 26.
175. GJC to Howard Christian, 17 February 1936, GJC Papers, Folder 33.
176. GJC to Clara Gordon, 13 February 1936, GJC Papers, Folder 26; see also GJC to H.B. Popham, Roseau, 9 April 1936, GJC Papers, Folder 138.
177. GJC to Dr [R.A.] Hoyte, 1 June 1936, GJC Papers, Folder 37.
178. GJC to M.T. Morphy, Salisbury, Southern Rhodesia, 1 June 1936, GJC Papers, Folder 37.
179. GJC to Mrs Leung, 25 January 1937, GJC Papers, Folder 27.
180. GJC to Franz Dove, 12 December 1938, GJC Papers, Folder 78; GJC to Dr G.A. Bushy, 12 December 1938, GJC Papers, Folder 82.
181. GJC to Howard Christian, 10 May 1939, GJC Papers, Folder 61.
182. GJC to R.U. Riley, 23 June 1939, GJC Papers, Folder 273.
183. GJC to Howard Christian, 21 July 1939, GJC Papers, Folder 59.
184. GJC to Howard Christian, 21 August 1939, GJC Papers, Folder 59.
185. GJC to Essi, 7 November 1939, GJC Papers, Folder 152; GJC to Howard Christian, 28 November 1939, GJC Papers, Folder 59.
186. M.D. Reece to GJC, 15 December 1939, GJC Papers, Folder 62.
187. GJC to M.D. Reece, 13 January 1940, GJC Papers, Folder 67.

188. GJC to Howard, 4 January 1940, GJC Papers, Folder 28; GJC to Howard Christian, 11 January 1940, GJC Papers, Folder 53.
189. GJC to Beau, 3 January 1940, GJC Papers, Folder 70.
190. GJC to M.D. Reece, 13 January 1940, GJC Papers, Folder 67.
191. [GJC to Dr Beausoleil], 15 January 1940, GJC Papers, Folder 70.
192. GJC to Mrs Leung, 18 January 1940, GJC Papers, Folder 28.
193. GJC to Dr A.E.C. Beausoleil, 19 January 1940, GJC Papers, Folders 67 and 70.
194. GJC to Barbara Gordon, 10 February 1940, GJC Papers, Folder 28.
195. [GJC] to Dr A.E.C. Beausoleil, Tafo, via Kumasi, 10 February 1940, Folder 70.
196. GJC to Howard Christian, 28 February 1939, GJC Papers, Folder 114.
197. GJC to Essie, 16 September 1937, GJC Papers, Folder 33.
198. GJC to Dr A.E.C. Beausoleil, 19 January 1940, GJC Papers, Folder 67 and 70.
199. GJC to Edu Sam, 10 February 1940, GJC Papers, Folder 64.
200. GJC to Dr Peter Christian, 13 February 1940, GJC Papers, Folder 144.
201. GJC to Miss Laura Lecointe, Coulibistrie, Dominica, "My dear Coumere", 13 February 1940, GJC Papers, Folder 67.
202. GJC to Mr C. Vaughan Charles, Washington, USA, 6 March 1940, Folder 64.
203. "Beau" to "My dear GJ", Tafo, 27 March 1940, GJC Papers, Folder 64.
204. [Dr Beausoleil] to Howard Christian, 19 April 1940, GJC Papers, Folder 277.
205. The service was held at St Andrew's Anglican Church, although Christian was Roman Catholic. According to the oral record, Mami Abba was of the view that he was denied a Catholic funeral, because he was not married under Catholic rites. Grace Christian, interview with Margaret Rouse-Jones, 8 August 2007, OPReP Collection. See also "Funeral Service in St Andrew's Church Sekondi on the Occasion of the Burial of the Late Hon. G. J. Christian, Thursday 18 April 1940 at 4 p.m.", GJC Papers, Folder 218.
206. Obituary [Notice re George James Christian], Sekondi, 18 April 1940, GJC Papers, Folder 276.
207. Howard Christian to Angela Christian, 19 September 1948, GJC Papers, Folder 298.
208. "R.I.P. Hon. George James Christian" [acknowledgements and notice of final obsequies], Sekondi, 30 April 1940, GJC Papers, Folder 61.
209. Howard Christian to Essi Christian, 25 February 1943, GJC Papers, Folder 126.
210. J. Bart-Plange, Kumasi-Ashanti, to Essi Christian, "From the Family Record", 8 February 1967, GJC Papers, Folder 171.
211. Legislative Council Debates Session 1940, October 1940, 5–6, National Archives of Ghana, Accra.
212. W.P. Gillam (Gold Coast Machinery and Trading Company Limited) to the Honourable Colonial Secretary, 25 April 1940, GJC Papers, Folder 33. A note in

red pencil written across the bottom of this document states that "this idea was given effect to by Government".
213. Gordon Rohlehr, "National Heritage Library: Catalyst for Sovereignty and Literacy", in *Transgression, Transitions, Transformation: Essays in Caribbean Culture* (San Juan, Trinidad and Tobago: Lexicon, 2007), 385–91. Gordon Rohlehr is emeritus professor of West Indian literature at the University of the West Indies, St Augustine, Trinidad and Tobago.
214. The George James Christian Papers were donated to the University of the West Indies, St Augustine, and were officially handed over by his granddaughter Mrs Estelle Appiah in a ceremony at the Alma Jordan Library (formerly the Main Library) on 22 June 2005.
215. The Hon. M. Eugenia Charles, "National Pride", speech by prime minister of Dominica on the occasion of the twelfth anniversary of independence, 3 November 1990. Eugenia Charles Fonds, University of the West Indies, Cave Hill, Barbados.
216. [George James Christian to Joseph O. Bowers], 6 April 1940, GJC Papers, Folder 64.

Selected Bibliography

Adi, Hakim, and Marika Sherwood. *Pan-African History: Political Figures from Africa and the Diaspora since 1787.* London: Routledge, 2003.

Agyemang, Fred. *Accused in the Gold Coast.* 2nd ed. Ghana: Waterville, 1972.

Amos, Alcione M. "The History of the Afro-Brazilian Community in Togo: With Special Emphasis on the Olympio Family". In *Back to Africa.* Volume 1, *Afro-Brazilian Returnees and Their Communities,* edited by Kwesi Kwaa Prah, 121–44. CASAS Book Series No. 69. Cape Town: Centre for Advanced Studies of African Society, 2009.

Baptiste, Fitzroy André. "Developments in African History and the African Diaspora at the University of the West Indies, 1968–1998: A Personal Odyssey". In *Caribbean Perspectives on African History and Culture,* edited by Richard Goodridge, 3–4. Cave Hill, Barbados: Department of History and Philosophy, University of the West Indies, 2004.

Barrow, A.H. *Fifty Years in Western Africa: Being a Record of the Work of the West Indian Church on the Banks of the Rio Pongo.* New York: Negro Universities Press, 1969. Original edition, London: Society for Promoting Christian Knowledge, 1900.

Boadi-Siaw, Samuel. "The Afro-Brazilian Returnees in Ghana". In *Back to Africa.* Volume 1, *Afro-Brazilian Returnees and Their Communities,* edited by Kwesi Kwaa Prah, 145–48. CASAS Book Series no. 69. Cape Town: Centre for Advanced Studies of African Society, 2009.

Braithwaite, Lloyd. *Colonial West Indian Students in Britain.* Kingston: University of the West Indies Press, 2001.

Buell, Raymond Leslie. *Liberia: A Century of Survival, 1847–1947.* Philadelphia: University of Pennsylvania Press, 1947.

Cardinall, A.W. *The Gold Coast 1931: A Review of conditions in the Gold Coast in 1931 as compared with those of 1921, based on figures and facts collected by the Chief Census Officer of 1931, together with a Historical Ethnographical and Sociological Survey of the People of that Country.* Chapter 7, Non-African Population. n.p., 1931.

Chamberlain, Mary, ed. *Caribbean Migration: Globalised Identities.* London: Routledge, 1998.

Charles, John-Baptiste. Manuscript autobiography. Eugenia Charles Fonds, University of the West Indies, Cave Hill, Barbados.

Clover, David. "The West Indian Club Ltd: An Early 20th Century West Indian Interest in London". *The Society for Caribbean Studies Annual Conference Papers*, edited by Sandra Courtman, 8 (2007).

Cowper, Francis. *A Prospect of Gray's Inn*. 2nd rev. ed. London: GRAYA, on behalf of Gray's Inn, 1985.

Dominique, Mary Ursula. *From a Small Beginning: Autobiography of Ma Baba*. Transcribed and written by Natalie Charles Andrew, with illustrations by Ronald Deschamps. N.p., 1983. Reprint, Roseau, Dominica: Tropical Printers, 2007.

Dyde, Brian. *A History of Antigua: The Unsuspected Isle*. London: Macmillan, 2000.

Ephson, Isaac S. *Gallery of Gold Coast Celebrities 1632–1958*. Accra, Ghana: Ilen, 1969–1971.

Flax, Olva. *The Influence of Church and School upon the Antiguan Society*. [Antigua]: Antigua Archives Committee, [1984?].

Gold Coast Handbook 1937. N.p.: Gold Coast Government, 1937.

Goodridge, Richard, ed. *Caribbean Perspectives on African History and Culture*. Cave Hill, Barbados: Department of History and Philosophy, University of the West Indies, 2004.

Green, J. "Caribbean Influence in the Gold Coast Administration in the 1900s". *Ghana Studies Bulletin* 2: 10–16.

Guggisberg, Frederick Gordon. *The Gold Coast: A Review of the Events of 1920–1926 and the Prospects of 1927–1928*. Accra: C. Fairweather, Government Printer, 1927.

Hall, Peter. *Autobiography of Rev Peter Hall, First Moderator of the Presbyterian Church of Ghana*. Accra: Waterville Publishing House, 1965.

Harris, Joseph, ed. *Global Dimensions of the African Diaspora*. 2nd ed. Washington, DC: Howard University Press, 1993.

———. "Return Movements to West and East Africa: A Comparative Approach". In *Global Dimensions of the African Diaspora*, edited by Joseph Harris, 51–64. 2nd ed. Washington, DC: Howard University Press, 1993.

Honychurch, Lennox. *The Dominica Story: A History of the Island*. Roseau: Dominica Institute, 1984.

Jenkins, Ray. "'West Indian' and 'Brazilian' Influences in the Gold Coast–Ghana, c. 1807–1914: A Review and Reappraisal of Continuities in the post-Abolition links between West Africa and the Caribbean and Brazil". Paper presented to the Twelfth Annual Conference of the Society for Caribbean Studies, Hoddesdon, Hertfordshire, UK, 12–14 July 1988.

Kimble, David. *A Political History of Ghana: The Rise of Gold Coast Nationalism, 1850–1928*. Oxford: Oxford University Press, 1963.

Leyel, Peter. "A Distinguished Barbadian: The Story of My Grandfather, Sir George Campbell Deane, Kt". *Journal of the Barbados Museum and Historical Society* 58 (2012).
Lieck, Albert, ed. *Trial of Benjamin Knowles.* Edinburgh: William Hodge, 1933.
Marley, Rita, with Hettie Jones. *No Woman No Cry: My Life with Bob Marley.* New York: Hyperion, 2004.
Mathurin, Owen Charles. *Henry Sylvester Williams and the Origins of the Pan-African Movement, 1969–1911.* Westport, CT: Greenwood, 1976.
Maynard, G.G. Oliver. *A History of the Moravian Church, Eastern West Indies Province.* Trinidad: Yuille's Printerie, 1968.
Merriman, Nick, ed. *The Peopling of London: Fifteen Thousand Years of Settlement from Overseas.* London: Museum of London, 1993.
Noel, Ronald Courtney. "Henry Sylvester-Williams: A New Inquiry into an Old Hero". MPhil thesis, University of the West Indies, St Augustine, Trinidad, 2006.
Philip, Ira P. *HAKIM, Son of Mazumbo: The Extraordinary Life of Hakim Gordon.* Warwick, Bermuda: Writers' Machine, 1995.
Prah, Kwesi Kwaa, ed. *Back to Africa.* Volume 1, *Afro-Brazilian Returnees and Their Communities.* CASAS Book Series no. 69. Cape Town: Centre for Advanced Studies of African Society, 2009.
———. *Back to Africa.* Volume 2, *The Ideology and Practice of the African Returnee Phenomenon from the Caribbean and North-America to Africa.* CASAS Book Series No. 92. Cape Town: Centre for Advanced Studies of African Society, 2012.
Redkey, Edwin S. *Black Exodus: Black Nationalist and Back-to-Africa Movements, 1890–1910.* New Haven and London: Yale University Press, 1969.
Report of the Pan-African Conference. London: Pan-African Association, 1900.
Rohlehr, Gordon. "National Heritage Library: Catalyst for Sovereignty and Literacy". In *Transgression, Transitions, Transformation: Essays in Caribbean Culture*, edited by Gordon Rohlehr, 385–91. San Juan, Trinidad and Tobago: Lexicon, 2007.
Rouse-Jones, Margaret D. "History at the Personal Level: Tesserae in the Mosaic of Caribbean Social History". *Caribbean Quarterly* 58, no. 1 (March 2012): 65–86.
Rouse-Jones, Margaret D., and Estelle M. Appiah. "West Indian Patriot in West Africa: A Study of George James Christian of Dominica and the Gold Coast". In *Caribbean Heritage*, edited by Basil A. Reid, 195–206. Kingston: University of the West Indies Press and the Reed Foundation, 2012.
———. "West Indian Returnees and Their Communities: Examples from the Gold Coast in the Nineteenth and Twentieth Centuries". In *Back to Africa.* Volume 2, *The Ideology and Practice of the African Returnee Phenomenon from the Caribbean and North-America to Africa*, edited by Kwesi Kwaa Prah, 380–406. Cape Town: Centre for Advanced Studies of African Society, 2012.

Russell, Horace O. *The Missionary Outreach of the West Indian Church: Jamaican Baptist Missions to West Africa in the Nineteenth Century*. Volume 3 of *Research in Religion and Family*. New York: Peter Lang, 2000.

Sampson, Magnus J., ed. *West African Leadership: Public Speeches Delivered by J.E. Casely Hayford*. London: Frank Cass, 1969.

Sherwood, Marika. *Origins of Pan-Africanism: Henry Sylvester Williams, Africa, and the African Diaspora*. London: Routledge, 2011.

Smith, Edwin W. *Aggrey of Africa: A Study in Black and White*. New York: Richard R. Smith, 1930.

Tachie-Menson, C.W. *Brief History of the St. George's (Seccondee) Lodge No. 3851 of Ancient, Free and Accepted Masons, English Constitution 1918–1939*. Sekondi: Hope Press, 1939.

———. *Freemasonry in the Gold Coast*. N.p., 1953.

Vassady Jr, Bela. "The Role of the Black West Indian Missionary in West Africa, 1840–1890". PhD dissertation, Temple University, 1972.

Wariboko, Waibinte. *Ruined by "Race": Afro-Caribbean Missionaries and the Evangelization of Southern Nigeria, 1895–1925*. Trenton, NJ: Africa World Press, 2007.

Warner-Lewis, Maureen. *Central Africa in the Caribbean: Transcending Time, Transforming Cultures*. Kingston: University of the West Indies Press, 2003.

———. "The West Indian Anglican Mission to West Africa". Typescript, 2010.

———. "West Indian Memories of Life in West Africa as Agents of the British Colonial Enterprise". Paper presented at Heritage: Its Management and Preservation, Eighth Symposium, Social History Project, Department of History and Archaeology, University of the West Indies, Mona, 2008.

Williams, C. Kingsley. *Achimota: The Early Years*. Accra, Ghana: Longmans of Ghana, 1962.

Wyse, Akintola. "The Sierra Leone Krios: A Reappraisal from the Perspective of the African Diaspora". In *Global Dimensions of the African Diaspora*, edited by Joseph Harris, 339–68. 2nd ed. Washington, DC: Howard University Press, 1993.

Index

Abbensetts, C.E.M., 59, 61, 66, 70, 90, 129, 150, 151, 153, 162, 202, 203, 209–12
Abbontiakoon Mines Limited, 114
Accra, Christiansborg District, 40, 57
Accra Ice Company, 65
Accra Magisterial District Probation Committee, 71
Accra Teacher Training Institution, 4
Achimota College and School, 26, 45, 57, 62, 64, 69, 70, 72, 147, 176, 244n144; correspondence between GJC and Dr Aggrey regarding, 82–90; death of Dr Aggrey and memorials, 89–90; employment of GJC's daughters at, 96–100; employment practices at, 99, 100–101; establishment of, 80–82; experience of GJC's sons as students at, 93–95
Achimota School, 84, 85, 87, 91, 94, *103*, 261n2
Ackon, Mary Aba (wife of GJC), 32–33, *75, 76*
African and Eastern Trade Corporation, 138
African Association, the, 20, 23, 136. *See also* Pan-African Association
African diaspora. *See* African returnees
African returnees: as missionaries, 2, 3; from Barbados, 202–4; from Brazil, 3–4, 300n69; from British Guiana, 202; from Dominica, 204–7; from Jamaica, 3; from St Lucia, 200–202; from Trinidad and Tobago, 2, 197–200; from the West Indies, 195, 207–8; to Ghana, 3, 4–5; to Nigeria, 2, 4; to Sierra Leone, 2, 248n49
African Union Company, 25, 136, 243n133
Afro-Brazilian returnees, 3–4, 300n69
Aggrey, Dr James Emmanuel Kwegyir: and establishment of Achimota College and School, 80–82; and friendship with GJC, 26, 34, 49, 82–90, 101, *103*; death of, 89. *See also* Dr Aggrey Memorial High School
Aggrey House, London, 191
Aggrey Memorial School, 95
Agomanya Convent, 207
Ambaah, E.H., 128
Anglo African Corporation, 141, 201
Apaloo, Modesto, 94
Apatu, Lena, 65
Ariston Gold Mines (1929) Limited, 114
Armah, Dr Joseph Ersuah, 65–66, *78*, 181, 217
Armah, Josephine Martha (daughter of GJC). *See* Christian, Josephine Martha

313

Ashanti Administration Ordinance: No. 1 of 1902, 122, 126; Criminal Procedure Ordinance, 126
Ashanti, king of (the Asantehene), 116
Ashanti region, 58, 112, 158, 187; map of, *29*; West Indian migrants in, 195, 198, 203, 212
Ashanti, legal system of, 114, 117–23, 126–32. *See also* Rex *v.* Dr Knowles
Auguste, Dr E.L., 58, 198, 199, 200, 203, 209, 210, 212
Awoonor-Williams, F., 91
Awoonor-Williams, Nora, 59
Awotwi, Chief, 108–9

"Back to Africa" movement, 1–2
Bannerman, C.E. Woolhouse, 130
Baptist Missionary Society: British (1841), 2–3; American, 187
Baptiste, Fitzroy André, 1
Barclays Bank, 111, 113, 270n70. *See also* Colonial Bank
Barton, Mr Justice, 26, 59, 217
Basel Missionary Society (1843), 3
Bay St Louis, Mississippi, 205
Beausoleil, Dr A.E.C. (GJC's personal physician), 58, 61, 68, 144, 151, 197, 199, 200, 203, 208, 213, 215–18, 219
Bekyire Yankeh II (Omanhin of Dutch Sekondi), 113
Blyden, Edward, 2
Boadi-Siaw, Samuel, 3
Boham, Frances Maame Franswa (wife of GJC), 32, 33, 75
Boland, Virginia, 31, 74
Bonitto, J.S., 4
Bouchier, Reverend Father, 58
Bowers, Reverend Joseph O., 1, 204–7, 223, 224, 301n88
Bowers, Sheriff M., 14, 204

Brown, Bishop J.W., 26
Brown, Dr, and League of Coloured Peoples, 45
Browne, Innes, 111, 114
Brazil, returnees from, 3–4, 300n69
Buckle, J., 23
Burke, Christiane (Chrissie), 31, 39, 47–48, 135, 227, 258n286
Busby, Dr George, 64, 95, 144, 198, 199, 200, 209, 211, 212
Busby, Margaret, 64, 227, 247n24.
Busby, Sarah Helena (daughter of GJC). *See* Christian, Sarah Helena
Bushe, H.G., 130

Callender, Walter, 203; guardian of Margaret, 203–4
Campbell, Robert, 2
Cape Coast, 4, 104, 131, 186, 220
Cassada Garden Estate, Dominica, 135
Central Wassau Gold Mines Limited, 114
CERES Medal of the United Nations Food and Agricultural Organization, 69
Chapel Square (Elmina), 33, 64
Chappelle, Charles W., 25, 144, 243n133
Charles, Dame Eugenia, 7, 223
Charles, John-Baptiste, 7
Cheapside Syndicate Limited, 35, 141, 201
Christian, Angela Ambah (daughter of GJC), 32, 36, 43–45, 68–70, 75, 100, *103*, 152, *166*; and GJC's satisfaction with, 68–70
Christian, Clara Marguerite (daughter of GJC), 31, 36–37, 50–52, 62–63, *74*, 77, 99, 152, *167*
Christian, Ebenezer Kwesi (son of GJC), 32, 33, 64, *75*, 77; as Freemason, 165
Christian, Edward Clifford (son of

GJC), 32, 62, 68, 72–73, 75, 79, 90, 93–95, 100, *102*
Christian, Essi Matilda (daughter of GJC), 32, 35, 42–46, 50, 57, 59–61, 67–68, 70–71, 75, 77, *78*, 85, 95, 100–101, 152, 165, *166*, 228
Christian, Ferdinand Francisco (son of GJC), 32, 62, 68, 71–72, 75, 79, 93–95, 100, 147, 152, 153, 244n147; relationship with Rev. Bowers, 204
Christian, George James: accolades, 132, 164–65, 220–22; as benefactor, 143–45; as businessman, 134–36; criminal defence cases, 105, 116, *133*; early years in Dominica, 13–14; as Freemason, 133, 160–65, *168*; as honorary consul for Liberia, 134, 157–60, 165, 170; illness and death, 213–20, *226*; legal career, 105–32; legal work for mining industry, 114–16, 117; as member of the Legislative Council for Sekondi, 170, 172, *194*; property law cases, 106–7, 108–9, 113; role in the Benjamin Knowles case, 117–31; student days in London, 17–22; as Western Province Teachers' Union's legal counsel, 113–14. *See also individual names of children and colleagues*
Christian, George James Sr (father of GJC), 9–14
Christian, George Kwesi (son of GJC), 32, 56, 75
Christian, Herminie Eccuah (daughter of GJC), 42, 56–57, 75, 76, 85–86
Christian, Howard Kojo (son of GJC), 32, 42–47, 59–61, 66–68, 75, 76, 77, *78*, 100–101, *102*, 152, 160, *166*; assumed patriarchal responsibilities after death of GJC 30, 67
Christian, Joseph (son of GJC), 32–33, 35, 41–43, 62, 64–65, 75, 76, *78*, 92–93, 152, *166*
Christian, Josephine Martha (daughter of GJC), 32–33, 35, 41–43, 62, 65–66, 75, 76, *78*, 152, *166*
Christian, Maude Mary (daughter of GJC), 31, 35, 37, 74, 77, 134; Aggrey's appreciation of, 83–85, 88–89; education and early employment, 39–40; illness and death, 57–59, 97, 200; impact of death on GJC, 57–59; involvement in life of Netelka Packwood, 146–47; memorials and donations after death of, 145, 212, 220, *226*
Christian Maternity Home, 65
Christian, May (niece of GJC), 31, 38–39, 258n285, 258n286
Christian, Peter Charles (son of GJC), 31, 35–36, 55 74, 76, 135, 148, 150–51, 213, 250n78, 258n285, 258n286; education and dental practice of, 38–39, 44, 49, 53–54; as Freemason, 164; GJC's disappointment with, 63
Christian, Sarah Helena (daughter of GJC), 64, 75, 76, 96–99, *103*, 152, *166*
Christian, Ulric (son of GJC), 16, 31, 56, 74, 245n4
Church Council of Christ the King Catholic Church, 70
Clarke, Dr C. Belfield, 55, 212
Cockburn, Captain Joshua, 49, 142; as litigant in US Supreme Court property rights case, 146
Colonial Bank, 4, 111–12, 139, 142. *See also* Barclays Bank
Colonial government, 130, 280n100
Colonial Missionary Society, 190
Companion of the Order of the Volta, 207

Congregation of Sisters of the Handmaids of the Divine Redeemer, 206, 207
Congregational Church, 190
Convent of the Faithful Virgin, Roseau, Dominica, 39
Convention People's Party, 131
Cools-Lartigue, Alex R., 197, 277n7
Council of Legal Education, 66, 121
Criminal Procedure Ordinance. *See* Ashanti Administration Ordinance No. 1 of 1902
Cuffee, Paul, 2
Curtis, Campbell and Company, 139–40, 150, 214

Dadson, J.E., 105
Daily Mail, the: reporting on *Rex v. Knowles*, 119, 122, 125–27, 131
Deane, George Campbell, 202–3
Dick, Mrs R.E., 42, 251n107, 208–9
Dick, Robert Ebenezer, 42, 302n95, 162, 207–8
Dietrich, Henry, 108, 209
Diocese of St John's-Basseterre, West Indies, 207
District Grand Lodge of the Gold Coast, 162–64
Dr Aggrey Memorial High School, 90
Dominica: children of GJC born in, 30–31, 53, *74*; relatives of GJC living in, 30, 36, 47; GJC and remittances sent to, 147–48; society, 7–8; social and political climate, 1860s, 10–13
Dominica House (Sekondi), 25–27, *28*, 32, 34, 63, 68, 146, 151, 198, 209–10, 212, 220, 249n54
Douglas, Horace, 50, 66, 109, 117, 122, 124, 128, 129, 150, 175, 181
Douglin, Canon Philip H., 2

Douglass, Frederick, 223n7
Douthwaite, Dennis W. (steward of Gray's Inn), 17, 18
Dove, Franz, 61, 66, 98, 112, 116, 125, 129, *133*, 141, 151, 201, 251n107
Doyle, Thomas, 12
Dulwich College, 42

Edwin, Chief Kojo (Odikro of Poassi), 113
Elmina. *See* Chapel Square, Elmina
Effia Nkwanta Hospital, 212
Endsleigh Hospital, 57
Evans-Anfom, Dr Emmanuel, 94, 262n12, 267n116
Everard, Reverend, 16–17

Farquhar, Reverend Charles W., 14, 20, 239n49, 239n54
Fenyi, Cecilia Ajuah, 32, 75
Forster, Essi Matilda (daughter of GJC). *See* Christian, Essi Matilda
François, George Joseph, 35, 45, 63, 70, 94, 97, 98, 127, 141, 150–51, 181, 196, 197–98, 203, 210–11, 215, *225*; co-founder of the Anglo African Corporation, 200–201
François, John, 94
Fraser, Reverend Alexander G., 80–81, 88, 90–93, 96, 172, 263n21
Freeling, Governor, 13
Freeman, Reverend T.B., 4
Freemasons, 14, 53, 64, 134, 160–65, *168*, 208, 212–13, 286n222
French, Abba Lucy (Mami Abba) (wife of GJC), 27, 32, 34–36, 48, 59, 70, *75*, *76*, 83, *102*, 151–52, 218, 220
French, J.W. (father-in-law of GJC), 34, 145

Ga society, 4
Garvey, Marcus, 2
Ghana: returnees to, 3, 4–5, 301n88; map of, 29; post-independence era, 69–70, 72–73; pre-independence era, 27, 44, 65–66, 72, 101, 118, 200, 201, 212, 288n16; Reverend Bowers's work in, 206–7; marriage types in, 246n16. *See also* Rex *v.* Dr Knowles; West Indians
Ghana Broadcasting Corporation, 71
Ghana Education Service, 261n2
Ghana Girl Guides, 71
Ghana Medical School, 72
Giles Hunt and Company, 111–12
Gold Coast Bar Association, 129
Gold Coast Colony: judicial system of the, 118, 120–21, 130. *See also* Ashanti, legal system of
Gold Coast High Commission in London, 69
Gold Coast Leader, the: reporting on construction of Dominica House 25; reporting on legal counsel of GJC, 105; reporting on election defeat of GJC, 170
Gold Coast Lodge No. 773, 161
Gold Coast Regiment, 185
Gold Coast Selection Trust Limited, 114
Gold Coast society, 25, 127, 169, 170, 175, 180, 187–88, 192, 220. *See also* West Indians
Gordon, Clara Marguerite (daughter of GJC). *See* Christian, Clara Marguerite
Gordon, Edgar, 37, 51–52, 249n63
Grace, Canon, 98
Gray's Inn, 17–20, 22, 50, 69, 70, 104, 121, 124, 150, 220, 242n106
Green, Jeffrey, 4
Greenfield, Thomas J. (barrister of Gray's Inn), 18

Greenwood, Lord, 66
Greeves, Affleck, 215
Guggisberg, Governor Frederick Gordon, 49, 80–82, 92, 184
Guggisberg House, 95

Hallet, Hollis, 51
Hampton Institute, 36, 38
Handbook of the Gold Coast, 7
Handmaids of the Divine Redeemer, the Sisters of the, 206–7
Harrison College, Barbados, 202
Hayford, Joseph Ephraim Casely, 169–71, 185, 287n3
Hill, Colonel S.J., 3
Howard University, 38, 40–41, 44, 49, 54; GJC donation to, 144
Hoyte, Cunliffe Malcolm Gustave, 198–99, 203, 209, 211, 223
Hoyte, Dr Ralph Allen Sergeant Sr, 198–99, 200, 203, 209–12, 223
Hoyte, Dr Ralph Jr, 199
Huggins, H. Dudley, 196, 209, 296n15
Hypolite, Mr, 31

Imperial College of Tropical Agriculture, 175, 296n15
Inner Wheel Club of Accra, 71
Innes Browne and Company, 111
Inns of Court, GJC admission to, 18
International School Cantonments Committee, 71

J.J. Peele and Company, 116
Jackson, Dr J.H., 153–54
Jackson, Dr William Walrond, 3
Jenkins, Ray, 4

King's School, Rochester, 42
Kingsford, Major G.T., 59, 163

Koens, Jan, 160, 165
Korle Bu Hospital, 34, 55, 72, 145
Knowles, Dr Benjamin, 117–31, 132
Kumasi Garage Company, 112
Kwahu Mining Company, 114
Kwame Nkrumah University of Science and Technology, 261n2, 262n12
Kwaw Koom, Chief Odikro, 107–8
Kwesi Andoh II, Chief, 91

La Sagesse Convent School, 42, 51
Lagos Observer, the: reporting on GJC participation in Pan-African Conference, 21–22
Lake, Obiagele, 4
Langridge, Arthur (barrister of Middle Temple), 18
Laudat, Sylvanie (mother of GJC), 9, 236n5
Lazare, Emmanuel, 254n185
League of Coloured Peoples, 45, 190–91
Lecointe, Laura, 31, *74*, 148, 219
Leeward Islands, 39
Leung, Francis Stanislaus: and GJC at Gray's Inn, 17, 19; as law partner of GJC, 25, 104, 131, 195, 203, 213, 241n80, 267n5, 296n13
Leung, Mrs Hedwig, 26, 109–12, 125, 142, 151, 218; as guardian of GJC's children in London, 41–43, 49, 52, 140
Lever Brothers of Nigeria, 138
Lewis, George Stanley, 45, 141, 197, 203, 208, 209–10, *226*, 228, 234n21, 252n132, 299n62; businesses established in the Gold Coast, 200–202
Lewis, Sir Arthur (Nobel laureate), 45, 252n132, 299n62
Liberia, 38, 154; nationalism in, 288n16; GJC as honorary consul for, 134, 157–60, 165, 170

Lincoln's Inn, 104
Lockhart, Constance, 63, 148, 211, 282n131
Love, Robert, 2

Maidstone Prison, 126, 131
Mami Abba. *See* French, Abba Lucy
Mansu stool, 114
Mansour, John, 110–11, 197
Mansour, John (son of GJC), 32, *79*, 247n24
Maria Grey Teacher Training College, 100
Marley, Rita, as returnee to Ghana, 5
Masons. *See* Freemasons
McCarthy, Judge Mr L.E.V. (solicitor general), 70, 98
McCaskie, N.L., 66
McKay, Claude, 2
Menzies, G.K., 191
Mero Estate, Dominica, 134
Mico Chapel Fund, Jamaica, 145
Mico Training College, Antigua, 9, 10, 14, 17, 20, 43, 205
Millers Limited, 138
Mobil Oil Ghana Limited, Essi Forster as corporate legal adviser to, 71
Montgomery Ward and Company, 25
Moody, Dr Harold A., 45, 294n118; founder of the League of Coloured Peoples, 190–1
Moore, Richard B., 2
Moravian Church, 3, 9
Murrell, J.H., 58, 91, 189, 200, 202–3, 211
Muss, Leo, 24, 147
Muss, Leonard, 24, 195

Nanwa Gold Mines, 116
National Congress of British West Africa, 171, 287n3, 288n16

National Union of Empire Africans, 191
Native Administration Revenue
  Ordinance, 176
Nigeria: Islam practiced in, 174;
  nationalism in, 288n16; returnees to,
  2, 4
Nurses and Midwives (Accra) Schools
  Board of Governors, Essi Forster as
  chairman of, 71
Nkrumah, Kwame, 66, 131

Oberlin College, 36
Ochesco Industries, 64
Oddfellows organization, 14, 16, 160–61
Old Year's Night, celebration of by GJC
  and friends, 210, 218
Order of the British Empire: awarded to
  Moira Stuart, 62; awarded to Margaret
  Busby, 64; awarded to C.M.G. Hoyte,
  198

Packwood, Netelka. *See* Sam, Netelka
  Packwood
Padmore, George (of Trinidad), 2
Padmore, George (of Liberia), 26
Palm Oil Estates, 113
Pan-African Association, 20–22, 197. *See
  also* African Association
Pan-African Conference (1900), 20–22
Peele, Captain, 59
Pemberton, His Honour Thomas Sholto,
  11, 12–13
Peters, Reverend R.E. and Mrs
  Henrietta, 7, 49, 94, 160, 165; and the
  West African Industrial Academy,
  152–57, 187
Phelps Stokes Fund, 81
Phillips, Grace Fehintola (daughter of
  Anglican Bishop S.C. Phillips), 72

Phipps, Richard Emmanuel, 20, 95,
  197–98, 209
Pickering and Berthoud, 136, 141
Pine, Governor Benjamin (of Dominica),
  13, 238n39
Prah, Kwesi Kwaa, 1–2
Prince of Wales College and Achimota
  School. *See* Achimota College
Princess Marie Louise Hospital at Korle
  Wokon, 202
Project Hope of America, 72

Queen Mary's Hospital, Carshalton, 42
Quist, E.C., 98
Quist, Rosamund, 210, 228, 303n118

racial prejudice, discussion of: at
  Achimota College, 96–99, 100–101; in
  UK 46, 67; in job promotion, 196–97;
  and wage discrimination, 267n116
Rawle, Richaw, 3
Reece, Maurice, 23–24, 143, 150, 196,
  209, 217, 218
Reeves, Fred, 16, 17–18, 19
Rex v. Dr Knowles, 117–31
Rio Pongas Mission (1855), 3
Rita Marley Foundation, 5
Roberts, Julian C., 199–200
Robinson, Alexander, 11–12
Rodger Club (Accra), 90
Romain, Jeanvillia, 9, 236n9
Roseau Town Council, Dominica, 135
Royal Infirmary, Scotland, 64, 99
Royal Society of Arts (London), 191
Russwurm, John, 2

St Augustine's Seminary, 204–5
St George Lodge, Dominica, 149, 164
St George's Lodge, Sekondi, 162, 163,
  165, 212

St Joseph School, Dominica, 14
St Kitts, Oddfellows in, 161
Sam, Chief Alfred, 2
Sam, Netelka Packwood, 146–47, *166*, 281n106
Sarbah, John Mensah, 104, 132
Savary, Justice, 26, 198
Saxton, Commander, 59
Scottish United Presbyterian mission (1846), 2
Seale-Hayne Agricultural College, Newton Abbot, Devon, 42, 64, 92
Secondom House, Dominica, 136, 212
Senegambia region, Anglican missionaries to, 3
Serrant, Felina, 16, 31, *74*, 245n13
Sekondi House, Dominica, 63, 135, 212
Selwyn-Clark, Dr, 58, 97
Shillingford, Howell, 15, 19, 135
Sierra Leone, 23, 104, 198; returnees to, 2, 248n49; nationalism in, 288n16; GJC's children educated in; 32, 33, 35, 40–41, 56, 65
Simmonds, Dr, 23, 144, 196, 199, 298n43
Sisserou Award of Honour, Dominica, awarded to Bishop Bowers, 207
Slater, Sir A. Ransford, 125, 130
Smart, L.A., 107, 209, 214
Smyly, Sir Philip Crampton (chief justice of the Gold Coast), 23–24, 125, 132, 242n114
Society of the Divine Word, 205
Stuart, Moira, 62, 236n4
Sugar Planters Experiment Station, Sophia, British Guiana, 196
Swanzy Limited, 138

Tabom. *See* Afro-Brazilian returnees
Takoradi Harbour and Town Ordinance (Acquisition of Lands) 1921, 106
Takoradi Harbour Scheme, 24, 106–7, 137, 185, 199
Tarkwa Banket West, 114
Tarquah Trading Company, 138
Tew, Sir Mervyn, 116
Thomas-Hope, Elizabeth, 5
Todd, K.W., 26

University of Dublin, Ireland, 72

Wariboko, Waibinte, 2
Warner-Lewis, Maureen, 3
Wasaw, Upper and Lower, 115
Webster, Reverend Harry, 89
West African Diamond Syndicate, 114
West African Industrial Academy, 7, 94, 152–57, 187
West India Committee, 190
West Indian Club Limited, 189–90
West Indians: and discrimination in the Gold Coast, 127–28, 213; as returnees to Africa, 4–5; contributions to the Gold Coast society, 127–28, 208–13
Western Province Bar Association, 188
Western Province Teachers' Union, 113
Wharton, H., 4
Williams, Henry Sylvester, 2, 17, 18, 22, 23, 197, 243n123; as founder of the African Association (London), 20
Windsor House, Bermuda, 35, 51, 62
Wood, Samuel Richard, 7
World War 1, 108, 118, 185, 198, 201
World War 2, 46, 67, 94
Wynne-Baxter and Keeble, 124
Wyse, Akintola J.G., 248n49

Yoruba. *See* Brazil, returnees from

Zoombo. *See* Lazare, Emmanuel

www.ingramcontent.com/pod-product-compliance
Lightning Source LLC
Chambersburg PA
CBHW021818300426
44114CB00009BA/227